GUIDE TO REFERENCE
Essential General Reference and Library Science Sources

ALA Editions purchases fund advocacy, awareness,
and accreditation programs for library professionals worldwide.

GUIDE TO REFERENCE

**Essential General Reference
and Library Science Sources**

JO BELL WHITLATCH and
SUSAN E. SEARING, Editors

AN IMPRINT OF THE
AMERICAN LIBRARY ASSOCIATION
CHICAGO • 2014

© 2014 by the American Library Association

Printed in the United States of America

18 17 16 15 14   5 4 3 2 1

Extensive effort has gone into ensuring the reliability of the information in this book; however, the publisher makes no warranty, express or implied, with respect to the material contained herein.

ISBNs: 978-0-8389-1232-4 (paper); 978-0-8389-1994-1 (PDF); 978-0-8389-1995-8 (ePub); 978-0-8389-1996-5 (Kindle). For more information on digital formats, visit the ALA Store at alastore.ala.org and select eEditions.

Library of Congress Cataloging-in-Publication Data
Guide to reference : essential general reference and library science sources / Jo Bell Whitlatch and Susan E. Searing, Editors.
     pages cm
   Includes bibliographical references and indexes.
   ISBN 978-0-8389-1232-4 (alk. paper)
   1. Reference books—Bibliography. 2. Reference sources—Bibliography. 3. Reference services (Libraries) I. Whitlatch, Jo Bell. II. Searing, Susan E.
   Z1035.1.G885 2014
   011.02—dc23   2014013098

Cover design by Alejandra Diaz. Image © Anita Ponne/Shutterstock, Inc.

Text design in the Berkeley and Helvetica typefaces. Composition by Scribe, Inc.

♾ This paper meets the requirements of ANSI/NISO Z39.48-1992 (Permanence of Paper).

CONTENTS

FOREWORD

The American Library Association has long been a source for authoritative bibliographies of the reference literature for practicing librarians, library educators, and reference service trainers. ALA's *Guide to Reference Books* was printed in eleven editions over nearly a century, and was succeeded in 2009 by the online *Guide to Reference* (www.guidetoreference.org). The *Guide to Reference* segments, drawn from the online *Guide*, continue that tradition with expertly compiled, annotated bibliographies of reference works and serve as snapshots of the evolving content of the *Guide*.

Although intended for use largely in North American libraries serving institutions of higher education, the segments will also be valuable to public and school librarians, independent researchers, publishers and book dealers, as well as librarians outside North America, for tasks such as identifying sources that will answer questions, directing researchers, creating local instructional materials, educating and training LIS students and reference staff, and inventorying and developing reference collections. These guides provide a usably comprehensive, rather than exhaustive, repertory of sources as the foundation for reference and information services in today's higher education settings. They include works that can most usefully satisfy the vast majority of demands made on a reference service, while not altogether excluding "exotic" or little-known works that will meet only the unusual need.

In addition to providing classified annotated bibliographies, topical sections include editors' guides that orient readers to each subject, its scope and concerns, and the types of sources commonly consulted. The editors' guides will be useful to the generalist librarian and to the LIS student as background to the bibliographies or as intellectual frameworks for addressing reference questions.

The reader will find entries for works that are, for the most part, broadly focused; works on individual persons or with a narrow geographical or chronological focus are generally not included. Selection criteria favored titles published in the last twenty years; the reader may consult earlier printed bibliographies and indexes, such as the numerous print editions of the *Guide to Reference Books*, for many earlier and still important works. As libraries shift their print reference works to the general stacks or to remote locations, the online *Guide* and its older print editions may help to identify reference works that are no longer close at hand.

Sources in the *Guide* include websites, search engines, and full-text databases as well as the traditional array of encyclopedic, bibliographic, and compendious works. Online sources have replaced their printed versions for most librarians under most circumstances. A source only appears in one format; its annotation will identify the format options and describe the relationships between online and print versions. New reference works or editions are not automatically included in the *Guide*. Selection criteria favor sources that have stood some test of time and utility, as well as sources that are free but authoritative or sources that require purchase or licensing but are held at enough libraries to be reasonably available to readers of the *Guide*. The General Reference Works sections do not include the vast majority of discipline-specific sources that are covered in the History and Area Studies; Humanities; Science, Technology, and Medicine; or Social and Behavioral Sciences divisions; please consult the *discipline specific* volumes or the online *Guide* for specialized discipline sources.

The reader is encouraged to peruse the annotations of entries in the same subcategory as known items. An annotation may contain extensive cross references to related sources that are not described separately as well as comparisons to related sources, indications of appropriate audiences for the source, and other details that provide significant added value. In an attempt to balance inclusion and exhaustion, a source may be included in several but not necessarily all relevant subcategories.

This segment on Essential General Reference and Library Science Sources includes sources for each patron and librarian in every type of library. The first subsection on Essential General Reference Works draws from more than 5600 General Reference Works currently annotated in the online *Guide* and is intended to provide a basic set of the most useful general reference sources for librarians assisting patrons with their queries or, for patrons pursuing queries on their own. The subsection on Library Science includes the majority of works about library science that are currently represented in the online *Guide*.

We on the *Guide to Reference* team hope you find the segments helpful, and we welcome your comments at guidetoreference@ala.org. To get the full benefit of the comprehensive compilation in a wide range of subject areas as well as updates to each segment, we also encourage you to subscribe to the online *Guide*, where you have access to updated entries, annotations, user comments, and special features such as personal notes and lists. We regularly seek new editors, especially those who believe they can improve existing sections or develop new ones. Please check the website at www.guidetoreference.org for details on subscribing or volunteering to participate in the continuing development of the *Guide to Reference*.

Jo Bell Whitlatch
Guide to Reference
Division Editor for General Reference Works

CONTRIBUTORS

Donald Altschiller, History, Religion, Government Documents, and Military Affairs Bibliographer at Mugar Memorial Library, Boston University, serves as Contributing Editor for the Other General Reference Works section of the *Guide to Reference*.

Barbara M. Bibel, Reference/Collection Development Librarian and Consumer Health information Specialist (Medical Library Association certification) at the Oakland Public Library in California, serves as Contributing Editor for the Encyclopedias section of the *Guide to Reference*.

Christopher C. Brown, Professor, Reference Technology Integration Librarian/Government Documents Librarian, University of Denver, University Libraries, serves as Contributing Editor for the Government Publications section of the *Guide to Reference*.

Fred Burchsted, Research Librarian at Widener Library, Harvard University, serves as Contributing Editor for the Biography section of the *Guide to Reference*.

Rosanne M. Cordell, Associate Dean for Public Services at Northern Illinois University
Libraries, serves as Contributing Editor for the Bibliography—General; Printing and Publishing sections of the *Guide to Reference*.

Jennifer Duncan, Head of Collection Development at Utah State University in Logan, Utah, serves as Contributing Editor for the Periodicals section of the *Guide to Reference*.

Lili Luo, Associate Professor at the School of Library and Information Science at San Jose State University, serves as Contributing Editor for The Web as Reference Tool and Online General Reference Libraries sections of the *Guide to Reference*.

Mary K. Mannix, Maryland Room Manager, C. Burr Artz Public Library, Frederick County Public Libraries, serves as the Contributing Editor for the Genealogy section of the *Guide to Reference*.

Patrick Reakes, Chair, Humanities and Social Sciences Library at the University of Florida (UF), serves as Contributing Editor for the Newspapers section of the *Guide to Reference*.

Susan E. Searing, Interim Associate University Librarian for User Services at the University of Illinois, Urbana-Champaign, serves as Contributing Editor for the Library and Information Science section of the *Guide to Reference*.

Steven W. Sowards, Associate Director for Collections at the Michigan State University Libraries, serves as Division Editor for Social and Behavioral Sciences of the *Guide to Reference*.

Cynthia Thomes, Reference and Instruction Librarian, UMUC Library, University of Maryland University College, serves as Contributing Editor for the Dissertations section of the *Guide to Reference*.

Barry Trott, Director of Digital Services at the Williamsburg (Va.) Regional Library, serves as Contributing Editor for the Bibliography—Selection of Materials section of the *Guide to Reference*.

Melissa S. Van Vuuren, English and Humanities Librarian, Georgetown University Lauinger Library, serves as Contributing Editor for the Language Dictionaries section of the *Guide to Reference*.

Jo Bell Whitlatch, Faculty Emeritus, San Jose State University Library, serves as Division Editor for General Reference Works of the *Guide to Reference*.

Essential General Reference

Introduction: Essential General Reference Sources

The scope of Essential Sources can be described as reference sources that every librarian should know. The Essential General Reference Sources segment focuses upon the main reference sources that are most useful in answering common reference questions. The annotated sources in the section on Essential General Reference Sources are useful in a variety of ways:

1. Answering challenging reference queries;
2. Developing a valuable reference collection;
3. Serving as a resource for library school students learning basic sources: and
4. Providing a professional development tool for experienced reference librarians in assessing their knowledge of common general reference sources.

Excellent interviewing skills, search skills, and knowledge of sources are the most important factors in reference success. In an information age with many free search engines, the goal of reference success may be more difficult to obtain. Many users with adequate search skills and clearly defined information needs will not be the primary clientele for reference services. Therefore, reference queries now and in the future will require either very skillful interviewing and search skills to locate the information needed and/or excellent knowledge of reference sources. Most of the research related to reference success has been focused on the competencies related to Visibility/Approachability, Interest, Listening/ Inquiring, Searching, and Follow-up as outlined in the "Guidelines for Behavioral Performance of Reference and Information Service Providers" (http://www.ala.org/rusa/resources/guidelines/guidelinesbehavioral). Although current research has not focused on librarian knowledge of reference sources and relationship to reference success, librarian knowledge of reference sources still remains an important factor in many successful reference transactions.

Reference librarians have a responsibility for developing valuable reference collections, regardless of format. Local needs and circumstances should determine the final set of core works for individual libraries—the sources in your library that would be frequently used for certain types of queries as a place to start in locating information. Within these limitations Essential Sources will be useful in evaluating and updating basic reference collections.

Because Essential Sources is intended to serve as a valuable resource for library school students learning basic sources, we consulted the following works when selecting the annotated sources that are included:

- Bopp, Richard E. and Smith, Linda C. 2011. *Reference and Information Services: An Introduction,* 4th ed. Santa Barbara, CA: Libraries Unlimited.
- Cassell, Kay Ann, and Hiremath, Uma. 2013. *Reference and Information Services: An Introduction,* 3rd ed. Chicago: Neal-Schuman.
- Mulac, Carolyn M. 2012. *Fundamentals of Reference.* Chicago: American Library Association.
- Rabina, Debbie. 2013. Reference Materials in LIS Instruction: A Delphi Study. *Journal of Education for Library and Information Science,* 54(2): 108–123.

Many of the sources discussed in these publications are included in Essential Sources. Our expert editors, who selected the core sources included in each section of Essential Sources, also drew upon their own knowledge of the subject. The *Guide* is aimed primarily at a US English-speaking audience and this scope is reflected in our selection of basic reference sources. Rabina notes that lists of basic core sources do not consider local needs, the emphasis of a particular LIS program, or specific workplace needs (p. 119); within these limitations, Essential Sources will assist instructors and LIS students in learning basic reference sources.

For professionals keeping up in the field has always been important. But rapid changes in technology require even more emphasis on professional development in the 21st century. Most of the research related to reference success has been focused on the competencies as outlined in the "Guidelines for Behavioral Performance of Reference and Information

Service Providers." Yet, knowledge of reference sources still remains an important factor in many successful reference transactions. The importance of information sources is highlighted in the following excerpt from "Professional Competencies for Reference and User Services Librarians" (http://www.ala.org/rusa/resources/guidelines/professional):

Information Resources

Goal

A librarian assesses and evaluates resources in all formats in terms of objective standards and how well it meets the library's user needs.

Strategies

1. Assesses the content of resources in the print and virtual collections for accuracy and currency.
2. Determines the authority of these resources.
3. Identifies any bias or point of view in an information resource.
4. Evaluates new information sources appropriate for the primary users.
5. Reads reviews of new information resources to complement the librarian's own judgment.
6. Writes and publishes reviews of new information resources.

Along with search engines and search techniques, reference sources are continually evolving. Thus, knowledge and skills require constant updating. Experienced reference librarians will want to use this annotated list of sources to assess their knowledge of sources and to become acquainted with sources they have not previously used.

As an instructor who has taught both basic reference and advanced reference in the San Jose State University Graduate School of Library and Information Science, a practicing reference librarian, and a librarian who has conducted research in evaluation of reference services, I am delighted to present the *Guide* project of the most basic general reference sources. This project draws from more than 5600 annotated sources included in the General Reference Works division of the *Guide to Reference* (www. guidetoreference.org). Many present and past contributors have generously contributed their time and expertise to make the General Reference Works division of the *Guide* possible. I would like to acknowledge their efforts in this introduction. I particularly wish to thank my previous co-editor of the General Reference Works division, Charlotte Ford, as well as the many other contributors, including: Holly Ackerman, Rajwant Chilana, Kimberly Clarke, Madeline Copp, Amed Demirhan, Edward Fishwick, Malaika Grant, Jon Giulian, Jason Hardin, Fred Jenkins, Cynthia Johnson, Susan Kendall, Akram Khabibullaev, Lorrie Knight, Sean Knowlton, Robert Kusmer, David Langenberg, John Lawrence, Rachel Leket-Mor, Yasuko Makino, Mary Malloy, Terri Miller, Setsuko Noguchi, Michelle Oswell, George Paganelis, Jack O'Gorman, Rohayati Paseng, Lisa Pillow, Karen Peacock, Katalin Radics, Emily Ray, Emily Rogers, Amauri Serrano, Bonnie Simmons, Donna Smith, Lou Vyhnanek, Elizabeth Waraksa, Karen Wei, Sarah Wenzel, David M Westley, Helene Williams, Michael Witt, Tao Yang.

Jo Bell Whitlatch
Guide to Reference
Division Editor for General Reference Works

1

Bibliography

Rosanne M. Cordell and Barry Trott

Early and Rare Books

Book Collecting

BIBLIOGRAPHY

1 **Alibris for libraries.** http://library.alibris
.com/. Alibris. Emeryville, Calif.: Alibris.
1998–

Alibris provides selectors access to a broad selection
of used and out-of-print materials. In addition to
titles stocked by Alibris, the database searches the
inventories of over 7,500 booksellers worldwide,
offering access to over 60 million titles. Alibris provides a variety of tools to assist selectors, including
the ability to match want-lists to the Alibris database
and to create subject-centered collection reports on
titles in the database. Libraries can also order titles
from Alibris through their Interlibrary Loan (ILL)
systems, using OCLC's ILL Fee Management (IFM)
service (for more information, see http://library
.alibris.com/ill-program?cm_sp=lhs-_-services-_-ill).
Alibris also offers librarians access to used audiovisual
materials in a variety of formats, including CD, vinyl,
VHS, and DVD.

National Bibliographies and Catalogs

Europe

GREAT BRITAIN

2 **British national bibliography.** http://
www.bl.uk/catalogues/bnb/index.html.
British Library. London: British Library.
1950-
015.42   Z2001.B75

Most comprehensive publishing record of the United Kingdom and the Republic of Ireland, including
print since 1950 and electronic publications since
2003. Emphasizes mainstream monographs. Previously in print and CD-ROM. Includes most new
books, serials and forthcoming books. Excludes
government documents, music scores, maps,
AV, diaries, promotional material, and ephemera.
Z39.50 download of MARC records free.

IRELAND

3 **British national bibliography.** http://
www.bl.uk/catalogues/bnb/index.html.
British Library. London: British Library.
1950-
015.42   Z2001.B75

Most comprehensive publishing record of the United Kingdom and the Republic of Ireland, including print since 1950 and electronic publications since 2003. Emphasizes mainstream monographs. Previously in print and CD-ROM. Includes most new books, serials and forthcoming books. Excludes government documents, music scores, maps, AV, diaries, promotional material, and ephemera. Z39.50 download of MARC records free.

North America

CANADA

4   Canadiana. http://www.collectionscanada
.gc.ca/canadiana/index-e.html. National
Library of Canada. Ottawa, Ont.: National
Library of Canada. 1998– 1480-7378
Z1365; Z1365.C24

Comprehensive bibliography of Canadian publishing since 1950. Lists the more than 45,000 titles per year that are published in Canada, as well as those published elsewhere but of significance to Canada. Includes books, periodicals, pamphlets, sound recordings, microforms, music scores, government documents, theses, electronic documents, educational kits and video recordings, and forthcoming publications. Acts as portal to over 65 million pages of digital collections from Canadian libraries, archives, and museums. Supersedes the print and microfiche versions of *Canadiana*, which ceased in 1991 and 2000.

UNITED STATES

**5   Center for Research Libraries online
dissertations catalog.** http://www-apps
.crl.edu/catalog/dissertationSearch.asp.
Center for Research Libraries. Chicago:
Center for Research Libraries

Provides catalog records for more than 800,000 doctoral dissertations from more than 1,200 universities outside of the U.S. and Canada. Dissertations date from the 18th century to the present.

Dissertations acquired through exchange agreements and on a title-by-title basis by request.

Dissertations available via interlibrary loan and electronic document delivery, depending on

a patron's institution's CRL (Center for Research Libraries) membership status.

6   Library of Congress online catalog.
http://catalog.loc.gov/. Library of
Congress. Washington: Library of
Congress. 1990s

Z881.U5

Contains more than 16 million records for books, serials, manuscripts, maps, music, recordings, images, and electronic resources in the Library of Congress collections with keyword or browse searching. It is available via a Z39.50 server, and a new version of the catalog is also available: http://catalog2
.loc.gov/

The catalog includes records from the time between 1898 and 1980, which have an indicator that says "from old catalog." These older records may not be up to modern cataloging standards. The records for some older materials are available only on site in the Library's Main Card Catalog.

Librarians searching for name and subject authority information can search authorities (http://authorities.loc.gov/). Other libraries' catalogs and other Library of Congress databases, the Copyright Office (http://www.copyright.gov/records/), and the American Memory Project (http://memory.loc.gov/ammem/index.html) are linked.

**7   American book publishing record
cumulative, 1876-1949: An American
national bibliography.** R.R. Bowker
Company. New York: R.R. Bowker
Company, 1980. ISBN 0835212459
015.73   Z1215.A55

Contents: v. 1-10, Dewey Decimal classes 000-999; v. 11, Fiction, Juvenile fiction; v. 12, Non-Dewey Decimal classified titles; v. 13, Author index; v. 14, Title index; v. 15, Subject guide.

Designed as a retrospective supplement for *American book publishing record* and *American book publishing record cumulative, 1950-1977*, entries for this set were compiled from *A catalog of books represented by Library of Congress printed cards* and its supplements. A useful, subject-divided record of 75 years of American book publishing, the set also serves as a source for shared cataloging. All told, the bibliography includes nearly 625,000 titles. Government publications, subscription books, dissertations, new printings, serial publications, and pamphlets under 49 p. were excluded.

8   Booksinprint.com. http://www.books inprint.com/bip/. R. R. Bowker Company. New Providence, N.J.: R. R. Bowker. 2001–

Z1215

This source is an important reference and collection development tool. It contains bibliographic records for 5–6 million books, audio books, and videos. Includes in-print, out-of-print, and forthcoming titles. Entries include title, cover image, author, publication date, publisher, ISBN-10 and ISBN-13, status, binding, edition, etc. Readers can preview first chapters if the book is available from Dial-a-Book (http://www .dialabook.net/) or ebrary (http://www.ebrary.com/ corp/). Interface also includes Global Books In Print (http://www.globalbooksinprint.com/bip/).

Additional features include the ability to search a local library's catalog, and an additional subscription gives users access to reviews from Booklist Online (29), LibraryJournal.com Reviews (32), School Library Journal, and Choice Reviews Online (36). There are some concerns about inaccuracies with author, availablity, and ISBN data. Competition from online free bookstores means that libraries may choose not to subscribe. Amazon.com (27) has good bibliographic data and has secondhand and out-of-print books. Amazon also sells CDs and other consumer goods. A print version of the *Subject guide to books in print* (9) may be useful in collection development. A good source of information about books from the United Kingdom and other English-speaking countries is BookData Online.

9   Subject guide to Books in print.
R.R. Bowker Company. New York: R.R. Bowker Company, 1957– 0000-0159
015.73   Z1215.P973

Originally intended as a subject index to the *Publishers trade list annual* and as a companion to the author and title lists in Books in Print (8), this current trade bibliography has long been valued in its own right. Current editions classify some 2.8 million volumes by nearly 80,000 Library of Congress subject headings. Works to which the Library of Congress does not assign subject headings (e.g., fiction, poetry,

drama, and Bibles) are not indexed. Also includes contact information for over 77,000 publishers.

10   WorldCat. http://www.oclc.org/worldcat/ default.htm. OCLC. Dublin, Ohio: OCLC Online Computer Library Center
                                          Z695.83

WorldCat is the largest bibliographic database in the world. It was started in 1971 as part of the Ohio Library College Center, now Online Computer Library Center (OCLC). The database continues to grow rapidly with millions of records from thousands of libraries worldwide. See http://www.oclc .org/worldcat/statistics/default.htm for up-to-date statistics. All Library of Congress (6) bibliographic records are loaded in WorldCat, and since 1976, U.S. Government materials are also included.

Content includes books, Internet sites, visual, sound, and computer files, some articles, serials, archival materials, microforms, maps, scores, manuscripts, and various other materials. In addition, series title searches are a useful means of updating the printed *Titles in series* lists. The inclusion of LCSH, DDC, ISBN numbers, and URLs, where applicable, makes it an authoritative destination for checking bibliographic data. For items not found in World-Cat, the *NUC-pre 56* is still a viable option. WorldCat is also the means by which millions of interlibrary loans have been made. Export features are available for EndNote (http://www.endnote.com/), RefWorks (http://www.refworks.com/), and other bibliographic management software. WorldCat is available on the Internet as WorldCat.org, and OCLC has added a product called WorldCat Local (http://www.oclc .org/worldcat-local.en.html) to allow local libraries to use the worldcat.org interface to reflect their holdings.

Although the database has holdings from over 70,000 libraries worldwide, there is an obvious strength in the collections for the United States.

WorldCat is an essential reference source for all libraries.

Web Portals

11   The European library. http://www.the europeanlibrary.org/tel4/. The Conference of European National Librarians (CENL).

Den Haag, The Netherlands: Koninklijke Bibliotheek, National Library of the Netherlands

Z675.N2

A portal to the print and digital resources of 48 national libraries of Europe and leading European Research Libraries. Catalogs of more than 200 million resources , including 24 million pages of full text and nearly 120 million bibliographic records, are searchable. Advanced searching permits the user to specify which libraries are searched. Researchers can register for free to access metadata. Membership available to libraries.

12   Libweb: library servers via WWW.
http://www.lib-web.org. Thomas Dowling, OhioLINK. Seattle, Wash.; Dublin, Ohio: WebJunction. 1995–
005.75025; 025.3132025; 020.711025; 027.025

Directory of home pages of more than 8,000 libraries worldwide, organized geographically for browsing and searchable by library name, location, type (academic, public, special, school, national, state), and consortial affiliation. Another directory of library websites and online catalogs, Marshall Breeding's libweb-cats (http://www.librarytechnology.org/libweb cats/), lists more libraries, especially school libraries, but requires registration in order to use the advanced search feature.

13   WorldCat. http://www.oclc.org/worldcat/default.htm. OCLC. Dublin, Ohio: OCLC Online Computer Library Center

Z695.83

WorldCat is the largest bibliographic database in the world. It was started in 1971 as part of the Ohio Library College Center, now Online Computer Library Center (OCLC). The database continues to grow rapidly with millions of records from thousands of libraries worldwide. See http://www.oclc.org/worldcat/statistics/default.htm for up-to-date statistics. All Library of Congress (6) bibliographic records are loaded in WorldCat, and since 1976, U.S. Government materials are also included.

Content includes books, Internet sites, visual, sound, and computer files, some articles, serials, archival materials, microforms, maps, scores, manuscripts, and various other materials. In addition, series title searches are a useful means of updating the printed *Titles in series* lists. The inclusion of LCSH, DDC, ISBN numbers, and URLs, where applicable, makes it an authoritative destination for checking bibliographic data. For items not found in WorldCat, the *NUC-pre 56* is still a viable option. WorldCat is also the means by which millions of interlibrary loans have been made. Export features are available for EndNote (http://www.endnote.com/), RefWorks (http://www.refworks.com/), and other bibliographic management software. WorldCat is available on the Internet as WorldCat.org, and OCLC has added a product called WorldCat Local (http://www.oclc.org/worldcat-local.en.html) to allow local libraries to use the worldcat.org interface to reflect their holdings.

Although the database has holdings from over 70,000 libraries worldwide, there is an obvious strength in the collections for the United States.

WorldCat is an essential reference source for all libraries.

Printing and Publishing

Copy Preparation

14   The Chicago manual of style. 16th ed.
Chicago: The University of Chicago Press, 2010. 1 v. (various pagings).
ISBN 9780226104201
808.0270973   Z253.U69

The 16th ed. of this significant work (available online and in print) continues to be an authoritative "how to" source for authors and editors, but now also includes many additions to recognize that much of the publishing world is electronic and online. One of the guiding principles of this edition is "to recognize the continuing evolution in the way authors, editors, and publishers do their work . . . and to maintain a focus on those aspects of the process that are independent of the medium of publication."-Pref.

The manual has been organized into three sections: 1) process of writing, editing, and publishing, 2) style and usage, and 3) documentation. To facilitate navigation and ease of use, some sections have been combined while others have expanded. Some of the most notable inclusions and changes are: editorial requirements of electronic publications, role of electronic markup, copyright and permissions, including electronic rights, citing electronic sources, and an introduction to Unicode; hyphenation guidelines appear in a four-part table. Responding to reader requests, Chicago now recommends a uniform stylistic treatment of the main citation elements for both documentation systems.

Free companion website is available at http://www.chicagomanualofstyle.org, and subscribers can personalize their copies. For those who want to see the 1st ed. (1906), a PDF copy is available on the site.

15   Endnote. http://www.myendnoteweb
.com. Thomson Reuters. New York:
Thomason Reuters. 2013

Web access to Endnote software. Endnote Basic is free. Two gigabytes storage (up to 50,000 references). References can be imported from at least nine databases or created manually. Six citation and paper styles available. Subsets of citations called "groups" can be shared. Cite While You Write plug-in for Microsoft Word available. Option to build a Researcher ID to integrate with the Web of Science (368) databases. Endnote downloadable for fee. Five gigabytes file storage, unlimited reference storage, search of several hundred databases,automatic reference updating,and Find Full Text feature.

16   MLA handbook for writers of research papers. 7th ed. Joseph Gibaldi. New
York: Modern Language Association of
America, 2009. 292p.
ISBN 9781603290241
808.027   LB2369.G53

Gives detailed instructions for every step of research and writing process including numerous citation examples and formatting guidelines. Purchase of print includes web access to additional examples and searchable text of the full edition. Standard source to consult before using the MLA style manual and guide to scholarly publishing (17). Widely used by secondary and post-secondary institutions; should be considered essential for most libraries.

17   MLA style manual and guide to scholarly publishing. 3rd ed. Joseph
Gibaldi. New York: Modern Language
Association of America, 2008. xxiv, 336 p.
ISBN 9780873522977
808.027   PN147.G444

The new 3rd ed. of this essential work has been reorganized and revised. Contains guidance on writing scholarly texts, documenting research sources, submitting manuscripts to publishers, and a section that deals with legal issues surrounding publ. (e.g., copyright, fair use, and contracts). Also includes simplified citation formats for electronic sources.

**18   Publication manual of the American
Psychological Association. 6th ed.**
American Psychological Association.
Washington: American Psychological
Association, 2010. xviii, 272 p., ill.
ISBN 9781433805592
808/.06615   BF76.7

Now in its 6th edition, the APA manual remains an indispensable tool for research and writing in psychology and related disciplines. Revisions and updates reflect the current landscape of scholarship, especially the impact of the Internet and online technology: advice on how to cite digital source materials and audiovisual media, word-processing software, online submission to journals, and retention and sharing of digitized data. Also of interest: discussion of plagiarism issues, advice on copyright permission, and suggestions for cover letters when seeking publication.

A related title, the *APA Style Guide to Electronic References* focuses on the formatting and examples of citations for various types of electronic information from this edition of the full *Publication Manual*.

19   RefWorks. https://www.refworks.com/.
ProQuest. Bethesda, Md.: ProQuest. 2002-

Web-based bibliographic management system to gather, manage, store and share information. Generates citations and bibliographies. Bibliographic data can be imported from databases or entered into a form. Citations can be moved among user-created folders. Formats and creates bibliographies in standard and journal-specific styles. Write-N-Cite feature can be added to MS Word software. Works with Windows, Mac, UNIX, and Linux platforms.

20   Research and documentation online.
http://www.dianahacker.com/resdoc.
Diana Hacker, Barbara Fister. Boston:
Bedford/St. Martin's

                                       ZA4375

Includes guidelines for documenting sources following MLA, APA, Chicago, and CSE styles, with sample student papers illustrating how citation styles are applied. Presents tips for evaluating sources and a glossary of terms related to literature searching. Discusses research in humanities, social sciences, history, and sciences and recommends standard reference sources.

Printed version offers additional guidance on formulating research questions, mapping search strategies, and finding and evaluating sources: *Research and documentation in the electronic age*, 5th ed.

21 Zotero. http://www.zotero.org. Roy Rosenzweig Center for History and New Media. Fairfax, Va.: Roy Rosenzweig Center for History and New Media. 2009-
Bibliographic management download for Firefox browser. Three hundred megabytes of storage can be increased for fee. Can be synced among multiple devices and accessed from any browser. Collections can be shared with groups. Downloads automatically from searches in Firefox. Full text files, Web pages, and citations can be saved. User can add identifiers and tags.

Copyright

22 Copyright. http://www.copyright.gov/. Library of Congress. Washington: U.S. Copyright Office. 2004-

KF3004

Official U.S. copyright site located at the Library of Congress. Separate pages available include About Copyright (copyright basics, FAQs, current fees, etc.), Search Copyright Records (by title, author, etc.), Publications (circulars, forms, factsheets, reports, and studies), Licensing, Preregistration, How to Register a Work, How to Record a Document, Law and Policy, and Related Links (patents, trademarks, etc.).

The online catalog available at http://cocatalog .loc.gov/cgi-bin/Pwebrecon.cgi?DB=local&amp ;PAGE=First serves as the successor to the print *Catalog of copyright entries*. For older records, instructions are provided for online submissions for searches of all Copyright Office records, including earlier records not available online.

General Works
DIRECTORIES
North America

23 Publishers directory. http://gale .cengage.com/DirectoryLibrary/index.htm. Gale Research. Detroit: Gale Research. 1990s-
Online version of Gale's print *Publishers directory*. Covers "approximately 30,000 U.S. and Canadian publishers, distributors, and wholesalers"—*Factsheet*. Includes contact information (name, address, phone, fax, website, e-mail) as well as sales, number of employees, date founded, affiliates, mergers, number of new titles, total titles, ISBNs, subjects covered, key officers and personnel, special services, and branch offices. Includes ability to generate lists, is cross-searchable, and is a part of the Gale Directory Library. For more information about the product, see http://gale.cengage .com/pdf/facts/PublisherDir.pdf.

UNITED STATES

24 Literary market place online. http://www.literarymarketplace.com. R.R. Bowker Company. New York: R.R. Bowker Company. 1998-
Web version combining two directories: Literary Market Place: LMP and International Literary Market Place. Covers the book publishing industry in all subjects and includes information on companies, books, periodicals, awards, and events as well as contact information for publishers, literary agents, distributors and sales representatives, wholesalers, book producers, exporters and importers, manufacturers and printers, translators and interpreters, paper suppliers, remainder dealers, producers of reference books and magazines, literary associations, and societies.

Free users who register have full access to small presses and industry services. In the Publishers and Agents categories, free user access is limited to company names and addresses. Subscribers have access to full profiles of publishers and agents (these entries include addresses, phone/fax numbers, personnel listings, description, year founded, subsidiaries, and memberships). All users may use alphabetic browsing, keyword searching of all fields, and advanced search options.

Selection of Materials

Audiovisual Materials

25   **Bowker's complete video directory.** R.R. Bowker Company. , 1990- 1051–290X

Bowker's Complete Video Directory is a valuable tool for selectors of audiovisual materials. The current (2012) guide is primarily made up of a Title Index containing "information for over 73,000 feature films, other performing arts and entertainment events" and an Educational & Special Interest Video Title Index, with over 186,000 entries. Additional indexes provide access via Awards, Genre, Cast/Director, Spanish Language, Closed Captioning, Manufacturer/Distributor, and Subject. Also available as part of Bowker's Booksinprint.com (8).

26   **NICEM Film and Video Finder Online.** http://www.nicem.com/. National Information Center for Educational Media. Access Innovations, Inc. 1996-

The National Information Center for Educational Media's Film and Video Finder Online "contains over 440,000 bibliographic records, representing 640,000 items of nonprint materials that cover all subject areas, are intended for all age levels, and are disseminated in all formats of media." A subscription-based product, the database includes films, videocassettes, laser discs, CD-ROMs, audiocassettes, slides, filmstrips, overhead transparencies and DVDs, both in-print and out-of-print, from the early 20th century to the present day. Entries are searchable, and there are a variety of search limiters that can be applied. Results can be downloaded and printed. One caveat is that entries do not currently include reviews. A useful item for librarians putting together audiovisual resource collections.

REVIEWS

27   **Amazon.com.** http://www.amazon.com/. Amazon.com, Inc. Seattle, Wash.: Amazon.com. 1995–

With its worldwide reach and large catalog of materials, Amazon.com has become a useful tool for book selectors. Amazon provides quick access to lists of current popular fiction and best sellers as well as browsable guides to a wide range of nonfiction topics. Advanced searching can be done by author, title, ISBN, publisher, or key word and can be limited by format, subject area, language, and publication date. Listed titles generally include reviews from such sources as *Booklist*, *Library journal*, and *The publishers weekly*, as well as excerpts from newspaper reviews. Readers reviews are also part of the record. New and used titles are available, as well as listings of out-of-print materials. Amazon has a variety of options available for library purchasers in the corporate accounts section of the site. Amazon has international affiliates in Canada (http://www.amazon.ca/), the United Kingdom (http://www.amazon.co.uk/), France (http://www.amazon.fr/), Germany (http://www.amazon.de/), China (http://www.amazon.cn/), and Japan (http://www.amazon.co.jp/).

28   **Metacritic.com.** http://www.metacritic.com/. CNET Networks, Inc. San Francisco: CNET Networks. 1999–
                                                              N7475.M48

Serves as a reviewing source as well as a compilation of reviews by 60–70 well-respected critics. Excerpts of film, music, game, book, and television reviews published since 2001 in major newspapers and magazines can be read on the site, and links are provided to free full-text versions. In addition, site editors interpret these reviews using a 100-point scale, weight the scores based upon the prestige of the reviewer and/or publication, and calculate a "metascore" for each work. Users of the site may also contribute ratings, which are calculated separately. The database can be searched by the title of a specific work, the name of an individual involved, a genre, or metascore.

Books

BOOK REVIEW INDEXES

29   **Booklist online.** http://www.booklistonline.com/. American Library Association. Chicago: American Library Association. 2006–

Useful for reviews of current fiction, nonfiction, and reference materials, Booklist Online is a subscription database that "contains over 120,000 reviews and thousands of features dating back to 1992."—FAQ There is some free content, including feature articles, columns, and some current reviews. The bulk of the reviews are available only to subscribers. Reviews are arranged into broad categories of Adult Books, Books for Youth, Media, and Reference. Users can browse reviews in these areas by subject or use a variety of search tools to locate materials. Online content is derived from the long-running ALA publication *Booklist*.

30   Book review digest plus. http://www .ebscohost.com/academic/book-review -digest-plus. EBSCO Publishing. Ipswich, Mass.: EBSCO Publishing. 1999-

028.1   Z1035.A1

The Book Review Digest Plus database includes citations since 1983 to over two million reviews of more than 660,000 books. Many of the titles have review excerpts. About 10 percent of the reviews are full-text, and a fifth of the titles are annotated. Materials covered include "fiction, non-fiction, books for children, and reference works in the humanities, social sciences, and general sciences."—*Web site*. Coverage from 1905–82 is available in Book Review Digest Retrospective. Successor to *Book review digest*, used by selectors in both public and academic libraries since 1905 as a source for finding short summaries of reviews of fiction and nonfiction materials. Published until 2011 by the H. W. Wilson Company.

31   Book review index online plus. http:// www.gale.cengage.com/BRIOnline/index .htm. Gale/Cengage Learning. Farmington Hills, Mich.: Gale/Cengage Learning

Selectors will find over 5 million review citations, including over 634,000 full-text reviews, in Gale's online version of *Book review index*. This subscription database gathers review information from a core list of nearly 700 journals (http://gale .cengage.com/tlist/sb5122.xls). As of July 2007, book reviews from select blogs are also included. Book Review Index Plus includes "entire backfile of *Book Review Index*'s print content from 1965 to the present" (http://www.gale.cengage.com/BRIOnline/ explore_content.htm). The database is "OpenURL compliant, allowing subscribers to link to full-text reviews from other sources" (Web site).

32   LibraryJournal.com reviews. http:// reviews.libraryjournal.com/?ref=menu. Library Journal. New York: Reed Business Information

Useful for reviews of current fiction, nonfiction, and reference materials, LibraryJournal.com offers access to reviews from current and past issues of *Library journal*. Reviews are arranged into ten categories: Books, Genre Fiction, Graphic Novels, Computer Media, Reference, Professional Media, Magazine, Video/DVD, Audio, and Express Reviews. Within each category are chronologically arranged, thematic lists of reviewed titles from *Library Journal* back to 2005. For complete access to the *Library Journal* review database back to 1988, users must be subscribed to the print edition and register at the LibraryJournal.com site.

GUIDES

33   ARBAonline. http://www.arbaonline .com/. Westport, Conn.: Libraries Unlimited. 2003–

Database of librarian-authored reviews of reference books and electronic reference tools, 1997 to date. Updated monthly. Search interface offers multiple options, plus browsing by subject or latest monthly update. Access restricted to subscribers. Also issued in print since 1970 as *American reference books annual*.

34   Fiction Core Collection. http://www .ebscohost.com/public/fiction-core -collection. H.W. Wilson Company. Ipswich, Mass.: EBSCO Publishing. 2003-

H. W. Wilson's long-running collection guides have been brought together in digital form under EBSCO's Core Collections package (http://www .ebscohost.com/academic-alt/core-collections). The Fiction Core Collection includes author, out-of-print status, title, reprint publication data, publisher, ISBN, publication date, LCCN, sequel details, illustration note, publication history, and price for over 15,000 classic and contemporary works of fiction. The online edition includes book review citations and excerpts, book covers, advanced searching and sorting capabilities. Updated on a monthly basis. A useful resource for selectors and readers' advisors, particularly in public libraries, and can be useful for curriculum support in school media centers.

Titles are also available in print form from Grey House Publishing (http://www.hwwilsoninprint.com/core_collections.php).

35 Public Library Core Collection.
http://www.ebscohost.com/public/public -library-core-collection-nonfiction.
H. W. Wilson Company. Ipswich, Mass.: EBSCO Publishing. 2008-

H. W. Wilson's long-running collection guides have been brought together in digital form under EBSCO's Core Collections package (http://www .ebscohost.com/academic-alt/core-collections). The Public Library Core Collection: Nonfiction includes Author, Out-of-Print Status, Title, Reprint Publication Data, Publisher, ISBN, Publication Date, LCCN, Sequel Details, Illustration Note, Publication History, and Price for over 36,000 reference and nonfiction works for adults. The online edition includes book review citations and excerpts, book covers, advanced searching and sorting capabilities. Content is updated on a monthly basis. A useful resource for public library selectors in all nonfiction areas, and can be helpful for curriculum support in school media centers, especially at the middle and high school levels.

Titles in the Core Collection package are also available in print form from Grey House Publishing (http://www.hwwilsoninprint.com/core_collections .php).

36 Choice reviews online. http://www .cro3.org/. Association of College and Research Libraries. Chicago: American Library Association

Publishes "over 7,000 reviews" (*About Choice*) annually. Reviews concentrate on "academic books, electronic media, and Internet resources of interest to those in higher education" (*About Choice*). Available only to subscribers, the reviews in Choice Reviews Online are concise and authoritative and include full bibliographic information and useful recommendations for audience. Reviews are fully searchable, and users can apply a variety of limits to their searches. Users' profiles allow selectors to receive monthly e-mails of reviews tailored to their specifications. Users can check holdings in WorldCat (10), allowing them to determine what libraries in their area own a particular title. Other features include an annual list of Outstanding Academic Titles published in the previous year and bibliographic essays on current topics of interest. Online content is derived from *Choice* magazine.

37 Amazon.com. http://www.amazon.com/. Amazon.com, Inc. Seattle, Wash.: Amazon.com. 1995–

With its worldwide reach and large catalog of materials, Amazon.com has become a useful tool for book selectors. Amazon provides quick access to lists of current popular fiction and best sellers as well as browsable guides to a wide range of nonfiction topics. Advanced searching can be done by author, title, ISBN, publisher, or key word and can be limited by format, subject area, language, and publication date. Listed titles generally include reviews from such sources as *Booklist*, *Library journal*, and *The publishers weekly*, as well as excerpts from newspaper reviews. Readers reviews are also part of the record. New and used titles are available, as well as listings of out-of-print materials. Amazon has a variety of options available for library purchasers in the corporate accounts section of the site. Amazon has international affiliates in Canada (http://www.amazon.ca/), the United Kingdom (http://www.amazon.co.uk/), France (http://www.amazon.fr/), Germany (http:// www.amazon.de/), China (http://www.amazon.cn/), and Japan (http://www.amazon.co.jp/).

38 Booklist online. http://www.booklist online.com/. American Library Association. Chicago: American Library Association. 2006–

Useful for reviews of current fiction, nonfiction, and reference materials, Booklist Online is a subscription database that "contains over 120,000 reviews and thousands of features dating back to 1992."—FAQ There is some free content, including feature articles, columns, and some current reviews. The bulk of the reviews are available only to subscribers. Reviews are arranged into broad categories of Adult Books, Books for Youth, Media, and Reference. Users can browse reviews in these areas by subject or use a variety of search tools to locate materials. Online content is derived from the long-running ALA publication *Booklist*.

39 Booksinprint.com. http://www.books inprint.com/bip/. R. R. Bowker Company. New Providence, N.J.: R. R. Bowker. 2001–
Z1215

This source is an important reference and collection development tool. It contains bibliographic records for 5–6 million books, audio books, and videos. Includes in-print, out-of-print, and forthcoming titles. Entries include title, cover image, author, publication date, publisher, ISBN-10 and ISBN-13, status, binding, edition, etc. Readers can preview first chapters if the book is available from Dial-a-Book (http://www.dialabook.net/) or ebrary (http://www.ebrary.com/corp/). Interface also includes Global Books In Print (http://www.globalbooksinprint.com/bip/).

Additional features include the ability to search a local library's catalog, and an additional subscription gives users access to reviews from Booklist Online (29), LibraryJournal.com Reviews (32), School Library Journal, and Choice Reviews Online (36). There are some concerns about inaccuracies with author, availablity, and ISBN data. Competition from online free bookstores means that libraries may choose not to subscribe. Amazon.com (27) has good bibliographic data and has secondhand and out-of-print books. Amazon also sells CDs and other consumer goods. A print version of the *Subject guide to books in print* (9) may be useful in collection development. A good source of information about books from the United Kingdom and other English-speaking countries is BookData Online.

Reference Books

40   Booklist online. http://www.booklist online.com/. American Library Association. Chicago: American Library Association. 2006–

Useful for reviews of current fiction, nonfiction, and reference materials, Booklist Online is a subscription database that "contains over 120,000 reviews and thousands of features dating back to 1992."—FAQ There is some free content, including feature articles, columns, and some current reviews. The bulk of the reviews are available only to subscribers. Reviews are arranged into broad categories of Adult Books, Books for Youth, Media, and Reference. Users can browse reviews in these areas by subject or use a variety of search tools to locate materials. Online content is derived from the long-running ALA publication *Booklist*.

41   Choice reviews online. http://www.cro3 .org/. Association of College and Research Libraries. Chicago: American Library Association

Publishes "over 7,000 reviews" (*About Choice*) annually. Reviews concentrate on "academic books, electronic media, and Internet resources of interest to those in higher education" (*About Choice*). Available only to subscribers, the reviews in Choice Reviews Online are concise and authoritative and include full bibliographic information and useful recommendations for audience. Reviews are fully searchable, and users can apply a variety of limits to their searches. Users' profiles allow selectors to receive monthly e-mails of reviews tailored to their specifications. Users can check holdings in WorldCat (10), allowing them to determine what libraries in their area own a particular title. Other features include an annual list of Outstanding Academic Titles published in the previous year and bibliographic essays on current topics of interest. Online content is derived from *Choice* magazine.

42   LibraryJournal.com reviews. http://reviews.libraryjournal.com/?ref=menu. Library Journal. New York: Reed Business Information

Useful for reviews of current fiction, nonfiction, and reference materials, LibraryJournal.com offers access to reviews from current and past issues of *Library journal*. Reviews are arranged into ten categories: Books, Genre Fiction, Graphic Novels, Computer Media, Reference, Professional Media, Magazine, Video/DVD, Audio, and Express Reviews. Within each category are chronologically arranged, thematic lists of reviewed titles from *Library Journal* back to 2005. For complete access to the *Library Journal* review database back to 1988, users must be subscribed to the print edition and register at the LibraryJournal.com site.

43   The new Walford guide to reference resources: Volume 1: Science, technology, and medicine. 9th ed. Ray Lester. London: Facet, 2005–. xix, 827 p., ill. ISBN 1856044955
011.02   Z1035.1

"This book is the first volume of a series that succeeds *Walford's guide to reference material*, published . . . 1959 and 2000 by Library Association Publishing." The scope and format of this guide is much different from the "old Walford," and thus it would behoove librarians to keep both eds. on the shelf. This version concentrates on websites and on general interest resources, including many that aren't specific to science and technology. Includes current awareness sources and many monographs that aren't traditional reference sources, but rather are popular introductions to topics.

Volume 2: The social sciences was published January 2008; and *Volume 3: Arts, humanities, and general reference* is expected in 2015. For more information, see publisher's page at http://www.facetpublishing .co.uk/title.php?id=4998.

44   Recommended reference books for small and medium-sized libraries and media centers. 28th ed.
Shannon Graff Hysell. Littleton, Colo.: Libraries Unlimited, 1981– 0277-5948
011.02   Z1035.1.R438
A compilation of best titles reviewed in *American Reference Books Annual (ARBA) Online* (33) and recommended for purchase by small and medium-sized academic, public, or school libraries. Each annual edition features approximately 500 critical, signed reviews of print and electronic reference sources taken from ARBA and published in the previous two years. The reviews are in a classified arrangement by subject area with author/title and subject indexes. The focus is on materials that are both affordable and useful.

OUT OF PRINT BOOKS

45   Alibris for libraries. http://library.alibris .com/. Alibris. Emeryville, Calif.: Alibris. 1998–
Alibris provides selectors access to a broad selection of used and out-of-print materials. In addition to titles stocked by Alibris, the database searches the inventories of over 7,500 booksellers worldwide, offering access to over 60 million titles. Alibris provides a variety of tools to assist selectors, including the ability to match want-lists to the Alibris database and to create subject-centered collection reports on titles in the database. Libraries can also order titles from Alibris through their Interlibrary Loan (ILL) systems, using OCLC's ILL Fee Management (IFM) service (for more information, see http://library.alibris.com/ill-program?cm_sp=lhs -_-services-_-ill). Alibris also offers librarians access to used audiovisual materials in a variety of formats, including CD, vinyl, VHS, and DVD.

Periodicals

46   Directory of open access journals.
http://www.doaj.org. Lund University Libraries. Lund, Sweden: Lund University Libraries. 2003–
011.34
Directory of free, full-text, scholarly journals spanning most disciplines. Journals are international and multilingual in scope and must be peer reviewed or have an editorial review board. The database includes more than 10,000 journals, the majority of which are searchable at the article level. Browsable by title and subject tree. Entries link out to full-text content at the journal's homepage; records include title, subject, ISSN, publisher, language, related keywords, and year of first online issue available.

47   Magazines for libraries. Cheryl Laguardia, William A. Katz, Linda Sternberg Katz. New York: Bowker, 1969– 0000-0914
050.25   Z6941.M23; PN4832
The 22nd edition from 2013 of this venerable guide annotates and evaluates more than 5,300 periodicals. The substantive annotations are provided by a team of subject specialists. Entries are grouped into more than 200 subject categories, each with a brief introduction that discusses periodical publishing in that area. Entries include bibliographic information as well as an indication of what sources index the journal under review. Title and subject indexes. This volume is useful for public, university, college, junior college, school, and special libraries.

48   MediaFinder. http://www.mediafinder .com. Oxbridge Communications. New York: Oxbridge Communications
Directory of U.S. and Canadian periodicals including magazines, journals, newspapers, newsletters, and catalogs. Subscribers have access to "70,000 titles from major city dailies to fanzines, in 263 subject areas."—*About page* Searchable by keyword and subject but also by advertisement rates, publication type, print specification, circulation, subscription price, and whether or not the publisher rents the list. Browsable by subject category. Entries include a brief editorial description; names and contact information of key staff; and data about circulation, advertising, and the physical attributes of the publication itself

(number of pages, type of binding, etc.). Facilitates data export. Online version of the *Standard periodical directory* (372).

49   Ulrich's periodicals directory. http://www.ulrichsweb.com/ulrichsweb. R. R. Bowker. New Providence, N.J.: R. R. Bowker. 2001–

Z6941

Directory of periodicals from around the world, including magazines, journals, newsletters, newspapers, annuals, and irregular serials. Searchable by keyword, title, ISSN, and subject. Several browse options are available, including title, subject, electronic vendor, country of publication, language, place of publication, and classification. Each entry includes basic information about the title, such as a basic description, publisher information, circulation figures, peer-reviewed status, and start year. Specialized features of this site include details about other available formats, including all electronic availability options; indexing and abstracting sources, including retrospective; document delivery options; publisher and ordering information; advertising and rights information; and reviews of the publication. Updated daily. OpenURL compliant.

The print version is still available as a more economical choice. Published annually, it is arranged alphabetically within subject classification. Indexes include refereed serials, online periodicals, cessations, ISSNs, and titles.

This title has undergone a number of changes, as reported in Ulrich's itself. The title started publication as *Periodicals directory: A classified guide to a selected list of current periodicals foreign and domestic* (1932–38) and changed to *Ulrich's periodicals directory: A selected guide to current periodicals, inter-American edition* (1938–43), then to *Ulrich's periodicals directory* (1943–63), and finally to *Ulrich's international periodicals directory* (1966–2000). This last title incorporated *Irregular serials and annuals* (1967–87) in 1988.

Websites

50   Best free reference websites. http://www.ala.org/ala/mgrps/divs/rusa/sections/mars/marspubs/marsbestindex.cfm. RUSA

Machine-Assisted Reference Section (MARS). Chicago: American Library Association

Since 1999, the Machine-Assisted Reference Section (MARS) of ALA's Reference and User Services Division has created an annual list of the best free websites. All sites listed provide most or all of the information for free. Selected sites cover a wide range of subject areas of use to librarians and library users. Sites are selected based on their usefulness in responding to "ready reference" type questions, the authority of the organization providing the site, the unique nature of the information provided, and the "appropriate use of the web as a medium."—*MARS Selection Criteria*, http://www.ala.org/ala/mgrps/divs/rusa/sections/mars/marspubs/marsbestrefcriteria.cfm

Archived selections from 1999 onward are listed alphabetically, with a link to the MARS review. The current year's list is linked from the MARS home page. See http://www.ala.org/ala/mgrps/divs/rusa/sections/mars/index.cfm, under publications.

51   Fiction Core Collection. http://www.ebscohost.com/public/fiction-core-collection. H.W. Wilson Company. Ipswich, Mass.: EBSCO Publishing. 2003-

H. W. Wilson's long-running collection guides have been brought together in digital form under EBSCO's Core Collections package (http://www.ebscohost.com/academic-alt/core-collections). The Fiction Core Collection includes author, out-of-print status, title, reprint publication data, publisher, ISBN, publication date, LCCN, sequel details, illustration note, publication history, and price for over 15,000 classic and contemporary works of fiction. The online edition includes book review citations and excerpts, book covers, advanced searching and sorting capabilities. Updated on a monthly basis. A useful resource for selectors and readers' advisors, particularly in public libraries, and can be useful for curriculum support in school media centers.

Titles are also available in print form from Grey House Publishing (http://www.hwwilsoninprint.com/core_collections.php).

52   Guide to Reference. http://www.guidetoreference.org. Robert Henry Kieft, American Library Association. Chicago:

American Library Association. 2008-
Since its first publication in 1902, *The Guide To Reference* has been an essential source for selectors of reference materials in both academic and public libraries. The 12th edition, the first to be fully digital, carries on that tradition, offering annotations of print and online resources that are critical to libraries and library users today. Searchable and browsable. Offers links to important reference resources. The *Guide* is divided into six major categories: general reference works; humanities; social and behavioral sciences; history and area studies; science, technology and medicine; and interdisciplinary fields, with each primary heading broken down into further subcategories.

53 NoveList plus. http://www.ebscohost .com/novelist. EBSCO. Ipswich, Mass.: EBSCO Pub. 1994–
Requires paid subscription. Supplies information on over 200,000 works of fiction and non-fiction for all ages. Includes full-text book reviews, discussion guides, thematic and genre-based reading lists, and popularity rankings. Popular features include "author read-alike" lists, lists of award-winning and "best" titles in various categories, and recommendations from librarians. Searchable or browsable by author, title, series, Dewey number, appeal factors such as genre and tone, and more. Users may create a personal login to save title lists and to establish and manage alerts. A companion database, NoveList K–8 Plus, focuses on works for young readers. Both databases and more are available in the NoveList Complete package.

54 Public Library Core Collection. http:// www.ebscohost.com/public/public-library -core-collection-nonfiction.
H. W. Wilson Company. Ipswich, Mass.: EBSCO Publishing. 2008-
H. W. Wilson's long-running collection guides have been brought together in digital form under EBSCO's Core Collections package (http://www .ebscohost.com/academic-alt/core-collections). The Public Library Core Collection: Nonfiction includes Author, Out-of-Print Status, Title, Reprint

Publication Data, Publisher, ISBN, Publication Date, LCCN, Sequel Details, Illustration Note, Publication History, and Price for over 36,000 reference and nonfiction works for adults. The online edition includes book review citations and excerpts, book covers, advanced searching and sorting capabilities. Content is updated on a monthly basis. A useful resource for public library selectors in all nonfiction areas, and can be helpful for curriculum support in school media centers, especially at the middle and high school levels.

Titles in the Core Collection package are also available in print form from Grey House Publishing (http://www.hwwilsoninprint.com/core_collections .php).

55 The reader's advisor online. http:// www.readersadvisoronline.com/. Libraries Unlimited. Westport, Conn.: Libraries Unlimited. Searchable index of genre fiction titles. Includes all titles from the *Genreflecting* series.

56 Scout report archives. http://scout .wisc.edu/archives/. Internet Scout Project. Madison, Wis.: Internet Scout Project, Computer Sciences Department, University of Wisconsin-Madison
Since 1994, the Scout Report project (http://scout .wisc.edu/) has provided librarians and researchers with current awareness services focused on collecting accurate, authoritative, and useful web resources.

The Scout Report Current Issue (http://scout.wisc .edu/Reports/ScoutReport/Current/) is published every Friday and contains links to websites arranged in the categories of "Research and Education" and "General Interest." The listed sites each have a critical annotation that explores its usefulness. There are also links to network tools that might be of use to librarians and researchers. Additionally, special editions of the report are published occasionally to review specific subject areas or areas of interest.

The Scout Report Archives contains annotated listings of 24,480 items from the Scout Report back to 1994. The annotations and links are both browsable and searchable.

2 Biography

Fred Burchsted

Africa

Collective Biography

57   Dictionary of African biography.
Emmanuel K. Akyeampong, Henry
Louis Gates. Oxford; New York: Oxford
University Press, c2012. 6 v., ill.
920.06   CT1920.D52
The new Dictionary of African Biography is now
the leading source. The print ed. comprises 2126
200-3000 word entries in six volumes, covering a
wide range of occupations and including both living
(25%) and deceased figures, with 20% of the entries
on women. Figures from ancient times to the present
are covered from both North and Sub-Saharan Africa.
Those included had a significant impact on African
history and culture with available sources sufficient
to support a 500 word article. Most of the biographees are of Africans born in Africa, but some colonial figures and other non-Africans and members of
the diaspora are included. Each article has a brief list
of further readings.

Vol. 6 includes: Places of Birth or Major Involve-
ment, Periods of Activity (list of biographees by majors
eras), Occupation and Realms of Renown, Current
Heads of African Nations, Directory of Contributors, and General Index (pp. 353-592). Replaces the
incomplete Africana Dictionary of African Biography.
Also available as an e-reference edition as part of the
Oxford reference online (290) and in the Oxford

African American Studies Centers. Additional entries
are being added to the online version.

Asia

Asia (by country)

CHINA

Collective Biography

**58   Biographical dictionary of the People's
Republic of China.** Yuwu Song. Jefferson,
N.C.: McFarland & Company, Inc.,
Publishers, 2013. vii, 443 pages
951.05092/2 23   DS778.A1 B56 2013
Includes 588 individuals influential in Chinese life and
culture. Political emphasis but wide range of occupations represented. Sources are cited at the end of each
entry. Brief bibliography and name index.

Europe

Europe (by country)

GREAT BRITAIN

Collective Biography

**59   Oxford dictionary of national
biography.** http://www.oxforddnb.com/.
Oxford Univ. Press, British Academy.

Oxford; New York: Oxford University Press. 2004–

The Oxford Dictionary of National Biography (ODNB) is the preeminent source for biographies of deceased Britons and for significant travelers or resident foreigners. Over 55,000 articles, with substantial source lists including references to archival collections. Includes revised or rewritten entries for all 38,500 persons in the original *Dictionary of national biography* (DNB) and its suppl. Full text of all DNB articles linked from ODNB articles.

Each Jan., about 200 persons dying five years previously are added. In May and Oct., new persons from all eras are added. Includes many more women and representatives of unusual occupations (e.g., snooker player) than the DNB. About 10,000 (18%) entries have ports. Wealth at decease indicated and known ports. enumerated. People search offers searching by name, fields of interest (elaborate list at Open Full List), sex, places, dates, life events, and religious affiliation. Searches may be limited by presence of image. Full text search available. ODNB website offers free *Oxford biography index* (http://www.oup.com/oxforddnb/info/index/), searchable by name, that provides year of birth/death, and occupation for each person in the ODNB.

Oxford dictionary of national biography also available in print, covering persons dying through 2000, with contributor index only. The DNB and its supplements are indexed in Biography and Genealogy Master Index (82). Original DNB, without suppl., full text in Internet Archive at http://www.archive.org/.

For background on the old and new DNB, see R. Faber and B. Harrison's *The dictionary of national biography: A publishing history* (pp. 171–192 in *Lives in print: Biography and the book trade from the Middle Ages to the 21st century*) and Harrison's "A slice of their lives: Editing the DNB, 1882-1999" (*English historical review*, vol. 119 no. 484 (2004), pp. 1179-1201). See also J. Scherrer's "The most amusing book in the language: The dictionary of national biography" in *Distinguished classics of reference publishing*, and K. Thomas's *Changing conceptions of national biography: The Oxford DNB in historical perspective*.

60   Who's who and who was who. http://www.ukwhoswho.com/public/home.html. A and C Black. Oxford: Oxford University Press. 2007–

Offers online access to *Who's who* and *Who was who*. *Who's who*, the leading biographical source for living persons from Great Britain, was the pioneer work of the who's who type. From 1847–96 was a handbook of titled and official classes and included lists of names rather than biographical sketches. In 1897, called "First year of new issue," became a biographical dictionary of prominent persons in many fields. Has been developed and enlarged along these lines ever since. Principally British, but a few prominent names of other nationalities included. Biographies are reliable and fairly detailed; they give main facts, addresses, often telephone numbers and, in case of authors, lists of works.

Available through Oxfordonline. Print versions of *Who's who* and *Who was who* still published by A. C. Black.

Indexed (1974–present) in Biography and Genealogy Master Index (82). More information in L. K. Simon's "Afternoon Tea, Parliament, and Who's Who" in *Distinguished classics of reference publishing*.

Who was who, for the most part, offers the original sketches as they last appeared in *Who's who* (from 1897 to date) with the date of death added, but in a few instances additional information has been incorporated. Online version offers links to Oxford Dictionary of National Biography (59) entries. Updated online annually in December, although death dates are added for new *Who was who* entries monthly.

In print *Who was who*, entries for those whose death came to the editors' attention after the appropriate vol. was published are found in an addendum preceding the main alphabet. Indexed by *Who was who: A cumulated index, 1897–2000*, which provides an index to v. 1–10 of the series. Death dates that did not appear in *Who was who* have been added in the index when available. Dates for each vol. appear in the title. Contents: v. 1, 1897–1915 (6th ed., 1988); v. 2, 1916–28 (5th ed., 1992); v. 3, 1929–40 (2nd ed., 1967); v. 4, 1941–50 (5th ed., 1980); v. 5, 1951–60 (4th ed., 1984); v. 6, 1961–70 (2nd ed., 1979); v. 7, 1971–80 (1981); v. 8, 1981–90 (1991); v. 9, 1991–5 (1996); v. 10, 1996–2000 (2001); v. 11, 2001–5 (2006); v. 12, 2006-2010 (2011).

Full text of *Who was who* (v. 1–3, 1897–1940 only) in *British biographical archive* (Series 2).

RUSSIA (INCLUDING SIBERIA) AND THE FORMER USSR
Collective Biography

61 Biographical dictionary of the former Soviet Union: Prominent people in all fields from 1917 to the present. 2nd ed. Jeanne Vronskaya, Vladimir Chuguev. London; N.J.: Bowker-Saur, 1992. 661 p. ISBN 0862916216

920.047   CT1213

Includes about 7,000 persons, covering the full range of occupations, with emphasis on fine and performing arts, less on literary, academic, and political figures. Includes émigrés. Occupational index under 41 categories. 1st ed., titled *A biographical dictionary of the Soviet Union: Prominent people in all fields from 1917–1988* (1989), is indexed in Biography and Genealogy Master Index (82). Full text of 2nd ed. in *Biographisches archiv der Sowjetunion*.

Also see *The Soviet Union: A biographical dictionary*, which covers 1,400 individuals with good coverage of perestroika- and glasnost-associated figures and list of biographees by subject/profession (full text in *Biographisches archiv der Sowjetunion*).

62 Who's who in Russia and the new states. Rev. ed. Leonard Geron, Alex Pravda. London; New York: I. B. Tauris, 1993. ca. 525 p. ISBN 1850434875

920.047   CT1203.W47

Pt. 1 (40 p.) lists major gov. officials for 15 countries under their ministries, committees, and other organizational entities. Pt. 2 provides biographies for almost 7,000 individuals. Political emphasis but with some coverage of non-governmental/military figures. Biographies of 3 to 50 lines, depending on prominence and available information. One of the most carefully prepared of the books in this field.

Earlier ed.: *Tauris Soviet directory* (1989; full text in *Biographisches archiv der Sowjetunion*).

Several other books on the immediate post-Soviet period have more detailed entries on fewer figures:

Longman biographical directory of decision-makers in Russia and the successor states includes initial list of biographees by subject (e.g., dissident, writer) under each nation, and terminal name index. Indexed in Biography and Genealogy Master Index (82).

Who's who in Russia and the CIS republics is especially good on periodical editors and sports figures, and so helps balance the political/military emphasis of other sources. Appendix A lists biographees by occupation; Appendix B by organization of gov. affiliation; Appendix C lists recipients of honors and awards; Appendix D lists books mentioned in articles by title. Indexed in Biography and Genealogy Master Index (82).

Encyclopedia of contemporary Russian culture covers artists, writers, performers, journalists, some politicians, etc. Includes living and deceased persons. Many articles with references. Listed by area of activity.

SPAIN

Collective Biography

63 Dictionary of Hispanic biography. Joseph C. Tardiff, L. Mpho Mabunda, Rudolfo Anaya. New York: Gale Research, 1996. xxv, 1011 p., ill. ISBN 0810383020

920.046   CT1343.D53

Includes about 470 biographies with source lists, some with portraits, of living (about 70 percent) and deceased persons, from the 15th century to the present. Covers individuals from Spain (61), North America (187), and Latin America (222) from a wide range of occupations. Occupation, nationality/ethnicity, and subject indexes. Indexed in *Biography and genealogy master index* (82). Full text in *Biography in Context* (67) and in *Spanish, Portuguese, and Latin American biographical archive*.

International
Collective Biography

64 Almanac of famous people. Gale Research, Inc., Gale Group. Detroit: Gale Research, Inc., 1989- 1040-127X

920.02   CT104.B56

Tenth edition, 2011. Offers date/place of birth/death, nationality, occupation, and brief description for over 33,000 persons selected from Biography and Genealogy Master Index (BGMI) (82), together with references to collective biographies. Worldwide coverage, ancient to contemporary. Second volume includes indexes by year (entries arranged by month/day), by month and day, by place of birth/death, and by occupation. Month/day and place of birth/death, and occupation are not accessible in BGMI. Includes a wide range of occupations. A valuable source, especially for smaller libraries. Available online in Biography in context (67).

65 **Biographical dictionary.** http://www
.s9.com/biography/. S9.com. Andover,
Mass.: S9.com. 1996

Very brief information on over 33,000 person of all periods. Searchable by birth/death dates, positions held, professions, literary and artistic works, and other keywords. Although large and conveniently searchable, anyone may create or edit biographies, so it must be used with caution.

66 **The biographical dictionary of women
in science: pioneering lives from
ancient times to the mid-20th century.**
Marilyn Bailey Ogilvie, Joy Dorothy
Harvey. New York: Routledge, 2000. 2 v.,
xxxviii, 1499 p. ISBN 0415920388
509.22B   Q141.B5285

Two volumes. Profiles over 2500 women in science, in an attempt to be comprehensive, including not only award winners, but just scientists at a time when it was uncommon or frowned upon. Includes many nationalities not previously covered anywhere. Subjects are those who are dead or born before 1910. Alphabetical list of entries. Brief biography of facts and dates, akin to *American Men and Women of Science* style entry, then a page-length narrative is given, including list of sources used. Signed entries. Some entries are only one or two sentences. Indexes by country, time period, occupation, and subject. No illustrations.

67 **Biography in context.** http://www.gale
.cengage.com/InContext/bio.htm. Gale
Group. Farmington Hills, Mich.: Gale
Group. 2002–
CT104

Includes full text of many Gale and other reference books, including Contemporary Authors (77), *Contemporary black biography, Directory of American scholars* 10th ed. (2002), and *Dictionary of American biography*. Also includes biographical

articles from over 250 periodicals. The Person Search allows search by occupation, nationality, ethnicity, gender, birth/death year, and place. Formerly titled Biography Resource Center. The new version allows searching limited to individual reference titles.

68 **Biography reference bank.** http://www
.ebscohost.com/academic/biography
-reference-bank. EBSCO Publishing.
Ipswich, Mass.: EBSCO Publishing. 2001–
CT104

Combines content from Current Biography Illustrated (78), *World authors*, Biography Index (83), and Junior Authors & Illustrators, together with biographies from other reference publishers. Covers more than 600,000 persons, and tracks over two million records. Links to 300,000 full text articles, and includes 35,000 illustrations. Searches available include name, full text keyword, source, birth date, occupation, gender, place of origin, and ethnicity. Published until 2011 by the H. W. Wilson Company when EBSCO took over.

Ebsco also produces two smaller full text biography databases *Biography Reference Center* (http:// www.ebscohost.com/public/biography-reference -center) with over 461,000 full-text biographies and *Biography Collection Complete* (http://www.ebsco host.com/public/biography-collection-complete) with over 177,000 biographies.

69 **Chambers dictionary of political
biography.** John Ransley. Edinburgh,
Scotland, U.K.: Chambers, 1991. 436 p.
ISBN 0550172513
920.02   D108.C44

Presents the lives of 1,100 men and women who have shaped the modern political world. Each entry provides birth and death dates, official titles, and a brief paragraph highlighting the individual's career and accomplishments. Extensive cross-references, lengthy section of political quotations, and a very thorough glossary of political terms.

70 **Dictionary of literary biography.** Gale
Research. Detroit: Gale Research, 1978–.
ill., ports. 1096-8547
808   PS21.D5

An indispensable reference tool for literary research in far-reaching genres and crossing political borders, the articles in this series are often the first critical and biographical treatment of a literary figure. Volumes comprise a nation, region, or era and a genre, and a single author may be included in more than one volume. Essays run from 3,000 to 15,000 words, depending on the importance of the figure. Because of the broad inclusion of the series, many articles are the seminal writings on an author. Thorough biographies are accompanied by exhaustive bibliographies of an author's works, including first performances of plays for dramatists. Indexed in Gale's free Literary Index (http://www.galenet.com/servlet/LitIndex), it is available as an online resource (http://www.cengage.com/search/productOverview.do?Ntt=Dictionary+of+literary+biography||1020100476145070493 9786883975191010182l&N=197&Ntk=APG||P_EPI&Ntx=mode%2Bmatchallpartial) and in Literature resource center (LRC).

71   Dictionary of medical biography.
W. F. Bynum, Helen Bynum. Westport, Conn.: Greenwood Press, 2006. 5 v. (xl, 1415 p.), ill. ISBN 0313328773
610   R134.D57
Biographies, with mention of relevant scientific and social context, of healers, medical practitioners, and physicians from all cultures from ancient times to the present. Emphasis is on Western medicine, but also includes essays that provide an introduction to Chinese, Islamic, Japanese, South Asian, and Southeast Asian medicine, and entries on traditional and alternative medicine. Each entry includes brief bibliographies of primary and secondary literature references. Illustrations, name, and subject index. Also available as an e-book.

72   Dictionary of scientific biography.
Charles Coulston Gillispie, Frederic Lawrence Holmes, American Council of Learned Societies. New York: Scribner, 1980–1990. 18 v. ISBN 0684169622
509.22B   Q141.D5
New ed. publ. in December 2007, available as eight new print vols. Available online in two e-book versions, as the 8-vol *New Dictionary of Scientific Biography* or as the 26-vol. *Complete Dictionary of Scientific Biography* that consists of the 18-vol. original set

plus the 8 new vols. See details at http://www.gale.cengage.com/ndsb/about.htm.

Description based on set publ. 1980–90. Work is internat. in coverage, including scientists from all periods of history (excluding living persons), and encompassing the fields of astronomy, biology, chemistry, earth sciences, mathematics, and physics. Technology, medicine, and social sciences are only included as they relate to the above sciences. Focuses on scientists whose work made a difference to the discipline. Signed articles include bibliographies of original and secondary works. In some cases the article is the first or most comprehensive study of a figure's total contribution to science.

Vols. 15–18 are suppl., including more recent scientists or those whose entries were not ready for the main edition of the work, and including supplementary features, such as topical essays on the achievements of ancient civilizations.

New dictionary of scientific biography contains new articles about scientists dying after 1980 and earlier figures omitted from the original Dictionary together with articles updating, but not replacing, entries in the original. Unlike the original, psychology and anthropology are covered, with some sociology and economics.

73   Encyclopedia of life writing: Autobiographical and biographical forms. Margaretta Jolly. London: Fitzroy Dearborn, 2001. 2 v. (xlvii, 1090 p.) ISBN 157958232X
920.003   CT21.E53
Over 600 articles on genres (e.g., case histories, letters), themes (childhood, disability, identity), contexts (apartheid, Islam), and authors of life writing. Articles cover eras (classical) and regional traditions (Caribbean: Francophone; Japan: Heian period). Each article includes references. Thematic list broadly categorizes articles by chronology, region, and subject. Author, title, and subject indexes. Available through Credo Reference. *Encyclopedia of women's autobiography* is a similar but more specialized work.

For the current literature on life writing, see "Annual bibliography of works about life writing," which has appeared in the journal *Biography* since 1978. For French-language literature, see Philippe Lejeune's Autopacte (http://www.autopacte.org/), which offers bibliographies of personal writings. In print: *Bibliographie des études en langue française sur la littérature personnelle et les récits de vie* (1984–).

74   Great lives from history. Salem Press. Pasadena, Calif.: Salem Press, 2004–. 27 v. ISBN 1587651521

Worldwide coverage with European emphasis. About 330 persons per set in three- to four-page articles with annotated source lists. Good source for beginning researchers, especially for non-Anglo-American figures. Each biography includes "significance" section which places each life in historical context. Online description available at http://salem press.com/Store/ProdGroup/?ProductGroup.Id =16. Revised edition of *Dictionary of world biography* by Magill et al. Published or forthcoming (each in multiple volumes): *The ancient world*, *The Middle Ages*, *The Renaissance and early modern era, 1454–1600*, *The 17th century*,

The 18th century, *The 19th century*, *Notorious lives*, *The 20th century*.

75   The Harper encyclopedia of military biography. Trevor Nevitt Dupuy, Curt Johnson, David L. Bongard. New York: HarperCollins, 1992. viii, 834 p. ISBN 0062700154

355.00922B   U51.D87

Concise sketches of some 3,000 world military leaders from antiquity through the Kuwait War, usually ending with a paragraph evaluating the individual's character, abilities, and contributions. Articles with lists of primarily English-language sources. Indexed in *Biography and genealogy master index* (82).

Three more recent works cover fewer figures, often with longer articles: *Macmillan dictionary of military biography* (about 400 articles, no sources), *World military leaders: A biographical dictionary* by Grossman (about 215 articles with sources), *Who's who in military history: From 1453 to the present day* by Keegan et al. (roughly 650 articles, no sources, indexed [1st ed., 1976, only] in *Biography and genealogy master index*) (82).

76   Women in world history: A biographical encyclopedia. Anne Commire, Deborah Klezmer. Waterford, Conn.: Yorkin, 1999–2002.

17 v., ill. ISBN 078763736X

920.7203   HQ1115.W6

Covers over 10,000 women, living (born before 1927 only) and deceased, from antiquity to the present. Articles range from a paragraph to several pages; most have source lists, which include the location of personal papers. Abundant name cross-references provided, and each entry starts with a list of variant names. Many brief articles in side-boxes, sometimes in the main alphabetical sequence, but often with topically related entries, so the index must be used to find them. Authors are under-represented because there are many other sources for literary biography. Vol. 1 begins with 90 dynastic geneal. charts, grouped by country. The last vol. (v. 17) contains indexes. Indexed in Biography and Genealogy Master Index (82).

The same editors later produced *Dictionary of women worldwide: 25,000 women through the ages*, covering 25,000 women, with shorter entries.

CONTEMPORARY

77   Contemporary authors online. http://solutions.cengage.com/Gale/ Catalog/Fact-Sheets/?cid=14W-RF0329 &riba=14W-RF0329-7. Gale Research. Detroit: Gale Research. 1995–

Major source for around 116,000 living (or deceased since early 1960s) literary and nonliterary writers worldwide. Articles typically include short critical essay ("Sidelights"); brief who's who type personal information (including agent); awards; brief career summary; list of author's writings; books, articles (including reviews), and/or websites about the author; and sometimes a portrait.

In print *Contemporary authors*, new entries appear in *Contemporary authors* (CA); revisions of CA entries appear in *Contemporary authors, new revision series*. Cumulative index in print vol. and on free website (http://www.galenet.com/servlet/LitIndex). Indexed in Biography and genealogy master index (82). Full text in Biography in Context (67) and Literature Resource Center.

78   Current biography illustrated. http:// www.ebscohost.com/academic/current -biography-illustrated. EBSCO Publishing.

Ipswich, Mass.: EBSCO Publishing
CT 100

Online version of content from *Current biography* since 1940. Adds about 150 biographies annually of persons of various nationalities, professions, and occupations, who are currently prominent in their particular fields. Information generally includes full name, dates of birth/death, occupation and reason for newsworthiness, address, a biographical sketch of about 2,500 words, with port. and references to sources.

Published until 2011 by the H. W. Wilson Company. Successor also to *Current biography yearbook*, and Biography Reference Bank (68). Indexed in Biography and Genealogy Master Index (82).

79   The international who's who of women. Europa Publications Ltd. London: Europa Publications Ltd., 1992– 0965-3775

920.72   CT3235.I58

Current ed. provides the expected biographical facts concerning over 7,500 women who have been "under-represented" (*Foreword*) in works such as *The international who's who*—with which this work has little overlap. Information was derived from responses to questionnaires and was verified by the publisher. Substantial coverage of women from Third World and non-Western European/North American countries. Index, by broad career categories, identifies nationality of subjects.

First ed., 1992; 2nd ed., 1997; thereafter biennial. The 2nd ed. indexed in *Biography and genealogy master index* (82).

80   Who's who in the world. Marquis Who's Who, Macmillan Directory Division. Wilmette, Ill.: Marquis Who's Who, Macmillan Directory Division, 1971– 0083-9825

920.02   CT120.W5

Over 60,000 biographies in the current edition are drawn from "virtually every nation."—*Pref*. Invites comparison with *The international who's who* and includes many of the same names, though there is far less overlap than one might expect. Professional index by areas of activity. Included (1985–) in Marquis Who's Who on the Web and Biography in Context (67). Available online in Credo Reference.

Indexed in Biography and Genealogy Master Index (1974–) (82).

81   World Who's Who. http://www.world whoswho.com/public/views/home.html. Europa Publications Limited. London: Routledge. 2007–

Brief biographical data on prominent persons throughout the world. Almost 60,000 persons currently in online version. Access to online version accompanies print copy or available independently. Offers full-text searching. Includes entries for persons in recent editions (largely since 2000, some back to 1995) now deceased, together with selections from other Europa biographical titles.

Print version titled *International who's who*. Current ed. (77th, 2014) has over 25,000 entries. Introductory section on reigning royal families. 38th ed. (1974) to current ed. indexed in Biography and Genealogy Master Index (82).

See also *Who's who in the world* (80).

Indexes

82   Biography and genealogy master index. http://solutions.cengage.com/Gale/Catalog/Fact-Sheets/?cid=14W-RF 0329&riba=14W-RF0329-7. Gale, Cengage Learning. Farmington Hills, Mich.: Gale. 2001–

Z5305.U5

Essential first stop in biographical research. Indexes nearly 1,600 publ., largely biographical dictionaries and subject encyclopedias, and includes references on over 13.6 million people. Both current and retrospective works included. Subscription database. Indexes H. W. Wilson's Biography Index: Past and Present (83), which extends Biography and Genealogy Master Index's coverage to periodical articles. Birth/death dates given. Searches can be limited to articles with portraits.

Covers *American men and women of science* (from 1973– ; for earlier coverage see *American men and women of science: Cumulative index*), *Who's who* [Great Britain] (from 1974–) (60), *Who's who in America* (from 1973–) (92), *Who was who in America*, and other Marquis who's who publications. Also available in print.

This is the electronic version of the discontinued microform *Bio-base*.

83 Biography index. http://www.ebscohost
.com/academic/biography-index-past-and
-present. EBSCO Publishing. Ipswich,
Mass.: EBSCO Publishing. 2006
Z5301

Indexes English-language biographical material found in periodicals, individual and collective biographical books, selected *New York Times* obituaries, and other sources. Published until 2011 by the H. W. Wilson Company. Successor to the print format *Biography index* by Joseph publ. quarterly with annual cumulations and index by profession, which has been indexed in Biography and Genealogy Master Index (Gale/Cengage Learning) (82). Earlier content is offered in Biography Index Retrospective: 1905-1982.

Latin America and the Caribbean
Collective Biography

84 Dictionary of Hispanic biography.
Joseph C. Tardiff, L. Mpho Mabunda,
Rudolfo Anaya. New York: Gale Research,
1996. xxv, 1011 p., ill. ISBN 0810383020
920.046   CT1343.D53

Includes about 470 biographies with source lists, some with portraits, of living (about 70 percent) and deceased persons, from the 15th century to the present. Covers individuals from Spain (61), North America (187), and Latin America (222) from a wide range of occupations. Occupation, nationality/ethnicity, and subject indexes. Indexed in *Biography and genealogy master index* (82). Full text in *Biography in Context* (67) and in *Spanish, Portuguese, and Latin American biographical archive*.

North America
Collective Biography

**85 Obituaries.com: newspaper
Obituaries from the U.S. and Canada.**
http://www.obituaries.com. Legacy.com.
Evanston, Ill.: Legacy.com. 2006-

Offers free obituary searches for recent (2000-) US and Canadian obituaries. In the absence of obituaries, birth and death dates together with, where available, place of last residence are provided from the Social Security Death Index. Searches can be limited by state and by decade back to 1930.

United States

**86 Dictionary of American religious
biography. 2nd ed., rev. and enl. ed.**
Henry Warner Bowden. Westport, Conn.:
Greenwood Press, 1993. ix, 686 p.
ISBN 0313278253
209.22B   BL72.B68
First ed., 1977.

With a view to correlating "information on American religious figures from all chronological periods and most denominational or theological affiliations" (*Pref.*), the 2nd ed. presents biographical sketches of 550 deceased persons, thoroughly updating most of the original articles and adding 125 new biographies. For each biographee, available details of vital statistics, education, and career are briefly noted before a discussion of the life work and influence of the figure. Bibliographies at the end of the articles cite works both by and about a person. Appendixes: denominational affiliation and listing by birthplace. For living religious leaders, see *Religious leaders of America*.

Timothy L. Hall's *American religious leaders* includes articles on 270 persons from the 17th century to the present; written for the nonspecialist.

BIBLIOGRAPHY

**87 Cyndi's list of genealogy sites on the
Internet.** http://www.cyndislist.com.
Cyndi Howells, Cyndi Howells. Puyallup,
Wash.: Cyndi Howells. 1996–
025.04;929.1   CS21

The largest collection of genealogy links on the Internet with over 329,000 links (as of January 2014). Searchable by keyword. The alphabetically arranged categories are very useful research starting points. Especially handy for librarians when they have little experience with a genealogy topic. Free.

The "Biographies" section, under the main category index, offers a valuable list of links to biographical sites, including many state and regional sites, plus a link to the extensive "Obituaries" section.

COLLECTIVE BIOGRAPHY

88   American national biography online.
http://www.anb.org/. American Council of Learned Societies, Oxford University Press. New York: Oxford University Press. 2000–
Preeminent source for well-known deceased Americans. Articles (several hundred to several thousand words) include lists of primary (with locations of manuscript collections) and secondary sources. Searchable full text and by birthplace, gender, birth/death dates, and occupations and realms of renown. Cross-references and ill., lacking in the print, are supplied in the online version.

The print *American national biography* covers about 17,450 people who died before 1996. About 100 entries on people who died since 1996, or otherwise omitted from the printed version, added every quarter to the online version. Biography and Genealogy Master Index (82) indexes original version and suppls. 1 and 2, but not additions to electronic version not yet incorporated into a suppls.

Print version has four indexes in v. 24: list of biographees, and biographees by contributor, birthplace, and "occupations and realms of renown." Occupations are not grouped, so one must scan the whole index to find all, say, scientific disciplines or religious denominations. *Supplements* I (2002) and II (2005), adding persons omitted from the main set and those who died since 1996, offer an improved cumulative occupational index listing occupations and "realms of renown" under 17 categories. No index to subjects and persons mentioned in articles, unlike the old *Dictionary of American biography* (DAB).

Although ANB articles largely replace those in the DAB and its suppls, some 9,000 persons in the DAB do not appear in the ANB because they were not selected for the ANB or their ANB articles have not yet appeared. The DAB is thus still essential for historical research. Persons selected for the ANB are much more ethnically diverse, and the ANB includes more women than the DAB. Significant temporary residents and foreigners of importance in U.S. history are included. Numerous reviews, including E. S. Morgan and M. Morgan's "Who's

really who" in *New York review of books* (v. 47, no. 4, pp. 38–43, March 9, 2000).

89   Dictionary of Hispanic biography.
Joseph C. Tardiff, L. Mpho Mabunda, Rudolfo Anaya. New York: Gale Research, 1996. xxv, 1011 p., ill. ISBN 0810383020
920.046   CT1343.D53
Includes about 470 biographies with source lists, some with portraits, of living (about 70 percent) and deceased persons, from the 15th century to the present. Covers individuals from Spain (61), North America (187), and Latin America (222) from a wide range of occupations. Occupation, nationality/ethnicity, and subject indexes. Indexed in *Biography and genealogy master index* (82). Full text in *Biography in Context* (67) and in *Spanish, Portuguese, and Latin American biographical archive*.

Contemporary

90   Marquis biographies online. http://www.marquiswhoswho.com/online-database/product-description. Marquis Who's Who Inc. New Providence, N.J.: Marquis Who's Who. 1985–
The Marquis who's whos are standard sources for contemporary biography. As they began in 1899 (with a historical vol. covering 1607–1896), they serve as retrospective biography as well. They contain concise biographical data, prepared according to established practices, with addresses and, in the case of authors, lists of works. The standards of admission are high, aiming to include the "best-known men and women in all lines of useful and reputable achievement," including (1) those selected on account of special prominence in creditable lines of effort, and (2) those included as a matter of policy on account of official position.

The several *Marquis who's who publications* began in 1899 with *Who's who in America* (WWA) (92). Biographies of selected deceased biographees were published in *Who was who in America* (WWWA). *Historical volume 1607–1896* was added to provide similar information for persons deceased before WWA began. Additional Who's who publications were added to provide more detailed information for regions of the United States and for certain professions. Most Marquis publications are indexed in

Biography and Genealogy Master Index (82) from 1974/75 (38th ed. of WWA).

Marquis Biographies Online includes entries from *Marquis who's who publications* since 1985 plus *Who's who in American history* (WWAH), which comprises WWWA covering 1897 to date plus the *Historical volume 1607–1896*. For persons with no post-1984 entries and not in WWAH, see the print versions of *Marquis who's who publications*. Searching of biographies since 1985 allows multiple search terms, including name, city/state/postal code/country of mailing address, occupation, birth date/place, death date/place, college/university, degrees, graduation year, hobbies/interests, political affiliation, religion, and keyword. Searching in WWAH (pre-1985 biographies) allows multiple search terms, including name, occupation, birth date/place, death date/place, keyword, and historical era limitation. A separate entry on WWA (92) discusses information in WWA not accessible through Marquis Biographies Online.

91   Who's who among African Americans.
Gale Research Inc. New York: Gale
Research, 1996– 1081-1400
920.073   E185.96.W52

From the first ed. for 1975–76 annually through the 28th ed. publ. in 2014, this well-done Gale title continues to be the standard reference for notable African Americans. Acquiring and keeping in an accessible location—not remote storage—is the classic example of why print publ.—on a year by year basis—are essential for biographical research on persons, living and dead.

About 10,000 entries in the 1st ed., increased to more than 19,600 in the current ed. Terminal obituaries section and geographic and occupational indexes. Information largely collected by questionnaires to the biographees. Current ed. available in Gale Virtual Reference Library (288). Indexed in Biography and Genealogy Master Index (82). Full text (25th ed., 2010) in Biography in Context (67).

An earlier work, *Who's who in colored America* (1st ed., 1927, to 7th ed., 1950) includes geographical and vocational listings. Full text in African American Biographical Database.

92   Who's who in America. [A.N. Marquis].
Chicago: A.N. Marquis, 1899– 0083-9396
920.073   E176.W642

Who's who in America (WWA) from 1985 to the present and *Who was who in America* (WWWA) are available via Marquis Biographies Online (90). However, some information, discussed below, in the pre-1985 WWA is not accessible in the online version. The print WWA was issued biennially 1899–1992/93 and annually 1994 to date. The 62nd ed. (2008) lists over 100,000 persons and has geographic and professional indexes. During Marquis' lifetime (he died in 1943), "worthy" professions were emphasized. Many religious figures are included, sports and entertainment less so (Babe Ruth and Mae West were not included, although entries were later added to WWWA). Marquis was, however, racially, ethnically, and religiously inclusive. Each edition is thoroughly revised, new biographies added and others dropped. All biographees from 1974 on are indexed in *Biography and genealogy master index* (82).

Biographees may disappear from WWA due to death (necrology list with most eds. since 2nd (1901/02) with 1960/61–1974/75 gap), transfer to "non-current status," or discontinuation. Non-current biographees (so-called through about 1959) remained in the Marquis database and might appear in regional who's whos or even reappear in WWA. They were persons of reduced "reference value" and were often retired. Lists of retirees (with entries in the previous ed.) appeared in eds. 42 (1982/83)–49 (1995). Discontinued biographees were removed from the database.

A separate vol. titled *Indices to, and vocational analysis of, the living biographees* (1952), offers lists of all living non-current biographees for eds. 1–22 and 23–26 (1950/51) and gives the last ed. in which they appear. Supplemented by *Indices and necrology* vols. containing lists of persons who had become non-current which were issued with eds. 27 (1952/53), 28 (1954/55), 29 (1956/57), and 30 (1958/59). *Indices and necrology* vol. for 30th ed. (1958/59) cumulates listings for eds. 27 (1952/53)–30 (1958/59). *Indices to, and vocational analysis of, the living biographees* plus *Indices and necrology* vol. for 30th ed. (1958/59) serve to index non-current biographees living during the 1950s.

The bulk of deceased WWA biographees appear in WWWA and are thus accessible via Marquis Who's Who on the Web. Some biographees were not transferred to WWWA on decease. These must be found in the print vols.

WWWA in Marquis Biographies Online allows

birth/death place searching only, not a geographic (mailing address in the original entries) search. Therefore the *Geographic index* in the pre-1985 print WWA is significant.

Monthly supplement

From Dec. 1939–Aug. 1959 a *Monthly supplement and international who's who* was published as a supplementary service, giving sketches concerned with "who's who in world news and why." A cumulated index to v. 1–10, titled *Index to the monthly supplement, 1939–1949* (also includes v. 11, 1950) was published separately and also in WWWA

(v. 2, p. 605–54; 1939–49 only). Lists of the *Monthly supplement* biographees appeared in the *Indices and necrology* vols. Biographees in the *Monthly supplement* did not necessarily receive entries in the regular biennial volumes.

Cedric Larson's *Who, sixty years of American eminence: The story of Who's who in America* supplies a history of this important publication. See also Albert Nelson Marquis' entry in the *American national biography* (88) and Leon Harris' "What's what with America's Who's who," *Smithsonian*, v. 12, no. 8 November, 1981, p. 204–221.

3

Core Geography

Steven W. Sowards

Atlases

93   Goode's world atlas. 22nd ed. Howard Veregin, J. Paul Goode, Rand McNally and Company. Skokie, Ill.: Rand McNally, 2010. 1 atlas (xii, 371, [1] p.), col. ill., col. maps. ISBN 9780528877544

912   G1021

Updates the 21st edition of 2005. Emphasizes physical and political maps, and maps showing resources and products. Includes "new thematic maps on global climate change, sea level rise, CO_2 emissions, polar ice fluctuations, deforestation, extreme weather events, infectious diseases, water resources, and energy production." Originated in the early 20th century as *Goode's school atlas*, frequently reissued thereafter. List of source materials. Glossary of foreign geographical terms. Index by subject to thematic maps, and index of place names with pronunciation and coordinates.

94   National Geographic atlas of the world. 9th ed. National Geographic Maps. Washington: National Geographic Society, 2011. 1 atlas (1 v. (various pagings)), col. ill., col. maps. ISBN 9781426206320

912   G1021

In addition to physical and political coverage, thematic maps deal with topics such as population, food, minerals, climate, and energy. Articles on the physical and natural world, and human activities (such as population, energy and health). Maps

of the oceans; sky maps; and the Moon and Mars based on NASA findings. Comprehensive place-name index. Appendixes deal with time zones, metric conversion, abbreviations, airline distances, and global temperature and rainfall statistics.

95   Oxford atlas of the world. George Philip & Son. New York: Oxford University Press, 1992-. 1 atlas (448 p.), color ill., color maps. ISBN 9780199328468

G1201

Updated and published annually each year in a new edition, since 1992: the version of 2013 is the 20th edition. Physical, political and thematic maps of continents, countries, regions and major cities. Employs both maps and satellite photographs. Covers political, economic, and demographic statistics; includes articles on topics of current interest such as the environment and population matters in major cities of the world. Contents organized in sections: world statistics, the oceans and seas, photographic images of Earth, gazetteer of nations, thematic world geography, major world cities, world maps, Europe, Asia, Africa, Australia and Oceania, North America, and South America. Astronomical information in brief. Gazetteer with facts in brief for world nations, including flags. Glossary. Index of places keyed to map locations, also showing latitude and longitude.

96   The Times comprehensive atlas of the world. 13th ed. Times Books (Firm). London: Times Books; Collins

Bartholomew Ltd., 2011. 1 atlas (1 volume (various pagings)), color illustrations, color maps.
ISBN 9780007419135

912   G1021

Regarded as the best of the English-language world atlases. 125 color plates provide photographic images of the continents from space, astronomical information, thematic maps on topics such as biodiversity and climate change, a brief history of mapmaking, and numerous maps for each of the continents and for the ocean regions of the world. Maps are produced by the firm of Collins Bartholomew. Geographical information includes elevation and water features. Political boundaries, urban areas and the transportation grid are superimposed. Each regional map is drawn at one of four consistent scales, allowing easy comparisons. New in this edition are more than 35 maps of major urban areas. Updated content since the 12th edition of 2007, with thousands of revised place names, and recording of geopolitical border changes and newly independent countries. Lists, such as longest rivers. Table for countries of the world, including small images of flags. Glossary. Index: for each named place or feature, the location on a plate is shown, as well as latitude and longitude.

97 Road atlas: United States, Canada, and Mexico. Rand McNally (Firm). Boston: Rand McNally, 1932– 0361-6509

629.281   G1201.P2

The *Rand McNally road atlas* has been published annually since 1932: the 2014 edition will be the 90th. Driving maps for each state with inset details for larger cities and urban areas; for the Interstate system; and for Canadian provinces and key cities. Coverage of Mexico is a single page. Map keys distinguish types of highways and roads, highway numbers, mileage along road segments, and points of interest including parks. Index of cities by state, with population and key to map location. Mileage and driving time charts between major places. Appears in several versions, including "large scale" and *Motor carriers' road atlas*.

General Works

98 Companion encyclopedia of geography: From local to global. 2nd ed.

Ian Douglas, Richard J. Huggett, C. R. Perkins. London: Routledge, 2007. 2 v. (xxxvii, 1022, xlviii p.), ill., maps.
ISBN 9780415431699

910   G116.C645

Adds to and complements the 1st ed., *Companion encyclopedia of geography: The environment and humankind*, which was on a different theme. "Gives an integrated view of modern geography, drawing together many contemporary human and physical strands of the subject around the theme of place and change."—*Pref.* Contains 64 signed chapters arranged into six parts and two volumes. Vol. 1 contains four parts: the nature of place; forces for change; actors in the process; and examples of the nature, rate, and direction of change. Vol. 2 contains two parts: the geographical imagination; and responses to the geographical drivers of change. Index.

99 A dictionary of geography. 4th ed.
Susan Mayhew. Oxford; New York: Oxford University Press, 2009. 551 p., ill., maps.
ISBN 9780199231812

910.3   G63

More than 3,500 definitions, of which 300 are new to this edition. Reflects new information in areas such as climate change, economic geography and geographic information systems (GIS). Provides continued and updated coverage of terms from a wide range of topics such as cartography, ecology, development, migration, and meteorology. Bibliography, and points to relevant web sites. Available as an e-book.

100 The dictionary of human geography. 5th ed. Derek Gregory. Malden, Mass.: Blackwell, 2009. xvi, 1052 p., ill.
ISBN 9781405132879

304.203   GF4

Fully revised edition covering concepts, topics, organizations and subfields of human geography (urban, cultural, economic, Marxist, etc.), with some 300 new entries. Articles are signed (with initials). Explains complex terms and vocabulary, aimed at an academic audience. Includes citations to sources for suggested readings, as well as maps, diagrams, a lengthy bibliography of books and articles, and a detailed index. Available as an e-book.

101 Encyclopedia of geography. Barney Warf. Thousand Oaks, Calif.: Sage

Publications, 2010. 6 v. (lv, 3398 p.), ill. (some col.), maps (some col.)
ISBN 9781412956970
910.3   G63

Over 1,200 signed entries by more than 900 contributors. Six volumes cover physical geography; human geography; nature and society; methods, models and GIS; history of geography; and people, organizations and movements. Emphasizes interdisciplinary aspects of the field, and relevance for new trends such as globalization, geospatial technology, environmental awareness, and the impact of the Internet on relationships at a distance. Suggestions for further reading. Index. Includes a short atlas. Available as an e-book.

102   GEOBASE. http://www.elsevier.com/ elsevier-products/geobase. Elsevier Science, Geo Abstracts. New York: Elsevier Science. 1991-
GE220

The largest and most comprehensive English-language bibliographic database in the discipline of geography. GEOBASE is not only one of the most important reference resources for searching current geographical literature, but is also one of the more important sources in related subjects such as ecology, environmental studies, geology, and oceanography. Scope of coverage is worldwide, with over 2,000 journals fully covered and 3,000 selectively covered from 1980 to present. More than 2,000 books, monographs, conference proceedings, and reports are also covered. Contains nearly 1.5 million records, most with abstracts. Produced by Elsevier Science and includes *Ecological abstracts*, *Geographical abstracts: Human geography*, *Geographical abstracts: Physical geography*, *Geological abstracts*, *Geomechanics abstracts*, *International development abstracts*, and *Oceanographic literature review*.

The database is available online (via OCLC First-Search, DIALOG, or Engineering Village 2) or on CD-ROM. The material within the database is also contained in the aforementioned print journals.

For literature before 1980, the paper indexes that preceded GEOBASE must be consulted. *Geographical abstracts: Human geography* was the result of the merger of the following indexes: *Geographical abstracts. D, Social and historical geography* and *Geographical abstracts. F, Regional and community planning*. *Geographical abstracts: Physical geography* was the result of the merger of *Geographical abstracts. A, Landforms and the quaternary*, *Geographical abstracts. B, Climatology and hydrology*, and *Geographical abstracts. G, Remote sensing, photogrammetry, and cartography*.

103   Geographic information: How to find it, how to use it. Jenny Marie Johnson. Westport, Conn.: Greenwood Press, 2003. x, 216 p., ill., maps.
ISBN 9781573563925
0016.91   G116

Currently one of the best general guides to the subjects of geography and cartography available in the English language. Analyzes each resource thoroughly and explains each topic or concept comprehensively yet clearly. Chapters include a bibliography of print resources and a list of online references. Indexed.

104   A guide to countries of the world. 3rd ed. Peter Stalker. New York: Oxford University Press, 2010. 421 p.
ISBN 9780199580729
G 103.5   910.3

Covers more than 200 nations, in alphabetical order. Concise entries provide an outline map; a tabular summary of key data such as population (including proportions of ethnic, linguistic or religious minorities), GDP per capita, and life expectancy; and notes about current social, political and economic trends. Appendices include indicator tables for health, economic and education data, and lists of international organizations. Earlier editions published as *A-Z of countries of the world* and *Handbook of the world*. Available as an e-book.

105   The student's companion to geography. 2nd ed. Alisdair Rogers, Heather A. Viles. Malden, Mass.: Blackwell Publishers, 2003. xv, 395 p., ill.
ISBN 0631221328
G116.S78 910

An introduction to the discipline consisting of 61 signed chapters provided by 65 widely recognized experts from Australia, Canada, New Zealand, Singapore, the United Kingdom, and the United States. Organized in six parts: why study geography, what are geographers doing, studying geography, geography in context, a geographical directory, and expanding horizons. Each chapter includes a list of references. General index.

106   The world factbook. National Foreign
        Assessment Center (U.S.), United States.
        Washington: Central Intelligence Agency,
        1981–. maps (some color). 0277-1527
        910.5   G122.U56a
Continues *National basic intelligence factbook*
(1977–80).

For each country of the world (in alphabetical
order), provides brief data on geography, people,
government, economy, membership in international
intergovernmental organizations, communications,
transportation, and defense forces. Small maps of
each country; regional maps in color. Includes introductory notes, definitions, and abbreviations.

Also available for download at https://www
.cia.gov/library/publications/the-world-factbook/
index.html.

Geographic Information Systems

**107   A to Z GIS: An illustrated dictionary
        of geographic information systems.
        2nd ed.** Tasha Wade, Shelly Sommer.
        Redlands, Calif.: ESRI Press, 2006. xvi,
        268 p., color ill. ISBN 1589481402
        910.285   G70.212.A86
Containing over 1,800 entries and about 400 illustrations, this work "was designed to be a comprehensive technical dictionary for GIS students and
professionals alike."—*Pref.* Definitions provided by
over 150 subject experts; includes seven in-depth
essays. First ed., 2001.

**108   Encyclopedia of geographic
        information science.** Karen K. Kemp.
        Los Angeles: SAGE Publications, c2008.
        xxv, 558 p., ill., maps.
        ISBN 9781412913133
        910.285   G70.212.E53
Includes 230 entries, with an average length of 1,350
words. Topics covered range from relatively simple to
highly complex concepts that might only be of interest to a high-end practitioner. Entries are authored
or coauthored by 164 scientists, supervised by four
editorial advisory board members and an overall editor. Cross-references and reading lists at the end of
each entry provide guidance for follow-up research.
Not heavily illustrated.

Available as an e-book.

109   Encyclopedia of GIS. Shashi Shekhar,
        Hui Xiong. New York: Springer, c2008.
        xxxix, 1370 p., ill. ISBN 9780387359755
        910.285   G70.212.E534
Divided into 41 fields, each one an important subar-
ea within GIS–*Pref.* Contains around 300 items with
723 figures and 90 tables. The A–Z format entries
are authored or coauthored by 325 scientists, supervised by 41 field editors and two editors. Cross-
references and reading lists at the end of each entry
provide guidance for follow-up research. Available as
an e-book.

110   Geospatial platform. http://www.geo
        platform.gov/. Federal Geographic
        Data Committee. Reston, Va.: Federal
        Geographic Data Committee. 2013-
                                       G70.212
Led at this time by the Federal Geographic Data
Committee (FGDC), the U.S. government has
experimented with a series of geospatial data sites,
including *Geospatial one-stop* and *Geodata.gov.* As of
2013, the *Geospatial platform* or *Geoplatform* is the
most comprehensive online portal to U.S. federal,
state, and local geospatial information and data, with
more than 80,000 data sets. The site offers access
to downloadable data, map galleries, links to state-
based data portals, downloadable software, and lists
of agencies.

111   GIS dictionary. http://resources.arcgis
        .com/glossary. Redlands, Calif.: ESRI. 2005
Free dictionary or glossary published by ESRI, producers of ArcGIS software. Most entries are one or
two sentences in length. ". . . includes terms from
GIS operations such as analysis, data management,
and geocomputation; from rapidly evolving uses
of GIS for modeling, GIScience, and Web-based
GIS; and from the GIS foundation fields of cartography, spatial statistics, computer science, survey-
ing, geodesy, and remote sensing. This online GIS
Dictionary also includes ESRI software-specific
terminology."—*Website*

Historical Maps

112   American memory. http://memory.loc
        .gov/ammem/gmdhtml/gmdhome.html.

Library of Congress: Geography and Map Division. Washington: Library of Congress. 1999–

A Web site and database of over 10,000 high-quality digital images of maps from the collections of the Geography and Maps Division of the Library of Congress. The general focus is Americana and cartographic treasures. However, there are also several distinct themes, including cities and towns (primarily panoramic maps), conservation and environment, discovery and exploration, cultural landscapes (including the American Colonization Society's Liberian maps), military battles and campaigns (primarily American Revolution and Civil War), and transportation and communication (railroads). Images are high-resolution MrSID or JPEG2000 files that may be downloaded and viewed offline. Fully cataloged images may be searched or browsed by collection theme, geographic location, subject, creator, or title.

113   Atlas of the historical geography of the United States. http://dsl.richmond .edu/historicalatlas/. Charles Oscar Paullin, John Kirtland Wright, Robert K. Nelson, Carnegie Institution of Washington, American Geographical Society of New York. Richmond, Va.: Digital Scholarship Lab, University of Richmond. 2013
911.73   G1201.S1

Paullin's 1932 *Atlas of the historical geography of the United States* was the first adequate atlas of American history, combining over 600 maps on 166 plates with explanatory text. Recently digitized in georectified format by the DSL with the support of the Andrew W. Mellon Foundation. The online format allows zooming to enlarge images, and rapid comparison of related maps in series such as those showing growth of the states and territories from 1790-1910, population density based on census figures from 1790-1930, trends in immigration, trends in imports/exports, presidential election returns at the county level from 1824-1928, and the growth of agriculture and industry. Reprints 47 historically important maps dating from 1492-1867, and street plans of seven major cities dating from 1775-1803.

114   Atlas of world history. 2nd ed. Patrick K. O'Brien, Philip's Map Studio. New York: Oxford University Press, 2010. 1 atlas (312 p.), ill. (some col.), col. maps.

ISBN 9780199746538
909   D21.5

Updates the first edition of 2002. Some 450 color maps with explanatory text, covering the ancient world, the medieval world, the early modern world, the age of revolutions, and the 20th century and today. Illustrates the geographic aspect of developments in politics, economics, culture and religion. Bibliography. Detailed table of contents and extensive index including place names on the maps.

115   Atlases: Department of History, United States Military Academy. http://www .westpoint.edu/history/SitePages/Atlases .aspx. Department of History, United States Military Academy. West Point, N.Y.: United States Military Academy

Provides online access to numerous maps illustrating the military history of the United States and the history of warfare, from ancient times to the war in Iraq. Maps vary in scope from strategic coverage, to tactical analyis of specific battles, sometimes with multiple maps covering the action of a single day. Some of these maps, up through the Korean War, appear in print in *The West Point atlas of American wars* by Vincent J. Esposito (1959). Also includes detailed coverage of the campaigns of Napoleon, and selective coverage of other conflicts of interest including the Arab/Israeli wars and the campaigns of Julius Caesar.

116   Historical atlas of the United States. National Geographic Society. Washington: National Geographic Society, 1988. ISBN 0870447475
911.73   G1201.S1.N3

The centennial edition of the National Geographic Society's atlas, this is not superseded by the 2004 edition, *National Geographic historical atlas of the United States* (118), and it is still worth retaining and using. Heavily illustrated with reproductions of paintings, charts, graphs, photographs, maps with relevant text, chronologies, and time lines. An accompanying portfolio contains 18 maps for regions and for the entire United States. The presentation in six major areas (the land, people, boundaries, economy, networks, communities) is interspersed with five chronological sections: 1400–1606, 1607–1788, 1789–1860, 1861–1916, and 1917–88. The bibliography cites sources for the illustrations and text of each page and the consultants used. Topical index for illustrations and text.

117 Historical atlas of the United States: with original maps. Derek Hayes, University of California Press. Berkeley, Calif.: University of California Press, 2007. 1 atlas (280 p.), ill. (chiefly col.), maps (chiefly col.) ISBN 9780520250369

911/.73   G1201.S1

Text built around more than 500 historical maps, drawn or published at the time of the topics under discussion. Grouped into some 60 chapters on themes such as exploration of the New World, Western expansion, Native Americans, America's wars, highway and air travel, and urban growth. Bibliography. Index.

118 National Geographic historical atlas of the United States. Ronald M. Fisher, National Geographic Society. Washington: National Geographic Society, 2004. 1 atlas (240 p.), ill. (some col.), chiefly col. maps. ISBN 0792261313

911.73   G1201.S1.F5

Quite different in presentation from the 1988 centennial edition of the *National Geographic historical atlas of the United States* (116); the presentation here is strictly chronological. Sections include "Age of rediscovery, 1400–1749," "New people in a new world, 1750–1799," "Forming a more perfect union, 1800–1849," "A nation comes of age, 1850–1899," "A nation at war, 1900–1949," "Decades of change, 1950–present." Covers the controversial 2000 presidential election and U.S. military activities in Iraq up through the 2003 capture of Saddam Hussein. The narrative is more issue driven (displacing Native Americans, Prohibition) than that of the 1988 edition, with completely different maps and photos. More approachable with the single chronological organization.

Name Sources

119 Canadian geographical names data base. http://www4.rncan.gc.ca/search-place-names/name.php. Natural Resources Canada; Ressources Naturel Canada, Canadian Permanent Committee on Geographical Names. Ottawa, Ont., Canada: Natural Resources Canada. 1997–

Searchable database of 350,000 Canadian place names officially recognized by the Geographical Names Board of Canada (GNBC), for use in maps, charts and texts. "12% of these records are names of populated places and administrative areas; 60% are water features (e.g. lakes, rivers, bays) and 21% are terrain features (e.g. mountains, capes, valleys)." Database may be queried by name, coordinates, unique identifier code or rectangular area, or through browsing an alphabetical list. Provides latitude and longitude, and indicates location by province and county. Formerly *Geographical names of Canada*.

120 The Columbia gazetteer of the world. http://www.columbiagazetteer.org/. Saul B. Cohen, Columbia University. New York: Columbia University Press. [2001]–

910.3   G103.5

Successor to the print *Columbia gazetteer of the world*. Contains some 170,000 entries. Database may be searched by key word, type of place, and placename. Covers names for both physical and political sites and locations. Typical entries indicate the geographical location, dimensions and borders of an area, economic information, demographics, historical background, and alternative spellings or names.

121 Geographic names information system (GNIS). http://geonames.usgs.gov/domestic/index.html. U.S. Geological Survey, United States Board on Geographic Names. Reston, Va.: U.S. Geological Survey. 2001–

E155

For locations within the United States. Developed by USGS in conjunction with the U.S. Board on Geographic Names (US BGN). Serves as the official repository for domestic geographic names data. Contains information about both physical and cultural geographic features. Searchable by name, location, class, and federal feature ID number. Brief entries include latitude and longitude, elevation, and any variant versions of place names. For similar information on places outside the United States, use the GEONET names server (122).

122 GEOnet names server. http://earth-info.nga.mil/gns/html/. U.S. National

Geospatial-Intelligence Agency, U.S. Board on Geographic Names. Springfield, Va.: Defense Mapping Agency. 1996-

G103.5

This gazetteer -- "the official repository of standard spellings of all foreign geographic names, sanctioned by the United States Board on Geographic Names (US BGN)" -- is the largest and most comprehensive digital database of geographic feature names, covering the world outside the United States (for U.S. place names, see the USGS Geographic names information system) (121). Supports searching by place name, and by browsing online maps. This database stems from the printed gazetteers compiled and published by the Army Map Service and the Foreign Names Committee of the US BGN beginning during the Second World War. More than 100 printed foreign country gazetteers produced by the Foreign Names Committee are available from the U.S. Geological Survey.

123 Getty thesaurus of geographic names online. http://www.getty.edu/research/ tools/vocabulary/tgn/index.html. Getty Research Institute, Getty Research Institute. Los Angeles: Getty Information Trust. 1999–

910   G104.5

The best historical digital gazetteer. Includes over 900,000 records and 1.7 million place names, including historical names and alternative spellings (sometimes in non-Roman scripts). Identifies both physical features (such as rivers and mountains) and political or administrative entities (such as inhabited places or cities, but also names of regions, counties, states, and countries). Hierarchically structured: places are set in context as part of larger entities (for example: world, continent, nation, state, county, city); also indicates smaller constituent parts such as districts within a city. In light of the mission of the J. Paul Getty Trust, attention is paid to places important in the fields of art and architecture, and entries often describe the historical and cultural significance of a place, including brief notations about dates. Published sources of information are credited.

Online Maps

124 American memory. http://memory.loc .gov/ammem/gmdhtml/gmdhome.html.

Library of Congress: Geography and Map Division. Washington: Library of Congress. 1999–

A Web site and database of over 10,000 high-quality digital images of maps from the collections of the Geography and Maps Division of the Library of Congress. The general focus is Americana and cartographic treasures. However, there are also several distinct themes, including cities and towns (primarily panoramic maps), conservation and environment, discovery and exploration, cultural landscapes (including the American Colonization Society's Liberian maps), military battles and campaigns (primarily American Revolution and Civil War), and transportation and communication (railroads). Images are high-resolution MrSID or JPEG2000 files that may be downloaded and viewed offline. Fully cataloged images may be searched or browsed by collection theme, geographic location, subject, creator, or title.

125 The Atlas of Canada. http://atlas.nrcan .gc.ca/site/english/index.html. Natural Resources Canada. Ottawa, Canada: Natural Resources Canada. 2006

A comprehensive national atlas in digital format. Maps arranged by section and then by topic. For example, there are 12 topics within the *People & Society* section, such as "Age," "Education," "Family," "Housing," etc. Each topic has numerous maps and text. The primary sections of the atlas are *Environment*, *People & Society*, *Economy*, *History*, *Climate Change*, *Freshwater*, *Health*, *Reference Maps*, *Map Archives* (previous editions), and *Topographic Maps*. Also contains learning resources for teachers and students and free data (primarily base maps). 1st ed. in print format, 1906.

126 Atlas of the historical geography of the United States. http://dsl.richmond .edu/historicalatlas/. Charles Oscar Paullin, John Kirtland Wright, Robert K. Nelson, Carnegie Institution of Washington, American Geographical Society of New York. Richmond, Va.: Digital Scholarship Lab, University of Richmond. 2013

911.73   G1201.S1

Paullin's 1932 *Atlas of the historical geography of the United States* was the first adequate atlas of American history, combining over 600 maps on 166 plates with explanatory text. Recently digitized in georectified format by the DSL with the support of the Andrew W. Mellon Foundation. The online format allows zooming to enlarge images, and rapid comparison of related maps in series such as those showing growth of the states and territories from 1790-1910, population density based on census figures from 1790-1930, trends in immigration, trends in imports/exports, presidential election returns at the county level from 1824-1928, and the growth of agriculture and industry. Reprints 47 historically important maps dating from 1492-1867, and street plans of seven major cities dating from 1775-1803.

127 Atlases: Department of History, United States Military Academy. http:// www.westpoint.edu/history/SitePages/ Atlases.aspx. Department of History, United States Military Academy. West Point, N.Y.: United States Military Academy

Provides online access to numerous maps illustrating the military history of the United States and the history of warfare, from ancient times to the war in Iraq. Maps vary in scope from strategic coverage, to tactical analyis of specific battles, sometimes with multiple maps covering the action of a single day. Some of these maps, up through the Korean War, appear in print in *The West Point atlas of American wars* by Vincent J. Esposito (1959). Also includes detailed coverage of the campaigns of Napoleon, and selective coverage of other conflicts of interest including the Arab/Israeli wars and the campaigns of Julius Caesar.

128 Google Earth. http://earth.google.com/ index.html. Google (Firm). Mountain View, Calif.: Google. 2007-
TR810.K49

Primarily an online visualization tool that streams remotely sensed images of the Earth's surface. Not all photographic imagery is at the same resolution, so some areas seem blurry when magnified at a larger scale. However, it remains one of the most comprehensive compilations of high-resolution worldwide imagery available. Other geographic information is integrated into the system, such as roads, buildings, and various commercial establishments.

129 Google maps. http://maps.google.com/. Google (Firm). Mountain View, Calif.: Google. 2005–
G 1021   912

Free, interactive, printable online map service. Covers the United States and world nations, with zoom down to the street level. Other features include driving directions, business locators, traffic monitoring and aerial satellite photo views. Comparable to Yahoo! maps (136) and and MapQuest (130): these competing firms frequently update and enhance features on their products.

Google also offers a photographic "Streetview" in many cities. A primary difference between Google Earth (128) and Google Maps is the three-dimensional capabilities of the former.

Most features of Google Maps are available in versions for major world languages such as Spanish, French, and German; and for widely-used non-Roman scripts such as Chinese, Japanese, Korean, Russian (Cyrillic), Hebrew and Arabic.

130 MapQuest. http://www.mapquest.com/. MapQuest. Lancaster, Pa.; Denver, Colo.: MapQuest. 1996-
912   G1021

Free, interactive, printable online map service. Covers the United States and world nations, with zoom down to the street level. Other features include driving directions, business locators, traffic monitoring and aerial satellite photo views. Comparable to Google Maps (129) and and Yahoo! maps (136): these competing firms frequently update and enhance features on their products.

131 National atlas of the United States of America. http://nationalatlas.gov/. National Geospatial Program. Reston, Va.: U.S. Geological Survey. 1997–

nationalatlas.gov is an online portal containing dynamic and static digital maps of the U.S., articles, explanatory text, links to related authoritative websites, and raw data for GIS software. Maps and data are organized into the following broad themes: agriculture, biology, boundaries, climate, environment, geology, government, history, mapping, people, transportation, and water. Users can create their own maps by selecting layers to display using the "Map Maker" function.

132 Perry-Castañeda Library map collection. http://www.lib.utexas.edu/ maps/. Perry Castaneda Library. Austin, Tex.: University of Texas at Austin

Provides online access to a wealth of public domain maps, including federal documents and publications no longer under copyright. Links on the main Web page lead to collections of digitized maps covering the world, the various continents, the United States and individual states, and parts of Texas. Other sections provide historical, thematic and topographical maps. Content is drawn from sources like the CIA World factbook (106), the United States Geological Survey (135), and scanned atlases. Includes the complete text of the 1923 edition of William Shepherd's well-known Historical atlas, and the *National Atlas of the United States of America* published in 1970. The site also offers a changing array of maps covering geographic areas that are in the news.

133 SimplyMap. http://www.simplymap.com. New York: Geographic Research, Inc. 2005-
G3701.A25
Produces on-the-fly data-based maps through selection of locations and variables for demographic or marketing information. Categories of variables include census data, consumer expenditure, market segments, and retail sales. Use of a filter allows combination of two variables. Maps can be exported as GIF or PDF files, and data reports can be exported as Excel, DBF, or CSV. Access requires a subscription for authentication and creation of an individual account.

134 United Nations Cartographic Section, Department of Field Support. http://www.un.org/Depts/Cartographic/english/htmain.htm. United Nations. New York: United Nations. 1999–
Contains three types of digital maps in PDF: over 100 general reference maps of regions and countries, six thematic maps, and over 25 peacekeeping and truce-supervising deployment maps.

135 USGS. http://www.usgs.gov/. Geological Survey (U.S.), United States. Dept. of the Interior. Geological Survey. Reston, Va.: U.S. Geological Survey. 1996–
551.0223
The U.S. Geological Survey "collects, monitors, analyzes, and provides scientific understanding about natural resource conditions, issues, and problems"—*About USGS*. The USGS was founded in 1879 and serves as the primary science agency

of the Department of the Interior. Many newer publications are available free online as part of the USGS Publications Warehouse. The USGS has long been known as a major source of data and studies related to geology, water, energy, mineral resources, and natural disasters. However, the role and importance of the USGS has grown over time, most notably when it absorbed many of the functions of the U.S. Bureau of Mines and the National Biological Service during federal budget cuts of the 1990s. Operating within the USGS, the Biological Resources Discipline now conducts research on such topics as conservation, ecosystems, wildlife, genetics, and more, and these areas are also reflected in the wealth of information available on the USGS website.

The USGS plays a major role in the production and distribution of maps, aerial photographs, satellite imagery, and geospatial data. Their products include the popular 1 : 24,000-scale topographic quadrangle map series. Printed topographic, geologic, hydrologic, and other maps are searchable via the USGS website and may be purchased for a small fee. Digital downloads of many maps are available for free.

136 Yahoo! maps. http://maps.yahoo.com/. Yahoo! Inc. (Firm). Santa Clara, Calif.: Yahoo! Inc. 1996-
912   G1021
Free, interactive, printable online map service. Covers the United States and world nations, with zoom down to the street level. Other features include driving directions, business locators, traffic monitoring and aerial satellite photo views. Comparable to Google Maps (129) and and MapQuest (130): these competing firms frequently update and enhance features on their products.

Tourism

137 A companion to tourism. Alan A. Lew, Colin Michael Hall, Allan M. Williams. Malden, Mass.: Blackwell, 2004. xviii, 622 p., ill. ISBN 0631235647
910.01   G155.A1
Contains 48 chapters divided into six parts focused on "the major research and theoretical subject areas of tourism studies."—*Pref.* Each chapter is signed

and has a list of references. Index. Available as an e-book.

138   Dictionary of travel, tourism and hospitality. 3rd ed. S. Medlik. Oxford, U.K.; Boston: Butterworth-Heinemann, 2003. ix, 273 p., maps.
ISBN 0750656506
338.479103   G155.A1
Divided into seven parts. The largest (Pt. 1) is a dictionary of over 4,000 terms. Pts. 2 and 3 are definitions of international and national organizations. Pt. 4 is a biographical dictionary of people associated with the travel industry. Pt. 5 is a list of abbreviations. Pt. 6 is a table giving information on countries of the world. Pt. 7 is a bibliography of dictionaries, journals, directories, manuals, sources of statistics, and other books. Available as an e-book.

139   Dictionary of travel and tourism. http://www.oxfordreference.com/view/10.1093/acref/9780191733987.001.0001/acref-9780191733987. Allen Beaver. Oxford; New York: Oxford University Press. 2012. ISBN 9780191733987
910/.3   G155.A1
6,500 entries identify and define industry terms, the names of technical practices, acronyms and abbreviations, and association names. Revises and updates the 2005 CABI edition, *Dictionary of travel and tourism terminology*, with additional information about topics such as procedures of the TSA, branding and social media, and Web-based developments such as Expedia Travel Agents Affiliate Program (TAAP). Written from a British perspective, but global in coverage.

140   Encyclopedia of tourism. Jafar Jafari. London; New York: Routledge, 2000. xxxv, 683 p. ISBN 0415154057
338.4791   G155.A1
"A quick reference source or guide to the wide range of basic definitions, concepts, themes, issues, methods, perspectives, and institutions embraced by tourism in its disparate manifestations."—*Introd.* Contains over 1,200 signed entries. Entries are arranged alphabetically. Many cross-references, *see*

also listings, and suggestions for further reading. Index. Available as an e-book.

Travel Guides

141   Baedeker's travel guides. Baedeker (Firm). Ostfildern, Germany: Baedeker
The Baedeker's series of travel guides, originally published in German in the 19th century but also prominently published in English, were pioneering travel works. Older editions are now prized for historical value and as collectibles. Often published in collaboration with other firms or organizations. Numerous individual volumes cover countries, regions or major cities, with information about sights, hotels, restaurants and travel. Maps. For a complete list of current volumes available in German, see http://www.baedeker.com/. A smaller number of English-language titles have been published in English in recent years, through partnership with Mairdumont and Marco Polo Travel Publishing.

142   Blue guides. Blue guide travel monographs. London: Somerset Books
In this series of travel publications, the emphasis is on destinations with architectural, artistic, historical and archaeological appeal. Provides high quality, detailed floor plans, diagrams, maps, and photographs to educate the traveller. Individual volumes typically cover a single city, or a region within a country. The majority of titles deal with European locations. Scholarly in tone. Hotel, restaurant and transportation information is held to a minimum. For a complete list of currently available volumes, see http://www.blueguides.com/.

143   Bradt travel guides. Bradt (Firm). Chalfont St. Peter, U.K.: Bradt Travel Guides
Offers more than a hundred guide books; the same publisher also produces books about destinations, and guides to wildlife. Content includes background sketches of history and natural history, practical tips, comments on "sustainable" travel, etiquette advice, maps, notes about major sights, and information about accomodations, dining, shopping and nightlife. Good source for countries and regions that are

less traditional as destinations: recent volumes in the series have covered Nova Scotia, Bosnia & Herzegovina, Angola, Tajikistan, Abruzzo, the Faroe Islands, and Transylvania.

144 Fodor's guides. Fodor's Travel (Firm).
New York: Fodor's Travel

This extensive series of travel guides offers individual volumes that cover major cities, regions, countries, or whole continents, with more than 300 titles. Many are updated annually. Provides information about transportation, hotels, restaurants and destination sights: noted for thoroughness of coverage. Budget-seeking and discounts are not the highest priority here. For a complete list of currently available volumes, see http://www.fodors.com/.

145 Frommer's travel guides. Arthur
Frommer, Frommer Media LLC.
Hoboken, N.J.: John Wiley & Sons, Inc.

Volumes in this series provide extensive and detailed listings for tourist sights, hotels, and restaurants. Arthur Frommer introduced the concept of "Europe on $5 a Day" in 1957: obviously costs have since increased. Intended for adult travellers, rather than those strictly travelling light. Offers useful advice for novice travellers, including suggested itineraries. Individual volumes cover a country, a region, a major city, or a prominent destination. Each volume offers maps and an index. In 2013, Mr. Frommer reacquired rights to the series from Google. For a complete list of currently available volumes, see http://www.frommers.com/.

146 Let's go: the student travel guides.
Let's Go (Firm). Cambridge, Mass.;
Berkeley, Calif.: Let's Go; Distributed by
Publishers Group West

Launched in 1960 by students at Harvard, these guides remain oriented to younger travellers with content "written entirely for students by students" and including coverage of nightlife and hostels. The goal is still advice about low-budget travel for backpackers and others. Many but not all destinations in the series are in Europe, with quite a few in the United States. Typical volumes cover one country, one city, or a group of nearby cities. Some editions are updated only occasionally. While some other travel guides exist in e-book formats, *Let's Go* is the most committed to options

such as downloadable PDF versions. For a complete list of currently available volumes, see http://www.letsgo.com/.

147 Lonely planet travel guides. Lonely
Planet (Firm). London; Footscray,
Australia; Oakland, Calif.: Lonely Planet
Publications

Individual volumes typically cover single countries or sometimes geographic regions. Illustrated with simple maps that highlight important features. Originally popular with backpackers, and still valued for advice about travel on a minimal budget ("on a shoestring"). For a complete list of currently available volumes, see http://www.lonelyplanet.com/.

148 Michelin guides. Michelin (Firm).
Clermont-Ferrand, France; Greenville,
S.C.: Michelin

Published since 1900, beginning as a method to increase demand for automobile tires (the principal business of the company). Noted for their system of ratings based on one, two, or three stars. There are two series. Michelin Green Guides are comprehensive travel guides to countries or to regions within countries, offering cultural and historical background information, as well as restaurant and hotel recommendations. The less numerous Michelin Red Guides are limited to hotel and restaurant reviews, usually for specific major cities, and cover only establishments that meet specific criteria for quality. Maps are a strength. These guides remain strong resources for travel by car. For a complete list of currently available volumes, see http://www.michelintravel.com/michelin-guides/.

149 Rick Steves' Europe. Rick Steves.
Berkeley, Calif.: Avalon Travel

Travel guide coverage in this series is limited to Europe: by covering a smaller number of destinations, the ability to update the content is improved. Individual volumes tend to cover single countries, or sometimes geographical regions. Offers useful advice for planning a trip; especially helpful for novice travellers. Includes walking tour descriptions; hotel and restaurant information is not emphasized. Aimed at an adult audience, rather than students. Avalon Travel also publishes the *Moon travel guides*.

For a complete list of currently available volumes, see http://www.ricksteves.com/.

150   Rough guides travel guides. Rough Guides (Firm). London: Rough Guides
Most volumes in this series cover a single country or a major city. Presents historical and cultural background information. Hotel and restaurant information is minimal. Written from a British perspective, and primarily aimed at young adults, with features on nightlife. Advice for planning a trip may be helpful for novice travellers, with details about transportation options. For a complete list of currently available volumes, see http://www.roughguides.com/.

Web Tools

151   Expedia travel: vacations, cheap flights, airline tickets & airfares. http://www.expedia.com/. Expedia (Firm). Bellevue, Wash.: Expedia. 1996–
Makes it possible to compare costs for hotel rooms, airfares and car rentals, separately or in combination. The oldest and the largest of the internet-based travel services. Similar competing web sites include Travelocity (155), Priceline (153) and Orbitz (152), among others.

Features on Web-based portals of this kind change frequently, so it pays to examine available choices, read the fine print, and take time to explore options. There may be terms and conditions for some functions. Best practices for consumers include paying with credit cards, and printing all confirmation numbers and reservation information.

152   Orbitz travel: airline tickets, cheap hotels, car rentals, vacations. http://www.orbitz.com/. Orbitz Worldwide (Firm). Chicago: Orbitz Worldwide. 2001-
Makes it possible to compare costs for hotel rooms, airfares and car rentals, separately or in combination. Offers an automated Price Assurance feature. Similar competing web sites include Expedia (151), Travelocity (155) and Priceline (153), among others.

Features on Web-based portals of this kind change frequently, so it pays to examine available choices, read the fine print, and take time to explore

options. There may be terms and conditions for some functions. Best practices for consumers include paying with credit cards, and printing all confirmation numbers and reservation information.

153   Priceline.com: travel, airline tickets, cheap flights, hotels, hotel rooms, rental cars, car rental. http://www.priceline.com/. Priceline (Firm). Norwalk, Conn.: Priceline.com. 1998-
Shows comparative costs for hotel rooms, airfares and car rentals, separately or in combination. Similar competing web sites include Expedia (151), Travelocity (155), and Orbitz (152), among others. Distinguished by its blind bidding option, which lets shoppers trade away control of booking details in favor of potential discounts (the "Express Deal" option allows one to bypass the bidding).

Features on Web-based portals of this kind change frequently, so it pays to examine available choices, read the fine print, and take time to explore options. There may be terms and conditions for some functions. Best practices for consumers include paying with credit cards, and printing all confirmation numbers and reservation information.

154   Travelers' health: CDC. http://wwwnc.cdc.gov/travel. Centers for Disease Control and Prevention. Atlanta, Ga.: Centers for Disease Control and Prevention. 1995–
614.5   RA643
Health-related information from the U.S. government about destination locations, inspection scores for cruise ships, specific diseases, recommended vaccinations, and food and water safety. News alerts. Travel advice for children, seniors, and pregnant women. Full text of the latest edition of the CDC Yellow Book: *Health information for international travel.*

155   Travelocity: book travel for less. http://www.travelocity.com/. Travelocity (Firm). Southlake, Tex.: Travelocity. 1996-
Displays comparative costs for hotel rooms, airfares and car rentals, separately or in combination. Travelocity is noteworthy for its attention to rail travel options. Similar competing web sites include Expedia (151), Priceline (153) and Orbitz (152), among others.

Features on Web-based portals of this kind change frequently, so it pays to examine available choices, read the fine print, and take time to explore options. There may be terms and conditions for some functions. Best practices for consumers include paying with credit cards, and printing all confirmation numbers and reservation information.

156 Travel.State.Gov. http://travel.state .gov/. Bureau of Consular Affairs, U.S. Department of State. Washington: U.S. Department of State

Divided into five primary sections. The first two sections provide information on international travel for U.S. citizens, including registration at the U.S. embassy or consulate, travel requirements, and tips. Also information on document requirements, including information on applying for or renewing passports. The third section, on visas, provides information for foreign visitors and immigrants traveling to the United States. The fourth section relates a variety of information concerning children and family issues including intercountry adoption and international parental child abduction. The fifth section deals with law and policy issues concerning Americans traveling or living abroad. Other important information includes travel warnings and "Consular Information Sheets" for each country. "Consular Information Sheets" include information about entry and exit requirements, medical facilities, and crime.

157 World Tourism Organization. http:// www.unwto.org/. World Tourism Organization. Madrid, Spain: World Tourism Organization. 2006–

A service of the United Nations. Large tourism website. Includes over 900 online publications within the online *UNWTO ELibrary* at http://www .wtoelibrary.org/home/main.mpx. Links include the full text of the *UNWTO tourism highlights* annual with useful statistical reports and projections for tourism expenditure and trends in destinations.

4 Dissertations

Cynthia Thomes

Bibliography

International

158 Center for Research Libraries online dissertations catalog. http://www-apps .crl.edu/catalog/dissertationSearch.asp. Center for Research Libraries. Chicago: Center for Research Libraries

Provides catalog records for more than 800,000 doctoral dissertations from more than 1,200 universities outside of the U.S. and Canada. Dissertations date from the 18th century to the present.

Dissertations acquired through exchange agreements and on a title-by-title basis by request.

Dissertations available via interlibrary loan and electronic document delivery, depending on a patron's institution's CRL (Center for Research Libraries) membership status.

159 Networked Digital Library of Theses and Dissertations (NDLTD). http:// www.ndltd.org/. Networked Digital Library of Theses and Dissertations, Virginia Polytechnic Institute and State University. Blacksburg,Va.: Networked Digital Library of Theses and Dissertations (NDLTD). 1990s-
LB2369 378.05; 808.02; 025.04

NDLTD, an international organization composed of universities, research institutions, national libraries, consortia, and partner organizations, promotes the adoption, creation, use, dissemination, and preservation of electronic theses and dissertations (ETDs). Provides various links, including general information on ETDs, under "About," as well as information about how to find, build, and manage open-access ETDs (under "Thesis Resources").

160 Open access theses and dissertations (OATD). http://oatd.org/. Open Access Theses and Dissertations Steering Committee. Winston-Salem, N.C.: Open Access Theses and Dissertations. 2013-

Provides access to more than 1.8 million open-access theses and dissertations published around the world, with metadata provided by more than 800 participating universities, colleges, and research institutions. Full text of theses and dissertations is available from the original host site, not from OATD.

161 OpenThesis. http://www.openthesis .org/. OpenThesis.org. OpenThesis.org

Contains bibliographic information for dissertations, theses, and other academic documents from U.S. and international institutions. Full text available for a small percentage of documents.

Creating a free account provides users with advanced search features and with the option to store documents and searches, set up alerts, and upload and manage their own documents.

North America

UNITED STATES

162 PQDT open (ProQuest dissertations and theses open). http://pqdtopen. proquest.com/. ProQuest. Ann Arbor, Mich.: ProQuest. 2007-
Provides free access to the full text of dissertations and theses whose authors opted to make their work available as open access.

Contains a small subset of the documents available in *ProQuest dissertations and theses* (163).

163 ProQuest dissertations and theses (PQDT). http://www.proquest.com/en-US/catalogs/databases/detail/pqdt.shtml. ProQuest. Ann Arbor, Mich.: ProQuest. 2000s-

AI3

Indexes virtually all U.S. dissertations going back to the 19th century. Since 1980 entries have searchable 350-word abstracts; full-text as well as 24-page "previews" available for many dissertations since 1997. Essential starting point for any U.S. dissertation search.

Also includes citations to masters' theses with searchable 150-word abstracts since 1988 as well as a growing number of foreign dissertations.

Bibliographic records and abstracts are also available on CD-ROM and in print from ProQuest Dissertation Publ. Paper counterparts and predecessors include *Dissertation abstracts international* (monthly), *Masters' abstracts international* (bimonthly), and *Comprehensive dissertation index* (annual). See earlier editions of the *Guide* for publishing history.

Guides and Manuals

164 Networked Digital Library of Theses and Dissertations (NDLTD). http://www.ndltd.org/. Networked Digital Library of Theses and Dissertations, Virginia Polytechnic Institute and State University. Blacksburg, Va.: Networked Digital Library of Theses and Dissertations (NDLTD). 1990s-

378.05; 808.02; 025.04   LB2369

NDLTD, an international organization composed of universities, research institutions, national libraries, consortia, and partner organizations, promotes the adoption, creation, use, dissemination, and preservation of electronic theses and dissertations (ETDs). Provides various links, including general information on ETDs, under "About," as well as information about how to find, build, and manage open-access ETDs (under "Thesis Resources").

5 Encyclopedias

Barbara M. Bibel

English Language Encyclopedias

165 Encyclopaedia Britannica online.
http://www.britannica.com/.
Encyclopaedia Britannica. Chicago:
Encyclopaedia Britannica. 2001–
Has three sites: Encyclopaedia Britannica Online Academic Edition at http://info.eb.com/products/britannica-academic-edition/ (which includes Merriam-Webster's collegiate dictionary and thesaurus (249) but does not include children's encyclopedias), Encyclopaedia Britannica Online Public Library Edition at http://info.eb.com/products/britannica-public-library-edition/ (includes adult and children's search pages for *Encyclopaedia Britannica, Britannica concise encyclopedia*, and *Compton's*) and Encyclopaedia Britannica Online School Edition at http://info.eb.com/products/britannica-school/ (includes *Britannica elementary, Compton's*, and *Encyclopaedia Britannica*, as well as teacher resources). All include dictionaries and a thesaurus, an atlas, links to articles and websites, and personal workspace feature for creating research projects. "World Data Analyst," "Year in Review Browse," and daily features also included. Britannica produces a print edition of *New encyclopaedia Britannica* every two years. *Compton's by Britannica* appears in print every two years also.

A free version, Britannica.com, offers the beginning part of most articles without charge: http://britannica.com/ A subscription is required to obtain the full article, unless an entire article is hyperlinked from another website.

166 Wikipedia. http://www.wikipedia.org/.
San Francisco: Wikimedia Foundation.
2001–

AE5

"Free encyclopedia that anyone can edit." Available in many languages with varying amounts of content. Provides extensive guidelines but little oversight to assure that contributors follow them. Some articles by experts on arcane subjects are unique and accurate. Lack of editorial oversight means users should verify information elsewhere and not make Wikipedia the only source consulted.

167 World book online reference center.
http://www.worldbookonline.com/. World
Book. Chicago: World Book. 2005–
Includes the complete World Book Encyclopedia plus over 8,500 articles specially created for the online version, more than 12,000 ill. and maps, 100 videos, 10,000 sounds, and 100 360-degree panoramas, as well as 7,000 Web links. Also has Back in Time (13,000 historic articles from past eds.), *Enciclopedia estudiantil hallazgos* (Spanish-language version of *The world book student discovery encyclopedia*), parent, teacher, and student resources, special reports (500 in-depth feature articles), Surf the Ages (fictitious historical websites), periodical articles from *EBSCO content solutions, World book dictionary*. Today

in History, Through the Year (activities and articles about each month), and World Book Research Libraries (primary source documents). Continuous updating. Print edition available annually from World Book.

Comprehensive Sets

168 AccessScience. http://www.access science.com/. Columbus, Ohio: McGraw-Hill. 2000–

1097-8542

Providing access to over 8,000 articles (from the former *McGraw-Hill encyclopedia of science and technology*), this resource also includes 110,000 dictionary terms from the *McGraw-Hill dictionary of scientific and technical terms*, biographies of leading scientists, research updates from the *McGraw-Hill yearbooks of science and technology*, updates from *Science news*, videos, and more. A high quality, convenient scientific dictionary/encyclopedia. Pricing based on institution size.

McGraw-Hill provides several sub-platforms for its e-books, including AccessAnesthesiology, AccessEmergencyMedicine, AccessEngineering, AccessMedicine, AccessPediatrics, AccessPharmacy, AccessPhysiotherapy,and AccessSurgery.

169 Encyclopaedia Judaica. 2nd ed. Fred Skolnik, Michael Berenbaum. Detroit: Macmillan Reference USA; Keter, 2007. 22 v., ill. (some color), maps (some color) ISBN 9780028659282

909.04924   DS102.8.E496

First ed., 1972; 10 yearbooks and two supplementary volumes, 1973–1994; CD-ROM version, 1997.

The definitive reference work for Judaic studies. Includes about 22,000 entries on people, places, events, topics, concepts, and texts. More than 2,600 entries are new to this edition; over half of the remainder were substantially revised. Note that this edition of the *EJ* includes an entire volume providing extensive coverage for the state of Israel and expanded coverage of women; it is also a rich resource on the Holocaust. Entries range from a paragraph to very substantial essays; all include bibliographies. Every volume includes a list of abbreviations and a glossary. The final volume includes a full thematic outline of all entries that is very useful for those seeking all the relevant entries

on a broad topic. This is followed by an index that will also guide users to topics discussed only within larger entries. Some items found in the earlier edition have been omitted, so it is sometimes worth consulting both editions.

Also available as an e-book, which offers the advantage of keyword searching.

170 Encyclopedia Americana. Scholastic Library Publishing. Danbury, Conn.: Scholastic Library Publishers, 1829–. 30 v., ill. (some color); maps (some color) ISBN 0717201392

031   AE5.E333

History: First published in 1829. First ed. in 1903–4, 16 v. unpaged; several partial revisions, especially an edition in 22 v. published in 1912 under the title *The Americana*, which included some new articles and changes in others. The 1918–20 edition was a complete revision, which is the basis of succeeding editions. Now has a continuous revision policy. From 1979 to 2003 the imprint was Grolier; in 2004 it became Scholastic.

A good, comprehensive general encyclopedia. Most articles are signed and have bibliographies. There are many maps and illustrations. This encyclopedia's major strength is its coverage of the United States. Available online as part of the Grolier Online suite.

171 Encyclopedia of religion. 2nd ed. Lindsay Jones. Detroit: Macmillan Reference USA, 2005. 15 v., ill. ISBN 0028657330

200.3   BL31.E46

First. ed., 1987.

A standard work treating theoretical (doctrines, myths, theologies, ethics), practical (cults, sacraments, meditations), and sociological (religious groups, ecclesiastical forms) aspects of religion; includes extensive coverage of non-Western religions. The second edition contains about two-thirds of the articles from the first edition (retained or revised) and 600 new articles. Signed articles, many quite substantial, by an international group of contributors conclude with extensive bibliographies. Many composite entries treat two or more related topics. This edition includes 14 "visual essays" on such topics as sacred time, which are scattered out of sequence throughout the volumes. An alphabetical list of entries appears in v. 1.

Vol. 15 provides a synoptic outline of contents, an extensive general index, and a group of 21 articles received too late to be included in the main set.

The *Encyclopedia of religion* is partial successor to the *Encyclopaedia of religion and ethics* by Hastings et al., a work that was largely concerned with theoretical aspects of religion. However, some articles in the earlier work remain useful for historical purposes.

A digital version is available through the Gale Virtual Reference Library (288).

172   Stanford encyclopedia of philosophy.
http://plato.stanford.edu/. Edward N. Zalta, Center for the Study of Language and Information. Stanford, Calif.: Metaphysics Research Lab, Center for the Study of Language and Information, Stanford University. 1995– 1095-5054
B51

The most substantial, authoritative, and scholarly open-access online encyclopedia in philosophy (and possibly in any field), though far from complete with at least half of its more than 2,000 projected entries not yet assigned or submitted. Lengthy articles—typically equivalent to 5–40 printed pages—are the norm, as are extensive bibliographies. The SEP's intended scope encompasses the full range of philosophical topics, including non-Western, though contributions to date concentrate mainly on Western philosophy. So far, the SEP is fulfilling its promise as a dynamic reference work, as many existing articles have already been updated or revised at least once. Older versions of articles are archived in periodic "fixed editions" of the SEP maintained on its website. The principal site at Stanford University is mirrored by sites in Australia, the Netherlands, and the United Kingdom.

Factbooks and Compendiums

Almanacs and Yearbooks

173   Famous first facts: A record of first happenings, discoveries, and inventions in American history. 6th ed. Joseph Nathan Kane, Steven Anzovin, Janet Podell. New York: H. W. Wilson, 2006. xvii, 1307 p., ill. ISBN 0824210654
031.02   AG5.K315

Aims to establish the earliest date of various occurrences, achievements, inventions, etc. First published in 1933, this current edition contains more than 7,500 entries, is arranged into 16 topical chapters, and has five indexes. Each chapter is arranged alphabetically by subtopic ("Daily Life" includes "Birth," "Children," "Death," "Sewing," etc.). The five indexes are by subject, year, day, personal name, and geography. Each entry describes or explains the event or invention and provides the date. Some entries include the source of information.

174   Guinness world records. Guinness World Records Ltd. New York: Guinness World Records Ltd., 1956–. ill. (some color) ISBN 1904994121
AG243.G87

Has undergone many title changes and various publishers: *Guinness book of superlatives* (1956–1960s); *Guinness book of world records* (1962–1989; 1996–1997); *Guinness book of records* (1990–1995; 1998).

A compendium of information, grouped by topic, concerning the longest, shortest, tallest, deepest, fastest, etc., in relation to natural features, manmade structures, people, events, and achievements. Indexed. Some content is also available at http://www.guinnessworldrecords.com/.

175   Notable Last Facts: A Compendium of Endings, Conclusions, Terminations, and Final Events. William H. Brahms. Haddonfield, N.J.: Reference Desk Press, 2005. ISBN 9780976532507
031.02   AG105

A counterpart to *Famous First Facts* (173) this compendium offers 16,000 notable last facts organized by subject. An extensive table of contents and a comprehensive index make it easy to find the necessary material.

176   Old Farmer's Almanac. Robert Bailey Thomas. Dublin, N.H.: Old Farmer's Almanac, 2014. ISBN 9781571986030
031.02

The oldest continuously published almanac in the United States contains a wealth of information about the weather, phases of the moon, gardening, recipes, and folk lore. There are U.S. and Canadian editions. It is also available as an e-book and online: http://www.almanac.com/

177   Sports illustrated . . . almanac.
Sports Illustrated. New York: Bishop
Books, 2002–. ill. 1056-7887
GV741.S768

This all-in-one-volume source of sports records provides team and individual records for major sports as well as the less popular, such as swimming, figure skating, bowling, tennis, horse racing, motor sports, boxing, archery, cycling, etc. Each sport is covered separately, with a brief descriptive essay, then the statistics.

178   Whitaker's almanack. Joseph Whitaker.
London: A. & C. Black, 1869–. ill.
ISBN 0713676590
AY754.W5

Former title: *An almanack for the year of our Lord*, but generally known as *Whitaker's almanack*. Began publishing in 1869.

Focuses on information about the United Kingdom's social, political, and economic structure. Organized by topics such as the royal family, peerage, regional government, local government, heritage, etc. Other sections include information about other countries, including statistics and currencies and exchange rates; events of the past year; a general reference section. Includes index.

179   The world almanac and book of facts.
World Almanac Books. New York: World
Almanac Books, 1868–. ill., maps.
ISBN 0886879957, 0084-1382
317   AY67.N5W7

Title and publisher vary. Began publishing in 1868 by New York World; publication was suspended in 1876. Publication revived in 1886 by Joseph Pulitzer (from 2007 edition, copyright statement).

One of the most highly regarded American almanacs. Contains statistics on social, industrial, political, financial, educational, and other subjects; political organizations; societies; historical lists of famous events; etc. A handbook with which reference workers should be familiar. Alphabetical index at the front of each volume.

Internet Resources

180   Infoplease.com. http://www.infoplease
.com/. Information Please LLC. Boston:
Information Please LLC. [1998–]

The site contains an almanac, atlas, dictionary, encyclopedia, thesaurus, and timelines, in addition to special resources for schoolchildren (a "homework center" and Infoplease.com's site for children, Factmonster.com). Full-text searching is available for the entire site, or for a specific type of source (e.g. almanac or dictionary). Includes a biography section, providing access by profession, as well as "People in the News" extending back to 1997. For statistics, the original sources are noted; the site also provides internal links to related statistics available on the site. The print equivalent of the almanac portion of the site is *The time almanac*.

6 Genealogy

Mary K. Mannix

International

Compendiums

**181 International vital records handbook.
6th edition ed.** Thomas Jay Kemp.
Baltimore: Genealogical Publishing Co.,
2013. xvi, 697 p., forms.
ISBN 9780806319810
2013 929/.1   CS42.7.K46

Contains addresses, application forms, and ordering
information for vital records in the United States, the
U.S. Trust Territories, and worldwide. Telephone,
fax numbers, e-mail, and URLs are included where
available. While much of this information is online,
this provides quick, easy access for researchers.

Internet Resources

**182 Cyndi's list of genealogy sites on the
Internet.** http://www.cyndislist.com.
Cyndi Howells, Cyndi Howells. Puyallup,
Wash.: Cyndi Howells. 1996–
025.04;929.1   CS21

The largest collection of genealogy links on the
Internet with over 329,000 links(as of January
2014). Searchable by keyword. The alphabetically
arranged categories are very useful research starting
points. Especially handy for librarians when they
have little experience with a genealogy topic. Free.

The "Biographies" section, under the main category index, offers a valuable list of links to biographical sites, including many state and regional sites,
plus a link to the extensive "Obituaries" section.

183 FamilySearch. http://www.familysearch
.org/default.asp. Church of Jesus Christ
of Latter-Day Saints. Salt Lake City, Utah:
Church of Jesus Christ of Latter-Day Saints

"Product of the world's largest repository of genealogical information."-Family History Library, in Salt
Lake City; free of cost. The search section includes:
historical record collections(some are searchable scans,
some browsable scans, others simply indexes); user-
submitted genealogies, FamilySearch catalog (Family History Library), Family history books (full-text
books from eight leading genealogy libraries), and the
research wiki. Genealogies retrieves records from the
ancestral file and the Pedigree Resource File. Historical Records consists of 1709 collections as of January
2014, including Census; also includes material from
International Genealogical Index. Researchers can also
find the nearest Family History Center, where materials may be ordered from Salt Lake City. Some full-text
books can only be accessed at a FHC or partner library.
Researchers can also create free accounts for building
their own family trees. Serves as gateway for volunteer
indexing projects.

184 Find a grave. http://www.findagrave
.com/index.html. Jim Tipton, Find a grave.

Provo, Utah: Ancestry.com 929.5
The most well-known crowd-sourcing site for locating graves and cemeteries. Often includes photographs of tombstones and added content, such as obituaries and family data. Can search by cemetery or name of deceased. As of January 2014, includes information from over 400,000 cemeteries from 200 countries, over 111,000 grave records. Not all cemeteries are covered in their entirety. Includes section on famous graves. Also, yearly necrologies interesting epitaphs, interesting monuments, posthumous reunions, and claim to fame. Acquired by Ancestry.com in 2013, remains free.

Names

Surnames

BRITISH AND AMERICAN

185 Dictionary of American family names.
Patrick Hanks. Oxford; New York:
Oxford University Press, 2003. 3 v.
ISBN 0195081374
929.40973   CS2485.D53
Pioneering effort to explain the history and origin of the 70,000 most frequent family names in the United States, together with some rarer names of historical or etymological importance. Gives the basic facts about family names, summarizing where the name came from, what it meant at the time it came into existence, and its history. Short essays at the beginning of vol. 1 cover naming practices in the world's leading languages and cultures. Hanks claims that "over 85% of Americans will find an entry for their surname in DAFN." Also available online in Oxford reference (290).

North America

United States

BIBLIOGRAPHIES

**186 Passenger and immigration lists
index: a guide to published arrival
records of about 500,000 passengers
who came to the United States
and Canada in the seventeenth,**
eighteenth, and nineteenth centuries.
1st ed. P. William Filby, Mary K. Meyer.
Detroit: Gale Research Co., 1981. 3 v.
(xxxv, 2339 p.)
929/.373   CS68.F537
Guide to published records of millions of immigrants who came to the New World between the sixteenth and the mid-twentieth centuries. Over thirty annual supplements (published 1982–2013), nearly five million names indexed. Bibliography in each volume. A "preliminary edition" was published 1980. This work "brings together in one alphabet citations to information about passengers . . . whose names appear in a broad collection of published passenger lists or naturalization records" (*Introd.*). Entry usually gives name, age, place and year of arrival or of naturalization record. Supplements have been published annually and cumulated as: ——. *1982–85 cumulated supplements* (1985, 4 v.); ——. *1986–90 cumulated supplements* (1990, 3 v.); ——. *1991–95 cumulated supplements* (1995, 3 v.); ——. *1996–2000 cumulated supplements* (2000, 3 v.).; ——. *2001–2005 cumulated supplements* (2005, 3 v.) Available in Ancestry.com, but not in the *Ancestry Library Edition*.

GUIDES

**187 A genealogist's guide to discovering
your female ancestors: special
strategies for uncovering hard-to-find
information about your female lineage.**
Sharon DeBartolo Carmack. Cincinnati:
Betterway Books, 1998. 152 p.
ISBN 1558704728
929.1082   CS14.C38
One of many useful guides to family history research by Carmack, a professional genealogist. The first one to offer special strategies and research techniques for tracing female genealogy. Suggests effective methods for determining maiden names and accessing official documents that can specify facts about maternal ancestors, but its content includes research techniques for individuals of either sex.

**188 Guide to genealogical research in
the National Archives of the United
States. 3rd ed.** Anne Bruner Eales, Robert
M. Kvasnicka. Washington: National
Archives and Records Administration,

2000. vii, 411 p., ill. (some col.), maps.
ISBN 1880875241

016.929/1/072073   Z5313.U5U54; CS68

A comprehensive guide to materials of genealogical interest located in the National Archives in Washington, D.C., and in some 20 National Archives and Records Administration facilities around the country. Military records, records relating to particular groups (Native Americans, African Americans, and civilian government employees), and other useful records. Two appendices—a list of record groups cited and a list of microform publications cited—as well as useful reproductions of records described, make this an indispensable guide to significant genealogical resources. Census microfilm information no longer as useful. Indexed.

Should be supplemented with information available at the NARA website: http://www.archives.gov/research/genealogy/index.html

189   Hidden sources: family history in unlikely places. Laura Szucs Pfeiffer. Orem, Utah: Ancestry, 2000. xviii, 292 p., ill., maps. ISBN 0916489868

929/.1/072073   CS14.P48

A guide to little-known records that can provide information about ancestors, such as adoption records, bankruptcy records, records of coroner's inquests, fraternal organization records, indenture records, licenses, orphan asylum records, and patent records. While discussions are not comprehensive, it is a useful introduction to a variety of sources. Includes selected readings. A companion to *The Source* (192) and *Printed Sources* (190), although less scholarly.

190   Printed sources: a guide to published genealogical records. Kory L. Meyerink. Salt Lake City, Utah: Ancestry, 1998. xiv, 840 p., ill. ISBN 0916489701

016.929/373   Z5311.P75;CS9

Essential companion volume to *The Source* (192) (which covers "original" records, such as censuses and vital records). *Printed Sources* covers secondary sources—where to find them, what is in them, and how to use them. Secondary works include those giving background information (how-to books and atlases), finding aids, printed original works, and compiled information. Three appendices provide information on CD-ROMs, major U.S. genealogical

libraries, and genealogical publishers and booksellers. Although some of the sources included are now available online in digitized format or have been superseded by online publications, the general discussion of secondary sources is still valuable.

191   Revolutionary war pensions awarded by state governments 1775-1874, the general and federal governments prior to 1814, and by private acts of Congress to 1905. Lloyd DeWitt Bockstruck. Baltimore: Genealogical Publishing Co., 2011. xxiv, 1042 p. ISBN 9780806318691

331.25/291355   E255.B67

Provides access to material previously unavailable in one location. Data reconstructs records lost in 1800 and 1814 fires. 16,500 pensioners included along with 15,000 others.

192   The source: a guidebook of American genealogy. 3rd rev. ed. Loretto Dennis Szucs, Sandra Hargreaves Luebking. Provo, Utah: Ancestry, 2006. ISBN 1593312776

929/.1072073   CS49.S65

Considered by many to be the most important reference book for genealogists, serves as a detailed guide to every category of "original" source material—manuscript, microfilm, published record groups, and online databases—currently available for genealogical research between the beginnings of European colonization in America and 1910. Each chapter is written by an expert on a particular type of record. Substantive revision of the previous edition. Four completely new chapters have been added—"Computers and Technology," "General References and Guides," "Colonial English Research," and "Colonial Spanish Borderland Research"—and several chapters have been entirely rewritten. Separate bibliographic and subject indexes of the previous ed. are now consolidated in one index, p. 937–965. Along with *Printed Sources* (190) and *Hidden Sources* (189), this is indispensable to the committed genealogist.

193   They became Americans: finding naturalization records and ethnic origins. Loretto Dennis Szucs. Salt Lake City, Utah: Ancestry, 1998. viii, 294 p., ill. ISBN 091648971X

929.1072073   CS47.S96

Well-written research guide to naturalization records that leads the genealogical researcher through the many kinds of records created at different times in the country's history and explains how to find these records and interpret them. An appendix provides a chronology of immigration by ethnic group, changes in immigration law, and changes in the law affecting women and their citizenship.

HANDBOOKS; MANUALS

**194 Evidence explained: citing history sources from artifacts to cyberspace.
2nd ed.** Elizabeth Shown Mills. Baltimore: Genealogical Publishing Co, 2009. 885 p, ill.
907.2 22   D5.M55 2009
The definitive genealogy style guide for sourcing. A genealogy or local history researcher will locate precise directions for citing a wide variety of source types. Archives and artifacts; business and institutional records; cemetery records, census records, church records, local and state records: courts, governance, licenses, registrations, rolls, vital records, property and probate; national government records; books, CDs, maps, leaflets, videos, legal works government documents, periodicals, broadcasts, and web miscellanea. Also of use are chapters on the fundamentals of evidence analysis and the fundamentals of citation. This second edition provides new information on citing digital media.

INDEXES

195 Biography and genealogy master index. http://solutions.cengage.com/Gale/ Catalog/Fact-Sheets/?cid=14W -RF0329&iba=14W-RF0329-7. Gale, Cengage Learning. Farmington Hills, Mich.: Gale. 2001–
Z5305.U5
Essential first stop in biographical research. Indexes nearly 1,600 publ., largely biographical dictionaries and subject encyclopedias, and includes references on over 13.6 million people. Both current and retrospective works included. Subscription database. Indexes H. W. Wilson's Biography Index: Past and Present (83), which extends Biography and Genealogy Master Index's coverage to periodical articles.

Birth/death dates given. Searches can be limited to articles with portraits.

Covers *American men and women of science* (from 1973– ; for earlier coverage see *American men and women of science: Cumulative index*), *Who's who* [Great Britain] (from 1974–) (60), *Who's who in America* (from 1973–) (92), *Who was who in America*, and other Marquis who's who publications. Also available in print.

This is the electronic version of the discontinued microform *Bio-base*.

196 Periodical source index. Allen County Public Library. Fort Wayne, Ind.: Allen County Public Library Foundation, 1987– 1065-9056
929/.1/016   CS1.P47
Annual. See also the historical volume, covering 1847–1985. Known as *PERSI*. The largest and most widely used index of articles from genealogy and local history periodicals in the world. It is the only tool that tracks many of these periodicals. Created by the Allen County Public Library, which has one of the largest collections of such periodicals in print, this annually updated publication and database has become the largest of its kind. In addition to print, it is also available on microfiche, and online at Ancestry.com and HeritageQuest Online (197).

INTERNET RESOURCES

197 HeritageQuest online. http://heritage questonline.com/. ProQuest Information and Learning Company, Heritage Quest (Society). Ann Arbor, Mich.: ProQuest
929.373   CS44
Library subscription service from ProQuest Information and Learning Company. Includes set of digitzed U.S. census schedules (some searchable, others must be browsed), full-text family and local histories, *PERSI* (*Periodical Source Index*) (196), selected records from Revolutionary War pension and bounty land warrant application files, and Freedman's Bank records (1865-1874), which was founded to serve African Americans, and {record} (*United States Congressional Serial Set*). Must be accessed through a library; most libraries provide remote access. Not all censuses are indexed; only 1880 is indexed by every person in household.

Government Publications

Christopher C. Brown

International

General Works

LIBRARY RESOURCES

**198 Worldwide government directory, with
international organizations.** National
Standards Association. Bethesda, Md.:
National Standards Association, 1987–.
maps. 0894-1521
351.2025   JF37.L345

Continues *Lambert's worldwide government directory,
with inter-governmental organizations.* Publisher varies.
Pt. 1 serves as a directory, organized alphabetically
by country, to government officials in more than 170
countries. Includes addresses, phone numbers, and
forms of address. Pt. 2 provides alphabetical entries
for international organizations. No index.

As of June 2013, no longer available online - see:
http://library.cqpress.com/world-powerbase/.

International Governmental Organizations

UNITED NATIONS

General Works

CATALOGS AND INDEXES

**199 Official document system of the United
Nations.** http://documents.un.org/.

Dag Hammarskjöld Library. New York:
United Nations. 2001–

The digital repository and retrieval system for U.N.
documents (i.e., masthead documents and official
records). These include meeting records, letters,
reports, and other texts intended mainly for member states' delegates and U.N. staff. Contains all
resolutions and decisions of the General Assembly,
Security Council, and Economic and Social Council (ECOSOC) in the organization's six official languages. Includes the vast majority of all documents
published since 1993, but one or more translations
of many items is lacking. Most documents issued
before 1993 have not yet been digitized for ODS.
Records in UNBISnet for documents published since
1993 ordinarily contain links to the corresponding
texts in ODS.

Includes three search interfaces. The advanced
search provides access by language, document symbol, publication and release date, session and agenda
item number, subject, title keyword, and full-text
keyword. Search fields in the so-called simple search
include only language, document symbol, full-text
keyword, and publication date. The global search
uses the Google search engine to target the full text
of U.N. documents published from 1993 to date.

The resolutions and decisions of the General
Assembly, Security Council, ECOSOC, and Trusteeship Council adopted from 1946 to 1993, as well
as certain periodicals, are stored separately in ODS.
The aforementioned periodicals include the daily

journals of the U.N. offices at New York, Geneva, and Vienna, and the daily lists of documents issued in Geneva and Vienna. To access these, users must select the appropriate database on the left half of the advanced search interface.

STATISTICS

200 UNdata. http://data.un.org. United
Nations Statistics Division. New York:
United Nations. 2008–

HA155

Provides simultaneous access to datasets derived from 14 statistical databases produced within the U.N. System. Subject matter includes population, labor, education, energy, agriculture, industry, tourism, trade, and national accounts. Its content may be accessed in four ways. Both the keyword and advanced searches identify and retrieve data by source (e.g., Unesco statistics), year, country, region, and miscellaneous keyword, but the advanced search does so more precisely. The Explorer offers hierarchical navigation within each database. Finally, the user may browse profiles created for each country. UNdata also contains a statistical profile of each country. The UN Statistics Division (UNSD) will ultimately include the statistical resources of national governments. UNdata usually hosts only part of a database's content, so it does not replace UN Comtrade, the National Accounts Main Aggregates Database, and other statistical systems created by the U.N. and related intergovernmental organizations. The lone exception is the UN Common Database, which has been rendered obsolete.

Other Governments

General Works

LIBRARY RESOURCES

**201 Worldwide government directory, with
international organizations.** National
Standards Association. Bethesda, Md.:
National Standards Association, 1987–.
maps. 0894-1521
351.2025   JF37.L345
Continues *Lambert's worldwide government directory,*

with inter-governmental organizations. Publisher varies. Pt. 1 serves as a directory, organized alphabetically by country, to government officials in more than 170 countries. Includes addresses, phone numbers, and forms of address. Pt. 2 provides alphabetical entries for international organizations. No index.

As of June 2013, no longer available online - see: http://library.cqpress.com/world-powerbase/.

United States

202 American memory. http://memory.loc
.gov/. Library of Congress. Washington:
Library of Congress. [1994]–

E173

The American Memory project provides free access to "written and spoken words, sound recordings, still and moving images, prints, maps, and sheet music that document the American experience"—"Mission and history" page. Collections can be browsed by broad topics including African American History, Architecture, Cities & Towns, Government & Law, Immigration, Literature, maps, presidents, sports & recreation, war, and women's history. Browsing by date from 1400 to present and by geographic area is also available. Keyword searching across all collections is possible as well. The wealth of historical information includes textual materials such as congressional documents from 1774-1875, woman suffrage scrapbooks, historical American sheet music, historical maps, selected early motion pictures, dozens of digitized print collections, and sound recording dating back to the Civil War era.

203 Occupational outlook handbook.
http://www.bls.gov/ooh/. United States
Bureau of Labor Statistics. Washington:
U.S. Department of Labor. 1998–
331   HD8051
Biennial official government estimate of trends and potential employment in 800 occupations. Browsable by major Occupation Groups (such as Healthcare or Media & Communication), by rate of pay, by projected rate of job growth, by projected absolute number of new jobs, or alphabetically. Searchable by rate of pay, level of required education, and anticipated numbers of new openings. Entries for each occupation indicate median pay, required education or credentials, number of jobs nationally,

and anticipated growth. Launched in print in 1949, and available on the Web since 1998. Reprints are sold by private publishers as well.

204 Official congressional directory.
W. H. Michael, United States. Washington: U.S. Government Printing Office, 1888–. ill., maps. 0160-9890
328.73073025   JK1011
Superintendent of Documents classification: Y 4.P 93/1: l/. Publ. 1809–86 as *Congressional directory.* Some current editions bear that title. Directories for some sessions issued in rev. eds. Supplements accompany some volumes. From 1865, printed at the Government Printing Office; before that by private firms. Volumes for 97th Congress completed under the direction of the Joint Committee on Printing. Volumes since 1995 (104th Congress) available electronically.

Contains (1) biographical sketches of members of Congress, arranged by state; (2) state delegations; (3) congressional ZIP codes; (4) terms of service; (5) committees, membership, and days of meetings; (6) joint committees; (7) committee assignments; (8) boards, commissions, and advisory organizations; (9) statistical information (e.g., sessions of Congress, votes cast for legislators); (10) the Capitol (e.g., officers of the Senate and House, capitol buildings and grounds); (11) executive departments; (12) independent agencies; (13) judiciary; (14) District of Columbia government; (15) international organizations; (16) foreign diplomatic representatives and consular offices in the United States; (17) U.S. diplomatic and consular offices; (18) press galleries, rules, representatives entitled to admission; (19) maps of congressional districts. Individual name index. Recent online content at http://purl.access.gpo.gov/GPO/LPS11679.

205 Statistical sites on the World Wide Web. http://www.bls.gov/bls/other. htm. U.S. Bureau of Labor Statistics. Washington: U.S. Bureau of Labor Statistics. 1998-
Links to official government statistical offices all over the world, including Web sites from more than 140 countries and from international agencies such as Afristat, East African Community (EAC), European Union Eurostat, Food and Agriculture Organization (FAO), International Energy Agency (IEA),

International Labour Organization (ILO), Organization for Economic Cooperation and Development (OECD iLibrary), United Nations International Computing Centre, United Nations Statistical Division, UN Economic Commission for Europe (UN/ECE) Statistical Division, UN Industrial Development Organization Statistics, and World Health Organization Statistical Information System (WHOSIS). Also links to sites of major U.S. federal statistical agencies, including Bureau of Economic Analysis, Bureau of Justice Statistics, Bureau of Labor Statistics, Bureau of Transportation Statistics, Census Bureau, Economic Research Service, Energy Information Administration, National Agricultural Statistics Service, National Center for Education Statistics, National Center for Health Statistics, Statistics of Income from the IRS, and FedStats (213). Excellent starting point for researchers.

Federal Publications

CATALOGS AND INDEXES

206 Historical census browser. http://mapserver.lib.virginia.edu/. University of Virginia. Library. Geospatial and Statistical Data Center., United States. Bureau of the Census., Inter-university Consortium for Political and Social Research. Charlottesville, Va.: Geospatial and Statistical Data Center, University of Virginia Library.

HA181

Provides population counts by category from the U.S. decennial census beginning with 1790 and ending with 1960, by states (excluding the District of Columbia and the territories) and in some cases at the county level. Data is categorized under General Population, Ethnicity/Race/Place of Birth, Education & Literacy, Agriculture, Economy/Manufacturing/Employment, and Slave Population, and each of these headings covers multiple detailed groupings. Simple-to-construct queries generate detailed counts by location for attributes such as gender, race, and country of birth, farm acreage, or school attendance. Tabulated information can be mapped at the state level, or at the county level within states for some census years. Figures based on historical volumes of the U.S. Census of Population and Housing.

Early Period to 1893

207 ProQuest Congressional. http://cisupa
.proquest.com/ws_display.asp?filter
=Congressional%20Overview. ProQuest
(Firm). Ann Arbor, Mich.: ProQuest. 2011
JK1021

Provides comprehensive indexing to publications
of the U.S. Congress including *Congressional record*,
published and unpublished hearings, congressional
reports and documents, the Serial Set, Congressional
Research Service (CRS) Reports, committee prints,
congressional bills and public laws, the United
States Code and legislative histories (1969-present).
Available for additional purchase are digital content
in PDF format to the collections. Allows for cross-
searching of the ProQuest *Executive branch documents*
collection (1789-1932) in subscribed libraries.

Includes all material covered in the CD-ROM
index Congressional Masterfile 2, as well as the print
index *CIS index annual*. Additional modules are online
versions of Congressional Masterfile 1, *CIS index to
unpublished US House committee hearings* (1833-1936,
1937-46, 1947-54, 1955-58, 1959-64, and 1965-68
with 1947-64 supplement), *CIS index to unpublished
US Senate committee hearings* (1823-1964, 1965-68,
1969-72 with 1913-68 supplement, 1973-76), *CIS
Senate executive documents and reports*, *CIS U.S. congressional committee hearings index*, *CIS U.S. congressional committee prints index*, and *CIS U.S. serial set index*.

1893 to Present

208 ProQuest Congressional. http://cisupa
.proquest.com/ws_display.asp?filter
=Congressional%20Overview. ProQuest
(Firm). Ann Arbor, Mich.: ProQuest. 2011
JK1021

Provides comprehensive indexing to publications
of the U.S. Congress including *Congressional record*,
published and unpublished hearings, congressional
reports and documents, the Serial Set, Congressional
Research Service (CRS) Reports, committee prints,
congressional bills and public laws, the United
States Code and legislative histories (1969-present).
Available for additional purchase are digital content
in PDF format to the collections. Allows for cross-
searching of the ProQuest *Executive branch documents*
collection (1789-1932) in subscribed libraries.

Includes all material covered in the CD-ROM
index Congressional Masterfile 2, as well as the
print index *CIS index annual*. Additional modules
are online versions of Congressional Masterfile 1,
CIS index to unpublished US House committee hearings
(1833-1936, 1937-46, 1947-54, 1955-58, 1959-64,
and 1965-68 with 1947-64 supplement), *CIS index
to unpublished US Senate committee hearings* (1823-
1964, 1965-68, 1969-72 with 1913-68 supplement,
1973-76), *CIS Senate executive documents and reports*,
CIS U.S. congressional committee hearings index, *CIS
U.S. congressional committee prints index*, and *CIS U.S.
serial set index*.

EXECUTIVE BRANCH

209 The American presidency project.
http://www.presidency.ucsb.edu/. John
Woolley, Gerhard Peters, University of
California. Santa Barbara, Calif.: University
of Caifornia. 1999–
JK511

An essential no-fee, online resource for anyone who
has an interest in the U.S. presidency. Papers and
documents from George Washington to Barack
Obama, 1789–2012, are consolidated into a single
searchable database. As of October 24, 2013, the
archive had 104,107 records, and it is continually
being updated. Executive orders, proclamations,
press conferences and briefings, Saturday radio
addresses, fireside chats, veto messages, signing
statements, radio and television correspondents din-
ners, debates, party convention addresses, party platforms, State of the Union addresses and messages,
inaugural addresses, and addresses to Congress,
the nation, the United Nations, and foreign legis-
latures are included, as are college commencement
addresses.

Several search options exist: (1) keyword Boolean, which can be limited by date, document
category, and/or president; (2) select document
type, document number, and year; (3) browse by
document category, date, and/or president. Other
important features include unique data and media
archives, elections information, and links to presidential libraries.

**210 Catalog of federal domestic
assistance.** https://www.cfda.gov/.

U.S. General Services Administration, Governmentwide Information Systems Division. Washington: U.S. General Services Administration

The online version of the *Catalog of Federal Domestic Assistance* is a searchable and browsable version of what is contained in the print version comprising over 3,000 pages. This federal assistance is available to state and local governments, private profit and non-profit organizations, and individuals. Assistance for project grants, direct loans, provision of services, training, and federal employment is described, together with links to web sites and contact information are provided.

The "Project Grants" section (under Find Programs) is the most pertinent for students, academics, and others seeking financial support. Project grants can include "fellowships, scholarships, research grants, training grants, and traineeships" among other types of support.

Related website: Grants.gov.

211   County business patterns. http://www .census.gov/econ/cbp/. U.S. Census Bureau. Washington: U.S. Dept. of Commerce, Economics and Statistics Administration, U.S. Census Bureau. [1999]–
330.973   HC106.82.C68

Provides a searchable database for business establishments and their numbers of employees for all counties and zip codes. Organizes data for 1998 to recent by NAICS codes, and data for 1994 to 1997 by SIC codes.

Print editions of older *County business patterns* publications available in larger depository libraries.

212   Federal register. http://www.gpo.gov/ fdsys/browse/collection.action?collection Code=FR. U.S. National Archives and Records Administration, Office of the Federal Register. Washington: National Archives and Records Administration, Office of the Federal Register. 0097-6326
353.005   KF70

Official repository for the daily publication of all newly adopted rules and regulations, proposed rules, and notices of federal agencies and organizations, executive orders, and other presidential documents. When a regulation is codified, it is part of the *Code*

of federal regulations. As many federal rules, codes, and regulations affect business establishments, this is a necessary resource. For example, information on business rates and terms, trademarks, or even the *Federal register* notice describing changes adopted for NAICS 2007.

Online access to issues 1994 (v. 59) through the most current. Issues prior to 1994 available at Federal depository libraries.

Subscriber access to the complete digitized *Federal register*, from its earliest date of publication, is available from HeinOnline.

213   FedStats. http://www.fedstats.gov/. U.S. Federal Interagency Council on Statistical Policy. Washington: Interagency Council on Statistical Policy

HA37.U55

FedStats provides a portal to publicly available statistics produced by more than 100 U.S. government agencies, including agriculture, census, education, health and human services, interior, justice, labor, transportation, and the treasury. It permits several access points to the agency sites, including an A–Z subject index, keyword searching, and federated searching across agency websites. This outstanding resource also provides a link to online versions of frequently requested publications such as the *Statistical abstract of the United States* (218) and the *State and metropolitan area data book.*

214   Government assistance almanac. J. Robert Dumouchel. Washington: Foggy Bottom Publications, 1985– 0883-8690
353.0082/025   HC110.P63; G69

An easy-to-use version of the *Catalog of Federal Domestic Assistance* (CFDA) (210). Published annually. Presents information on over 2,000 programs from CFDA in a condensed format for ease of use. Each covered program includes federal program number and title, types of available assistance, program objectives and permissible uses of funds, eligibility criteria, range of amounts awarded, summary of recent activity, and contact information.

215   Handbook of U.S. labor statistics: employment, earnings, prices, productivity, and other labor data. Bernan Press. Lanham, Md.: Bernan Press, 1997– 1526-2553
331.0973021   HD8051.H36

While this data can be found in other Bureau of Labor Statistics sources such as http://www.bls.gov/, these print volumes conveniently place the most useful labor statistics in one source. Includes statistics on employment (status, earnings, characteristics, experience, contingent and alternative work arrangements), projections by industry and occupation, productivity and costs, compensation, prices and living conditions, consumer expenditures, safety and health, labor management relations, and foreign labor and prices. Available as an e-book.

216 ProQuest statistical abstract of the United States. ProQuest. Lanham, Md.: Bernan Press, 2013. 1025 p.
ISBN 9781598885910
HA 202   317.3

Successor to the important federal publication. When the U.S. government cut funding for the Statistical Abstract of the United States (218) published by the Census Bureau, over the objections of librarians and researchers, ProQuest launched this replacement edition as an annual publication beginning with 2013. Intentionally mimics the format, scope and organization of the original resource. Remains an excellent source for the most current possible data on population, government finance, the economy, and even for some international statistics. Original source publications for figures in tables are indicated. Appendixes include a guide to sources of statistics, state statistical abstracts, and foreign statistical abstracts; discussion of metropolitan and micropolitan statistical areas; and a table of weights and measures. Index. Also available in an online edition, from which the data tables can be retrieved in PDF. http://proquest.libguides.com/statisticalabstract

217 Social explorer. http://www.social explorer.com/. Queens College (New York, N.Y.).; Department of Sociology. New York: Oxford University Press. 2005
HB3505

Commercial product. Provides access to demographic information from current and historical census data. Users can create tables from decennial census data from the first census in 1790 through the most recent census, as well as all the American Community Survey data files. Largely follows the original *American FactFinder* (219) interface, which makes it very intuitive to use. Mapping feature available to visually display data from any of the tables, e.g. a slide show showing income changes within census tracts over a period of many decades can be created. Includes tools for data visualization, saving of projects, and downloading of data sets. New data added soon after it is released by the Census Bureau. Some content accessible free-of-charge, but a subscription necessary to take advantage of all of the features.

218 Statistical abstract of the United States. U.S. Dept. of the Treasury, Bureau of Statistics, U.S. Dept. of Commerce and Labor, Bureau of Statistics, U.S. Bureau of Foreign and Domestic Commerce, U.S. Bureau of the Census, U.S. Census Bureau. Washington: U.S. G.P.O., 1878–2012. ill. 0081-4741
317.3   HA202

A single-volume work presenting quantitative summary statistics on the political, social, and economic organization of the United States. Statistics given in the tables cover a period of several years. Indispensable in any library: it serves not only as a first source for statistics of national importance but also as a guide to further information, as references are given to the sources of all tables. Includes a table of contents arranged by broad subject areas and a detailed alphabetical index. Also available online from the Census Bureau at http://www.census.gov/compendia/statab/.

In 2011, the Census Bureau announced that publication of the Statistical Abstract would cease after the 2012 edition due to federal budget cuts. In 2012, ProQuest announced plans to publish equivalent print and online versions. Under the title ProQuest Statistical Abstract of the United States (216), this new work began to appear with 2013.

Supplement: *County and city data book.*

GUIDES

219 American factfinder. http://factfinder2.census.gov/. U.S. Census Bureau. Washington: U.S. Census Bureau. [1999–]
317.3   HA181

American FactFinder (AFF) contains data on U.S. population and housing (from the decennial censuses from 2000 and 2010, as well as the American Community Survey) and economic data from the 2002 and 2007 Economic Censuses. In the new version of AFF the 1990 census has been removed. Social Explorer can be used to access the 1990 census and all other older census data. Users will find the current version significantly easier to user than the previous release. Before using FactFinder users should have a clear idea of the various Census programs and the data availability.

The Community Facts search reveals basic information for a state, county, city, or zip code. The simple Guided Search is a stepped approach to the complex available data. Experienced users will appreciate the Advanced Search functions, where users can start at any number of places including topics like Census program, Census dataset, population features (e.g. age, sex, education, employment, income), housing features (housing counts, financial characteristics), or if economic census data is desired, NAICS codes can be used. Durable URLs can be generated for most of the data tables, making it easy to refer to tables at a later time.

220 Data.gov. http://www.data.gov/. United States. General Services Administration. Washington: General Services Administration. 2009-

025.02   JK501

Includes nearly 100,000 data sets from executive agencies. Can be searched and downloaded in a wide variety of file formats. Provides keyword searching which can be limited by location, dataset type, tags, file format, community, organization type, and organization, with or without first doing a word search. Data sets are from the federal government, state governments, local governments, universities and other entities. The data sets are primarily science-related, with major content focusing on geology, oceanography, meteorology, and climatology. The largest data contributors are the National Oceanic and Atmospheric Administration (NOAA), National States Geographic Information Council (NSGIC) GIS inventory, and the U.S. Geological Survey.

221 FDsys, Federal Digital System: America's authentic government information. http://www.gpo.gov/fdsys/. United States. Government Printing Office. Washington: United States. Government Printing Office. 2011-

Formerly *GPO access*. Provides free online access to official publications from all three branches of the U.S. government. Legislative branch: legislative publications including bills, debate (*Congressional record*), reports, documents, public and private laws, history of bills, House and Senate rules and manuals, and *United States statutes at large*. Executive branch: *Federal register* (212), *Code of federal regulations*, *Public papers of the president*, *Weekly compilation of presidential documents*, *Commerce business daily*, *Economic indicators*, and Treasury issuances. Judicial branch: Supreme Court decisions, selected appellate opinions.

Coverage dates vary by collection, but generally covers mid-1990s to present. Addition of older content is ongoing.

Browse by each collection individually, or search database as a whole. Searching extends to the full text of each document. Search results can be limited by collection, date published, government author, location, and more.

222 The United States government manual. U.S. Office of the Federal Register. Washington: Office of the Federal Register, National Archives and Records Service, General Services Administration, [1973-]. ill. 0092-1904

353   JK421.A3

Official organizational handbook of the federal government. Gives information on the agencies of the legislative, judicial, and executive branches as well as quasi-official agencies, international organizations in which the United States participates, and relevant boards, commissions, and committees. Agency entries usually list the chief officials; describe the agency's purpose and role in the federal government, its history and authority, and its programs and services; and give information about the agency's consumer activities, contracts and grants, employment, publications, etc. Also provides organizational charts and several appendixes and reprints the Declaration of Independence and the U.S. Constitution. Name and agency/subject indexes. Available as an e-resource at http://www.gpo.gov/fdsys/browse/collection.action?collectionCode=GOVMAN as well as at http://www.usgovernmentmanual.gov/.

223 USA.gov. http://purl.access.gpo.gov/GPO/LPS89189. General Services Administration (U.S.). Washington: U.S. General Services Administration. 2000-

USA.gov is the U.S. government's searchable gateway to online government information, resources, and services. Known as FirstGov from 2000 to 2006, USA.gov is organized by audience, subject, and government department, with links to sites from federal agencies and state, local, and tribal governments and organizations.

LEGISLATIVE BRANCH

224 Congress.gov: United States legislative information. http://beta.congress.gov/. Washington: Library of Congress. 2014-
KF45.C37

Soon to be the replacement for the Library of Congress' portal to legislative information. Provides records of bills, legislative actions, *Congressional Record* debate.(Older THOMAS (227) content has not yet been added to Congess.gov.) Includes legislation from the 103rd Congress of 1993. Intuitive new interface. After search terms have been entered, results can be further limited by session of Congress, Chamber of Congress (House or Senate), legislation type, subject, status of legislation (whether it became law or some other status), committee, sponsor/cosponsor, and political party. Integrates a browsable pictorial directory of current members of Congress with the legislative database.

225 ProQuest Congressional. http://cisupa .proquest.com/ws_display.asp?filter =Congressional%20Overview. ProQuest (Firm). Ann Arbor, Mich.: ProQuest. 2011
JK1021

Provides comprehensive indexing to publications of the U.S. Congress including *Congressional record*, published and unpublished hearings, congressional reports and documents, the Serial Set, Congressional Research Service (CRS) Reports, committee prints, congressional bills and public laws, the United States Code and legislative histories (1969-present). Available for additional purchase are digital content in PDF format to the collections. Allows for cross-searching of the ProQuest *Executive branch documents* collection (1789-1932) in subscribed libraries.

Includes all material covered in the CD-ROM index Congressional Masterfile 2, as well as the print index *CIS index annual*. Additional modules are online versions of Congressional Masterfile 1,

CIS index to unpublished US House committee hearings (1833-1936, 1937-46, 1947-54, 1955-58, 1959-64, and 1965-68 with 1947-64 supplement), *CIS index to unpublished US Senate committee hearings* (1823-1964, 1965-68, 1969-72 with 1913-68 supplement, 1973-76), *CIS Senate executive documents and reports*, *CIS U.S. congressional committee hearings index*, *CIS U.S. congressional committee prints index*, and *CIS U.S. serial set index*.

226 ProQuest legislative insight. http:// proquest.libguides.com/quick_start _legislative_insight. ProQuest (Firm). Ann Arbor, Mich.: ProQuest. 2011-
KF49.P76

Presents federal legislative histories including all bill versions, debate (*Congressional Record*), congressional reports and documents, hearings, committee prints, public laws, presidential signing statements as well as Congressional Budget Office (CBO), General Accounting Office / Government Accountability Office (GAO), and Congressional Research Service (CRS) reports. Document references have accompanying PDF full-text files. Part A covers legislative histories from 1929 to 2013; Part B focuses on laws prior to 1929 as well as histories that were not originally included in Part A.

Also includes a table for historic sessions of Congress, a popular names locater for names of laws, and background on the legislative process. Searchable by keyword or by numbers (Public Law, *Statutes at Large* citation, or enacted bill number). Browsing can be done by session of Congress.

227 THOMAS. http://thomas.loc.gov/home/ thomas.php. Edward F. Willett, Library of Congress, United States. Washington: Library of Congress. [1995–]
025.06   KF49.T56

Search for bills by keyword, status, bill number, or sponsor for the current Congress. Search bills from multiple congresses for the 101st Congress (1989) forward; separate search interfaces are provided for Public Laws, Congressional Record, presidential nominations, committee reports, roll call votes, and treaties. Table of appropriations bills available for FY 1998 forward. Links to current activity in Congress, educational materials, and to a detailed explanation of the legislative process. In late 2014, THOMAS is slated to be replaced by a new Congress.gov (224) site.

228   U.S. Congressional serial set. http://
www.readex.com/content/us-congressional
-serial-set-1817-1994. Chester, Vt.: Readex
                                    KF12
Established in 1815 as the place to gather together
documents of Congress. Beginning with the 15th
Congress in 1817, the Set included House and Senate Report and Documents, and at various times in
its history also included selected Executive Branch
documents. The retrospective *American State Papers*
series was published from 1832-1861 to gather
together documents from 1789-1838 that had not
been included in the earlier Serial Set volumes. Two
competing vendors have produced digital versions
of the Serial Set and *American State Papers*. Readex's
U.S. Congressional Serial Set has created a digital serial set with carefully controlled indexing of personal
names, names of congressional acts, geographic
names, and subjects. Provides separate modules for
Serial Set maps and the *American State Papers*. Pro-
Quest Digital Serial Set is part of the larger *ProQuest
Congressional* (207) product and contains maps and
the American State Papers within the same module.

The Readex Serial Set covers 1817-1980 and is
searchable by keyword and browsable by subjects,
authority controlled personal names, legislative act
names, geographic names, publication category,
congressional standing committee, and session of
Congress. Number searching is also available for
retrieving documents by serial set volume number or
document number.

General Works

BIBLIOGRAPHY

229   Library of Congress online catalog.
http://catalog.loc.gov/. Library of
Congress. Washington: Library of
Congress. 1990s
Z881.U5
Contains more than 16 million records for books, seri-
als, manuscripts, maps, music, recordings, images,

and electronic resources in the Library of Congress
collections with keyword or browse searching. It is
available via a Z39.50 server, and a new version of the
catalog is also available: http://catalog2.loc.gov/

The catalog includes records from the time
between 1898 and 1980, which have an indicator
that says "from old catalog." These older records
may not be up to modern cataloging standards. The
records for some older materials are available only on
site in the Library's Main Card Catalog.

Librarians searching for name and subject
authority information can search authorities (http://
authorities.loc.gov/). Other libraries' catalogs and
other Library of Congress databases, the Copyright
Office (http://www.copyright.gov/records/), and the
American Memory Project (http://memory.loc.gov/
ammem/index.html) are linked.

GUIDES

230   ProQuest statistical insight. http://
cisupa.proquest.com/ws_display.asp?filter
=Statistical%20Overview. ProQuest.
Ann Arbor, Mich.: ProQuest. 2010-
                                    HA202
Formerly published by Congressional Information
Service (CIS), and as LexisNexis statistical. Includes
content formerly found in American statistics index
(ASI) for U.S. government pupblications, Statistical
reference index (SRI) for statistics published by U.S.
state governments and private organizations, Index
to international statistics (IIS) for international information, and the interactive *Statistical datasets* online
product, which includes demographic data searchable on a geographical basis. Access is authenticated
and limited to subscribers. Available in three versions (Business, Reference and Complete) providing
access to between 200,000 and 500,000 tables. ASI
content begins with indexing in 1973, and links to
full text from 2004. SRI content begins with indexing in 1980, and links to full text from 2007. IIS
content begins with indexing in 1980, and links to
full text from 2007. Continuously updated online.

8 *Language Dictionaries*

Melissa S. Van Vuuren

English Language

231   Black's law dictionary. 9th ed ed.
Bryan A. Garner, Henry Campbell Black.
St. Paul, Minn.: West, 2009. xxxi, 1920 p.
ISBN 9780314199492
340.03   KF156.B53

The standard, ubiquitous legal dictionary. Updates the 4th edition of 2004: 2,000 new terms bring the total to 45,000 definitions of modern and historical legal terms, as well as over 3,000 legal quotations. The editor, Garner, maintains his status as a lexicographer with definitions based in actual usage, backed up by quotations. Provides West Key numbers to facilitate case-finding using West digests. Appendices include a table of legal abbreviations, assorted legal maxims, the texts of the U.S. Constitution and the Universal Declaration of Human Rights, lists of members of the United States Supreme Court, and a map of Federal Circuit court jurisdictions. Bibliography.

**232   Dorland's illustrated medical
dictionary. 32nd ed.** W. A. Newman
Dorland. Philadelphia: Saunders/Elsevier,
2012. xxvii, 2147 p., ill. (chiefly color)
ISBN 9781416062578
                                        R121.D73

First–22nd ed., 1900–51 had title: *The American illustrated medical dictionary*; 31st ed., c2007.

Designed to satisfy the conventional use of a dictionary; that is, to discover spelling, meaning, and derivation of specific terms and to assist in the creation of words by defining prefixes, suffixes, and stems. Includes a section on "Fundamentals of medical etymology." Reflects standard and current terminology, with official nomenclatures from various fields, e.g., for anatomy, *Terminologia Anatomica* (Federative International Committee on Anatomical Terminology), for enzymology (Nomenclature Committee of the International Union of Biochemistry and Molecular Biology on the Nomenclature and Classification of Enzymes), and several others as listed in the preface. Also includes eponyms, acronyms, abbreviations, pronunciation, cross-references, etc. 1,525 illustrations in this edition. Eight appendixes include, for example, selected abbreviations used in medicine, symbols, phobias, table of elements, units of measurements, and others. Accompanying CD-ROM contains supplementary appendixes, e.g., selected terms in anatomy, a listing of surgical equipment not covered in the main section (A-Z) of the dictionary, also audio phonetics for over 35,000 terms. Internet access to this dictionary is available for subscribers at http://www.dorlands.com. For health professionals and students in medicine, nursing, and allied health. Index to tables; Index to plates; Index to appendixes; extensive "notes on the use of this dictionary" in the beginning pages of the dictionary.

233   Encyclopaedia Britannica online.
http://www.britannica.com/.
Encyclopaedia Britannica. Chicago:
Encyclopaedia Britannica. 2001–

Has three sites: Encyclopaedia Britannica Online Academic Edition at http://info.eb.com/products/britannica-academic-edition/ (which includes Merriam-Webster's collegiate dictionary and thesaurus (249) but does not include children's encyclopedias), Encyclopaedia Britannica Online Public Library Edition at http://info.eb.com/products/britannica-public-library-edition/ (includes adult and children's search pages for *Encyclopaedia Britannica*, *Britannica concise encyclopedia*, and *Compton's*) and Encyclopaedia Britannica Online School Edition at http://info.eb.com/products/britannica-school/ (includes *Britannica elementary*, *Compton's*, and *Encyclopaedia Britannica*, as well as teacher resources). All include dictionaries and a thesaurus, an atlas, links to articles and websites, and personal workspace feature for creating research projects. "World Data Analyst," "Year in Review Browse," and daily features also included. Britannica produces a print edition of *New encyclopaedia Britannica* every two years. *Compton's by Britannica* appears in print every two years also.

A free version, Britannica.com, offers the beginning part of most articles without charge: http://britannica.com/ A subscription is required to obtain the full article, unless an entire article is hyperlinked from another website.

234 Merriam-Webster's visual dictionary.
Jean-Claude Corbeil. Springfield, Mass.: Merriam-Webster, 2012. 1112 p., color ill., maps in color. ISBN 9780877791515
423/.1   PE1629
Comprises 25,000 definitions and 8,000 illustrations across eighteen themes: astronomy, Earth, plants and plantlike organisms, animals, human being, food and kitchen, house, do-it-yourself and gardening, clothing, personal accessories and articles, arts and architecture, communications, office automation, transport and machinery, energy, science, society, and sports and games. Each theme further divides into sub-themes. Terms and brief definitions accompany the full-color illustrations, which have significantly improved in detail and quality since the last edition. The theme list, table of contents, and index to words facilitate access to the dictionary's contents.

235 Stedman's medical dictionary. 28th ed. Thomas Lathrop Stedman. Baltimore: Lippincott, Williams & Wilkins, 2006.

1 v. (various pagings); 1 CD-ROM, ill. (chiefly color) ISBN 0781733901
610.3   R121.S8
First ed., 1911, titled *A practical medical dictionary*; title of later editions varies slightly. 27th ed., 2000.

A standard work, frequently revised. Offers approx. 107,000 terms and definitions (5,000 terms new in this edition) and 1,500 images. Many color illustrations, including a 40-page anatomy atlas. Contains "extensive system of usage notes . . . alerting users to common errors of sense, spelling, and pronunciation, including confusion between words of similar form or meaning."—*Pref.* Appendixes include cancer classification systems, body mass and body surface calculations, abbreviations to use in medication orders, and others. This ed. includes CD-ROM, including the "Stedman's plus spellchecker 2006" and 300 LifeArt® medical clipart four-color images. Also available online via Credo Reference. The 29th ed. is due to be published in 2013.

Recent editions of other Stedman's dictionaries include *Stedman's medical dictionary for the health professions and nursing* (6th ed., 2008); *The American Heritage medical dictionary* (2007 ed.), formerly titled *The American Heritage Stedman's medical dictionary*; and *Stedman's medical abbreviations, acronyms and symbols* (5th ed., 2013).

236 Visual dictionary. rev. and updated ed.
New York: DK Publ., 2011. 672 p., color ill., maps in color. ISBN 9780756686833
423/.1   PE1629.U48
Designed with both generalists and specialists in mind, the dictionary comprises more than 30,000 terms in fourteen sections: the universe; prehistoric Earth; plants; animals; the human body; geology, geography, and meteorology; physics and chemistry; rail and road; sea and air; the visual arts; architecture; music; sports; and the modern world. Each broad section is then further subdivided into more specific sections. For instance, "The Human Body" breaks down into sections such as "body features," "skull," "skin and hair," and "digestive system." These discrete sections each begin with an introductory paragraph. The main emphases of each section, however, are the photographs and illustrations, which serve to define the vocabulary words. A comprehensive index lists all of the terms. Additionally the dictionary's appendix includes a political map of the world, time zones, plane and solid shapes, and useful data:

measurement units, conversions, scientific symbols and notations, powers of ten, algebraic rules, mathematical symbols, and temperature scales.

Also available as ebook.

Abbreviations

237 Abbreviations.com. http://www
.abbreviations.com. STANDS4, LLC.
STANDS4, LLC. 2001?-

Claims to be the "Web's largest and most comprehensive directory and search engine for acronyms, abbreviations and initialisms on the Internet." Entries are crowd-sourced from volunteer editors. Contents may be searched by abbreviation, term, or word in term. This user-friendly website also allows users to browse alphabetically or by the following categories: academic and science, business and finance, community, computing, governmental, Internet, miscellaneous, regional, medical, and international. Each broad category is further subdivided into more specific topics. Entries include citation information in MLA, APA, and Chicago styles.

238 Abbreviations dictionary. 10th ed.
Dean Stahl, Karen Kerchelich, Ralph
De Sola. Boca Raton, Fla.: CRC Press,
2001. xviii, 1529 p. ISBN 0849390036
423.1   PE1693.D4

Lists the full forms of abbreviations, acronyms, appellations, contractions, etc., from the realms of computing and technology, science, and a broad range of other fields; pastimes; groups; the government; and the military. Contains 15,000 new terms to bring the total number of references to 300,000, and entries are in alphabetical as well as numeric order. Definitions are given when necessary. Complements the standard abbreviations reference *Acronyms, initialisms and abbreviations dictionary: A guide to acronyms, abbreviations, contractions, alphabetic symbols, and similar condensed appellations* (240). Also available as an e-book.

239 Acronym finder. http://acronymfinder
.com/. Mike Malloy. Estes Park, Colo.:
Mountain Data Systems. 1997-
423.1   P365

Claims to be the largest "human-edited collection available" for acronyms and abbreviations. Contents may be searched or browsed through an A-Z index.

Includes abbreviations, acronyms, and initialisms for information technology, science and medicine, military and government, organizations and schools, business and finance, and slang and pop culture.

Also consult the following print volumes, which may contain entries not included in this site: *Acronyms, initialisms, and abbreviations dictionary* (240), *Reverse acronyms, initialisms, and abbreviations dictionary* (241), and *International acronyms, initialisms, and abbreviations dictionary*.

**240 Acronyms, initialisms and
abbreviations dictionary.** Gale Research
Company. Detroit: Gale Research,
1976- 0270-4404
423.1   P365.A28

The venerable language expert and critic H. L. Mencken once remarked about "the characteristic American habit of reducing complete concepts to starkest abbreviations"—*Pref.* This massive dictionary includes mostly U.S. terms but also some Canadian and British usage. Covers international, national, regional, and state associations, political action committees, research centers, and stock exchange terms, among many other subjects. Helpful for some obsolete terms. Excellent feature: many terms include source citations. Also available online through the Gale Virtual Reference Library (288).

See also *Reverse acronyms, initialisms and abbreviations dictionary* (241), where terms are arranged alphabetically by the meaning of the acronym. For terms specific to foreign countries, see *International acronyms, initialisms and abbreviations dictionary*.

**241 Reverse acronyms, initialisms,
and abbreviations dictionary: A
companion volume to Acronyms and
initialism dictionary, with terms
arranged alphabetically by meaning
of acronym.** Ellen T. Crowley, Robert
C. Thomas. Detroit: Gale Research,
1972- 0270-4390
423.1   PE1693.G3

Since many acronyms do not clearly suggest the full name of the organization, this valuable source arranges the entries alphabetically by meaning.

A companion volume to *Acronyms, initialisms, and abbreviations dictionary* (240) and *International acronyms, initialisms, and abbreviations dictionary*.

American

242 The American Heritage dictionary of the English language. 5th ed. Boston: Houghton Mifflin Harcourt, 2011. xxvii, 2084 p., ill. (some col.), maps, ports. ISBN 9780547041018

423   PE1628.A623

This updated edition contains cumulative additions and revisions made since the 4th ed. was released in 2000. Includes about 10,000 new words and senses. Descriptive notes throughout the dictionary cover synonyms, usage, word histories, and regionalisms, as well as biographical and genealogical information, world currencies, and chemical elements. Guide to grammar and style. Thousands of sample sentences illustrate meanings. Visually appealing, the dictionary offers 4,000 illustrations, drawings, and maps.

Includes introductory essays: "Variation and change in our living language" by John K. Rickford, and "Usage in the American Heritage Dictionary" by Steven Pinker. Etymologies are often linked to appendices tracing the words of Indo-European and Semitic origin back to their roots in prehistory. These appendices have also been published separately as the American Heritage dictionary of Indo-European roots.

"This dictionary is highly recommended for its comprehensiveness, its pleasing layout, and its currency." (*Library Journal*, 11/15/2011)

243 Dictionary.com. http://dictionary.reference.com. InterActiveCorp. InterActiveCorp. 1995

Claims to be "the most-visited, most trusted, online dictionary" (*About Us*) with 50 million monthly users worldwide. Contents are both licensed from standard dictionaries publishers such as American Heritage, Harper Collins, and Random House and created by in-house lexicographers. Entries comprise headwords, pronunciation keys, parts of speech, definitions, word origins, pronunciation, and related forms. Features a word of a day and provides a blog, a daily crossword, word games, crossword solver, and browser tools, widgets, and third-party plug-ins to support use of the website. Also available as a mobile app.

244 Fowler's modern English usage. Rev. 3rd ed. H. W. Fowler, R. W. Burchfield. Oxford; N.Y.: Oxford Univ. Pr., 2004. 873 p.

ISBN 0198610211

428.003   PE1628.F65

Burchfield revises Henry Watson Fowler's 1926 *Dictionary of Modern English Usage*, a well-loved guide to usage, grammar, and word choice. While Burchfield retains many features of Fowler's original work, the third revised edition has been "largely rewritten" (*pref.*) to reflect modern English. Individual entries comprise headwords, part of speech, and usage notes, and may have pronunciation. Uses the International Phonetic Alphabet (IPA), and provides a key to pronunciation. Includes cross-references. In addition to the entries proper, this single-volume work has guides to abbreviations and symbols, bibliographical abbreviations, and a supplement to the 1996 3rd edition.

245 Onelook dictionary search. http://www.onelook.com/. Robert Ware, Datamuse. Hilton Head Island, S.C.: Datamuse

Indexing 900 online dictionaries that define 5 million terms, this is more of a search engine to words and phrases than a true online dictionary. A search on a word does not lead to a listing of definitions; instead, users are directed to a list of dictionaries that offer definitions of the word searched.

The online dictionaries indexed include such English language standards as the Merriam Webster's Online Dictionary, 11th ed. (http://www.merriam-webster.com/) and the American Heritage Dictionary of the English Language, 4th ed. as well as dozens of other dictionaries in French, German, and Spanish. Online dictionaries are chosen according to a selection policy, using these criteria: available, free, unique, high quality, commercially neutral, intellectually honest, designed to inform with a high contents/ads ratio.

Special features include searching for translated words and phrases, a reverse dictionary, and a "crossword puzzle mode" using wildcards.

246 Random House Webster's unabridged dictionary. 2nd ed., rev. and updated ed. Random House Reference. New York: Random House Reference, 2005. xxvi, 2230 p., ill., maps. ISBN 0375425993 PE1625.R3

First ed., 1966.

Comprised of 315,000 entries (which include biographical and geographical terms, abbreviations, foreign words and phrases, historical events, and the arts and literature), with 750,000 sample phrases and sentences and 2,400 ill. Special features discuss word usage, pronunciation, synonyms and antonyms, regionalisms, and commonly confused words. A new words section, found at the front of the work, covers 1,000 new words. Focus is on American English, but also reflects English used in Britain, Canada, and Australia. A CD-ROM of the dictionary is available. Libraries that already own the 2001 ed. do not need to purchase the 2005 ed., as the content is the same.

247 Webster's third new international dictionary of the English language, unabridged: a Merriam-Webster. Philip Babcock Gove. Springfield, Mass.: G. & C. Merriam Co., [1961]. 56a, 2662 p., illus. (part col.) col. port.

423   PE1625.W36

"A completely new work, redesigned, restyled and reset."—*Pref.* Vastly different from the 2nd ed.; Probably the most controversial reference book of the generation, both attacked and defended in the newspaper and the periodical press. Because of its departures from accepted dictionary practices, thorough familiarity with the introduction is essential to using this text. Major points to observed include the following:

Usage: Presents the language as currently used, with a novel concept of acceptability of usage, construction, pronunciation, etc.; therefore, much is included; often without qualification, which (particularly at the time of the work's original publication date) was regarded by many as colloquial, vulgar, or incorrect.

Scope: Includes some 100,000 new entries, with new scientific and technical terms especially well-represented, but the total has been reduced from 600,000 to 450,000 because many obsolete and rare words have been dropped; the divided page system has been abandoned; abbreviations are included in the main alphabet; the gazetteer and the biographical dictionary have been dropped; excludes all proper nouns; proper adjectives remain, all in lower case. An 8-page "Addenda" section of new words was added to the 1966 printing; that section was increased to 16 pages in 1971, to 32 in 1976, to 48 in 1981, 56 in 1988, and to 90 in 2002. The most current printing includes a new label—ISV for International Scientific Vocabulary—to denote current words of uncertain origin.

Treatment of words: Individual definitions are generally clear and to the point; meanings are given as before, chronologically, with earlier usage first;

etymologies have been expanded; pronunciations are given as used in "general cultivated conversational usage as well as in formal platform speech"; regional pronunciations are also frequently shown; indications of pronunciation is given by a newly devised system with the key only in the the the introduction, not on each page; the devices to indicate word division, stress, and hyphenization have been revised and are explained and illustrated in the introduction; punctuation and indentation are at a minimum.

Quotations: Abundant illustrative quotations, updated, and almost exclusively from recent sources, many of them popular. Author-only citations.

Also available as an online subscription–*Merriam Webster unabridged*: http://unabridged.merriam-webster.com

DESK DICTIONARIES

248 Merriam-Webster's advanced learner's English dictionary. Springfield, Mass.: Merriam-Webster, 2008. 1994 p., ill. (some col.) ISBN 9780877795513

423.1   PE1628.M354

Designed specifically for English-language learners, this dictionary covers both British and American English in roughly 100,000 entries and more than 160,000 usage examples with an emphasis on words used in daily life. Definitions are brief and written for clarity. Entries comprise headwords, pronunciations, spelling, definitions, synonyms and antonyms, examples, forms and tenses, grammatical labels, and cross-references. Three-thousand basic English terms are underlined in blue. Additionally includes information on geographical names, English grammar, irregular verbs, contractions, prefixes and suffixes, English word roots, words that are often confused, spelling rules, spelling of different sounds in English, a handbook of style, common first names, money, numbers, weights and measures, dates, holidays, envelope addresses, pronunciation symbols, and e-mail, letters, memos, and resumes.

249 Merriam-Webster's collegiate dictionary. 11th ed. Merriam-Webster, Inc. Springfield, Mass.: Merriam-Webster, Inc., 2003. 1623 p., ill. ISBN 0877798095

423 21   PE1628.M36

First ed., 1898. Frequently reprinted.

Small margins and small font are minor drawbacks to this dictionary of contemporary English. Compiled from the corpus of nearly 16 million citations at Merriam Webster's, the eleventh ed. of this dictionary covers 165,000 entries (10,000 new words and senses) and more than 700 ill. Many entries include the date the word was first used in print sources; definitions are given in historical order, rather than with the most common definition first. Two important changes are noted in this ed.: all standard variations of a word are now at the main entry, and abbreviations and chemical elements are now found in the body of the dictionary. At the front of the dictionary are an extensive section on how to use the dictionary, an essay on English lexicography, a guide to pronunciation, list of abbreviations used, and pronunciation symbols; the work ends with a list of foreign words and phrases, 6,000 biographical names, and 12,000 geographical terms. Includes a style guide, signs, and symbols in science and technology.

The online edition of this dictionary, at http://www.merriam-webster.com/premium/mwcollegiate/, is updated annually. The site is based on the print version of the dictionary and is available by subscription. Words can be searched, bookmarked, printed, and e-mailed; the site also includes listings of rhymes and antonyms, prefixes and suffixes, a thesaurus, medical desk dictionary, a Spanish-English dictionary, style guide, and word games.

Also available through Encylopaedia Britannica online (165).

250   New Oxford American dictionary.
    3rd ed. Angus Stevenson, Christine A.
    Lindberg. Oxford; New York: Oxford
    University Press, 2010. xxvi, 2018 p., [46]
    p. of plates, ill., maps.
    ISBN 9780195392883
    423   PE1628.N429
Very usable dictionary of American English with an attractive layout with more than 350,000 words, phrases, and senses. Includes specialist vocabulary for American plants and animals as well as more than 5,000 place-name entries, 4,000 biographical entries, and nearly 3,000 other proper names. Each entry begins with the principal meaning(s) of the word, organized by importance in present day English. After the main definition—core sense—entries generally

include additional word meanings, a pronunciation guide, grammatical usage, and etymology.

Ready Reference section of 45 pages is located between pages 972 and 973 of the A-Z dictionary. Includes British and American terminology; Arabic, Hebrew, and Russian alphabets; chemical elements; weights and measures; U.S. historical documents; U.S. Presidents; U.S. Chief Justices; landmark U.S. Supreme Court cases; U.S. states, countries of the world, and world maps.

This edition includes 2,000 new words, senses, and phrases, as well as new word trend charts featuring usage of rapidly changing words and phrases, such as the changing image from negative to positive of words "geek" and "nerd." Primary source for material is the Oxford English Corpus, a database of more than 2 billion words.

Also available in Oxford reference online (290). 1st ed. 2001.

English

251   The American Heritage dictionary for
    learners of English. Houghton Mifflin.
    Boston: Houghton Mifflin, 2002. xxiii,
    999 p., ill. ISBN 0618249516
    423.21   PE1628.A6229
Adapted from the *American Heritage dictionary of the English language* and designed for learners of English as a second language at the intermediate and advanced levels. Contains more than 40,000 words and phrases with brief definitions and sample sentences. Includes homonyms and synonyms. Small number of entries also include black and white illustrations. Appendix includes guides to irregular verbs and punctuation.

Companion volumes *American Heritage thesaurus for learners of English* and *American Heritage dictionary of idioms for students of English*.

252   The American Heritage dictionary of
    the English language. 5th ed. Boston:
    Houghton Mifflin Harcourt, 2011. xxvii,
    2084 p., ill. (some col.), maps, ports.
    ISBN 9780547041018
    423   PE1628.A623
This updated edition contains cumulative additions and revisions made since the 4th ed. was released in 2000. Includes about 10,000 new words and

senses. Descriptive notes throughout the dictionary cover synonyms, usage, word histories, and regionalisms, as well as biographical and genealogical information, world currencies, and chemical elements. Guide to grammar and style. Thousands of sample sentences illustrate meanings. Visually appealing, the dictionary offers 4,000 illustrations, drawings, and maps.

Includes introductory essays: "Variation and change in our living language" by John K. Rickford, and "Usage in the American Heritage Dictionary" by Steven Pinker. Etymologies are often linked to appendices tracing the words of Indo-European and Semitic origin back to their roots in prehistory. These appendices have also been published separately as the American Heritage dictionary of Indo-European roots.

"This dictionary is highly recommended for its comprehensiveness, its pleasing layout, and its currency." (*Library Journal*, 11/15/2011)

253 Fowler's modern English usage. Rev. 3rd ed. H. W. Fowler, R. W. Burchfield. Oxford; N.Y.: Oxford Univ. Pr., 2004. 873 p. ISBN 0198610211

428.003   PE1628.F65

Burchfield revises Henry Watson Fowler's 1926 *Dictionary of Modern English Usage*, a well-loved guide to usage, grammar, and word choice. While Burchfield retains many features of Fowler's original work, the third revised edition has been "largely rewritten" (*pref.*) to reflect modern English. Individual entries comprise headwords, part of speech, and usage notes, and may have pronunciation. Uses the International Phonetic Alphabet (IPA), and provides a key to pronunciation. Includes cross-references. In addition to the entries proper, this single-volume work has guides to abbreviations and symbols, bibliographical abbreviations, and a supplement to the 1996 3rd edition.

254 Oxford English dictionary: the definitive record of the English language. http://www.oed.com. Oxford University Press. Oxford: Oxford University Press. 2000–

PE1625

Comprised of the full-text of the *Oxford English dictionary* (OED), Second edition, plus the full-text of the three vols. of the Additions (that work-in-progress on the dictionary since 1989) and the

quarterly updates of 1,800 new or revised words (the OED's Revision Program, begun in 1993, aims to review and update every word and sense of the dictionary). Searching is very robust, and ranges from the ability to conduct simple word searches to using Boolean operators and wildcards; users can search the 2nd ed. solely, or the new edition of the OED—in progress since 2000. Possible to search by entry date; within quotations (by date, author, source); by pronunciation; by etymological references to particular languages; and within parts of speech.

Entries can be compared by rev. entries of the new edition of the OED with entries from the 2nd ed. to observe any changes in the use or study of the word. Provides access to the *Historical Thesaurus of the Oxford English Dictionary*. A single entry or a page of entries can be e-mailed to subscribers and nonsubscribers alike. Individual and institutional subscriptions available.

DESK DICTIONARIES

255 The Chambers dictionary. 12th ed. London: Chambers Harrap, 2011. xxiv, 1848 p. ISBN 9780550102416

423   PE1628.C41745

Provides concise definitions in a portable volume. Entries include headwords, pronunciation, part of speech label, definition(s), and etymology, and may also have subheads, alternative forms, hyphenation, inflections, classification labels, grammatical information, panels, and prefix, suffix, and combining forms. In addition to the entries proper, the dictionary includes information on the history of English, varieties of English, a guide to using the dictionary, spelling rules, non-English characters, a pronunciation chart, and abbreviations. Concludes with appendixes of foreign phrases and quotations, alphabets, Roman numerals, chemical elements, SI units, Beaufort scale, Mohs scale, earthquake severity measurement scales, wine bottle sizes, wedding anniversaries, mathematical symbols, planets, and major planetary satellites. Provides a "Word Lover's Miscellany" and a "Wordgame Companion."

256 Collins English dictionary: complete and unabridged. 11th ed. HarperCollins. Glasgow, Scotland, U.K.:

HarperCollins, 2011. xx, 1899 p. 423.
ISBN 9780007437863

Based on the 525-million-word Bank of English database. Defines the newest words and phrases to enter the English language; covers not only British English, but regionalisms and dialects of English as well. Copious language notes assist with word selection, and etymological notes detail word histories.

A free, online version of the dictionary is available at http://www.collinsdictionary.com. Offers more than 130,000 entries with definitions, word origins, synonyms, translations, example sentences, usage trends, and audio. The online version includes a thesaurus and translation tool along with the dictionary and covers both British and American English.

257 Oxford dictionary of English. 3rd ed.
Angus Stevenson. New York: Oxford Univ. Press, 2010. 2069 p.
ISBN 9780199571123
423   PE1628.O8675

Boasts more than 350,000 words, phrases, and senses, including 2,000 new phrases, senses, and words. The majority of additions derive from changes in computing, mobile technology, media, finance, the environment, and informal language and slang. Based on the British National Corpus, which represents modern English usage in both its spoken and written forms. Entries may comprise part of speech, core senses, subsenses, encyclopedia information, register, regional uses, spelling and alternate spelling, usage notes, word histories, verb inflections, plural forms, and cross-references. Word trends, showing shifts in popularity and usage of a particular word, are also included throughout the dictionary. The center of the volume includes a reference section. Also available online in *Oxford Reference Online* (290).

Etymology

258 The Facts on File encyclopedia of word and phrase origins. 4th ed.
Robert Hendrickson. New York: Facts on File, 2008. ISBN 9780816069668
422.03   PE1689.H47

Unique sample of 12,500 English words and phrases from more than 200 countries where English is the official language. Entries represent all the ways words and phrases come into being: language and dialects that have enriched English, newly coined words, slang, and place and animal names. Features new to this edition include more words and phrases from classical sources as well as a larger selection of current slang. Index.

Idioms, Slang, and Usage

259 The Cambridge guide to English usage. Pam Peters. Cambridge, U.K.; New York: Cambridge University Press, 2004. xi, 608 p., ill. ISBN 052162181X
423.1   PE1464.P47

The *Guide* describes how English is used in the 21st century; regional and global differences between American, Australian, Canadian, and U.K. English are highlighted. The 4,000 alphabetical entries, based on the Cambridge International Corpus and the British National Corpus, discuss words or sets of words and general topics on language, editing, and writing. The nine appendixes cover topics including proofreading and formatting letters and memos, units of measurement and conversion tables, and the International Phonetic Alphabet. Also available as an e-book.

260 Fowler's modern English usage. Rev. 3rd ed. H. W. Fowler, R. W. Burchfield. Oxford; N.Y.: Oxford Univ. Pr., 2004. 873 p.
ISBN 0198610211
428.003   PE1628.F65

Burchfield revises Henry Watson Fowler's 1926 *Dictionary of Modern English Usage*, a well-loved guide to usage, grammar, and word choice. While Burchfield retains many features of Fowler's original work, the third revised edition has been "largely rewritten" (*pref.*) to reflect modern English. Individual entries comprise headwords, part of speech, and usage notes, and may have pronunciation. Uses the International Phonetic Alphabet (IPA), and provides a key to pronunciation. Includes cross-references. In addition to the entries proper, this single-volume work has guides to abbreviations and symbols, bibliographical abbreviations, and a supplement to the 1996 3rd edition.

261 Green's dictionary of slang. Jonathon Green. Edinburgh, Scotland, U.K.:

Chambers, 2010. 3 v.
ISBN 9780550104403
427.09   PE3721.G677

Most reliable and authoritative source of English language slang. Includes slang for the last 500 years. Covers the United Kingdom, America, Australia, New Zealand, Ireland, the Anglophone Caribbean, and South Africa. Does not cover India. Provides definitions of over 100,000 words with citations to support every word. Entries generally contain the following elements: headword, part of speech label, alternative forms, etymology, usage label, definition(s), citation(s). Some entries include slang terms related to or derived from the main headword. Selected bibliography in v.3 has about 6,000 works and is arranged in two sections: 1. printed material (including books, newspapers, periodicals, comics) and 2. Internet (p. 2203-2204).

Winner of the Dartmouth Medal. Distributed in North America by Oxford University Press.

262 The new Partridge dictionary of slang and unconventional English. 2nd ed. Eric Partridge, Tom Dalzell, Terry. Victor, Eric Partridge. London; New York: Routledge, 2013. 2 v. (2506 p.)
ISBN 9780415619493
427.003 23   PE3721.P3 2013

Covering slang and unconventional English used in the English-speaking world since 1945, this standard slang dictionary comprises more than 60,000 entries, including 1,000 new entries from the U.S., U.K., and Australia. The second edition reflects how social media are changing the English language through initialisms, abbreviations, non-standard spelling, numbers and symbols replacing letters, and emoticons. Entries include head words, part of speech, senses, definitions, glosses, country of origin, date, cross-references, and citations. Entries are arranged alphabetically in an easily browsed layout. The second volume concludes with a section on numeric slang and a 21-page bibliography of sources.

An online version is available as *Partridge slang online*: http://partridgeslangonline.com

New Words

263 Netlingo. http://www.netlingo.com/. Erin Jansen. Santa Monica, Calif.: NetLingo. 1994–

Dubbed the "semantic storehouse of cyberspace," NetLingo records technology terms used in the computing, Web, and high tech industry communities. Since its inception in 1994, NetLingo has grown to more than 6,000 words and more than 2,000 emoticons, acronyms, and text messaging shorthand. The dictionary is organized into categories such as "Online Jargon," "Net Technology," "Software," "Hardware," and "Websites," although it's possible to browse alphabetically as well as search for terms. While the home page is packed with a good deal of information, it is easy to navigate, with clear headings and white space. Definitions are culled from observed current usage of standard technology terms, key computing texts, and suggestions from NetLingo users. According to the site's creator, the definitions are "written by a woman using layman's language everyone can understand."—*About NetLingo*

Regional and Dialect

AMERICAN

264 Dictionary of American regional English. Frederic G. Cassidy, Joan H. Hall. Cambridge, Mass.: Belknap Press, 1985–2013. v. 1–6, ill., maps.
ISBN 0674205111
427.973   PE2843.D52

Covers American English as spoken across the United States and is indispensable to the study of words, pronunciations, and phrases that vary from one region to another. The first four volumes, covering the letters A through Sk-, were published 1985–2002; in 2012 a fifth volume was published, which covers the remainder of the alphabet and contains an extensive bibliography (p. 1147-1244). Only the fifth volume incorporates Internet sources. The bibliography, arranged by author, includes thousands of published sources quoted in the five volumes of DARE. Compiled mainly from responses to a lengthy questionnaire (reprinted in the introduction) administered in 1,002 communities in the United States. Concentrating on colloquialisms, regional usages, dialect and ethnic terms, and out-of-the-way meanings, "DARE does not treat technical, scientific, or other learned words or phrases—or anything else that could be considered standard"—*Introd.* Entries include pronunciations, variant forms, etymologies, and information about regional and social distributions, including maps indicating geographical distribution of usages.

A sixth volume was published in January 2013, completing the set. The final volume includes contrastive geographic and social maps, an index to entry labels from volumes 1-5, the DARE Questionnaire, and a data summary of responses to the questionnaire. An index of labels by region, usage and etymology, and a list of index terms that were used in the entry labels in the first five volumes of DARE is available online: http://dare.wisc.edu.

An online version is available from Harvard University Press at: http://daredictionary.com.

Synonyms and Antonyms

265 Roget's international thesaurus. 7th ed.
Barbara Ann Kipfer. New York: Collins, 2010.
xxv, 1282 p. ISBN 9780061715228
423/.1 PE1591.R73
This rev. 7th ed. of the world's best-selling thesaurus organizes 464,000 synonyms, antonyms, and related words (3,000 of them new to this ed.) into 15 subject classes (such as body, senses, science & technology, space travel) and 1,075 categories (clusters of words that are similar in meaning). Users are directed from an alphabetical index to a numbered category to get to the appropriate word; illustrative quotations are provided to make meanings more clear. Cross references are plentiful. Seventh edition includes many new words and phrases for both general, scientific and technical terms.

Up to date; the best thesaurus available.

Foreign Languages

Chinese

BILINGUAL

266 Oxford language dictionaries online.
http://www.oxfordlanguagedictionaries
.com/. Oxford: Oxford University Press.
2007–

PE1635
Subscription database containing fully searchable bilingual dictionaries for Chinese, French, German,

Italian, Russian, and Spanish. Bi-directional searching permits translation from English to any one of the other languages and the reverse. Within the definition screen, results are also displayed for the following additional languages: Portuguese, Japanese, Korean, Polish, Russian, Thai, and Arabic.

Searching is by simple keyword as well as advanced search options. Results include definitions, usage examples and audio pronunciation. While based on British English, the database enables searching and cross-links with American spelling.

Links are also provided from results to the many-faceted Oxford "Tools and resources" on the Web covering such aspects as "life and culture," "grammar and vocabulary," "writing and word games," and "teaching and learning" for the various foreign languages; and the "Oxford language web," which graphically displays in the form of a wheel simultaneous translation of a given English word into all 12 languages noted above.

English definitions also provide a link to Oxford Reference Online (290) that displays the definition contained in the *Oxford dictionary of English*, 2nd ed. rev.

French

BILINGUAL

267 Oxford language dictionaries online.
http://www.oxfordlanguagedictionaries
.com/. Oxford: Oxford University Press.
2007–

PE1635
Subscription database containing fully searchable bilingual dictionaries for Chinese, French, German, Italian, Russian, and Spanish. Bi-directional searching permits translation from English to any one of the other languages and the reverse. Within the definition screen, results are also displayed for the following additional languages: Portuguese, Japanese, Korean, Polish, Russian, Thai, and Arabic.

Searching is by simple keyword as well as advanced search options. Results include definitions, usage examples and audio pronunciation. While based on British English, the database enables searching and cross-links with American spelling.

Links are also provided from results to the many-faceted Oxford "Tools and resources" on the Web covering such aspects as "life and culture," "grammar and vocabulary," "writing and word games," and "teaching and learning" for the various foreign languages; and the "Oxford language web," which graphically displays in the form of a wheel simultaneous translation of a given English word into all 12 languages noted above.

English definitions also provide a link to Oxford Reference Online (290) that displays the definition contained in the *Oxford dictionary of English*, 2nd ed. rev.

German

BILINGUAL

268   Oxford language dictionaries online.
http://www.oxfordlanguagedictionaries
.com/. Oxford: Oxford University Press.
2007–

PE1635

Subscription database containing fully searchable bilingual dictionaries for Chinese, French, German, Italian, Russian, and Spanish. Bi-directional searching permits translation from English to any one of the other languages and the reverse. Within the definition screen, results are also displayed for the following additional languages: Portuguese, Japanese, Korean, Polish, Russian, Thai, and Arabic.

Searching is by simple keyword as well as advanced search options. Results include definitions, usage examples and audio pronunciation. While based on British English, the database enables searching and cross-links with American spelling.

Links are also provided from results to the many-faceted Oxford "Tools and resources" on the Web covering such aspects as "life and culture," "grammar and vocabulary," "writing and word games," and "teaching and learning" for the various foreign languages; and the "Oxford language web," which graphically displays in the form of a wheel simultaneous translation of a given English word into all 12 languages noted above.

English definitions also provide a link to Oxford Reference Online (290) that displays the definition contained in the *Oxford dictionary of English*, 2nd ed. rev.

Italian

BILINGUAL

269   Oxford language dictionaries online.
http://www.oxfordlanguagedictionaries
.com/. Oxford: Oxford University Press.
2007–

PE1635

Subscription database containing fully searchable bilingual dictionaries for Chinese, French, German, Italian, Russian, and Spanish. Bi-directional searching permits translation from English to any one of the other languages and the reverse. Within the definition screen, results are also displayed for the following additional languages: Portuguese, Japanese, Korean, Polish, Russian, Thai, and Arabic.

Searching is by simple keyword as well as advanced search options. Results include definitions, usage examples and audio pronunciation. While based on British English, the database enables searching and cross-links with American spelling.

Links are also provided from results to the many-faceted Oxford "Tools and resources" on the Web covering such aspects as "life and culture," "grammar and vocabulary," "writing and word games," and "teaching and learning" for the various foreign languages; and the "Oxford language web," which graphically displays in the form of a wheel simultaneous translation of a given English word into all 12 languages noted above.

English definitions also provide a link to Oxford Reference Online (290) that displays the definition contained in the *Oxford dictionary of English*, 2nd ed. rev.

Korean

270   Oxford language dictionaries online.
http://www.oxfordlanguagedictionaries
.com/. Oxford: Oxford University Press.
2007–

PE1635

Subscription database containing fully searchable bilingual dictionaries for Chinese, French, German, Italian, Russian, and Spanish. Bi-directional searching permits translation from English to any one of the other languages and the reverse. Within the definition screen, results are also displayed for the following additional languages: Portuguese, Japanese, Korean, Polish, Russian, Thai, and Arabic.

Searching is by simple keyword as well as advanced search options. Results include definitions, usage examples and audio pronunciation. While based on British English, the database enables searching and cross-links with American spelling.

Links are also provided from results to the many-faceted Oxford "Tools and resources" on the Web covering such aspects as "life and culture," "grammar and vocabulary," "writing and word games," and "teaching and learning" for the various foreign languages; and the "Oxford language web," which graphically displays in the form of a wheel simultaneous translation of a given English word into all 12 languages noted above.

English definitions also provide a link to Oxford Reference Online (290) that displays the definition contained in the *Oxford dictionary of English*, 2nd ed. rev.

Language Translation Sites

271 Google translate. http://translate.google.com. Google (Firm). Mountain View, Calif.: Google. 2000s-

Using machine translation software developed by Google, the Google translate service provides a free translation by looking at patterns in many texts previously translated by human translators. As of 2014, supports 80 languages from Afrikaans to Zulu.

Note that machine translation is word for word and will not convey the nuances that humans give to language. Occasionally special programs need to be downloaded or installed to properly translate some texts.

Information on languages Google supports, translation tools, and updates on the *Google Translate Blog* are available at: http://translate.google.com/about/intl/en_ALL/

Russian

BILINGUAL

272 Oxford language dictionaries online. http://www.oxfordlanguagedictionaries.com/. Oxford: Oxford University Press. 2007–

PE1635

Subscription database containing fully searchable bilingual dictionaries for Chinese, French, German, Italian, Russian, and Spanish. Bi-directional searching permits translation from English to any one of the other languages and the reverse. Within the definition screen, results are also displayed for the following additional languages: Portuguese, Japanese, Korean, Polish, Russian, Thai, and Arabic.

Searching is by simple keyword as well as advanced search options. Results include definitions, usage examples and audio pronunciation. While based on British English, the database enables searching and cross-links with American spelling.

Links are also provided from results to the many-faceted Oxford "Tools and resources" on the Web covering such aspects as "life and culture," "grammar and vocabulary," "writing and word games," and "teaching and learning" for the various foreign languages; and the "Oxford language web," which graphically displays in the form of a wheel simultaneous translation of a given English word into all 12 languages noted above.

English definitions also provide a link to Oxford Reference Online (290) that displays the definition contained in the *Oxford dictionary of English*, 2nd ed. rev.

Spanish

BILINGUAL

273 Oxford language dictionaries online. http://www.oxfordlanguagedictionaries.com/. Oxford: Oxford University Press. 2007–

PE1635

Subscription database containing fully searchable bilingual dictionaries for Chinese, French, German, Italian, Russian, and Spanish. Bi-directional searching permits translation from English to any one of the other languages and the reverse. Within the definition screen, results are also displayed for the following additional languages: Portuguese, Japanese, Korean, Polish, Russian, Thai, and Arabic.

Searching is by simple keyword as well as advanced search options. Results include definitions, usage examples and audio pronunciation. While based on British English, the database enables searching and cross-links with American spelling.

Links are also provided from results to the many-faceted Oxford "Tools and resources" on the Web covering such aspects as "life and culture," "grammar and vocabulary," "writing and word games," and "teaching and learning" for the various foreign languages; and the "Oxford language web," which graphically displays in the form of a wheel simultaneous translation of a given English word into all 12 languages noted above.

English definitions also provide a link to Oxford Reference Online (290) that displays the definition contained in the *Oxford dictionary of English*, 2nd ed. rev.

Thai

274 Oxford language dictionaries online.
http://www.oxfordlanguagedictionaries.com/. Oxford: Oxford University Press. 2007–

PE1635

Subscription database containing fully searchable bilingual dictionaries for Chinese, French, German, Italian, Russian, and Spanish. Bi-directional searching permits translation from English to any one of the other languages and the reverse. Within the definition screen, results are also displayed for the following additional languages: Portuguese, Japanese, Korean, Polish, Russian, Thai, and Arabic.

Searching is by simple keyword as well as advanced search options. Results include definitions, usage examples and audio pronunciation. While based on British English, the database enables searching and cross-links with American spelling.

Links are also provided from results to the many-faceted Oxford "Tools and resources" on the Web covering such aspects as "life and culture," "grammar and vocabulary," "writing and word games," and "teaching and learning" for the various foreign languages; and the "Oxford language web," which graphically displays in the form of a wheel simultaneous translation of a given English word into all 12 languages noted above.

English definitions also provide a link to Oxford Reference Online (290) that displays the definition contained in the *Oxford dictionary of English*, 2nd ed. rev.

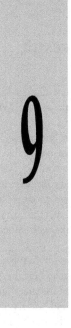

9 Newspapers

Patrick Reakes

Bibliographies, Union Lists, and Directories

Europe

GREAT BRITAIN

275 **The Waterloo directory of English newspapers and periodicals, 1800–1900.** http://www.victorianperiodicals .com/series2/PurchaseInformation. asp. John North. Waterloo, Ont.: North Waterloo Academic Press

Series two (of an expected series of five) includes a total of 50,000 entries, including 9,000 facsimile title pages and 48,000 personal names. Library locations are provided for the United Kingdom and North America. Indexes are provided by title, subject, place of publication (by town and county), issuing body, and people. Also includes a family tree for all titles related through mergers, common issuing bodies, or title changes. Fee-based online edition is updated daily. Also available in CD-ROM and print versions.

International

276 **Willing's press guide.** London: Willing Service, 1928– 0000-0213
072   Z6956.E5W5

Previously published in two volumes. Currently three volumes: U.K., Western Europe (except U.K.), and world (except U.K. and Western Europe). Lists approximately 65,000 titles, covering regional and national daily, weekly, and Sunday newspapers; Internet media and relevant websites; special-interest titles; journals and directories; and broadcast media. Entries include publishers' details, contact names, circulation data, subscription rates, advertising rates, summary of contents, readership/target audience data, etc. Multiple indexes.

North America

277 **Gale directory of publications and broadcast media.** Gale Research Inc., Gale Group. Detroit: Gale Research Inc., 1990–. maps. 1048-7972
302.2302573   Z6951.A97; PN4867

Supersedes and assumes the edition numbering of (1) Ayer directory of publications (title varies: 1930–69, *N. W. Ayer and Son's directory of newspapers and periodicals*; 1970–71, *Ayer directory: Newspapers, magazines . . .*; absorbed *Rowell's American newspaper directory* in 1910); (2)*The IMS . . . Ayer directory of publications* (1986) (called *The IMS directory of publications*). The earlier titles continue to be valuable for verification and research.

Covers United States and Canada. Arranged alphabetically by state (for Canada, by province), then by city. For print media, information includes publisher, address and telephone, beginning date, description, advertising rates, circulation, online availability, etc.; for broadcast media, call letters and frequency, address, format, advertising rates, etc. Special features include detailed subject index to print media, including type of publication (college, black, women, trade, etc.); subject index to radio station format; list of features editors of daily newspapers with at least 50,000 circulation, arranged alphabetically by state, then by city. Name and keyword index. Update issued midway between editions.

Also available electronically as a searchable subscription database via the *Gale directory library*. Entries in the electronic version are categorized as either an organization, a publication, or a database, with the data in the entries varying depending on the entry type. Includes 18,000 broadcast media organizations, 12,000 newsletters, and 12,500 newspaper entries. Broadcast media organizations are defined as television stations, radio stations, or cable television companies.

Indexes and Databases

International

278 Factiva. http://www.dowjones.com/ factiva/. Dow Jones & Co. New York: Dow Jones and Reuters. [2001–]

HG4515.9

Full-text articles from wire services such as Dow Jones and Reuters, major American and world newspapers such as the *New York Times*, leading business newspapers such as the *Wall Street Journal*, and a wide range of periodicals including *Barron's* and *Forbes*. Provides industry snapshots for more than 100 categories such as insurance, steel production, or alternative fuels; current and recent stock and currency price quotes (with graphing capability); and company snapshots for tens of thousands of worldwide firms. Content is in 28 languages.

279 InfoTrac custom newspapers.
http://www.cengage.com/search/ productOverview.do?Ntt=infotrac| |56907758516800931649079511 912012679&N=197&Ntk=APG| |P_EPI&Ntx=mode%2Bmatchallpartial. Thomson Gale. Farmington Hills, Mich.: Thomson Gale. 1998–

Searchable subscription database providing customizable cover-to-cover full-text coverage of

approximately 1000 newspapers, including international, U.S. national, regional, and local newspapers.

280 LexisNexis academic. http://www .lexisnexis.com/en-us/products/lexisnexis -academic.page. LexisNexis (Firm). Bethesda, Md.: LexisNexis. 1984-

KF242.A1

Searchable full-text subscription database that includes full text of articles from more than 2,500 newspapers, news from more than 300 local and regional newspapers, blogs and other web sources via WebNews, broadcast transcripts from the major radio and TV networks; national and international wire services; campus newspapers; polls and surveys; and over 600 newsletters. Non-English language news sources available in Spanish, French, German, Italian, and Dutch. Dates of coverage vary by individual source, with newspapers updated daily. Legal content includes federal and U.S. state statutes and cases, including Supreme Court decisions since 1790; some 800 law reviews; federal regulations; Shepherd's citations; and selective international coverage. Business content includes company information for 80 million public, private and international firms; profiles of 58 million executives; SEC filings; and industry profiles.

281 NewsBank's Access world news. http:// www.newsbankcolleges.com/colleges/ product.cfm?product=75. NewsBank, inc. Naples, Fla.: NewsBank, inc.

D860.A34

Searchable full text of over 2,000 local, state, regional, national, and international news sources, many unavailable elsewhere in electronic form. Updated daily. Indexing excludes paid advertising, paid obituaries, and photos/graphics. Dates of coverage vary by individual source; 1977 is the earliest date available. Map-based user interface can be customized to highlight specific title lists or groups (i.e., states, regions, languages, etc.). Searchable by headline, name, topic, keyword, date, and author. Foreign language titles are translated into English.

282 Newspaper source plus. http://www .ebscohost.com/public/newspaper-source -plus. EBSCO Publishing. Ipswich, Mass.: EBSCO Publishing. 2000s-

Searchable online subscription database providing partial or cover-to-cover full text for approximately 1000 national and international newspapers. Also includes selected newswires, and television and radio news transcripts from selected major broadcast entities.

United States

283 **Ethnic newswatch.** http://www.proquest .com/products_pq/descriptions/ethnic _newswatch.shtml. ProQuest Information and Learning. Ann Arbor, Mich.: ProQuest

Searchable, full-text collection of over 250 national and regional newspapers, magazines, and journals of the ethnic and minority press. Focus is on African American, American Indian, Asian American, and U.S. Latino publications, though periodicals from Jewish, Arab American, Eastern European, multi-ethnic communities, and other minority groups are also included. Search capabilities available in both English and Spanish, as well as the option to search by specific ethnic group. Coverage starts in 1990, with the companion database, Ethnic Newswatch: A History, extending coverage back to 1960.

284 **The New York Times index.** Ann Arbor, Mich.: Proquest LLC, 1913– 0147-538X

071.471   AI21.N45

Frequency varies. Index coverage begins in 1913, with *Prior series* coverage providing indexing in book form from 1851 to 1912.

Subject index giving exact reference to date, page, and column, with cross-references to names and related topics. Indexes the Late City edition, which is used for microfilming and bound files. Beginning in 1978, quarterly cumulations of the index are issued for the first three quarters of the year, with the annual volume "serving, in effect, as the fourth quarterly cumulation covering the entire year."

For more detailed information on the *Index*, see Grant W. Morse, *Guide to the incomparable New York Times index*, which describes filing rules, headings, subheadings, cross-references, special features, and changes to the *Index* over the years.

Fully searchable page images of the complete *New York Times* from 1851 to 2003 are available in ProQuest Historical Newspapers (285). Searchable full text (although not original page images) is also available in a number of other commercial database services, including ProQuest Newspapers, Factiva (278), LexisNexis academic (280), and America's Newspapers from NewsBank. Searchable archives back to 1851 are also available via the *New York Times* website: http://www.nytimes.com/ref/membercenter/nytarchive.html

See also *Personal name index to "The New York Times index," 1851–1974* and 1975–2003 supplement.

285 **ProQuest historical newspapers.** http://www.proquest.com/products_pq/ descriptions/pq-hist-news.shtml. ProQuest. Ann Arbor, Mich.: ProQuest. 2001–

E173

Searchable full text and full image subscription database with indexing and digitized page images of every issue of each paper cover-to-cover. Currently includes thirty six papers, including national, international, black and American Jewish titles, either singly or in combination with the others. Available papers include *New York Times* (1851–2004), *Wall Street Journal* (1889–1990), *Washington Post* (1877– 1991), *Chicago Tribune* (1849–1986), *Boston Globe* (1872–1924), *Atlanta Constitution* (1868–1932), *Hartford Courant* (1764–1984), *Christian Science Monitor*(1908–94), and the *Chicago Defender* (1909– 75). Continuing coverage of many of these, as well as other newspapers, provided by ProQuest National Newspapers.

286 **ProQuest newsstand.** http://www .proquest.com/en-US/catalogs/databases/ detail/newsstand.shtml. Ann Arbor, Mich.: ProQuest. 1996-

Abstracting and indexing are available for more than 1370 newspapers, with full text available for 1270 of these. Earliest coverage begins in 1977. Features exclusive access to eighty-five Gannett newspapers and content is customizable with state/regional packages or major national titles.

10 Online General Reference Libraries

Lili Luo

287 ipl2: information you can trust. http://www.ipl.org/. The iSchool at Drexel
Launched in January 2010, merging the collections of freely available Internet resources from the Internet Public Library (IPL) and the Librarians' Internet Index (LII). Currently hosted by Drexel University's College of Information Science & Technology, and a consortium of colleges and universities with programs in library and information science are involved in designing, building, creating and maintaining its collections and services.

Grouped into five sections: resources by subject, newspapers and magazines, special collections, for kids and for teens. Allows for keyword searches or browsing the directory under each section. Provides a reference service titled "Ask an ipl2 Librarian", where users can submit their questions and receive reference help. Provided by students in library and information science degree programs and volunteer information professionals.

Online Collections of Reference Texts

288 Gale virtual reference library. www.gale.com/gvrl. Gale Cengage Learning, Cengage Learning. Farmington Hills, Mich.: Gale Cengage Learning. 2002–

An electronic library containing thousands of reference titles from more than 100 publishers, covering most-studied subject areas, suitable to public, academic, school, and special libraries. Subscriber chooses individual titles for their electronic collection instead of purchasing an entire package. Works can be searched individually or across user-chosen texts or all works. Entries are available in a standard HTML view that includes graphics from print sources or in PDF format. Cross-references from the original print sources are now hyperlinks; cross-searching between reference works and some other Gale electronic products available.

289 Infoplease.com. http://www.infoplease.com/. Information Please LLC. Boston: Information Please LLC. [1998–]
The site contains an almanac, atlas, dictionary, encyclopedia, thesaurus, and timelines, in addition to special resources for schoolchildren (a "homework center" and Infoplease.com's site for children, Factmonster.com). Full-text searching is available for the entire site, or for a specific type of source (e.g. almanac or dictionary). Includes a biography section, providing access by profession, as well as "People in the News" extending back to 1997. For statistics, the original sources are noted; the site also provides internal links to related statistics available on the site. The print equivalent of the almanac portion of the site is *The time almanac*.

290   **Oxford reference online.** http://www
.oxfordreference.com/. Oxford University
Press. Oxford; New York: Oxford
University Press. 2002–

Large full-text selection of Oxford University Press's
reference works. Libraries can choose from a Core
or Premium Collection (the Premium Collection
includes all the core titles plus selected titles from
the *Oxford companion* series and the *Oxford dictionary of quotations*). Users can search entry titles,
full-text, people, and dates, and may choose to
search the entire database, a subject collection, or
specific titles. Search result screens offer further
refinement by subject facets. Each individual entry
gives hyperlinked cross-references to related terms
and lists of adjacent results within the same reference work. Oxford Reference Online also offers a
cross-reference tool within each entry: highlighting
a term and clicking "cross-reference" will perform
an entry heading search across the entire database. Other features include a 20th century timeline (available in Premium Collection) and links to
external websites relevant to each book and subject
in the database.

11 Other General Reference Works

Donald Altschiller

291 The Internet movie database (IMDb).
http://www.imdb.com. Internet Movie
Database, Ltd. Los Angeles: Internet Movie
Database, Ltd. 1994–

Largest web database of films (approximately
500,000 theatrical releases, made-for-television, and
direct-to-video). Television series and live action
games are also included. Each entry includes cast
and crew data, plot summaries, alternative titles,
production companies, filming locations, genres,
awards, IMDb user evaluations, as well as links to
standard reviewing sources, trivia, quotes, numerous
photos, etc. The search engine allows direct searching by name (performer, character, creative crew),
quotes, and plots. Other information about each
production is searchable by key word.

A similar, somewhat smaller database is All Movie
Guide (http://www.allmovie.com/). Here, specialized search tools for filming locations, costars, technical processes used, genre, and time period produce
cleaner search results when seeking film lists based
upon these criteria.

292 Robert's rules of order newly revised.
11th ed., a new and enlarged ed. / by
Sarah Corbin Robert . . . [et al.] ed.
Henry M. Robert III, Sarah Corbin Robert,
Daniel H. Honemann, Thomas J. Balch.
Philadelphia: Da Capo Press, 2011. lii,
716 p. ISBN 9780306820212
060.4/2   JF515

Still the standard work on parliamentary procedure,
despite the presence of several competitors. Contains rules, along with explanations, illustrations,
and interpretations to aid the reader. Index offers
subject access to rules and related issues. There
are numerous editions and versions on the market:
this is the "authorized" edition. Covers conduct of
business, meetings and quorums, motions, voting,
nominations and elections, the roles of officers and
boards, and bylaws. Includes charts and tables with
sample forms and guides to navigating the system.

293 Social register. Social Register
Association (U.S.). New York: Social
Register Association, [1977]-. v. ISBN 12
0-940281-26-0, 1071-3905
E154.7.S655 012

The Social Register is a directory of names and
addresses of socially prominent American families.
The origins go back to the 19th-century "visiting lists
of prominent individuals and their families." Individual books were published annually until 1976, when
they were consolidated into a single definitive book
listing the nation's foremost families.

Almost 25,000 entries are included in the winter
edition published by the Association every November.
These listings, which are primarily domestic but include
international references as well, record the following:

- the educational backgrounds
- maiden name

• club affiliations of listed persons, and the names given to estates or grand residences.

The Summer edition published in May lists names of yachts, specifications, and country of registration. The distribution of this volume is indeed puzzling, as the columnist and author Cecil Adams wryly notes: "Here we have the 30,000 snootiest families in the country, and they consent to put their addresses and phone numbers in a book available in the public library."

The summer edition contains seasonal information as well as "Dilatory Domiciles" and a list of yachts and their owners. (Online description.) The text is also available online. http://www.social registeronline.com

Associations, Societies, and Academies

Abbreviations

294   Acronym finder. http://acronymfinder .com/. Mike Malloy. Estes Park, Colo.: Mountain Data Systems. 1997-
P365 423.1

Claims to be the largest "human-edited collection available" for acronyms and abbreviations. Contents may be searched or browsed through an A-Z index. Includes abbreviations, acronyms, and initialisms for information technology, science and medicine, military and government, organizations and schools, business and finance, and slang and pop culture.

Also consult the following print volumes, which may contain entries not included in this site: *Acronyms, initialisms, and abbreviations dictionary* (240), *Reverse acronyms, initialisms, and abbreviations dictionary* (241), and *International acronyms, initialisms, and abbreviations dictionary*.

295   Acronyms, initialisms and abbreviations dictionary. Gale Research Company. Detroit: Gale Research, 1976- 0270-4404
423.1   P365.A28

The venerable language expert and critic H. L. Mencken once remarked about "the characteristic American habit of reducing complete concepts

to starkest abbreviations"—*Pref.* This massive dictionary includes mostly U.S. terms but also some Canadian and British usage. Covers international, national, regional, and state associations, political action committees, research centers, and stock exchange terms, among many other subjects. Helpful for some obsolete terms. Excellent feature: many terms include source citations. Also available online through the Gale Virtual Reference Library (288).

See also *Reverse acronyms, initialisms and abbreviations dictionary* (241), where terms are arranged alphabetically by the meaning of the acronym. For terms specific to foreign countries, see *International acronyms, initialisms and abbreviations dictionary*.

296   Reverse acronyms, initialisms, and abbreviations dictionary: A companion volume to Acronyms and initialism dictionary, with terms arranged alphabetically by meaning of acronym. Ellen T. Crowley, Robert C. Thomas. Detroit: Gale Research, 1972– 0270-4390
423.1   PE1693.G3

Since many acronyms do not clearly suggest the full name of the organization, this valuable source arranges the entries alphabetically by meaning.

A companion volume to *Acronyms, initialisms, and abbreviations dictionary* (240) and *International acronyms, initialisms, and abbreviations dictionary*.

General Works

297   Encyclopedia of associations. Gale Research. Farmington Hills, Mich.: Gale Cengage Learning, 1961- 0894-3869
061.3   Z5055.U4; AS22.E53

In 1954, Frederick Ruffner, a sales representative, was looking to find the name and address of an organization and was shocked to learn that no such directory existed at that time. He then self-published an encyclopedia of associations and founded Gale Publishing, which soon became one of the largest reference book publishing companies in U.S. history. The company was bought and is now known as Gale Cengage Learning.

The Encyclopedia of associations is published annually and is still the preeminent source for information on nonprofit U.S. membership organizations of national scope. Each entry includes organization name, address, phone number, primary official's name and title; fax number, when available; founding date, purpose, activities, and dues; national and internat. conferences; and more. Alphabetical name and keyword index.

Companion volumes: *Encyclopedia of associations: Regional, state, and local organizations.* and *Encyclopedia of associations: International organizations.*

All these editions are available electronically in the Gale Directory Library (http://www.gale.cengage.com/DirectoryLibrary/available.htm).

Etiquette

298 Emily Post's etiquette: manners for a new world. 18th ed. Peggy Post, Emily Post. New York: William Morrow, 2011. xi, 723 p., ill. ISBN 9780061740237

BJ1853.P6395

A nonfiction bestseller on its first publ. in 1922. The authors, descendants of Emily Post, update the manual to incorporate modern technology and mores, e.g., Facebook, Twitter, same-sex couples, etc. Besides these contemporary issues, this book also includes the classic etiquette issues: correct use of names and titles, official forms of address, dress codes, invitation wording, dining etiquette, and wedding planning.

"The book defines etiquette in today's real-life terms and brings it down to earth"—*A note to readers.*

Available electronically from *Gale Directory Library.*

Full-text of the original ed. is available through Bartleby.com at http://www.bartleby.com/95/index.html.

Foundations and Philanthropic Organizations

Directories

UNITED STATES

299 Catalog of federal domestic assistance. https://www.cfda.gov/.

U.S. General Services Administration, Governmentwide Information Systems Division. Washington: U.S. General Services Administration

The online version of the *Catalog of Federal Domestic Assistance* is a searchable and browsable version of what is contained in the print version comprising over 3,000 pages. This federal assistance is available to state and local governments, private profit and non-profit organizations, and individuals. Assistance for project grants, direct loans, provision of services, training, and federal employment is described, together with links to web sites and contact information are provided.

The "Project Grants" section (under Find Programs) is the most pertinent for students, academics, and others seeking financial support. Project grants can include "fellowships, scholarships, research grants, training grants, and traineeships" among other types of support.

Related website: Grants.gov.

300 Foundation Center. http://www.foundationcenter.org. Foundation Center. New York: Foundation Center. 1990s-

The preeminent website for foundation and corporate funding information. Foundation Directory Online, now includes a free search tool that has replaced Foundation Finder, providing public access to essential information about nearly 90,000 foundations and over 250,000 IRS Forms 990-PF.

Funder profiles include:

- Address and contact information
- Fields of interest
- Program areas
- Fiscal information

While the above information is free, access to most of the site requires a subscription. Useful sections on proposal writing, nonprofit management, training courses, and book lists. Addresses and contact information for Foundation Center offices in Atlanta, Cleveland, New York, San Francisco, and Washington, D.C.; lists of libraries and community foundations that offer Foundation Center print and electronic resources. Although some pages have needlessly slick graphics and occasionally appear cluttered, this site is a treasure trove of essential information for grantseekers.

The *Foundation directory* is also available in print.

General Works

301 Black firsts: 4,000 ground-breaking and pioneering historical events. 3rd ed. Jessie Carney Smith. Detroit: Visible Ink Press, 2013. xiii, 833 p., ill. ISBN 9781578593699
920.009296/073 B   E185.B574

A prodigious and meticulously compiled work first published in 1994 under the title *Black Firsts: 2,000 years of extraordinary achievement* and updated in 2002, this third edition with a new subtitle updates much of the historical information found in the earlier editions. For this edition, the compiler made a "deliberate focus on women who have been overlooked in our history far too often." In addition to citing specific accomplishments that made a person a "first", many entries provide background information on the person or the event. Available electronically in *Credo reference*

302 The Columbia Granger's world of poetry. http://www.columbiagrangers .org/static/about. William Harmon, Columbia University. New York: Columbia University Press. 1999–
PN1022

Electronic counterpart to the century-long indexing tradition of the print *Columbia Granger's index to poetry* (previous titles: *Index to poetry*, *Granger's index to poetry*; since 1996 effectively published as a two-volume work as *The Columbia Granger's index to poetry in anthologies* and *The Columbia Granger's index to poetry in collected and selected works*).

This online resource combines several standard poetry indexes published by Columbia University Press. In an easily navigable Web format, researchers have access to *The classic hundred poems* and *The top 500 poems*, both annotated anthologies; eds. 8–13 of *The Columbia Granger's index to poetry in anthologies*; eds. 1 and 2 of *The Columbia Granger's index to poetry in collected and selected works*; and *The Columbia Granger's index to African-American poetry*. The online resource includes biographical information for authors, critical context, and a glossary.

303 CRC handbook of chemistry and physics. CRC Press. Boca Raton, Fla.: CRC Press, 1913–. ill. 0147-6262
540.202   QD65.H3

"The overall philosophy of the Handbook remains to provide broad coverage of all types of data commonly encountered by physical scientists and engineers."—*Pref.* Web version of this workhorse of scientific handbooks is available through the publisher (http://www.hbcpnetbase.com) as part of CRCnetBASE and allows searching by property or substance.

304 Essay and General Literature Index. http://www.ebscohost.com/academic/ essay-general-literature-index. Ipswich, Mass.: EBSCO Publishing. 0014-083X
080.16016   AI3.E752

Indexes authors and subjects of essays appearing in collections back to 1985; Essay and General Literature Index Retrospective (http://www.ebscohost .com/archives/wilson-archives/essay-and-general-li terature-Retrospective) is an add-on providing access to the earlier print indexing from 1900 to 1984. Coverage spans the entire range of the humanities and social sciences, including literary works, art history, drama, and film. Indexes single and multi-author collections, plus selected annuals and serials published in the U.S., Canada, and Great Britain.

305 The Europa world year book. Europa Publications Limited. London: Europa Publications Limited, 1989– 0956-2273
391.184   JN1

Despite the title, covers all countries of the world. Issued annually in two volumes, with v. 1 covering international organizations and the first group of alphabetically arranged country entries and v. 2 the remainder of the country entries. Information on the United Nations, its agencies, and other international organizations followed by detailed information about each country, arranged alphabetically in each volume, giving an introductory survey, a statistical survey, the government, political parties, the constitution, judicial system, diplomatic representation, religion, press, publishers, radio and television, finance, trade and industry, transport, and tourism. Vol. 1 ends with an index to international organizations; v. 2 includes a country index.

Published as *Europa year book* prior to 1989. Similar Europa publications with a regional focus are the

Regional surveys of the world, including *Africa south of the Sahara*, *Central and south-eastern Europe*, *Eastern Europe, Russia, and Central Asia*, *The Far East and Australasia*, *The Middle East and North Africa*, *South America*, *Central America, and the Caribbean*, *South Asia*, *The USA and Canada*, and *Western Europe*. The electronic version of this resource, Europa World Plus, includes both the year book and the regional surveys as well as continual updates on recent elections, recent events, and a featured country. It also provides the capability to search and create tables of comparative statistics for the countries in the database.

306 Gale virtual reference library. www
      .gale.com/gvrl. Gale Cengage Learning,
      Cengage Learning. Farmington Hills,
      Mich.: Gale Cengage Learning. 2002–
An electronic library containing thousands of reference titles from more than 100 publishers, covering most-studied subject areas, suitable to public, academic, school, and special libraries. Subscriber chooses individual titles for their electronic collection instead of purchasing an entire package. Works can be searched individually or across user-chosen texts or all works. Entries are available in a standard HTML view that includes graphics from print sources or in PDF format. Cross-references from the original print sources are now hyperlinks; cross-searching between reference works and some other Gale electronic products available.

307 Injury facts. National Safety Council,
      National Safety Council. Itasca, Ill.:
      National Safety Council, 1999-. http://
      shop.nsc.org/Books-and-Manuals-Injury
      -Facts-2012-Book-CD-Kit-P9.aspx, color ill.
      1538-5337
      312 13   HA217.A4; HV676.A1 A2
A unique and authoritative source covering current occupational, motor vehicle, home, community, state and international injury statistics, both fatal and nonfatal,and the associated costs.

New content for 2013 includes graphic displays of overall injury fatality and of workplace injury data. Also includes new data on the safety impact of OSHA inspections; workplace nature of injury and part of body injuries; motor vehicle crashes by time of day and day of week and childhood drownings.

Also available in searchable CD format or as a book and CD combo kit. See http://shop.nsc.org/.

308 The Merck manuals. http://www
      .merckmanuals.com//. Merck and Co.
      Whitehouse Station, N.J.: Merck and Co.
      1995–
"A trusted source for medical information. . . ."
—*Website*

Overview of the various titles and editions of the Merck manuals, organized in categories by user group, with information about online availability, online in other languages, as printed book or PDA download, and appropriate links. The full-text online versions are periodically updated, with a listing of the last review date on the bottom of each topic page. Intended for medical professionals and health consumers. Under "healthcare professionals" lists the *Merck manual of diagnosis and therapy* (available online, online in other languages, mobile version, and as printed book); under "patients and caregivers" lists the *Merck manual home health handbook* (available online, online in other languages, mobile version(s), and also as printed book). Information previously found in *Merck manual of geriatrics* (2000) and *Merck manual of health and aging* (2004) has been incorporated into the appropriate sections of the *Merck manual of diagnosis and therapy* and *Merck manual home health handbook*. Other Merck publications include, for example, *Merck index*, *Merck veterinary manual*, and several others.

MerckEngage® http://www.merckengage.com/, (formerly Mercksource), is a related website intended for healthcare consumers as a good starting point, together with MedlinePlus. It provides information concerning medical conditions, health news, searches topics in Spanish. Its "resource library" and "health tool" tabs provide additional useful information.

309 Play index. http://www.ebscohost.com/
      academic/play-index. EBSCO Publishing.
      Ipswich, Mass.: EBSCO Publishing. 2006–
      Z 5781   792
Online version of standard Wilson title, indexing "more than 30,000 plays written from Antiquity to the present and published from 1949 to the present; includes mysteries, pageants, plays in verse, puppet performances, radio and television plays, and classic drama." A special feature provides linking to selected websites containing full text, criticism, etc. Published until 2011 by the H. W. Wilson Company, now available via EBSCOhost system.

310   Short story index. http://www.ebscohost
.com/academic/short-story-index. EBSCO
Publishing. Ipswich, Mass.: EBSCO
Publishing
016.80883/1   Z5917.S5; PN3373

Indexes more than 117,000 stories from more than
4,200 collections and anthologies, as well as an
additional 12,000 stories from periodicals. Contains
full text of more than 1,600 short stories. Search by
author, title, subject, keyword, date, literary technique, source, or any combination. Subject access
includes theme, locale, narrative technique or device
(such as surprise endings, dialect stories, parodies,
story-within-a-story), and genre. Entries feature links
to other works by the author and other stories in the
source collection. Earlier content indexed in Short
Story Index Retrospective: 1915-1983. Published
until 2011 by the H. W. Wilson Company.

311   Sports: The complete visual reference.
Francois Fortin. Willowdale, Ont.; Buffalo,
N.Y.: Firefly Books, 2000. xi, 372 p.
ISBN 1552095401

Beautifully ill. with color photos, charts, and other
graphics, this concise visual resource covers 127
sports, including traditional events, plus many others such as rock climbing, surfing, and motor sports.
Each entry includes the history, rules and strategies,
equipment, techniques, playing area, and environment for the sport.

**312   The Statesman's year-book: the
politics, cultures and economies of
the world.** Frederick Martin, John Scott
Keltie, Isaac Parker Anderson Renwick,
Mortimer Epstein, S. H Steinberg, John
Paxton, Barry Turner. London: Palgrave,
1864-. maps (pt. folded, pt. color).
0081-4601
320   JA51

Concise and reliable manual of descriptive and statistical information about countries of the world and
major international organizations. Currently covers close to 200 NGOs (including the U.N. and its
agencies, and the E.U. and its constituent parts),
major think tanks, and 194 countries. For the U.S.,
Canada and the U.K., individual entries cover each
state, province or possession. For agencies, provides
addresses and URLs. Updated annually: 2014 marks
the 150th edition, making this a useful resource

for comparative time series. Sections for each country include a map, historical overview, population
figures, a sketch of recent political events, a list of
current government leaders (including cabinet minis-
ters), an economic summary with statistics, addresses
for selected embassies, and a short bibliography of
statistical and reference sources. Index. Also available
as an e-book: http://www.statesmansyearbook.com/.

Directories

**313   Cole Directory (Titles vary by
city).** http://www.coledirectory.com.
Cole Information. Omaha, Neb.: Cole
information

In 1947, a businessman named Jack Cole started to
publish a set of "criss-cross" directories to various
U.S. cities. These directories list a city's residents
by address and also by telephone number. Useful
for small business owners in planning a marketing
strategy.

Mr. Cole ingeniously employed his staff to use
I.B.M. punch cards to input the information, turning
a telephone book into a database. The Cole Directories now cover about 200 cities, and are published in
print and digital formats.

Available by paid subscription.

314   The college blue book. Macmillan
Information. New York: Macmillan
Information, 1923–. maps (part color).
0069-5572
378.73   LA226.C685

Leading directory of American and Canadian colleges.
In five volumes. Vol. 1, *Narrative descriptions*, provides
information for over 3,000 institutions, with entries
arranged by state or province. Vol. 2, *Tabular data*,
outlines facts on enrollment, admissions policies, stu-
dent/faculty ratio, calendar system, library holdings,
dormitory and other facilities, work-study opportunities, and accreditation. Vol. 3, *Degrees offered by college
and subject*, identifies courses of study leading to a
certificate or degree. Vol. 4, *Occupational education*,
provides information for over 6,500 trade, technical,
business, and other proprietary schools, as well as
junior and community colleges that offer vocational
and occupational programs. Vol. 5, *Scholarships, fellowships, grants, and loans*, identifies financial aid
from corporate, government, and voluntary sources.

Vol. 6, *Distance learning* (new with the 29th ed.), includes descriptions of distance learning media, strategies for choosing, applying to, and paying for programs, and a directory of nearly 3,000 degree and certificate programs at more than 1,000 institutions. Now available as an e-book through the Gale Virtual Reference Library (288).

315   Directories in print. Gale Cengage
       Learning. Farmington Hills, Mich.: Gale
       Cengage Learnng, 1989- 0899-353X
       Z5771.D55; AY2001
       |300 11   Q011.02/D
Formerly entitled *Directory of directories*, this work is the preeminent source for descriptive and contact information on directories published worldwide, but primarily in the United States. "Covers subjects ranging from A (accountants, air pollution, automotive engineering) to Z (Zambia, zoological societies)."—*Introd.* Supplement published regularly between new editions. Subject, title, and keyword indexes. "Alternative formats index" identifies directories available in computer-readable, microfiche, mailing label, Braille, and other non-traditional formats. Hundreds of additional directories (defunct, suspended and directories that cannot be located) are cited, with status notes, in the title/keyword index.

Available electronically from the *Gale Directory Library*.

316   Gale virtual reference library. www
       .gale.com/gvrl. Gale Cengage Learning,
       Cengage Learning. Farmington Hills,
       Mich.: Gale Cengage Learning. 2002–
An electronic library containing thousands of reference titles from more than 100 publishers, covering most-studied subject areas, suitable to public, academic, school, and special libraries. Subscriber chooses individual titles for their electronic collection instead of purchasing an entire package. Works can be searched individually or across user-chosen texts or all works. Entries are available in a standard HTML view that includes graphics from print sources or in PDF format. Cross-references from the original print sources are now hyperlinks; cross-searching between reference works and some other Gale electronic products available.

**317   International association of
       amusement parks & attractions.**

http://www.iaapa.org/find-an-attraction. International association of amusement parks & attractions. Alexandria, Virginia: International association of amusement parks & attractions
Published by the largest trade association serving the amusement industry, this website provides a unique link to a directory of amusement parks mostly located in the United States, but also including many facilities throughout the world. The free directory search will access amusement parks, entertainment centers, water and theme parks, and other venues.

While the directory does not contain a comprehensive listing, the site still provides much useful information (address, website, etc.) for library users wanting to find a particular facility.

318   Library and book trade almanac.
       [Information Today, Inc.]. Medford, N.J.:
       Information Today, Inc., 2009– 2150-5446
       020.5   Z731.A47
Title varies: 1956–58, American library annual [new series]; 1959–61, American library and book trade annual; 1962–88, The Bowker annual of library and book trade information; 1989-2008, The Bowker annual: Library and book trade almanac. Includes reviews of the year's events, trends, and legislation relevant to librarianship and publishing; reports from federal agencies and key organizations; statistics on placement and salaries of beginning librarians; scholarship and award winners; statistics on library expenditures, facilities, and rankings; statistics on publishing output and average prices of books; bibliographies of recent books in librarianship, bestsellers, and award-winning books; directories of library consortia and associations; and a calendar of conferences and book fairs. Indexes: organizations; subjects.

319   National ZIP Code directory. Lanham,
       Md.: Bernan Press, 1900s-
       ISBN 9781601758828, 0191-6971
Published by the U.S. Postal Service until 2004, Bernan Press now issues the National ZIP Code Directory containing updated information on new residential numbers, new street names, and new ZIP Codes.

Published in two comprehensive volumes. In addition to ZIP Code listings, Volume 1 contains instructions on how to find ZIP Codes in the Directory and how to properly address your mailings.

Volume 2 contains information on symbol abbreviations, mail services, classes of mail, among other content.

The U.S. Post Office provides online access to a free directory, searchable by address, company or city:

https://tools.usps.com/go/ZipLookupAction !input.action

320 Peterson's annual guides: graduate study. Peterson's Guides. Princeton, N.J.: Peterson's Guides, 1966–. ill. 0163-6111
LB2371 378/.1553/02573

Issued in six books (titles vary slightly). Vol. 1, Peterson's guide to graduate and professional programs: an overview. Vol. 2, *Graduate programs in the humanities, arts, and social sciences*. Vol. 3, *Graduate programs in the biological sciences*. Vol. 4, *Graduate programs in the physical sciences, mathematics, agricultural sciences, the environment, and natural resources*. Vol. 5, Graduate programs in engineering and applied sciences. Vol. 6, *Graduate programs in business, education, health, information studies, law, and social work*.

Institutional profiles in the first volume provide basic information about colleges and universities in the United States, Canada, and American territories offering graduate work; first volume serves both as a basic reference source and as foundation for the other volumes in the series. Includes a directory of graduate and professional programs by field, a directory of institutions and their offerings, profiles of institutions, and "close-ups" of selected institutions, which include information about the faculty.

Also marketed in online form. Some free services are online at http://www.petersons.com/graduate-schools.aspx such as information about selecting and applying to a graduate program, advice about tests like the GRE, and tips for financial aid.

321 ReferenceUSA. http://www.referenceusa.com/. infoUSA (Firm). Omaha, Neb.: infoUSA Inc. 1999-
HF5035

Business directory covers 24 million U.S. businesses, 4 million new business, and 1.5 million Canadian businesses. White pages cover 89 million U.S. residents, and 12 million Canadian residential households. Identifies over 800,000 U.S. health care providers. Most used for the ability to download customized lists of companies from searches by geography, size of business, sales volume, number of employees, and executive gender.

322 Sports reference. http://www.sports-reference.com. Sports Reference, LLC. Philadelphia: Sports Reference, LLC. 2000-

The title of this website seems on the mark: users can easily and quickly retrieve sports statistics. Since members of the staff have degrees in applied mathematics and statistics (and posses a love of sports!), users can probably safely assume the general accuracy of the site.

First launched as Baseball-Reference.com in April 2000 and then Pro-Football-Reference.com in December of 2000 and later Basketball-Reference.com in April of 2004.

Sean Forman (math and computer science professor) formed Sports Reference, Inc., in October of 2004; and in December of 2007, the three groups joined forces to create Sports Reference LLC.

Currently, this easy-to-navigate free site covers baseball, basketball, professional and college football, and hockey.

323 Washington information directory. Congressional Quarterly Inc. Washington: CQ Press [etc.] ISBN 9780872895003, 0887-8064
975.30025   F192.3.W33

First publ. in 1975, this work is an essential source for finding information about the three branches of the U.S. government (executive, legislative, and judicial) and nongovernmental organizations located in Washington, D.C. Arranged by topical chapters (e.g., "Business and Economics"; "Health"; "Science and Technology") Lists executive agencies, members of the U.S. House of Representatives and Senate, congressional committees and subcommittees, and private organizations. Each entry includes a brief description of the agency or committee, the address, telephone, e-mail, website, fax, and names of key officers. Especially useful is a chart listing the libraries at federal departments and agencies with phone numbers. "Ready Reference" section contains lists of governors and other state and local officials, foreign embassies, U.S. ambassadors and State Department desk officers. Excellent source for locating Internet sites. Name, organization, and subject indexes.

Facebook and Twitter information for some legislators. Online version at http://www.cqpress.com/.

**324 Worldwide government directory, with
international organizations.** National
Standards Association. Bethesda, Md.:
National Standards Association, 1987–.
maps
0894-1521   JF37.L345 351.2025

Continues *Lambert's worldwide government directory,
with inter-governmental organizations.* Publisher varies.
Pt. 1 serves as a directory, organized alphabetically
by country, to government officials in more than 170
countries. Includes addresses, phone numbers, and
forms of address. Pt. 2 provides alphabetical entries
for international organizations. No index.

As of June 2013, no longer available online - see:
http://library.cqpress.com/world-powerbase/.

Holidays and Anniversaries

325 Chase's . . . calendar of events.
New York: McGraw-Hill, 1994–. ill.
ISBN 9780071489034, 0740-5286
394   GT4803.C48

Created by William Chase, a newspaper librarian
and his brother, Harrison, more than a half-century
ago, this reference work has emerged as the standard
source for finding sponsored days, weeks, and months
(Sweet Potato Month, Neurosurgery Outreach Month,
etc.) in addition to holidays, historic anniversaries, and
other noteworthy events. Probably a major source for
print and electronic journalists reporting on unusual
commemorations or sponsored events. Contains more
than 12,500 entries arranged chronologically by calendar date. CD-ROM included in vol. since 1998.
Supplementary information and the history of the publication is available at: http://www.chases.com but the
site doesn't provide full-text access to the work. Also
includes birthdays of notable individuals. Combined
keyword, name, and holiday index. A unique source.

Proverbs

326 The dictionary of modern proverbs.
Charles Clay Doyle, Wolfgang Mieder,
Fred R. Shapiro. New Haven, Conn.: Yale
University Press, 2012. xiv, 294 p.

ISBN 9780300136029
398.9/2103   PN6421.D69

Compiled by scholars of proverbs, quotations and
linguistics, this work is an impressive collection of
English-language proverbs originating in the 20th and
21st centuries. The more than 1400 individual entries
are organized alphabetically by keywords, with information about the earliest datable appearance, origin,
history and meaning of each proverb. Each entry cites
dictionaries or compilations that note the item. An
outstanding and unique reference source.

Quotations

**327 Bartlett's familiar quotations:
a collection of passages, phrases,
and proverbs traced to their sources
in ancient and modern literature.**
18th ed. John Bartlett, Geoffrey O'Brien.
New York: Little, Brown, and Co., 2012.
lxi, 1438 p. ISBN 9780316017596
808.88/2   PN6081.B27

First published in 1855 by a Massachusetts book-
seller, this eighteenth edition of this classic work
significantly expands the coverage to include quotations about mass journalism, recording, movies,
radio and television broadcasting, and the Internet.
Also expands international coverage to include writers from Europe, Asia, Africa and Latin America
and "unknown figures who have given utterance
to phrases that continue to make inroads as only
the most eloquent or startling or suggestive or even
unsettling quotations can." —(Pref.)

**328 The Oxford dictionary of American
quotations.** Hugh Rawson, Margaret
Miner. Oxford; New York: Oxford
University Press, 2006. xii, 898 p.
ISBN 9780195168235
081.03   PN6081.A623

Revised and expanded edition of the 1996 *American Heritage dictionary of American quotations* and
compiled by the same co-editors, this volume contains more than 6,000 quotations—about 30% are
annotated—which are arranged by topic, unlike
Bartlett's (327) and other quotation works which
are organized by author. Misattributed quotations
from the 1996 volume have been corrected. Some

categories include specific cities and states, in addition to contemporary events, e.g., Iraq War, etc. Keyword and author indexes and numerous cross-references.

Available electronically in *Oxford reference online* (290).

329 Oxford dictionary of quotations. 7th ed ed. Elizabeth Knowles. Oxford; New York: Oxford University Press, 2009. xxvi, 1155 p.

2009 082 22   PN6080.O95

First published in 1941, this venerable reference work includes quotations found in Oxford World's Classics and other annotated editions of classic works, along with modern and contemporary entries. 20,000 entries from 2,500 authors. Despite Ralph Waldo Emerson's admonition: "I hate quotations. Tell me what you know." (p.315), this work is a treasure trove for the intrepid scholar and researcher and also a delight for the casual browser. Most quotations include a source citation. Many quotations from foreign literatures are given both in their original language as well as English translation. Especially noteworthy: Sidebars feature film lines, misquotations, mottoes, newspaper headlines and slogans, among other topics, and cite the very hard-to-find exact source. Elegant and easy-to-read typography. Thematic keyword index.

Also available electronically: Oxford Reference Online (290).

330 The Yale book of quotations. Fred R. Shapiro, Joseph Epstein. New Haven, Conn.: Yale University Press, 2006. xxiv, 1067 p., ports. ISBN 0300107986

082   PN6081.Y35

Compiler of the *Oxford dictionary of American legal quotations* and profiled in the *Wall Street journal* (January 22, 1997) for his indefatigable research on legal footnotes, the Yale librarian Fred Shapiro has ascended to the highest ranks of quotation mavens.

Modeled on the *Oxford English dictionary* approach to documenting first word use, this work serves as an outstanding historical dictionary of quotations. Besides including quotations omitted from many classic works, the *Yale book of quotations* includes modern American popular culture, children's literature, sports, and computers among its 12,000 entries. Shapiro used eclectic sources to find and verify entries, including databases, the Internet, hundreds of quotation books, and the American Dialect Society e-mail list.

He relied on the "indispensable" *Oxford dictionary of quotations* (329) for pre-1800 citations; post-1800 quotations were rechecked and verified.

Arranged alphabetically by author or specific category (e.g., modern proverbs, radio and television catchphrases). Keyword index. Available on the web. http://quotations.yupnet.org/

Other important sources that involved extensive research on quotation origins include *Quote verifer* and *Brewer's quotations*.

12 Periodicals

Jennifer Duncan

Asia (by country)

China

INDEXES; ABSTRACT JOURNALS; DATABASES

331 China academic journals. http://
www.eastview.com/online/databasetitles.
Zhongguo zhi shi ji chu she shi gong
cheng. Beijing, China: Tsinghua University
China Academic Journals Electronic
Publishing House

Full text collection of more than 7,200 Chinese journals
from 1994 to the present. Limited retrospective coverage extends to 1979, but a deep backfile of many of the
titles is linkable through the Century Journals Project.
Available as a complete package or as separate subject
modules via the Internet or DVD-ROM. Distributed by
East View Publications in the United States.

Asia (by region)

Indexes; Abstract Journals; Databases

332 Bibliography of Asian studies. http://
ets.umdl.umich.edu/b/bas. Association
for Asian Studies. Ann Arbor, Mich.:
Association for Asian Studies
Z3001.DS5

The major index for materials related to East Asia,
Southeast Asia, and South Asia in the humanities, social sciences, and selected natural sciences, such as medicine, public health, geology,
and the environment. For 1971–91, the online
BAS contains the full data of the printed version
of the *Bibliography of Asian studies*, which includes
citations to Western language periodical articles,
monographs, chapters in edited volumes, conference proceedings, anthologies, and Festschriften.
Monographs published since 1992 are not included. Doctoral dissertations and master's theses
are seldom included. Keyword searching is available and is generally the most powerful way to
search BAS online. Entries can also be accessed
by author, subject, country, and journal title.
"Browse journal" provides information about the
years of coverage for each journal in the BAS. To
assist searchers, the subject classification in the
BAS is available online at http://bmc.lib.umich.
edu/bas/Help/subjects

The BAS began as an annual bibliography, the
Bulletin of Far Eastern bibliography, in 1936. In 1941,
the scope extended to Southeast Asia, and in 1955,
to South Asia. From 1956–91, the BAS appeared as a
fifth number of the *Journal of Asian studies*. G.K. Hall
published the *Cumulative bibliography of Asian studies*,
1941–65 and 1966–70, organized by subject, with
author indexes.

Europe (by country)

Great Britain

BIBLIOGRAPHIES; UNION LISTS; DIRECTORIES

333 **The Waterloo directory of English newspapers and periodicals, 1800–1900.** http://www.victorianperiodicals.com/series2/PurchaseInformation.asp. John North. Waterloo, Ont.: North Waterloo Academic Press

Series two (of an expected series of five) includes a total of 50,000 entries, including 9,000 facsimile title pages and 48,000 personal names. Library locations are provided for the United Kingdom and North America. Indexes are provided by title, subject, place of publication (by town and county), issuing body, and people. Also includes a family tree for all titles related through mergers, common issuing bodies, or title changes. Fee-based online edition is updated daily. Also available in CD-ROM and print versions.

INDEXES; ABSTRACT JOURNALS; DATABASES

334 **The Wellesley Index to Victorian Periodicals, 1824-1900.** http://www.proquest.com/en-US/catalogs/databases/detail/wellesley.shtml. Walter E. Houghton, ProQuest Information and Learning Company. Ann Arbor, Mich.: ProQuest Co. 2005-

The Wellesley Index covers 45 significant British periodicals beginning with the inception of *Westminster Review* (1824)through the end of the 19th century. In total, it includes more than 78,000 attributions by approximately 12,000 authors. One of the unique features of this resource is the identification of authors of anonymous works, a common attribute of Victorian periodical articles. The database is both browsable and searchable by author and pseudonym. It is also searchable by article title, periodical title, and periodical subject. Poetry is not indexed. Links to full text in Periodicals Archive Online (363) or British Periodicals when both databases are subscribed. Included as a datafile within the C19 (352) database.

The Wellesley Index was originally published in print with the same title by the University of Toronto press between 1965 and 1988, with a CD-ROM published in 1999 by Routledge to incorporate additions and corrections through 1997. The print volumes are readily available via interlibrary loan for those without access to the online version.

Russia (including Siberia) and the Former USSR

INDEXES; ABSTRACT JOURNALS; DATABASES

335 **Letopis zhurnalnykh statei.** http://www.eastview.com/PERI/product.asp?sku=P13. Vsesoiuznaia knizhnaia palata. Minneapolis, Minn.: Eastview Information Services

The standard Russian periodical index covering scholarly publications in the humanities, sciences, and social sciences. Current online access is available beginning with 1998 as part of the Russian National Bibliography module residing on the Universal Database platform from Eastview Information Services. Free online access is available through Indiana University for the time periods 1956–72 and 1973–75 at http://webapp1.dlib.indiana.edu/letopis/search.jsp?lang=en. Coverage of earlier content is available only through the print index, which began in 1927.

International

Abbreviations

336 **Periodical title abbreviations.** C. Edward Wall, Leland G. Alkire, Gale Research. Detroit: Gale Research, 1969–2006. 0737-7843
050.148   Z6945.A2.P47; PN4832

Annual two-volume set providing international coverage of periodical abbreviations for all disciplines. Vol. 1 lists abbreviations in alphabetical order together with the full title. Vol. 2 lists periodical titles alphabetically together with abbreviation. Although this title ceased in 2006, it is still useful for identifying abbreviations in citations, particularly in older works.

Bibliographies; Union Lists; Directories

337 Benn's media. Benn Business
Information Services. Teddington, U.K.:
Hollis, 1846–
0968-4557   P88.8 072
Arranged alphabetically within broad subject areas, each entry includes contact information, circulation figures, advertising rates, an editorial profile, and a readership profile. Currently issued in three volumes representing the United Kingdom, Europe (excluding the United Kingdom), and the world. The set includes directory information for more than 100,000 media listings from more than 208 countries.

Published under several titles: initially as *Newspaper press directory* (1846–1976); changed title to *Benn's press directory* (1978–82); divided into *Benn's press directory, United Kingdom* and *Benn's press directory, international* (1983–85); both volumes changed titles to *Benn's media directory, United Kingdom* (1986–91) and *Benn's media directory, international* (1986–91); merged to form *Benn's media directory* (1992).

338 Directory of open access journals.
http://www.doaj.org. Lund University
Libraries. Lund, Sweden: Lund University
Libraries. 2003–
                              011.34
Directory of free, full-text, scholarly journals spanning most disciplines. Journals are international and multilingual in scope and must be peer reviewed or have an editorial review board. The database includes more than 10,000 journals, the majority of which are searchable at the article level. Browsable by title and subject tree. Entries link out to full-text content at the journal's homepage; records include title, subject, ISSN, publisher, language, related keywords, and year of first online issue available.

**339 Early periodical indexes:
Bibliographies and indexes of
literature published in periodicals
before 1900.** Robert Balay. Lanham, Md.:

Scarecrow Press, 2000. xxx, 317 p.
ISBN 0810838680
011.34   Z6941.B35; PN4801
Comprehensive annotated bibliography of about 400 titles providing indexing to articles published before 1900. Most cited references are to subject bibliographies rather than traditional periodical indexes. Subject matter is completely multidisciplinary, covering the humanities, social sciences, and sciences, and the bibliography itself is arranged by classified subject. Includes four indexes: author, title, subject, and dates of coverage.

**340 The international directory of little
magazines & small presses.** http://
ebooks.dustbooks.com/id.php?fnc=xix.
Paradise, Calif.: Dustbooks
The International Directory of Little Magazines and Small Presses published its 49th edition for 2013-2014 and continues the print version of this title, which ceased in 2011. Publishers included generally lean toward the avant garde in literature, commentary, and art. Entries for little magazines and small book publishers provide typical directory information such as contact information, average press runs, book seller discounts, and subject coverage. Editors often provide brief descriptions as well. The online version is browsable by publisher name, geographic location (both U.S. states and countries), and subject areas.

341 Magazines for libraries. Cheryl
Laguardia, William A. Katz, Linda
Sternberg Katz. New York: Bowker,
1969– 0000-0914
050.25   Z6941.M23; PN4832
The 22nd edition from 2013 of this venerable guide annotates and evaluates more than 5,300 periodicals. The substantive annotations are provided by a team of subject specialists. Entries are grouped into more than 200 subject categories, each with a brief introduction that discusses periodical publishing in that area. Entries include bibliographic information as well as an indication of what sources index the journal under review. Title and subject indexes. This volume is useful for public, university, college, junior college, school, and special libraries.

342 MLA directory of periodicals. http://
www.mla.org/bib_periodicals. Modern

Language Association of America. New York: Modern Language Association of America. 2000-

Provides as full information as available on journals and series that fall within the scope of the *MLA international bibliography* (361). Entries list addresses, phone and fax numbers, e-mail addresses, frequency of publication, descriptions of scope, circulation figures, subscription prices and addresses, advertising information, links to current online content, peer review, and submission guidelines. The *Directory* also provides statistics on the number of articles and book reviews published each year, as well as how many are submitted.

Distributed as an electronic database through Gale, EBSCO and ProQuest; previously available in print.

343 Ulrich's periodicals directory. http:// www.ulrichsweb.com/ulrichsweb. R. R. Bowker. New Providence, N.J.: R. R. Bowker. 2001–

Z6941

Directory of periodicals from around the world, including magazines, journals, newsletters, newspapers, annuals, and irregular serials. Searchable by keyword, title, ISSN, and subject. Several browse options are available, including title, subject, electronic vendor, country of publication, language, place of publication, and classification. Each entry includes basic information about the title, such as a basic description, publisher information, circulation figures, peer-reviewed status, and start year. Specialized features of this site include details about other available formats, including all electronic availability options; indexing and abstracting sources, including retrospective; document delivery options; publisher and ordering information; advertising and rights information; and reviews of the publication. Updated daily. OpenURL compliant.

The print version is still available as a more economical choice. Published annually, it is arranged alphabetically within subject classification. Indexes include refereed serials, online periodicals, cessations, ISSNs, and titles.

This title has undergone a number of changes, as reported in Ulrich's itself. The title started publication as *Periodicals directory: A classified guide to a selected list of current periodicals foreign and domestic* (1932–38) and changed to *Ulrich's periodicals*

directory: A selected guide to current periodicals, inter-American edition (1938–43), then to *Ulrich's periodicals directory* (1943–63), and finally to *Ulrich's international periodicals directory* (1966–2000). This last title incorporated *Irregular serials and annuals* (1967–87) in 1988.

344 Willing's press guide. London: Willing Service, 1928– 0000-0213 072 Z6956.E5W5

Previously published in two volumes. Currently three volumes: U.K., Western Europe (except U.K.), and world (except U.K. and Western Europe). Lists approximately 65,000 titles, covering regional and national daily, weekly, and Sunday newspapers; Internet media and relevant websites; special-interest titles; journals and directories; and broadcast media. Entries include publishers' details, contact names, circulation data, subscription rates, advertising rates, summary of contents, readership/target audience data, etc. Multiple indexes.

345 WorldCat. http://www.oclc.org/worldcat/ default.htm. OCLC. Dublin, Ohio: OCLC Online Computer Library Center Z695.83

WorldCat is the largest bibliographic database in the world. It was started in 1971 as part of the Ohio Library College Center, now Online Computer Library Center (OCLC). The database continues to grow rapidly with millions of records from thousands of libraries worldwide. See http://www.oclc.org/ worldcat/statistics/default.htm for up-to-date statistics. All Library of Congress (6) bibliographic records are loaded in WorldCat, and since 1976, U.S. Government materials are also included.

Content includes books, Internet sites, visual, sound, and computer files, some articles, serials, archival materials, microforms, maps, scores, manuscripts, and various other materials. In addition, series title searches are a useful means of updating the printed *Titles in series* lists. The inclusion of LCSH, DDC, ISBN numbers, and URLs, where applicable, makes it an authoritative destination for checking bibliographic data. For items not found in WorldCat, the *NUC-pre 56* is still a viable option. WorldCat is also the means by which millions of interlibrary loans have been made. Export features are available for EndNote (http://www.endnote .com/), RefWorks (http://www.refworks.com/), and other bibliographic management software. WorldCat is available on the Internet as WorldCat.org, and OCLC has added a product called WorldCat Local (http://www.oclc.org/worldcat-local.en.html) to allow local libraries to use the worldcat.org interface to reflect their holdings.

Although the database has holdings from over 70,000 libraries worldwide, there is an obvious strength in the collections for the United States.

WorldCat is an essential reference source for all libraries.

346 **The writer's market.** Cincinnati, Ohio: F & W, 1922– 0084-2729
808.0250977178   PN161.W83
Directory of book and magazine editors (primarily United States) and guide to writing for publication. Entries are arranged in two primary sections: consumer magazines and trade, technical, and professional journals. Each of these groups is further subdivided by subject and then arranged alphabetically. Each entry includes addresses for queries, what the publication pays, descriptions of what the publication is looking for, and specifics on what to send. A list of literary agents is also included. Online access available for individual subscriptions at http://www.writersmarket.com/.

Indexes; Abstract Journals; Databases

347 **ABI/Inform global.** http://www.il.pro quest.com/products_pq/descriptions/abi_inform_global.shtml. ProQuest. Ann Arbor, Mich.: ProQuest. 1971-
HF54.7.A25
ABI/Inform, an early and important entrant in the bibliographic database marketplace, has expanded coverage and changed platforms over the years: access today of course is via the Web. Indexing and abstracting of business periodicals, some economics periodicals, as well as other periodicals related to business. Periodical coverage extends back as far as 1923 in some cases. Sold in several versions: extent of content varies with price.

ABI/Inform global covers more than 3,700 publications, with more than 2,600 available in full text. Includes 18,000 business-related dissertations, some 5,000 business case studies, the *Wall Street Journal* since 1984, and *EIU ViewsWire*.

ABI/Inform complete includes more than 6,000 periodicals, 30,000 business-related dissertations, the *Economist* and *Wall Street Journal*, 100,000 working papers from sources like OECD, and analysis of industries, markets and countries.

ABI/Inform research covers over 1,800 journals, with more than 1,200 available in full text.

ABI/Inform dateline offers some 280 periodicals, with more than 230 available in full text. These include journals, newspapers, trade magazines and regional sources.

A comparable and competing product is Business source elite (351).

348 **Academic search complete.** http://www.ebscohost.com/academic/academic-search-complete. EBSCO. Ipswich, Mass.: EBSCO
Residing on the EBSCOhost platform, this is one of the largest multidisciplinary indexing, abstracting, and full-text periodical resources available. The database includes more than 13,000 abstracted and indexed titles, many of them scholarly in nature. Of these, more than 9,000 are full text, and many include searchable cited references and PDF images of the original pages. Coverage varies by title but may go back to the initial issue. Titles are primarily in English. More limited coverage is available through Academic Search Premier and Academic Search Elite.

349 **America.** http://www.ebscohost.com/academic/america-history-and-life-with-full-text. Eric H. Boehm, American Bibliographical Center. Ipswich, Mass.: EBSCO Publishing. 1964–
016.917   Z1236; E171
The major bibliographic reference resource to the history of the United States and Canada from prehistory to the present. Covers about 1,800 journals published worldwide; 90% of coverage is English-language history journals, plus selected journals from major countries, and state and local history journals. All abstracts are in English. Articles, monographs, media, reviews, and dissertations and theses included. Advanced search provides thesauri for subject, author/editor, language, and journal name fields. Keywords, titles, publication dates, time periods, and entry numbers can also be searched. Publication began in 1964, with more than 530,000 entries in the database. Retrospective coverage from

1954 is complete, and more is being added on a project basis.

350 Business and company ASAP. http://www.gale.cengage.com/pdf/facts/bcprof.pdf. Gale Cengage (Firm). Farmington Hills, Mich.: Gale Cengage. 1999–
HF5030

Combines company data, a corporate directory, and business news with backfiles extending back to 1980. Searchable by keyword, subjects, or SIC codes. For more information, such as industry reports and profiles in greater depth, and information on a larger number of companies, consider Business insights: essentials.

351 Business source elite. http://www.ebscohost.com/academic/business-source-elite. EBSCO Publishing. Ipswich, Mass.: EBSCO. 1997- 1092-9754
338   HF5001

Comprehensive indexing of a wide range of business-related periodicals, reports and news sources. EBSCO publishes several versions of its business database product, with content that varies in extent and pricing. All include access to a *Regional business news* collection. All resources are delivered over the Web.

Business Source elite covers more than 1,100 business periodicals, including Harvard Business Review, and more than 10,000 Datamonitor company profiles. Over 1,000 journals are full text. Backfiles from 1985.

Business Source complete indexes some 2,000 peer-reviewed business journals and over 1,800 trade periodicals, many in full text, with some coverage from as early as 1886; over a million company profiles; market reports, industry reports and economic reports on individual countries; and 9,000 case studies.

Business Source premier covers some 2,200 periodicals, with some full text going back to 1965, and a smaller array of marketing, industry, company and country reports.

Business source corporate is a similar product marketed to companies, with full text from 2,700 periodicals, and numerous company, industry and country profiles and reports.

Successor to the print-format *Business periodicals index* (1959-) and online *Business abstracts* (1991-), published until 2011 by the H. W. Wilson Company.

Incorporates older content formerly found in *Business periodicals index retrospective* (1913-1982).

A similar and competing product is ABI/Inform global (347).

352 C19, the nineteenth century index. http://c19index.chadwyck.co.uk. Chadwyck-Healey Ltd. Ann Arbor, Mich.: ProQuest Information and Learning Co. 2005-

Indexes 15.6 million articles published in more than 2,500 journals. Searchable by keyword, title keyword, author, date, periodical title, and periodical subject. Browsing is available for *Poole's index to periodical literature* (385) and the *Wellesley index to Victorian periodicals, 1824–1900*. Composed of the above mentioned two indexes, plus the following: *American periodical series* (381), *British periodicals*, and *Periodicals index online* (364). Links to JSTOR (360).

In addition to indexing periodicals, the database also includes books, archives, newspapers, and "official publications" through the following indexes: *Nineteenth century short title catalogue*, *Nineteenth century microfiche project*, *House of Commons parliamentary papers*, *ArchivesUSA*, and *Palmer's index to the Times*.

353 ERIC. http://www.eric.ed.gov/. U.S. Department of Education. Washington: U.S. Department of Education

National education database sponsored by the U.S. Department of Education. Presently the largest education database in the world, ERIC contains over one million citations covering research documents, journal articles, books, technical reports, program descriptions and evaluations, and curricular materials in the field of education. Also includes abstracts, citations, and selective full-text. Earlier print versions were available as *Current index to journals in education* and *Resources in education*. Electronic versions are available through several different vendors, as well as freely available through the government website. The *Thesaurus of ERIC descriptors* is embedded in each database.

354 FRANCIS. http://www.inist.fr/?Francis-74&lang=en. Institut de l'Information Scientifique et Technique du Centre National de la Recherche Scientifique (INIST-CNRS). Vandoeuvre-les-Nancy,

France: Institut de l'Information Scientifique et Technique of the Centre National de la Recherche Scientifique (INIST-CNRS)

Indexing multilingual and multidisciplinary sources from 1984 forward. Coverage is approximately two-thirds humanities and one-third social sciences. In addition to 4,300 periodicals, the database indexes books and book chapters, conference papers, French dissertations, exhibition catalogs, legislation, teaching materials, and reports. More than 80% of citations include an abstract. Published in print as *Francis bulletin signalétique: 527, Histoire et sciences des religions*, but available online from Ovid, ProQuest, and EBSCO.

355 Gale directory of databases. Gale
Research. Detroit: Gale Research,
1993– 1066-8934
025.040296   QA76.9.D32G36
Contents: v.1, pt.1-3, Online databases; v.2, pt.1-3, Portable databases. Formed by the merger of *Computer-readable data bases*; *Directory of online databases*; and *Directory of portable databases*. Vol. 1 consists of an alphabetical list of online databases, with separate directories of producers and online services. Database entries include database name; producer with address and telephone number; contact person or department; type of database (e.g., full text, numeric); description of content; subject coverage; frequency of updating; options for online access. Indexes: geographic; subject; master (i.e., current and former names of databases, producers, and services). Vol. 2 consists of separate alphabetical directories by format (CD-ROM, DVD, diskette, magnetic tape, handheld, and batch access database products); content and organization are similar to v. 1. Also available online through Gale's Ready Reference Shelf, the Gale Directory Library, and Proquest's Dialog database catalog.

356 Historical abstracts. http://www.ebsco
host.com/academic/historical-abstracts
-with-full-text. Eric H. Boehm, American
Bibliographical Center. Ipswich, Mass.:
EBSCO Publishing. 1955–
016.90982   D299.H512
Formed by the merger of (1971-2003): *Historical abstracts: Part A: Modern history abstracts, 1450-1914*

(0363-2717); (1971-2003): *Historical abstracts: Part B: Twentieth century abstracts, 1914 to the present* (0363-2725); both of which superseded in part (1955-1971): *Historical abstracts* (0018-2435).

Provides coverage of topics in world history (excluding the United States and Canada) from 1450 CE to present. Indexes approx. 2,600 academic historical journals in over 40 languages back to 1955. All abstracts in English, regardless of language of publication. Also indexes and abstracts articles from magazines, books, dissertations, and collections. Can search by keyword, author, journal/article title, subject, publication date, publication type, and time period.

Topics in American and Canadian history are indexed in companion database America: History and Life (349).

357 IBZ online. http://www.degruyter.com/
view/db/ibz. Berlin: De Gruyter
                                                  AI3
International index of scholarly humanities and social science articles published in more than 40 countries and more than 40 languages. Abstracts are included for much of the database. In addition to general bibliographic citations, entries include subject headings and references in German and English. The database currently indexes more than 6,000 periodicals, with retrospective coverage of more than 11,500 titles. German and English interfaces available. Covers 1983 forward.

For retrospective indexing, the print *Internationale Bibliographie der Zeitschriftenliteratur aus allen Gebieten des Wissens* covers 1965–99. This title is the merger of the earlier *Bibliographie der fremdsprachingen Zeitschriftenliteratur* (1911–64) and *Bibliographie der deutschen Zeitschriften-literatur* (1896–1964).

**358 International index to black
periodicals.** http://iibp.chadwyck.
com. Alexandria, Va.: Chadwyck-Healey.
1528-3143
305   Z6944.N39.I68
Indexes more than 150 scholarly and popular multidisciplinary journals from the United States, the Caribbean, and Africa. Abstracts are available from 1998 forward. More than 100 core journals are available in full text. Retrospective indexing dates to 1900. Access is on the Chadwyck-Healy interface through ProQuest.

359   **Journal Citation Reports.** http://
thomsonreuters.com/journal-citation
-reports/. Thomson Reuters, Institute
for Scientific Information. Philadelphia:
Thomson Reuters. 1994–

Analyzes the bibliometric characteristics of the journals indexed in the Web of Science (368). Measures include total citations in a year to a particular journal, its impact and immediacy indexes, total articles published, and the half-life for citations. This resource is used frequently to locate "high-impact" journals for researchers to publish in or consult regularly, and is often used in promotion determination for academic scientists. Journals are grouped according to their subject area, so comparisons can easily be made within a discipline. JCR is available in *Science* and *Social sciences* editions. Web formats, titled *JCR Web*, date back to 1994; print, CD-ROM, and microfiche formats to as late as 1975.

360   **JSTOR.** http://www.jstor.org. JSTOR.
New York: JSTOR. [1995?]–

Z6944.S3

JSTOR began as a multidisciplinary, full-text, electronic journal archive focusing on the social sciences, humanities, and general science. Several different journal collections are available, with approximately 120 titles in each: multiple arts and sciences modules; biological sciences; four business modules; ecology and botany; health and general sciences; language and literature; mathematics and statistics; Jewish studies; Ireland; and music. Subject collections may share overlap with the general arts and sciences modules and subscription profiles vary by library. Date coverage often does not include current issues. While coverage does begin with v. 1, no. 1, there is generally a moving wall of between one to five years between the last issue in the database and the most recently published volume.

JSTOR has also moved into providing access to current journals, scholarly monographs, and primary sources. The *Current Scholarship Program* serves as the primary access platform for over 40 scholarly journal publishers, linking current content to the existing JSTOR archive. *Books at JSTOR* makes available more than 20,000 ebooks from academic presses through individual purchase, demand driven acquisition, or the purchase of subject collections.

All content is provided as high-resolution scans.

361   **MLA international bibliography of
books and articles on the modern
languages and literatures.** http://www
.mla.org/bib_electronic. Modern Language
Association of America. New York:
Modern Language Association of America.
1925- 0024-8215

Z7006

Indexes published criticism and research from all over the world in any language with no restrictions as to place of origin, nor of publication, nor the original language of the works cited, nor as to the physical type or medium of works. Works on pedagogy of language, literature, and rhetoric and composition are included from 1998 onward. Also covers film, television, theater, linguistics, history of the book and folklore. For references to Greek and Latin literature see L'Annee philologique.

The *MLA bibliography* does not index book reviews. Dissertation abstracts are included if published in *ProQuest dissertations and theses (PQDT)* (163).

Distributed as an electronic database, containing all current entries as well as those published in print volumes from 1926 to 2008, through Gale, EBSCO and ProQuest.

Selections are made from various book sources and from a basic master list of several hundred periodicals in modern languages and literatures. For detailed information about the periodicals indexed in the *Bibliography* consult the *MLA directory of periodicals* (342). By 1963, listed books and articles in English, French, German, Spanish, Italian, Portuguese, Rumanian, the Scandinavian and Netherlandic languages, Celtic, and a selection of East European languages. Beginning with the issue covering publications of 1969, coverage was further extended.

362   **PAIS international.** http://www.proquest
.com/en-US/catalogs/databases/detail/pais
-set-c.shtml. ProQuest (Firm). Ann Arbor,
Mich.: ProQuest. 1915–

Z7163

Formerly known as Public Affairs Information Service. Provides indexing and abstracts for content from some 1,600 periodicals, as well as from books, statistical yearbooks, directories, conference proceedings, pamphlets, reports and government publications. Source publications may be in languages besides English, especially French, German, Italian, Portuguese or Spanish. Includes economic and social conditions, education, energy and resources, politics and government, health care policy, human rights, and international relations. Basic coverage is from 1972 to present; *PAIS archive* also is available, with coverage back to 1915. Also available as PAIS international in print.

363   Periodicals Archive Online (PAO).
http://www.proquest.com/en-US/catalogs/databases/detail/periodicals_archive.shtml. ProQuest Information and Learning Company. Ann Arbor, Mich.: Proquest Information and Learning Company

Growing full-text and full-image archive of more than 700 international scholarly journals, primarily in the social sciences and humanities. More than 60 non-English-language publications are included. Multi-disciplinary in scope, coverage goes back 200 years. Articles are full-text searchable, and periodical titles are browsable by issue. Several collections are available (multiple "general" collections as well as several subject collections), so access to specific content will depend on the modules subscribed by an institution. Can be cross-searched with Periodicals Index Online (364) when both modules are subscribed. This database was formerly known as PCI Full Text.

364   Periodicals index online. http://www.proquest.com/en-US/catalogs/databases/detail/periodicals_index.shtml. ProQuest Information and Learning Company. Ann Arbor, Mich.: ProQuest Information and Learning Company

300.05001.305   AI3

Index to more than 6,000 popular and scholarly social science and humanities periodicals going back more than 300 years and including more than 40 languages. Journals are indexed from the first issue forward to 1995. Also known as PIO, this database is cross-searchable with Periodicals Archive Online (363), and when both databases are subscribed, full text is linked where available. The database also links out to JSTOR (360). The database was formerly called *Periodicals Contents Index* (PCI) and now resides on the Chadwyck Healy interface via ProQuest.

365   PsycINFO. http://www.apa.org/psycinfo/. American Psychological Association. Washington: American Psychological Association. 1989- 0033-2887
150.5   BF1

The most comprehensive index to the professional and peer-reviewed literature of psychology, indexing over three million articles published in more than 2,500 journals, as well as numerous books, book chapters, and dissertations. Provides descriptive, non-evaluative abstracts, and assigns controlled vocabulary subject headings for each entry. Those headings follow the system in APA's *Thesaurus of psychological index terms*. Formerly published in print as *Psychological abstracts* (ceased with 2006). Marketed at one time as PsycLit. Coverage has varied widely over the history of this title, with extensive coverage of publications since the 1880s and selected earlier citations. Coverage of books and dissertations is limited prior to the 1990s: current book publication entries are limited to works in English. Most indexed journal content is in English, and APA guidelines call for English-language abstracts for foreign-language materials. The database replaces associated indexes such as *Cumulative author index to Psychological abstracts* (1959/63–1981/83) and *Author index to Psychological index, 1894–1935, and Psychological abstracts, 1927–1958*.

366   PubMed. http://www.ncbi.nlm.nih.gov/pubmed. U.S. National Center for Biotechnology Information, National Library of Medicine, National Institutes of Health. Bethesda, Md.: U.S. National Center for Biotechnology Information. 1996–

PubMed®, developed and maintained by the National Center for Biotechnology Information (NCBI) at the National Library of Medicine® (NLM). Provides a search interface for more than 20 million bibliographic citations and abstracts in the fields of medicine, nursing, dentistry, veterinary medicine, health care systems, and preclinical sciences. It provides access to articles indexed for MEDLINE® and for selected life sciences journals. PubMed subsets found under the "Limits" tab are: MEDLINE and PubMed central®, several journal groups (i.e., core clinical journals, dental journals, and nursing journals), and topical subsets (AIDS, bioethics, cancer, complementary medicine, dietary supplements, history of medicine, space life sciences, systematic reviews, toxicology, and veterinary science). "Link-out" provides access to full-text articles.

For detailed information see the PubMed fact sheet at http://www.nlm.nih.gov/pubs/factsheets/pubmed.html and also MEDLINE®/PubMed®

resources guide (http://www.nlm.nih.gov/bsd/pm resources.html) which provides detailed information about MEDLINE data and searching PubMed.

Information regarding the mobile version of this resource is part of NLM's Gallery of mobile apps and sites.

367 Scopus. http://www.scopus.com/. Elsevier Science Publishers. s.l.: Elsevier B. V.

Scopus provides powerful, user-friendly searching of the STM journal literature (21,000 titles), as well as websites, patents (25 million), conference proceedings, and book series. Includes tools to analyze, visualize, and compare research productivity based on publication output, such as *Citation Overview/Tracker*, *Author Identifier*, *Author Evaluator*, and *Journal Analyzer*. Scopus exceeds the Web of Science (368) in its breadth of coverage of the current journal literature but has inconsistent citation searching before 1996. See more details at http://www.elsevier.com/online-tools/scopus.

368 Web of science. http://wokinfo.com/products_tools/multidisciplinary/webofscience/. Thomson Reuters. Philadelphia: Thomson Reuters. 2001-

Z7401

The Web of Science (WoS) database is the platform for Thomson Reuter's suite of databases. The *Web of Science Core Collection Citation Indexes* include the Science Citation Index, the Social Sciences Citation Index, the Arts and Humanities Citation Index and Book Citation Index, which are available separately. Other databases are available on the platform, such as chemical indexes, Journal Citation Reports (359), Essential Science Indicators, and nonproprietary databases such as Medline and CAB Abstracts. In addition to standard indexing, "Cited Reference Search" discovers all the articles in the database that have cited a particular article. "Related Records" retrieves records that have cited a source common to the chosen record. The "Author Search" function is a work in progress, attempting to cluster results to provide author name disambiguation. Offers strong analytical tools to assess a results set: "Analyze Results" to rank records by selected fields, and the "Create Citation Report" function includes a calculation of the h-index impact measurement of records in the set. Includes access to EndNote Basic (15) bibliographic management software and to ResearcherID

to manage author name disambiguation. Permits cross searching of all subscribed databases. One of the greatest strengths and weaknesses of the WoS is that coverage is largely restricted to core and high-impact journals. Coverage years vary by database. The Web of Science superceded the Web of Knowledge platform name in January 2014.

Latin America and the Caribbean (by region)
Indexes; Abstract Journals; Databases

369 ClasePeriodica. http://www.oclc.org/support/documentation/firstsearch/databases/dbdetails/details/ClasePeriodica.htm. OCLC. México: Departamento de Bibliografia Latinoamericana de la Direccion General de Bibliotecas de la Universidad Nacional Autónoma de México

Z7163

Indexing from more than 2,700 periodicals published in Latin America and the Caribbean in Spanish, Portuguese, French, and English. CLASE (Citas Latinoamericanas en Ciencias Sociales y Humanidades) covers the social sciences and humanities, while PERIODICA covers science and technology. Coverage begins with 1975. The databases are available for individual searching through the Universidad Nacional Autónoma de México Dirección General de Bibliotecas at http://dgb.unam.mx/.

370 HAPI online. http://hapi.gseis.ucla.edu. UCLA Latin American Center. Los Angeles: UCLA Latin American Center. 1997-

973.046805 F1408

The online version of *HAPI: Hispanic American periodicals index*. As of 2013, HAPI covers more than 350 peer reviewed journals with content on Latin America, the Caribbean, Brazil, and U.S. Latinos. Historically, more than 600 periodicals have been indexed. Includes citations to articles, book reviews (through 2001), documents, and original literary works. Languages covered are English, Spanish, Portuguese, French, German, and Italian. Initially, indexing began with 1975, but a retrospective project bridged the gap with the cessation of *Index to Latin American periodical literature, 1929–1960*. The database has a thesaurus and provides links to some full text.

North America

Bibliographies; Union Lists; Directories

371 MediaFinder. http://www.mediafinder
.com. Oxbridge Communications.
New York: Oxbridge Communications
Directory of U.S. and Canadian periodicals including magazines, journals, newspapers, newsletters, and catalogs. Subscribers have access to "70,000 titles from major city dailies to fanzines, in 263 subject areas."—*About page* Searchable by keyword and subject but also by advertisement rates, publication type, print specification, circulation, subscription price, and whether or not the publisher rents the list. Browsable by subject category. Entries include a brief editorial description; names and contact information of key staff; and data about circulation, advertising, and the physical attributes of the publication itself (number of pages, type of binding, etc.). Facilitates data export. Online version of the *Standard periodical directory* (372).

372 The standard periodical directory.
Oxbridge Communications. New
York: Oxbridge Communications,
1965– 0085-6630
016.051   Z6951.S78
Single-volume directory of U.S. and Canadian periodicals including more than 63,000 magazines, journals, newsletters, directories, and newspapers. Published annually. Arranged alphabetically by title within subject groupings. Entries include contact information, brief description of publication, circulation information, start date, and online availability. Also available online as MediaFinder (48).

Indexes; Abstract Journals; Databases

373 Left index. http://www.ebscohost.com/
academic/the-left-index. Ipswich, Mass.:
EBSCO Pub.
016.33543   HX1

Indexing and abstracting for both popular and academic publications of the left. Includes book reviews, some full-text articles, and Web sites. Much of the information, especially from news sources, cannot be found in other indexes.

This is the online version of Left Index, which ceased in 1999. The electronic version, available through EBSCOhost currently includes over 500 titles with coverage extending back to the inception of the print in 1982.

"*Left Index* is a most impressive database, both in content and searchability." (*Choice*, May 2003). A Choice Outstanding Title.

374 MasterFILE premier. http://www.ebsco
host.com/public/masterfile-premier.
EBSCO Publishing. Ipswich, Mass.:
EBSCO Pub. 2002-
Designed for public libraries, this Masterfile includes almost 1700 full text periodicals of general interest as well as photos, maps, flags, primary source documents, and reference books. Some key titles are available with backfile content to 1975.

375 ProQuest central. http://www.proquest
.com/en-US/catalogs/databases/detail/
proquestcentral.shtml. ProQuest (Firm).
Ann Arbor, Mich.: ProQuest. 2008-
Provides access to more than 25 of ProQuest's subject area databases, giving broad, multidisciplinary indexing, abstracting, and full text coverage. Dates are from 1905 to present with over 19,000 total sources included. Primarily indexing periodicals, the database also includes market and industry reports, dissertations, news sources, working papers, and business profiles. Graphs, charts, images, and tables are also searchable.

376 Proquest Research Library. http://www
.proquest.com/en-US/catalogs/databases/
detail/pq_research_library.shtml. ProQuest
(Firm). Ann Arbor, Mich.: ProQuest
Information and Learning Company.
1998-
General periodical coverage for core academic subjects from 1971 forward. ProQuest Research Library indexes over 5,000 titles with more than 3,500 in full text. This is a smaller subset of the content available in the ProQuest Central (375) database.

United States

BIBLIOGRAPHIES; UNION LISTS; DIRECTORIES

377 Gale directory of publications and broadcast media. Gale Research Inc., Gale Group. Detroit: Gale Research Inc., 1990–. maps. 1048-7972

302.2302573   Z6951.A97; PN4867

Supersedes and assumes the edition numbering of (1) Ayer directory of publications (title varies: 1930–69, *N. W. Ayer and Son's directory of newspapers and periodicals*; 1970–71, *Ayer directory: Newspapers, magazines . . .* ; absorbed *Rowell's American newspaper directory* in 1910); (2)*The IMS . . . Ayer directory of publications* (1986) (called *The IMS directory of publications*). The earlier titles continue to be valuable for verification and research.

Covers United States and Canada. Arranged alphabetically by state (for Canada, by province), then by city. For print media, information includes publisher, address and telephone, beginning date, description, advertising rates, circulation, online availability, etc.; for broadcast media, call letters and frequency, address, format, advertising rates, etc. Special features include detailed subject index to print media, including type of publication (college, black, women, trade, etc.); subject index to radio station format; list of features editors of daily newspapers with at least 50,000 circulation, arranged alphabetically by state, then by city. Name and keyword index. Update issued midway between editions.

Also available electronically as a searchable subscription database via the *Gale directory library*. Entries in the electronic version are categorized as either an organization, a publication, or a database, with the data in the entries varying depending on the entry type. Includes 18,000 broadcast media organizations, 12,000 newsletters, and 12,500 newspaper entries. Broadcast media organizations are defined as television stations, radio stations, or cable television companies.

378 The literary press and magazine directory. Council of Literary Magazines and Presses. Brooklyn, N.Y.: Soft Skull Press, 1981–

808.81   Z6513

Directory providing editor, address, description, beginning publication date, price, and advertising rate for U.S. literary magazines. Includes little magazines. Previously published as *CLMP directory of literary magazines and presses* (2003–5), *Directory of literary magazines* (1984–2001), *CCLM literary magazine directory* (1983), *CCLM catalog of literary magazines* (through 1982), and *Catalog of literary magazines* (started in 1975).

Also available online at http://www.clmp.org/directory/.

INDEXES; ABSTRACT JOURNALS; DATABASES

379 Academic OneFile. http://www.gale .com/AcademicOneFile/. Gale Cengage Learning. Farmington Hills, Mich.: Gale

Multidisciplinary periodical database covering over 14,000 journals in multiple languages, many of them peer-reviewed. Over 6,000 journals are provided in full text. Content is provided as both HTML and PDF. The database integrates citation information from the Web of Science (368) database and information on impact factors from Journal Citation Reports (359) for those who subscribe to both products.

380 AltPressIndex. http://www.ebscohost .com/government/alternative-press-index. Alternative Press Centre. Baltimore: Alternative Press Centre

Indexing from 1969 forward to more than 300 alternative (liberal or radical) periodicals. Born out of the New Left of the 1960s, the focus is on writings examining the "theories and practices of radical social change." Indexed titles are interdisciplinary and include both scholarly and popular publications. Online access to the *Alternative Press Index* is available through the EBSCO platform.

381 American periodicals series online, 1740–1900. http://www.proquest.com/ products_pq/descriptions/aps.shtml. ProQuest Information and Learning Company. Ann Arbor, Mich.: ProQuest Information and Learning Company

AP2

Based on the original University of Michigan microfilm project, the database includes digitized images of more than 1,100 American magazines and journals beginning with 1741. Article citations and full text are searchable. Periodical titles are browseable, and records include annotated bibliographic descriptions for each title.

Many libraries might have access only to the original microfilm version with indexing in print. The print indexes are *Index to American periodicals of the 1700's: Keyed to University Microfilms APS I* and *Index to American periodicals of the 1800's: Keyed to University Microfilms APS II*; Jean Hoornstra's index to the microfilm also offers notes on the content and character of periodicals included in the collection and might be of use even for those accessing the text electronically.

382 **Government periodicals index.** http://cisupa.proquest.com/ws_display.asp?filter={CA69C782-1314-43D4-8ECC-4ECFA441A0A4}. LexisNexis. Ann Arbor, Mich.: ProQuest

Current coverage for more than 160 titles. Search by title, author, GPO item number, issuing agency, or SuDoc number. Records include basic bibliographic information, subject descriptors, and details about the publication (address, subscription cost, etc.). The subscription database links to the full text hosted at agency websites. Retrospective coverage extends to 1988.

383 **19th century masterfile.** http://history.paratext.com/. Paratext. Sterling, Va.: Paratext. 2002–

AI3

Provides access to bibliographic citations from Anglo-American literature published prior to 1930 through more than 70 contemporary reference sources such as *Poole's index to periodical literature* (385) and Jones and Chipman's Index to legal periodical literature (1786–1922). Several individual titles are also indexed such as *Harper's Weekly*, *Scientific American*, and the *North American Review Index*. The database also indexes books, newspapers and government documents from both the United Kingdom and the United States. The database also links out to primary sources such as ARTstor, JSTOR (360), HathiTrust, the American State Papers, Making of America, and Accessible Archives historical papers.

384 **Omnifile full text mega (H. W. Wilson).** http://www.ebscohost.com/academic/omnifile-full-text-mega. EBSCO Publishing. Ipswich, Mass.: EBSCO Publishing

Residing on the EBSCO platform, this aggregating database includes all indexing, abstracting, and full text from the following H. W. Wilson databases: Education Full Text, General Science Full Text, Humanities Full Text, Readers' Guide Full Text (387), Social Sciences Full Text, Wilson Business Full Text. Selected indexing and full text from the following databases is also included: Applied Science and Technology Full Text, Art Full Text, Biological and Agricultural Index Plus, Index to Legal Periodicals Full Text, Library Literature and Information Science Full Text. Coverage incorporates more than 5,000 journals going back to 1982 with full text coverage of more than 3,100 of these titles.

A more limited version of this database is available in Omnifile Select, which does not include indexing and abstracting of titles not available in full text.

385 **Poole's index to periodical literature. Rev. ed.** William Frederick Poole, William Isaac Fletcher, American Library Association, Library Association of the United Kingdom. Boston; New York: Houghton Mifflin, 1893. 1 v. in 2

AI3.P7

Indexes about 590,000 articles in 12,241 volumes of 479 American and English periodicals. The print version was published in six volumes between 1882 and 1908, covering the years 1802–81. Includes subject index only and provides no access articles by author. When the print version is used, *Poole's index date and volume key* is useful for determining which periodicals are indexed in specific volumes of Poole's. Available online through both C19 (352) (searchable by keyword, author, subject, and periodical title) and Nineteenth Century Masterfile (383) (keyword searchable).

386 **Project Muse.** http://muse.jhu.edu/journals. Johns Hopkins University Press. Baltimore: Johns Hopkins University Press. [1995]–

AC1100

Current and recent access to the full text of more than 500 scholarly humanities, arts, and social science journals. Through the advanced search it is possible to search individual titles, subject groups, or the entire database. Date coverage varies by title but is not intended to go back to v. 1. A growing list of participating publishers (currently at more than 120) is available at http://muse.jhu.edu/about/publishers. html. The entire complement of titles is available as the Premium Collection, and more limited subcollections are also available: Standard, Basic Research, Basic College, Humanities, and Social Sciences.

387 **Readers' guide full text, mega edition.**
http://www.ebscohost.com/academic/
readers-guide-full-text-mega-edition.
EBSCO Publishing. Ipswich, Mass.:
EBSCO Publishing
AI 3

Covers general-interest periodicals. This online version provides the full text of 250 titles as far back as 1994 and indexing for more than 450 periodicals as far back as 1983. *Readers' Guide Retrospective* (388) is an add-on providing access to the earlier print indexing from 1890 to 1982.

Published until 2011 by the H. W. Wilson Company. *Readers' Guide* began in 1901 as a print index for small libraries, covering at first only 15 of the more popular periodicals, and gradually extending its coverage. The list of periodicals indexed varies from volume to volume. Retrospective indexing for the last decade of the 19th century was later completed for *Nineteenth century readers' guide to periodical literature, 1890–1899.*

Articles are primarily indexed by subject heading, however author entries are provided for each article and works of fiction and poetry are also indexed by title. Inclusion of reviews varies by year. Maps, portraits, and illustrations are also indexed, whether or not accompanied by text.

Many libraries still hold the print version of this standard title, *The readers' guide to periodical literature*, and rely on their print backfiles for retrospective access. A more limited version of this database is available as Readers' Guide Full Text Select, http://www.ebscohost.com/academic/readers-guide-full-text-select.

388 **Readers' guide retrospective.** http://www.ebscohost.com/academic/readers-guide-retrospective. EBSCO Publishing, H. W. Wilson Company. 1997-

Covers the electronic backfile of *Readers' Guide to Periodical Literature* (387) corresponding to the print version. Provided through the EBSCO interface, indexing extends from 1890 to 1982 for more than 550 popular titles.

13 | *The Web as Reference Tool*

Lili Luo

389 Internet Archive. https://archive.org/.
   San Francisco: Internet Archive. 1996-
Non-profit digital library of Internet sites and other cultural artifacts in digital form. Officially designated as a library by the State of California in 2007. Provides free access to researchers, historians, scholars, the print disabled, and the general public. Also an activist organization, advocating for a free and open Internet.

Groups digital assets into five data clusters: Web, audio, video, live music, and texts. Users can upload and download digital material to each data cluster, but the majority of the material is archived automatically by its web crawlers. Includes a feature called the The Wayback Machine, which is a service that allows people to visit archived versions of Web sites. Visitors to the Wayback Machine can type in a URL, select a date range, and then begin surfing on an archived version of the Web.

Includes discussion forums on different subjects, where users can ask questions and have conversations about a certain topic. Reviews and rating system of digital assets. As of October 2012, its collection topped 10 petabytes.

Search Engines

390 Google Books. http://books.google.com/.
   Google
Google search service that searches the books and magazines, which Google has digitized and stored in its databases. Results can be viewed to different degrees depending on copyright terms. If a book is in the public domain, users may view it in full. Otherwise, users can only have restricted access to the book, viewing a limited number of pages or merely snippets (two to three lines of text).

Books and magazines can be browsed by subject. Displays related book lists, and associated common terms and phrases. Provides a user rating and reviews tool. Includes a personal library for each user to add book favorites. Includes information on where to find books, both in libraries and for purchase.

391 Google scholar. http://scholar.google
   .com. Sergey Brin, Larry Page, Google.
   Mountain View, Calif.: Google
Google Scholar is a Google search service that allows users to search for scholarly literature. The search engine crawls sources from academic publishers, professional societies, preprint repositories, universities, and other scholarly organizations to locate scholarly information such as peer-reviewed papers, abstracts, and theses. Search results are ranked by relevancy, which is determined by the weight of the full text of each article, the author, the publication that publishes the articles, and how often the article has been cited in other research literature. Google Scholar inherits the simple search interface and advanced search options of the classic Google search engine. It can also be connected with library subscription databases, enabling users

to access the full text of articles retrieved using Google Scholar.

Social Computing and Community-Based Sources

392 ipl2: information you can trust. http://www.ipl.org/. The iSchool at Drexel
Launched in January 2010, merging the collections of freely available Internet resources from the Internet Public Library (IPL) and the Librarians' Internet Index (LII). Currently hosted by Drexel University's

College of Information Science & Technology, and a consortium of colleges and universities with programs in library and information science are involved in designing, building, creating and maintaining its collections and services.

Grouped into five sections: resources by subject, newspapers and magazines, special collections, for kids and for teens. Allows for keyword searches or browsing the directory under each section. Provides a reference service titled "Ask an ipl2 Librarian", where users can submit their questions and receive reference help. Provided by students in library and information science degree programs and volunteer information professionals.

Library and
Information Sciences

Introduction:
Library and Information
Science Sources

Unique within the *Guide to Reference*, the Library and Information Science (LIS) category not only presents core reference tools but also features a broad sampling of books and websites that support specialized areas of professional practice. This dual approach follows a century-old model. Selected writings about reference librarianship were cited in the first edition of the *Guide* in 1902, and in subsequent editions books about other aspects of the profession were added. When Constance Winchell prepared the 7th edition in 1951, the library science category grew significantly. With the transition to the online database, the range of LIS topics expanded even further, reflecting the porous intellectual boundaries of the discipline and the emergence of new directions in the field.

General Works

The sources arranged in the sections under General Works are typical of the reference genres covered throughout the *Guide*—bibliographies, journal indexes, encyclopedias, dictionaries, directories, etc. Comparing these listings to earlier editions of the *Guide* reveals clearly how much the tools of librarianship have changed since the advent of the Web. For example, printed directories of libraries are increasingly rare, since up-to-date information on individual institutions can be found easily via search engines. The same dynamic is no doubt responsible for the absence of current biographical dictionaries of living librarians. Single-topic bibliographies are also a dying species, as online indexes and abstracts make it possible to conduct searches and customize bibliographies on nearly any subject. In these regards, LIS echoes trends in other disciplines. Still, one experiences a twinge of nostalgia upon realizing that this edition of the *Guide* is the first to omit a published set of rules for filing catalog cards.

Just as the advent of online information has diminished the need for certain types of sources, so has it elevated the usefulness of other types. For example, the websites of professional associations are typically rich with information, not just about an organization's internal doings but also about the issues on which it focuses. Association websites offer freely available resource lists, directories, job postings, checklists, and toolkits of many kinds. Along with other organizations and agencies, LIS-related professional associations promulgate standards and guidelines that support progress in the field. Major providers of standards are highlighted in a separate section under General Works, while additional specialized standards are cited in the appropriate sections under Professional Practice.

It has never been easier to stay abreast of new directions in LIS than it is today, thanks to the near-total migration of periodical publishing to the electronic environment, and to the use of online technologies to communicate in new, more immediate ways. Upon the occasion of preparing this printed volume, two new sections were added to the LIS General Works category, Periodicals and Blogs. Both present a very small and selective sample of the large number of resources available for current news, opinion, and scholarly research.

Professional Practice

The Professional Practice section is organized by specialization. In addition to recognizable reference genres like topical bibliographies and handbooks, it includes books and websites that contain useful checklists and reference-style appendixes. Content that is formatted for easy browsing and consultation is favored. Workbooks are excluded; textbooks are included only when they represent the best, most up-to-date overview of a subject. As a general rule, anthologies of reprinted articles and conference proceedings are excluded. However, a few anthologies of case studies (the oft-maligned "how we done it good" genre) and the occasional scholarly monograph do appear when they constitute the best current treatment of a topic.

Scattered throughout the Professional Practice sections are book series that cover multiple aspects of library work. These include the *How-To-Do-It Manuals* from ALA-Neal-Schuman, the *Crash Course* series from Libraries Unlimited, and the *Fundamentals* series from ALA Editions. Although too basic to be of use to seasoned professionals, these works provide students, new librarians, and paraprofessionals with introductions to key specialties and technical areas within the LIS field.

Some repetition of entries occurs across sections, but it has intentionally been kept to a minimum. For example, the section titled Digitization, Digital Libraries, and Information Technologies features resources of particular use to library IT staff and the developers of virtual libraries. Yet, because every specialization within the LIS profession has been transformed by technology, every section includes works about technology. For instance, the Cataloging and Classification section has a sub-section on metadata, and works about online searching are located in the Reference and Information Retrieval section. Similarly, while the Type of Library section highlights general materials about the management of academic, public, and specialized libraries, works in other sections sometimes slant toward a specific library type. Sources on information literacy, for example, are often narrowly addressed to either academic or K–12 librarians.

The Professional Practice category encompasses both traditional activities, such as reference and cataloging, and newer emphases, such as assessment, marketing, and services to diverse users. Because reference librarians are the core audience for the *Guide*, the Reference section is more extensive than other sections.

Acknowledgements

With rare exceptions, the entries in this section were selected and annotated by me alone, and I bear sole responsibility for any errors in fact or judgment. Nonetheless, LIS is an interdisciplinary field, and the *Guide* is a collaborative endeavor. In a few instances, I re-used entries prepared by the expert contributors to other sections; I am grateful to them. Jo Bell Whitlatch helpfully suggested several items for my consideration, and she provided a second opinion when I was undecided about the appropriateness of a particular source. *Guide* editor-in-chief Denise Beaubien Bennett likewise offered encouragement and excellent advice, as well as last-minute editorial acumen. Because the *Guide* (to borrow Ranganathan's famous dictum about libraries) is a growing organism, I welcome suggestions of additional sources to include in the online database.

Susan E. Searing
Guide to Reference
Contributing Editor for Library and Information Science

14 General Works

Bibliography

Editor's Guide: This section includes classic bibliographies in library science, arguably of interest only to readers seeking a comprehensive view of the field over time or at a particular point in its history. Also described here are more recent bibliographies on an assortment of specialized topics. As in most disciplines, fewer and fewer specialized bibliographies are being published in LIS, due to the ease of conducting tailored subject searches in online databases and digital repositories. See Library and Information Science > General Works > Indexes; Abstract Journals; Databases for the tools to create your own bibliography.

393 **American music librarianship: A research and information guide.** Carol June Bradley. New York: Routledge, 2005. xv, 382 p. ISBN 0415972914
016.02678   ML111.B773
Comprehensive bibliography of writings from the 1890s to 2000, arranged by broad topic: collection development and management; cataloguing and classification; administration; general studies; librarians; libraries; education for librarianship; professional organizations. Very brief annotations. Indexes: author; subject/name. Subsections titled "Bibliography," "Discography," and "Periodical indexes and related literature" have their own indexes.

394 **A bibliography of librarianship.** Margaret Burton, Marion E. Vosburgh, Library Association. London: The Library Association, 1934. 3 p., l., 176 p.
Z666.B96
Repr.: N.Y.: B. Franklin, [1970]. Annotated bibliography of the early literature of librarianship. Arranged by subject: library history, special libraries, libraries for children, library practice, the library profession, law, architecture, cooperation, bibliography, the book, paleography and archives, and general bibliographies of librarianship. Although selective, an invaluable source of information about library literature before 1934. Author and subject index.

395 **Bibliography of library economy: A classified index to the professional periodical literature in the English language relating to library economy, printing, methods of publishing, copyright, bibliography, etc., from 1876 to 1920.** H. G. T. Cannons. Chicago: American Library Association, 1927. 680 p.
016.02   Z666.C21
Repr. of 2nd (1927) ed.: N.Y.: B. Franklin, 1970.
   "The present volume is the result of the first systematic attempt to index the whole range of literature in the English language published in the Library periodical press. . . ."—*Pref.*

Includes citations to articles published in 65 professional periodicals and some articles from general periodicals. Classified index, supplemented by an alphabetical subject index. Continued by: *Library literature*. For author index, see: *Cannons' bibliography of library economy, 1876–1920: An author index with citations*. Electronic version of 1st ed. (London: S. Russell, 1910) available through the Internet Archive: http://www.archive.org/details/bibliographyofli00cannrich.

396 Controversial issues in librarianship: An annotated bibliography, 1960-1984. Mark Youngblood Herring. New York: Garland Publ., 1987. xx, 698 p. ISBN 0824085787

016.02   Z666.H44

Covers controversies over collections, library facilities, personnel, technology, cooperation and networking, library education, reference services, library management and finance, librarians and society (including censorship and intellectual freedom), and the profession. Excludes non-English material. Subjectively annotated. Entries are arranged by author within subject sections. Author/name and title indexes. Covers an important and contentious period in 20th century library history; to identify earlier and later works, consult standard LIS journal indexes.

397 Current cites. http://lists.webjunction.org/currentcites/. Roy Tennant, OCLC RLG Programs. San Mateo, Calif.: OCLC RLG Programs. 1990–. 1060-2356

Z678.9 025

A monthly current awareness service, featuring six to 12 recent publications selected and annotated by librarians.

398 Index to Festschriften in librarianship. J. Periam Danton, Ottilia C. Anderson. New York: R. R. Bowker, 1970. xi, 461 p. ISBN 0835202615

016.02   Z666.D35

Indexes approximately 3,300 articles in 283 festschriften published 1864–1966. Authors, editors, subjects, and cross-references appear in a single alphabet. Supplemented by: Joseph Periam Danton and Jane F. Pulis, *Index to Festschriften in librarianship, 1967–1975*, which, its title notwithstanding, also covers pre-1967 festschriften omitted from the earlier work.

For more recent indexing of festschriften issued as special issues of journals, consult *LISA: Library and information science abstracts* (505) or *Library & information science source* (502).

399 International bibliography of bibliographies in library and information science and related fields. Henryk Sawoniak, Maria Witt. München, [Germany]: K.G. Saur, [1999]–2003. v. , ISBN 3598111444

Z666.S32

Describes nearly 20,000 bibliographies devoted to librarianship and related topics. Vol. I, in three physical volumes, covers 1945–1978. Vol. II, also in three physical volumes, covers 1979–1990. Entries for both time periods are arranged in a detailed classification, with general works (e.g., bibliographies covering national LIS literatures, lists of theses) followed by bibliographies on particular disciplines, topics, and subtopics. Final volumes (I/3 and II/3) list writings about the development and documentation of LIS literature and include author, title, subject, and geographical indexes. Scope is international and multilingual, with strong coverage of Eastern and Western Europe.

400 Librarians in fiction: A critical bibliography. Grant Burns. Jefferson, N.C.: McFarland, 1998. v, 185 p. ISBN 078640499X

016.82080352092   Z2014.L45B87; PR151.L53

Critically assesses 343 English language novels, short stories, and plays for adult readers that feature librarians as characters. Includes bibliography of secondary works. Author/title index. To find lists that include more recent citations, search the Web for the words "librarians" and "fiction."

401 Libraries and information in the Arab world: An annotated bibliography. Lokman I. Meho, Mona A. Nsouli. Westport, Conn.: Greenwood Press, 1999. xi, 349 p. ISBN 031331098X

016.0209174927   Z666.M44

Describes writings on librarianship and information science in 21 countries, primarily in English, Arabic, and French, 1977–98. Within country sections, arrangement is by subject. Non-English titles in Western languages are translated. Arabic titles are transliterated but not translated, and many lack annotations. Indexes: author; title; subject. See also

Librarianship and information science in the Islamic world, 1966–1999: An annotated bibliography.

402   Libraries in American periodicals before 1876: a bibliography with abstracts and an index. Larry J. Barr, Haynes McMullen, Steven G. Leach. Jefferson, N.C.: McFarland, 1983. xx, 426 p. ISBN 0899500668

016.02   Z666.B33

A bibliography of nearly 1,500 articles about libraries in the U.S. and elsewhere, appearing in American periodicals prior to 1876. Abstracts articles of more than 150 words; includes shorter articles in their entirety. Arranged geographically, with comprehensive author, title, subject index.

For articles after 1876, consult H. G. T. Cannons, *Bibliography of library economy* (395).

403   Library services for distance learning: fifth bibliography. http://dlsfifthbib. wordpress.com. ACRL Distance Learning Section. Chicago: Association of College and Research Libraries (ACRL) Distance Learning Section. 2010?

Compiled by members of the ACRL Distance Learning Section. Continues bibliographies published in 1991, 1996, 2000, and 2005 with varying authors and titles. Arranged by topic and type of publication; sub-arranged by year, covering 2006-2009. All citations have abstracts.

404   The literature of the book: A select bibliography, with critical essays, of books by, about and for the book professions. Marlow, U.K.: Logos, [2005?] ISBN 1861564910

z279

An annotated bibliography of the best books, chosen by experts, on the "book professions." Covers nineteen specific topics related to the broad themes of authorship, editing, production, publishing, bookselling, librarianship, and readership. The individual lists serve as good introductions to topics such as the history of the book, indexing, book marketing, and electronic books. Includes a chapter on reference books for publishers.

405   Voya's five-foot bookshelf: essential books for professionals who serve

teens 2000 to 2012. 1st ed. RoseMary Hornold. Bowie, Md.: VOYA Press, 2013. 92 p. ISBN 9781617510106

Bibliography of recommended books for young adult librarians, including both library professional literature and books on adolescent development from related disciplines. Reprints reviews from *VOYA* [Voice of Youth Advocates] magazine. Arranged alphabetically by main entry, with an author/title index.

Biography

Editor's Guide: There is no current "who's who" publication devoted to LIS. Web searches will often yield resume-type information or personal websites for LIS academics, but finding biographical data about practicing information professionals can be difficult.

406   A biographical directory of librarians in the United States and Canada. 5th ed. Lee Ash, Bernhard A. Uhlendorf, Council of National Library Associations. Chicago: American Library Association, 1970. xviii, 1250 p. ISBN 0838900844

020.922   Z720.A4W47

For historical research. First ed. (1933)–4th ed. (1966) titled: *Who's who in library service* (N.Y.: H.W. Wilson). Useful because it includes many librarians not included in *Who's who in library and information services* (414) and provides biographical information about librarians for whom only abbreviated information is given in the *Directory of library & information professionals* (408). Presents highly condensed data on education, positions held (with dates), important career assignments, memberships in organizations, honors, publications, and principal areas of professional interest. No indexes.

407   Dictionary of American library biography. George S. Bobinski, Jesse Hauk Shera, Bohdan S. Wynar. Littleton, Colo.: Libraries Unlimited, 1978. xxxix, 596 p. ISBN 0872871800

020.922   Z720.A4D5

Biographical sketches (1,000 to 6,000 words each) of 302 men and women notable for "contributions of national significance to library development; writings that influenced library trends and activities; positions of national importance . . . ; major achievements in special fields of librarianship; significant scholarly, philanthropic, legislative, or governmental support or activity that affected American libraries."—*Pref.* Includes only people deceased as of June 30, 1976. Signed articles include bibliographies. *The supplement to the dictionary of American library biography* covers primarily individuals who died between June 30, 1976 and June 30, 1987. *Dictionary of American library biography, second supplement* extends coverage to 2000, with a cumulative name index to all volumes.

408 Directory of library and information professionals. American Library Association, American Society for Information Science. Woodbridge, Conn.: Research Publications, 1988. 2 v. ISBN 089235125X
020.922   Z720.A4D57

Vol. 1 covers 23,000 individuals. Entries include some or all of the following information—biographee's name, current position, previous positions, education, publications, achievements, honors, memberships, language proficiency, professional expertise or subject specialty, and consulting availability. Name, employer, and address supplied for an additional 20,000 individuals based on the American Library Association's membership files. Vol. 2 contains specialty, employer, consulting/freelance, and geographical indexes. Never updated, so useful only for historical research.

409 A directory of oral history tapes of librarians in the United States and Canada. Doris Cruger Dale, American Library Association. Chicago: American Library Association, 1986. xvi, 103 p. ISBN 0838904432
020.973   Z720.A4D34

Lists 205 recorded interviews held by 40 institutions, arranged alphabetically by institution, then by name of librarian. Entries include a brief biographical sketch of the interviewee, name of interviewer, date and length of interview, subjects covered and names of other librarians mentioned, as well as information regarding copyright, availability of transcript, and permission to cite. Personal name and subject indexes. For more recent works, search WorldCat for "librarians" as a subject and "oral history" as keywords.

410 International biographical directory of national archivists, documentalists, and librarians. 2nd ed. Jeffrey M. Wilhite, Todd J. Kosmerick, Laurie Scrivener, Susan Houck. Lanham, Md.: Scarecrow Press, 2000. xxi, 291 p. ISBN 0810837803
020.922B   Z720.A1156

First edition, 1997, ed. by Frances Laverne Carroll and Susan Houck (Lanham, Md.: Scarecrow Press). Arranged by country. Supplies background (education, career history, professional memberships, publications, etc.) on 317 directors of national libraries, archives, and documentation centers. Also provides a single-paragraph history of the institution. Indexes: institutions, people, and places.

411 Pioneers and leaders in library services to youth: a biographical dictionary. Marilyn L. Miller. Westport, Conn.: Libraries Unlimited, 2003. xvi, 267 p. ISBN 1591580285
027.626092B   Z720.A4P56

Intended to compensate for inadequate inclusion of youth services for librarians in *The dictionary of American library biography* (407). Reprints 40 profiles from the *DALB* and its supplements, and adds 57 new ones. All subjects are deceased. Signed essays cover family background, education, professional career and contributions, and includes a bibliography. Index to names and subjects.

412 Pioneers of library and information science. http://faculty.libsci.sc.edu/bob/ISP/isp.htm. University of South Carolina, College of Library and Information Science. Columbia, S.C.: University of South Carolina, College of Library and Information Science. [1996?]

Briefly profiles 102 individuals and 35 organizations "significant to the development of Information Science in North America during the period 1900 - 1970" and describes archival and manuscript collections.—*Purposes of the Project*

413 Salute to America's librarians. Marquis Who's Who, Inc. New Providence, N.J.: Marquis Who's Who, 2007. 64 p. ISBN 9780837972992
020.92/273   Z720.A4; S25

A slim, promotional volume containing some 500 profiles of prominent and award-winning librarians. Biographical data is presented in the dense, abbreviated style of *Who's Who in America* (92), from which the entries are derived.

414   Who's who in library and information services. Robert J. Beran, Sandra Whiteley, Joel M. Lee, American Library Association. Chicago: American Library Association, 1982. xiv, 559 p.
ISBN 0838903517
020.922B   Z720.A4W45

For historical research. A successor to *A biographical directory of librarians in the United States and Canada* (406) and its predecessor, *Who's who in library service*, 1st–4th eds. (1933–66). Includes "librarians and information scientists; archivists; library school faculty and other educators; scholars in subject specialties associated with libraries or library education programs; publishers, editors, and journalists whose primary activity is in librarianship and information fields; trustees; others who have made notable contributions to library and information services."—*User's Guide* Provides highly abbreviated data on employment history, education, membership in professional organizations, honors, and publications. Numerical codes indicate principal areas of professional activity. No indexes.

Blogs and News

Editor's Guide: Blogs are an unstable medium, but one uniquely useful for sharing up-to-the-minute information, generating conversations within the LIS professions, and providing a forum for exploring new ideas. This section includes entries for individual blogs as well as sites that host, or aggregate links to, multiple blogs. The blogs described here meet one or more of the following criteria:

a. They have a record of continuous publication and were actively maintained at the time at which this volume went to press;
b. They have won awards or appeared on "best" lists;
c. They are favorites of the editor or were recommended by expert colleagues.

415   ALA blogs. http://wikis.ala.org/readwrite connect/index.php/ALA_blogs. American Library Association. Chicago: American Library Association. 2008-

An alphabetical list of links to blogs sponsored by the American Library Association and its various units. Although a few of the links are dead, most of the blogs are active and thus good sources of information about the doings of ALA and/or the topics of interest to blogging unit. Among the livelier ALA blogs, and the subjects they cover, are:

- AASL blog (school libraries)
- ACRLog (libraries in higher education)
- ALSC blog (children's services)
- District Dispatch (government policy and legislation)
- The Hub: Your Connection to Teen Reads (young adult literature)
- Leads from LLAMA(administration and management)
- LITA blog (information technology)
- NMRT Notes(new members of ALA)
- OIF blog(intellectual freedom)
- Programming Librarian(library programs)
- RUSA News (reference and adult services)
- TechSource blog (information technologies)
- Visibility @ Your Library(public relations)
- YALSA blog(young adult services)

416   ALA news: press releases. http://www .ala.org/news/press-releases. American Library Association. Chicago: American Library Association. 2004-

A searchable, up-to-date archive of press releases from the American Library Association. In a typical month, ALA may issue 50-90 press releases about programs, publications, and awards, making this a good way to stay abreast of U.S. developments in librarianship and ALA's activities in particular.

417   Booklist: blogs. http://www.booklist online.com/blogs. Chicago: American Library Association

The American Library Association's reviewing journal, *Booklist* (29), hosts several blogs devoted to books, audiobooks, reading, reviewing, and the publishing industry.

418   INFOdocket. http://www.infodocket.com/. Gary Price, Shirl Kennedy. New York: Library Journal. [2012-]

Frequent postings to this service on the *Library Journal* (539) website convey "the latest information industry news and resources," including news about library initiatives and programs.—*Home page*.

419   **Library blog center.** http://salempress .com/Store/blogs/blog_home.htm. Salem Press. Ipswich, Mass.: Salem Press. [2010–]
Sponsored by Salem Press, this site hosts the Library Blog Awards and the Library Blog Directory. The awards, given annually since 2010, are nominated and voted on by the public, with expert judges making the final selection. Awards have been given in the following categories:

- General: In the Library with the Lead Pipe (2012); Librarian in Black (2011); Libraries and Transliteracy (2010)
- Academic: Musings About Librarianship (2012); Information Tyrannosaur (2011); No Shelf Required (2010)
- Public: Librarian by Day (2012); Swiss Army Librarian (2011); Agnostic, Maybe (2010)
- School: The Adventures of Library Girl (2012); The Unquiet Librarian (2011); Bib 2.0 (2010)
- Special: bizologie (2012)
- Institutional-academic: Scholarly Communications @ Duke (2012)
- Institutional-public: Eleventh Stack (2012)
- Local: Cecil Country Public Library (2011)
- Commercial: Neverending Search (2011)
- Newcomer: Hack Library School (2011)

Lists of runners-up and top nominees are posted. A special category, "Quirky," applies to "character-driven blogs covering an array of library topics that defy categorization." --*Home page*. The winners are: Screwy Decimal (2012); A Librarian's Guide to Etiquette (2011); Awful Library Books (2010).

The Center also maintains a directory of some 1,300 library-related blogs, searchable by keyword, topical focus, audience, and "type," i.e. independent or connected to an institution or association. Entries provide brief descriptions, screen shots, and links to the blogs.

420   **Library history buff blog: promoting the appreciation, enjoyment, and preservation of our library heritage.** http://libraryhistorybuff.blogspot.com/.

Larry T. Nix. Middleton, Wis.: s.n. 2008-
Larry T. Nix, a retired librarian, shares stories and images from American library history. The blog features a detailed A-Z index of persons, libraries, and topics. Nix also maintains a website at http://www .libraryhistorybuff.org.

421   **Lorcan Dempsey's weblog.** http:// orweblog.oclc.org/. Lorcan Dempsey. Dublin, Ohio: OCLC. 2003-
Lorcan Dempsey, an acknowledged thought leader in the library world, is vice-president and chief strategist at OCLC. He blogs about library services, collections, and the user experience in the networked information environment.

422   **Stephen's lighthouse.** http://www.stephens lighthouse.com. Stephen Abram. 2005-
Stephen Abram, well-known librarian and consultant, blogs about "library strategies for direction, marketing, technology and user alignment." --*Home page* He frequently re-posts infographics and links to research reports.

Dictionaries and Thesauruses

Editor's Guide: This section includes English, bilingual, and polyglot guides to the specialized language of LIS and areas of specialization within the field.

423   **ALA glossary of library and information science. 4th ed.** Michael Levine-Clark, Toni M. Carter. Chicago: American Library Association, 2012. viii, 280 pages ; 26 cm
020.3   Z1006.A48
First edition, *A.L.A. glossary of library terms: with a selection of terms in related fields* , 1943. Defines specialized terms and acronyms used by librarians and information professionals. Omits general terms related to administration, management, and computer technologies. Entries contain cross-references. Previous editions remain useful for definitions of obsolete terms. The 3rd edition (1983) has been translated into Spanish, Japanese, and Vietnamese.

424   **ASIS&T thesaurus of information science, technology, and librarianship. 3rd ed.** Alice Redmond-Neal, Marjorie M. K. Hlava, Jessica L. Milstead, American

Society for Information Science and Technology. Medford, N.J.: Information Today, 2005. xiii, 255 p. ISBN 1573872431

025.4902   Z695.1.I56M54

First ed., 1994, and 2nd ed., 1998, ed. by Jessica L. Milstead, titled *ASIS thesaurus of information science and librarianship*. Intended to be used "for indexing the literature of the field and for developing familiarity with the coverage of the domain."—*Guide to using the ASIS&T thesaurus*

In three sections: alphabetical listing, with USE, UF, BT, NT, and RT references; hierarchical index of preferred terms; and permuted index of both preferred and non-preferred terms. Optional CD-ROM includes complete thesaurus with software for searching and modifying it.

425 Concise dictionary of library and information science. 2nd ed. Stella Keenan, Colin Johnston. London: Bowker-Saur, 2000. x, 265 p. ISBN 1857392515

020.3020.3   Z1006.K39

First ed., 1996. Brief, exceptionally clear definitions for some 4,500 terms deemed important in the practice of library and information science professions. Notes synonyms.

426 Dictionary of bibliometrics. Virgil Pasquale Diodato. New York: Haworth Press, 1994. xiii, 185 p. ISBN 1560248521

020.3   Z669.8.D56

Brief explanations of some 225 terms related to the quantitative study of patterns in information distribution and use. Citations within definitions to publications that elucidate the term or concept. Name index.

427 Dictionary of information and library management. 2nd ed. Janet Stevenson. London: A and C Black, 2006. 229 p. ISBN 0713675918

         Z1006.D53

First ed., 1997, titled *Dictionary of library and information management*. Succinctly defines over 6,000 terms used by information workers. Includes many general English words as well as specialized vocabulary, and therefore may be most useful to non-native speakers. Supplementary material includes lists of classification systems, websites, U.K. copyright laws, book awards, and major U.K. newspapers and magazines.

428 Dictionary of information science and technology. 2nd ed. Mehdi Khosrowpour. Hershey, Pa.: IGI-Global, 2013. 2 volumes (cccxlii, 1005 pages)

020.03   T58.5.D499

Covers all aspects of information science and technology, including applications to education, government, and business. Defines over 12,000 words and acronyms. Definitions are taken from the publisher's other reference books; all definitions include source citations. Available as in ebook in *InfoSci-Books* (498) and other online packages from IGI Global. *InfoSci-Dictionary* (435), a subscription-based online resource from the same publisher, is continually updated.

First ed. 2006.

429 Dictionary of librarianship: including a selection from the terminology of information science, bibliology, reprography, higher education, and data processing: German-English, English-German. 3rd rev. and enl. ed ed. Eberhard Sauppe. München, [Germany]: K.G. Saur, 2003. xix, 524 p. ISBN 3598115504

020.3   Z1006.S3215

Translates nearly 29,000 terms. Teil I: German-English; teil II: English-German.

430 Dictionary for school library media specialists: a practical and comprehensive guide. Mary Maude McCain, Martha Merrill. Englewood, Colo.: Libraries Unlimited, 2001. xiii, 219 p. ISBN 1563086964

020.3   Z1006.M43

Intended as a comprehensive dictionary covering all aspects of library work in K-12 schools. Includes computer terminology and educational jargon. Numerous cross-references. Also available as ebook. For a more succinct and slightly newer dictionary, see *The essential school library glossary*.

431 A glossary of archival and records terminology. http://www.archivists.org/glossary/index.asp. Richard Pearce-Moses. Chicago: Society of American Archivists. 2005

Also published in print in the *Archival fundamentals series II* (621). Defines over 2,000 English language terms found in the archival literature, with an emphasis on electronic records. Includes acronyms and organizations. Provides citations to usage and notes relationships among terms.

432 Glossary of library and information science: English-Chinese/Chinese-English. Su Chen, Shi Deng. Munchen, [Germany]: K.G. Saur, 2006. xxi, 343 p. ISBN 3598116896
Z1006.G56

Part 1: English-Chinese. Part 2: Chinese-English. Includes terms and acronyms. Indicates when English terms are translated or used differently in Taiwan or Hong Kong.

433 Glossary of terminology in abstracting, classification, indexing, and thesaurus construction. 2nd ed. Hans H. Wellisch. Medford, N.J.: Information Today, 2000. vii, 77 p. ISBN 1573870943
025.3014   Z695.9.W435

First ed., 1996, titled *Abstracting, indexing, classification, thesaurus construction: A glossary.* Defines terms used in standards and professional texts, as well as terms for common types of documents and their parts. Many entries include examples of usage.

434 Harrod's librarians' glossary and reference book: a directory of over 10,200 terms, organizations, projects and acronyms in the areas of information management, library science, publishing, and archive management. 10th ed. Raymond John Prytherch. Aldershot, Hants, England; Burlington, Vt.: Ashgate, 2005. xi, 753 p. ISBN 0754640388
020.3   Z1006.H32

First ed., 1938. Compiler varies; title and subtitle vary slightly among editions. Defines over 10,200 terms in information management, library science, publishing, and management of archives. Includes acronyms. Lists associations with directory-type data (street address and/or URL, brief description). Although British in origin, provides good coverage of North American words and organizations.

435 InfoSci-dictionary. http://www.igi-global .com/e-resources/infosci-databases/infosci -dictionary/. Hershey, Pa.: IGI Global. 2005–. 2327–7149
020.03

A subscription-based, searchable database of more than 26,000 terms and definitions extracted from IGI Global's publications. Continually updated. Covers all aspects of information science and technology, including applications in business, education, government, health, and librarianship.

436 Library-related acronyms. http://www .ala.org/tools/library-related-acronyms. American Library Association. Chicago: American Library Association. [n.d.]

Maintained by the ALA Library. Decodes acronyms of ALA units, ALA publications, other library-related organizations, and abbreviations commonly used in the library literature. Most entries are linked to relevant websites.

437 A manual of European languages for librarians. 2nd ed. C. G. Allen. London; New Providence, N.J.: Bowker-Saur, 1999. xiii, 994 p. ISBN 1857392418
409.4   P380.A4

First ed., 1975. Intended for librarians who must work with materials in languages they do not know. Gives basic orthographic, grammatical, syntactic, and lexical information for 38 European languages, including Latin and ancient Greek. Arranged by language group: Germanic, Romance, Celtic, Greek and Albanian, Slavonic, Baltic, Finno-Ugrian, and other. For each language, a brief general introduction is followed by an analysis of title-page usage (conventions for authors' names, titles, numeration, edition and imprint statements, series and periodicals), a short systematic grammar, a glossary of basic words related to library materials, and a list of grammatical endings keyed to the grammar section. For Greek and Cyrillic alphabets, romanization is covered as well.

438 Multilingual archival terminology. http://www.ica.org/14282/multilingual -archival-terminology/multilingual-archival -terminology.html. International Council on Archives. Paris: International Council on Archives. [n.d.]

An interactive, online database of archival terms and definitions in 20 languages, including English.

439 ODLIS. http://bibpurl.oclc.org/web/4113. Joan M. Reitz, Libraries Unlimited, Inc. [Westport, Conn.]: Libraries Unlimited. [1996]–
020.03   Z1006.R45

Defines terms and acronyms in the various specializations within library and information science, along with relevant vocabulary concerning publishing, printing, the book trade, graphic arts, book history, literature, bibliography, telecommunications, and computer science. Reflects North American usage. Definitions include copious cross-reference links and links to external Web sources. A print version, *Dictionary for library and information science*, appeared in 2004.

440 Serials acquisitions glossary. http://www.ala.org/alcts/resources/collect/serials/acqglossary. Association for Library Collections & Technical Services, Serials Section, Acquisitions Committee. Chicago: American Library Association. 2005
           Z1006.S5

First edition, 1993. Defines terms used by librarians, vendors, and publishers of serials, with special attention to electronic publishing. Fifty-one page PDF file.

Directories of Institutions and People

Editor's Guide: The ability to search the Internet for addresses, hours, contact names, and basic institutional data has made edited directories of libraries and information centers largely unnecessary. Some directories, however, do provide a greater depth of information, contain subject indexing, or enable comparisons; such sources are described here. Printed membership directories of organizations were once frequently consulted reference tools but few are published now. When made available on association websites, data on individual members is typically accessible only to other members. (See Library and Information Science > General Works > Professional Associations for URLs.)

By Geographic Location
AFRICA

441 Directory of national libraries in Africa. http://www.nlsa.ac.za/Downloads_01/natlib/National%20Libraries%20of%20Africa%20Directory.pdf. Isabel Ringel. [Pretoria]: National Library of South Africa. 2013 978-0-7961-0118-1

One-hundred-fifty-one-page PDF. "A survey of national libraries or equivalent institutions in African countries." —*Title page* Expands on information in the NatLib database at http://nlsahopta.nlsa.ac.za/nla/index.html. Organized alphabetically by country. Entries include contact information, brief list of services, number of books and journals, and contact information for library and information associations in the country.

AUSTRALIA AND OCEANIA

442 Australian libraries gateway. http://www.nla.gov.au/libraries/index.html. National Library of Australia. Canberra, [A.C.T.], Australia: National Library of Australia

Developed by the National Library of Australia. Provides a directory of some 5,200 Australian libraries, both public and private. Includes addresses, contact information, linked URLs, and information about access and resource sharing. Search options are keyword, state, type of library, and broad subjects in collections. Libraries manage their own information.

EUROPE

443 ARCHON Directory. http://www.nationalarchives.gov.uk/archon. National Archives, Historical Manuscripts Commission. Kew, U.K.: The National Archives

This gateway to archives and record depositories throughout the United Kingdom, with some links to repositories in other countries, is maintained by the Historical Manuscripts Commission of the National Archives. Individual institution records include contact and access information, website URLs, online finding aids, and online accession lists.

The ARCHON search screen has fields for repository name and geographic area; unfortunately, there is no access by subject word. Use this site in conjunction with *British archives: A guide to archive resources in the United Kingdom*, which lists some unique collections and provides subject access.

444 Aslib directory of information sources in the United Kingdom. Aslib. London: Aslib, 1982–. 1743-8616

Z791.A1A82

First ed., 1928. Now published biennially. Fourteenth ed., 2006, identifies over 11,000 institutions and organizations in the United Kingdom that contain subject collections or provide information services. Entries include street address, phone number, e-mail address, URL, brief description of purpose, subject coverage, publications, and information about access. Arranged alphabetically, with a subject index and list of acronyms.

445 BaseBibliotek: directory of Norwegian libraries and their ILL associates abroad. http://www.nb.no/BaseBibliotekSearch/. Oslo, Norway: National Library of Norway

Provides a directory of Norwegian public, research, special, university, polytechnic, folk high school and secondary school libraries. Also includes libraries that participated in the Nordic/Baltic union catalogue of serials (NOSP -2005), and other foreign libraries lending in Norway or using the National Library services. Entries for Norwegian libraries are most complete, including full location and contact information, plus information about holdings and services. Choice of Norwegian or English interface.

446 A directory of rare book and special collections in the United Kingdom and the Republic of Ireland. 2nd ed. B. C. Bloomfield, Library Association. London: Library Association, 1997. xxiii, 740 p. ISBN 1856040631
026.090941   Z1029.D57

Arranged geographically. Listings contain address, phone number, business hours, conditions of admission, and research facilities, plus a brief history and description of the collection. Notes catalogs and publications. Comprehensive index. According to a post on the CILIP Rare Books and Special Collections Group's website (http://www.cilip.org.uk), a new edition is in preparation.

447 The directory of university libraries in Europe. Europa Publications. London: Europa Publications, 1999–
ISBN 1857430719

Z789.D565

Biennial; last issued in 2006. Companion volume to the Europa World of Learning database, which includes only very basic information on libraries. Arranged by country, then by city or region. Lists departmental, as well as main libraries. English translations are given for institutional names. Supplies address, phone number, fax number, e-mail address, and URL; date of founding; director's name; areas of subject specialization; holdings counts; opening hours; and access restrictions. Data for some libraries is incomplete. Indexes: universities; libraries with unique names.

448 The European library. http://www.theeuropeanlibrary.org/tel4/. The Conference of European National Librarians (CENL). Den Haag, The Netherlands: Koninklijke Bibliotheek, National Library of the Netherlands
Z675.N2

A portal to the print and digital resources of 48 national libraries of Europe and leading European Research Libraries. Catalogs of more than 200 million resources , including 24 million pages of full text and nearly 120 million bibliographic records, are searchable. Advanced searching permits the user to specify which libraries are searched. Researchers can register for free to access metadata. Membership available to libraries.

449 Libraries and information services in the United Kingdom and the Republic of Ireland. Facet. London: Facet Publ., 1st- ed. 1960–
Z791.A1L4

Annual. Provides contact names, addresses, telephone and fax numbers, e-mail addresses, and URLs for libraries in the United Kingdom, the Channel Islands, the Isle of Man, and the Republic of Ireland. Arranged by category: public library authorities; universities and institutes of higher education; selected government, national, and special libraries, plus library and information science schools; library organizations and agencies. Indexed by name and subject.

INTERNATIONAL

450 Directory of special libraries and information centers. http://www. gale.cengage.com/DirectoryLibrary/. Independence, Ky.: Gale Cengage Learning. 2008–

The 41st ed. (2013) lists more than 37,500 libraries and resource centers of government agencies, businesses, publishers, educational and nonprofit organizations, and associations worldwide. Provides addresses, phone and fax numbers, contact names, e-mail addresses, URLs, and founding dates, plus brief information on collections, staffing, and services. May be searched by library or company names, locations, words in descriptions, subjects, and more.

Issued annually in print since 1963. Volumes since 2008 are part of the online *Gale directory library*.

451 International librarianship: A basic guide to global knowledge access. Robert D. Stueart. Lanham, Md.: Scarecrow Press, 2007. xi, 247 p. ISBN 0810858762

020.621   Z672.S78

Provides directory-style information (e.g., contact data, founding year, mission) about international and national library associations; governmental and nongovernmental organizations and foundations with an interest in libraries; and national libraries and bibliographic services. Opening chapter addresses trends and issues in international librarianship. Final chapter discusses information policy. Index.

452 Libweb: library servers via WWW. http://www.lib-web.org. Thomas Dowling, OhioLINK. Seattle, Wash.; Dublin, Ohio: WebJunction. 1995– 005.75025; 025.3132025; 020.711025; 027.025

Directory of home pages of more than 8,000 libraries worldwide, organized geographically for browsing and searchable by library name, location, type (academic, public, special, school, national, state), and consortial affiliation. Another directory of library websites and online catalogs, Marshall Breeding's

lib-web-cats (http://www.librarytechnology.org/lib webcats), lists more libraries, especially school libraries, but requires registration in order to use the advanced search feature.

453 List of national and state libraries. http://en.wikipedia.org/wiki/List_of _national_libraries. s.l.: Wikipedia. [n.d.]

Lists national libraries alphabetically by country, including those fulfilling this function but not having the actual title. Provides links to the libraries' websites and serves as an index to fuller entries for many of the libraries within Wikipedia.

Formerly found on the IFLA website.

454 OpenDOAR: directory of open access repositories. http://www.opendoar.org. Lunds universitetsbibliotek, University of Nottingham. Nottingham, U.K.; Lund, Sweden: University of Nottingham; University of Lund. [2006]–

Descriptive list of more than 2,200 institutional and subject-based open-access repositories located around the world. Use the "Find" operation to locate a repository by subject, content type, repository type, software platform, location, or language. Use the "Content Search" operation to search the full text of materials located in the included repositories.

455 World guide to libraries. München, Germany; New York: DeGruyter Saur, 1966–. 2 v. 0936-0085

027.0025   Z721.63

Arranged by country, then by type of library. Provides name of institution (with English translation if necessary), address, telephone, telex and fax numbers, email address, URL, year founded, name of director, important holdings, special departments, and collection statistics for more than 42,500 libraries in over 200 countries. Includes national libraries; public libraries with over 50,000 volumes; general research libraries, school libraries, and professional libraries with over 30,000 volumes; university libraries with more than 60,000 volumes; and various types of special libraries with more than 8,000 volumes. Alphabetical index.

Issued as vol. 8 of *International handbook of documentation and information*. 27th edition (2013) in two print volumes or e-book format. First edition also carried German title, *Internationales Bibliotheksadress-buch.* 2nd (1968) through 8th (1987) eds. also carried German title, *Internationales Bibliotheks-Handbuch.*

456 World guide to library, archive, and information science associations. 3rd ed. Alexandra Meinhold, International Federation of Library Associations and Institutions. Berlin; New York: De Gruyter Saur, 2010. ISBN 9783110226379
020.62025   Z673.A1W67
Pt. 1: International associations, in alphabetical order. Pt. 2: National associations, organized by country. In addition to address, URL, officers, and other basic data, provides information on membership requirements, organizational structure, sources of financial support, major goals and objectives, activities, and publications. Indexes to association names, acronyms, official journals, officers, and subjects. Covers 603 associations. See also *Library associations around the world*, an online directory maintained by IFLA and ALA, for a selective list of major international, national and state associations, with contact information and links to their websites.

First edition, 1990, ed. by Josephine Riss Fang and Alice H. Songe. 2nd ed., 2005, ed. by Marko Schweizer. Succeeds *International guide to library, archival, and information science associations*, also ed. by Fang and Songe (1976, 1980).

457 World guide to library, archive and information science education. 3rd ed. Axel Schniederjürgen. München, Germany: K.G. Saur, 2007. 560 p. ISBN 9783598220357, 0344-6891
                                            Z668
First ed., 1985, titled *International guide to library and information science education*, edited by Josephine Riss Fang and Paul Nauta. 2nd ed., 1995, edited by Josephine Riss Fang, Robert D. Stueart, and Kuthilda Tuamsuk. Arranged by country. Profiles of institutions and their programs include street address, phone number, e-mail address, and URL; director's name; year founded; sources of funding; tuition rate; financial aids; numbers of staff, students, and graduates; requirements for foreign students; continuing education programs; accreditation; and details of degrees offered, including admission requirements, objectives, and content areas. Indexes: place names; names of schools.

Consult individual schools' websites for more current information. For lists of accredited North American schools, visit the websites of the American Library Association (553), and for school library media programs specifically, the National Council for Accreditation of Teacher Education (http://www.ncate.org).

458 World guide to special libraries = Internationales Handbuch der Spezialbibliotheken. München, [Germany]; New York: DeGruyter Saur, 1983–. 0724-8717
                                            Z675.A2W67
Issued biennially as vol. 17 of *Handbook of international documentation and information.* 2013 edition in 2 print v. or e-book format. Lists about 35,000 libraries worldwide by subject, then by country. Provides name of institution (with English translation if necessary), address, telephone, telex and fax numbers, email address, URL, year founded, name of director, important holdings, and collection statistics. Indicates if the library participates in interlibrary loan programs and the professional associations with which it is affiliated. Separately lists national libraries. Alphabetical index by library name.

LATIN AMERICA

459 Libraries and archives. http://lanic.utexas.edu/la/region/library/. Latin American Network Information Center (LANIC). Austin, Tex.: University of Texas. 1992–
A subpage of the LANIC website. Directory of Latin American regional-level bibliographic databases, digital libraries, libraries, and archives. Provides links to individual research libraries, arranged by country.

NORTH AMERICA

460 ALA handbook of organization. http://www.ala.org/aboutala/governance/handbook. American Library Association. Chicago: American Library Association. 1972–. 0002-9769
                                            Z673.A5

Requires American Library Association member login. Provides detailed information about the structure and governance of the association, including committee charges and membership; staff listings; conference dates and locations; policies; elected officers and Council members; awards and scholarships; and more. Published together with the *Member directory* (461), 1981–96. Published online only since 2009.

461 ALA member directory. http://www.ala .org/Template.cfm?Section=alamemberd irectory&Template=/MembersOnly.cfm &NavMenuID=6612&ContentID=108 815&DirectListComboInd=D. American Library Association. Chicago: American Library Association. [2003–]

Requires American Library Association member login. Provides job title, address, phone number, affiliations within ALA, and e-mail link. Published annually in print, 1949–2002; issued together with the *ALA handbook of organization* (460), 1981–96.

462 American library directory. http://www .americanlibrarydirectory.com. Information Today, Inc. Medford, N.J.: Information Today, Inc.

027.21   Z731

Detailed profiles, updated yearly, for more than 34,000 public, academic, special, and government libraries in the United States, Canada, and U.S. territories. Related organizations are also covered: networks, consortia, and other cooperative library organizations; library schools and training courses; library systems; libraries for the blind and physically handicapped; libraries for the deaf and hearing impaired; state and provincial public library agencies; state school library agencies; and U.S. armed forces libraries overseas. Entries vary in level of detail but typically include address, phone and fax number, e-mail address, URL, date of founding, network participation, holdings counts, income and expenditures, special collections, key personnel, special services, and hours of operation. May also list software and database vendors, library publications, size of population served, and annual circulation.

Searchable data fields include library/institution name, library type, geographic indicators (e.g.,

zip code, city), subject areas, names of personnel, job titles, and automation systems. Ranges may be specified for such data as number of staff, size of holdings, circulation, population served, and expenditures.

Free access to physical address data only. Annual paid subscription required for full access with download privileges.

Also issued in print biennially (1908–77), then annually (1978–present). The 2013/14 edition, in two volumes, is the 66rd. Subtitle, compiler, place of publication, and publisher have varied. Entries arranged geographically. Summary statistical information regarding public libraries precedes each state, region, and province division; total numbers of North American libraries by category are provided in the front matter of v. 1. Indexed by organizations and personnel.

463 Federal depository library directory. http://catalog.gpo.gov/fdlpdir/FDLPdir. jsp. United States., United States., United States. Washington: Library Programs Service, Superintendent of Documents, U.S. Government Printing Office. 2006– 027.002573   Z675.D4

A directory of regional and selective depositories for U.S. government publications. Offers three search modes: a clickable map; a basic keyword search; and an advanced search by data fields. Entries include: depository library number; Congressional district; type of depository; type of library (academic, public, etc.); size of library; parent institution; year of designation as a depository library; address; and contact information.

464 Tribal libraries in the United States: A directory of American Indian and Alaska Native facilities. Elizabeth Peterson. Jefferson, N.C.: McFarland, 2007. v, 130 p., maps. ISBN 008997002573 027.9780786429394   E97.8.P47

Lists 237 tribal libraries by state. All entries include contact information and background on the tribe's ethnology, enrollment, and land area. Questionnaire responses from some libraries provide additional information about hours, access, collections (including special collections of tribal and Indian resources), services, equipment, and staff, along with comments on the library's strengths, challenges, and role in the community. Bibliography. Index.

By Subject

465 **Directory of Archival Organizations in the United States and Canada.** http://www2.archivists.org/assoc-orgs/directory. Society of American Archivists. Chicago: Society of American Archivists. [n.d.]

Previously issued in print. Includes contact information, membership size, dues, brief description, and links to websites of seventy archivists' organizations at the national, regional, state/provincial, and local levels.

466 **Directory of government document collections & librarians. 8th ed.** American Library Association. Washington: Congressional Information Service, 2003. 0276-959X

011/.53   Z1223.Z7; D57

Published irregularly for the Government Documents Round Table, American Library Association. The eighth edition (2003) substantially updates the 7th ed. Section 1 is a geographic guide to libraries, documents collections, and staff. Additional indexes list institutions by type of collection: state, local, foreign, and international—and special collections; library schools offering government documents instruction; state documents authorities and data centers; professional organizations, and government offices; and personal names. Section XI lists each Federal Depository Library Program number with its corresponding library and directory entry number.

For updated details, see GPO Access directory at http://catalog.gpo.gov/fdlpdir/FDLPdir.jsp.

467 **Directory of LIS programs and faculty in the United States and Canada.** http://www.alise.org/lis-programs--faculty. Association for Library and Information Science Education. Chicago: Association for Library and Information Science Education. 2005–. 1555-9092

Z668.D55

A complete listing of the faculty of 60 North American schools of library and information science, along with the teaching and research areas of each faculty member keyed to ALISE's LIS Research Areas Classification Scheme (http://www.alise.org/classification-scheme). Now published only online. Available to ALISE members and to others upon payment. Similar information for earlier years in *Directory of the Association for Library and Information Science Education* (1983–2004), *Directory of the Association of American Library Schools* (1971–1982), and the fall or winter issue of the *Journal of education for librarianship* (1960–1970).

468 **Directory of special libraries and information centers.** http://www.gale.cengage.com/DirectoryLibrary/. Independence, Ky.: Gale Cengage Learning. 2008–

The 41st ed. (2013) lists more than 37,500 libraries and resource centers of government agencies, businesses, publishers, educational and nonprofit organizations, and associations worldwide. Provides addresses, phone and fax numbers, contact names, e-mail addresses, URLs, and founding dates, plus brief information on collections, staffing, and services. May be searched by library or company names, locations, words in descriptions, subjects, and more.

Issued annually in print since 1963. Volumes since 2008 are part of the online *Gale directory library.*

469 **Federal depository library directory.** http://catalog.gpo.gov/fdlpdir/FDLPdir.jsp. United States., United States., United States. Washington: Library Programs Service, Superintendent of Documents, U.S. Government Printing Office. 2006–

027.002573   Z675.D4

A directory of regional and selective depositories for U.S. government publications. Offers three search modes: a clickable map; a basic keyword search; and an advanced search by data fields. Entries include: depository library number; Congressional district; type of depository; type of library (academic, public, etc.); size of library; parent institution; year of designation as a depository library; address; and contact information.

470 **Federal library directory.** http://viewshare.org/views/FRD/directory. Library of Congress. Federal Research Division. 2011–

Directory of U.S. federal libraries and information resource centers around the world. May be searched by keyword or browsed using pull-down menus by library type, federal department, state, country, and size of collection. Includes over 1,100 entries for: scientific and technical libraries; national libraries; academic libraries; presidential libraries; and libraries affiliated with military bases, agencies, hospitals, parks, and more. For security reasons, excludes embassy libraries and limits information about prison libraries. For each entry, provides address, contact information, URL, hours, name of director, staff size, collection size, circulation and reference services, and a brief description. Also presents an interactive map and pie charts, which are best viewed in the Firefox web browser.

471 A guide to Slavic collections in the United States and Canada. Allan Urbanic, Beth Feinberg. New York: Haworth Information Press, 2004. 198 p. ISBN 0789022494
Z730.7.G85;
026/.9400974918/02573   DJK27
The first comprehensive survey and directory of Slavic collections in the United States and Canada since *East Central and Southeast Europe: A handbook of library and archival resources in North America* (1976). Information was gathered from Slavic bibliographers across North America by means of a survey, and each bibliographer was free to give details on special aspects of individual collections. More than eighty collections are described, including those at universities, large public libraries, and even smaller research institutes.

472 Information industry directory. Gale Research, Thomson Gale (Firm). Detroit: Gale Research, 1991–. 1051-6239
025.040294   Z674.3.E53
Comprehensive, international directory of database producers and other firms and organizations "involved in the production and distribution of information in electronic form."—*Title page* Descriptive listings, arranged alphabetically, provide contact data, company information, and details about individual products and services. Indexes include master name and keyword; function/service classifications; personal name; geographic; subject. A searchable online version of this directory is included in the *Gale directory library*.

Annual, in 2 vols. First through tenth editions, (1971–90) had title *Encyclopedia of information systems and services.*

473 International directory of libraries for the blind. http://ifla.jsrpd.jp/. Misako Nomura, Mayu Yamada, International Federation of Library Associations and Institutions; Section of Libraries for the Blind. [Tokyo]: Japanese Society for Rehabilitation of Persons with Disabilities (JSRPD). 2000
Searchable database. Provides contact information, holdings data (by type of material), and lending policies. Also available in print.

474 The librarian's yellow pages online. http://www.librariansyellowpages. com/. The Librarian's Yellow Pages, Inc. Bethesda, Md.: The Librarian's Yellow Pages. [1990–]
022.90285;   Z678.892.U6
025.21; 020.92
Provides a directory of suppliers of library materials, furnishings, and services. May be searched or browsed by category. Also published in print, free upon request. The *Library Resource Guide* provides similar information categorized by subject, also with a free print edition. Another tool, the *Buyers Guide* sponsored by *American Libraries* magazine, is online-only, with interactive features and both a basic and advanced search option, as well as browsable categories.

475 Library consultants directory online. http://libraryconsultants.org/. Denise Sisco Shockley, Robert Burgin
Directory of library consultants in the U.S., searchable by name, state, and area of expertise. As of late 2013, about 40 consultants were included. Provides basic contact information only. Also displays active requests for proposals (RFPs) from libraries for consulting services.

476 Library publishing directory 2014. http://www.librarypublishing.org/ resources/directory-library-publishing-services. Sarah K. Lippincott. Atlanta, Ga.: Library Publishing Coalition. 2013. ISBN 9780989911825
Z716.6

Identifies 115 academic libraries with active publishing programs, primarily in the United States and Canada. For each, provides contact information, URLs for websites and social media, overview of mission, year that publishing program began, organizational structure, staffing, funding sources, types of publications, media formats, disciplinary specialties, top titles, percent of journals that are peer-reviewed, campus partners, publishing software platforms, digital preservation strategy, additional services, and future plans. Includes a separate listing of platforms, tools, and service providers, with URLs, and an index to personnel. Also available as a printed book from Purdue University Press.

477   Special collections in children's literature: an international directory. 3rd ed. Dolores Blythe Jones, Association for Library Service to Children. Chicago: American Library Association, 1995. xxiii, 235 p., ill. ISBN 808899282
026.0838934544   Z688.C47S63
Describes 300 collections in the United States and 119 in other countries. The main listing of U.S. collections is arranged by state and city and supplies contact information and a brief summary of the collection's size and highlights. The subject listing serves as an index by authors' names and topics to the main listing. A separate geographic listing, without subject access, covers non-U.S. collections. The final index is a name index to all collections. Although some contact information is out-of-date, there is no more recent guide of similar depth to special collections of children's literature.

First edition, *Subject collections in children's literature* (N.Y.: Bowker, 1969), and 2nd ed., *Special collections in children's literature* (Chicago: A.L.A., 1982), compiled by Carolyn W. Field.

478   Tribal libraries in the United States: A directory of American Indian and Alaska Native facilities. Elizabeth Peterson. Jefferson, N.C.: McFarland, 2007. v, 130 p., maps. ISBN 9780786429394
027.008997002573   E97.8.P47
Lists 237 tribal libraries by state. All entries include contact information and background on the tribe's ethnology, enrollment, and land area. Questionnaire responses from some libraries provide additional information about hours, access, collections (including special collections of tribal and Indian resources), services, equipment, and staff, along with comments on the library's strengths, challenges, and role in the community. Bibliography. Index.

Encyclopedias

479   The American public library handbook. Guy A. Marco. Santa Barbara, Calif.: Libraries Unlimited, 2012. ISBN 9781591589105
027.473   Z731.M29
A one-volume encyclopedia of American librarianship. Includes 65 topical articles on the history, issues, and daily operations of public libraries, with bibliographic references; 75 biographies of persons who died before 2000; and brief profiles of 1,200 libraries. Alphabetical arrangement. Detailed name and subject index.

480   Encyclopedia of communication and information. Jorge Reina Schement. New York: Macmillan Reference USA, 2002. 3 v. (xxvii, 1161 p.), ill. ISBN 0028653866
302.203   P87.5.E53
Arranged alphabetically. Provides 280 signed entries, two to eight pages long, by 191 contributors.

Cover careers in communication and information fields; information science; information technologies; literacy; institutional studies (e.g., government policy); interpersonal communication; and library science. Also includes substantial coverage of media theory; institutional studies (e.g., democracy and the media); interpersonal communication (e.g., conflict and group communication); media effects (e.g., arousal processes and the media); and numerous other topics directly relevant to media studies.

Most entries include short bibliographies. Cross-references, some black and white photographs, subject index. Also available as an e-book via the Gale Virtual Reference Library (288).

481   Encyclopedia of information science and technology. 2nd ed. Mehdi Khosrowpour. Hershey, Pa.: Information Science Reference, 2009. 8 v., ill. ISBN 9781605660264
004.03   Z1006.E566

Less a traditional encyclopedia than a compendium of over 600 short state-of-the-art articles in numerous general and highly specialized areas of research and application. Signed articles include references and definitions for key terms. Indexes.

Also available as an e-book. E-book version includes multiple search options, including search within PDF full texts.

482 Encyclopedia of information systems.
Hossein Bidgoli. Amsterdam, The Netherlands; Boston: Academic Press, 2003. 4 v., ill. ISBN 9780122272400

004.03   QA76.15

Contains 200 peer-reviewed articles and 2,000 glossary entries on applications, artificial intelligence, data communications, database design and utilization, hardware and software, international issues, management support systems, office automation and end-user computing, social, legal, and organizational issues, systems analysis and design, and theories, methodologies, and foundations. Articles include an overview of the topic and further reading. Available as an e-book.

483 Encyclopedia of library and information sciences. http://www.informaworld.com/smpp/title~db=all ~content=t917508581. Marcia J. Bates, Mary Niles Maack. Boca Raton, Fla.: CRC Press. 2010. ISBN 9780849397110

020.3   Z1006

On the Taylor & Francis Informaworld platform. Introduction and topical table of contents available free-of-charge; other content by subscription only. Covers topics related to: archival science; bibliography; document and genre theory; informatics; information systems; knowledge management; library and information science; museum studies; records management; social studies of information. International in scope. Presents long, signed articles in A-Z order with bibliographies. Limited search function on initial screen, but advanced search options are available. Also published in print.

Approximately three-quarters of the entries in this 3rd ed. are new, so older editions are still useful, especially for library-focused entries.

484 International encyclopedia of information and library science. 2nd ed. John Feather, R. P. Sturges. London;

New York: Routledge, 2003. xxxii, 688 p., ill. ISBN 0415259010

004.03   Z1006.I57

Articles written by library and information science experts, largely from the United Kingdom and United States. Twelve chapter-length signed articles treat "central issues"—*Pref.*: communication; economics of information; informatics; information management; information policy; information professions; information society; information systems; information theory; knowledge industries; knowledge management; organization of knowledge. Medium-length signed articles deal with specific topics, and short, unsigned entries "define the basic concepts, activities and objects of the information world."—*Pref.* Includes brief biographies of influential individuals worldwide. All signed articles include bibliographical references. A to Z arrangement, with many *see also* references. Index to topics and authors of entries. List of abbreviations. Available as an e-book from various third-party suppliers.

First ed., 1997.

485 LISWiki. http://liswiki.org. John Hubbard. [s.l.]: liswiki.org. 2005–

Over 1,400 contributed articles. Anyone can add or edit content. Browseable by title or category, or searchable by keyword. Completeness and accuracy of information varies. Most entries contain external links for further reading, but many are merely brief definitions or stub entries awaiting fuller content.

486 World encyclopedia of library and information services. 3rd ed. Robert Wedgeworth. Chicago: American Library Association, 1993. xvii, 905 p., ill. ISBN 0838906905

020.3   Z1006.W67

Title varies: 1st ed. (1980) and 2nd ed. (1986) had title: *ALA world encyclopedia of library and information services*. Signed articles on the concepts, condition, and history of librarianship. International in scope; includes articles about 160 countries written by contributors from these countries, as well as 216 biographies of important library figures, living and dead. Articles are enhanced by hard-to-locate statistical data, many illustrations, and selective bibliographies. Dictionary arrangement with a comprehensive index. Although many entries would benefit from updating, still a useful and unparalleled work.

Factbooks and Compendiums

487 **The librarian's book of lists.** George M. Eberhart. Chicago: American Library Association, 2010. viii, 118 p., ill. ISBN 9780838910634

020   Z665.L565

For every librarian with a penchant for lists. A miscellany of useful information (e.g., the best blogs on libraries and books; frequently banned books; key dates in American library history) and bizarre facts (e.g., librarian ghosts; movies with the worst librarian stereotypes; birds that make library-related sounds).

488 **Library world records. 2nd ed.** Godfrey Oswald. Jefferson, N.C.: McFarland & Co., 2009. 327 p.

027   Z721.O79

Presents records, "firsts" and other facts related to: national libraries; public and subscription libraries; university and academic libraries; specialty libraries and archives; miscellaneous world records (such as notable people who have worked in libraries); books, periodicals, and bookstores; library buildings; library catalogs, databases, and technology; and LIS organizations and schools. The scope is international. Bibliography. Detailed index. Illustrated.

First ed., 2004.

489 **The whole library handbook 5: current data, professional advice, and curiosa about libraries and library services. 5th ed.** George M. Eberhart. Chicago: ALA Editions, 2013. v, 528 p., ill. ISBN 9780838910900

020.973   Z665.2.U6

Eclectic compendium of facts and figures about libraries and librarians, along with "a selection of the most informative, practical, and entertaining" recent writings on libraries.—*Pref.* Organized by broad themes: libraries; people; the profession; materials; operations; users; advocacy; technology; issues; librariana. Reprints many short, practical articles that summarize professional topics and offer tips. Because each edition contains primarily new material, older editions remain useful. Index to subjects and authors. Similar volumes, *The whole digital library handbook* and *The whole school library handbook 2*, reprint short works and

extracts from journal articles but have less value for ready reference.

First edition, 1991.

Guides to the Literature

490 **Cabell's directory of publishing opportunities in educational technology and library science.** http:// www.cabells.com. Beaumont, Tex.: Cabell Publishing. 2007- 2155-7632

381   Z286.E3

Identifies over 400 journals in the fields of library science and educational technology. For each, indicates whether submissions are peer-reviewed, the number of reviewers, the turnaround time for reviews, and the acceptance rate. Entries provide editor's name and contact information, launch date, frequency, ISSN, a link to the journal's website, and brief information about the submission process. Search options include topic, title keyword, acceptance rate, type of review, number of external reviewers, indexing in Journal Citation Reports or ERIC, fees, and publisher. Now only online.

491 **Library and information science: a guide to key literature and sources.** Michael F. Bemis. Chicago: ALA Editions, 2014. 280 p. ISBN 9780838911853

016.02   Z666.B38

For many years, the discipline of library and information science lacked a current, annotated bibliography that addresses the breadth of the field; this work fills the gap. Identifies 1,594 works, primarily printed books and periodicals but also selected websites and online resources. Generally cites works published between 2000 and 2012, although some older classics are included. "Emphasis is on usefulness and practicality for the working librarian."—*Intro.* Entries meriting annotations meet criteria of timeliness and authority, have "professional standing," and/or possess features of special value, such as tables or case studies. Additional resources are listed without annotations. Entries appear in 39 chapters that reflect sub-domains or topics within LIS, arranged alphabetically. Each chapter opens with a short list of relevant LC subject headings, followed by sections for books, periodicals, websites and databases, with occasional sidebars to spotlight historical or other related works. Treats many core topics, such as cataloging, information technology, and reference, which are likewise covered, albeit more selectively, in *Guide to reference* (52). Also covers a number of unique topics, including awards, historical studies, biographies and memoirs of librarians, career guides, ethics, humor, international librarianship, reading promotion, and librarians in popular culture. Appendices describe national, regional, and international professional associations, including the divisions and chapters of ALA. Index.

Indexes; Abstract Journals; Databases

Editor's Guide: This section includes subscription and free resources that index journal articles and other publications. Some include abstracts and some include full text. Also in this section are searchable, LIS-specific repositories of electronic documents.

492 CiteSeerX. http://citeseerx.ist.psu.edu/. NEC Research Institute, Pennsylvania State University, College of Information Sciences and Technology. University Park, Pa.: Pennsylvania State University, College of Information Sciences and Technology. [2007–]

A digital library that focuses primarily on the technical literature of computer and information science. Although this version is labeled "beta," CiteSeerX is a solidly established and highly ranked repository founded in 1997. Offers many advanced features, such as automatic citation indexing, the ability to search for data tables embedded in documents, and impact ranking of conferences and journals. Registered users may create a personal content portal, MyCiteSeerX, to enable alerts and other customized services.

493 dLIST: digital library for information science and technology. http://dlist.sir. arizona.edu. University of Arizona, School of Information Resources and Library Science, Learning Technologies Center, University of Arizona. Tucson, Ariz.: University of Arizona. 2002–

Z665
"[A] cross-institutional, subject-based, open access digital archive for the information sciences, including archives and records management, library and information science, information systems, digital curation, museum informatics, records management and other critical information infrastructures." --*Home page* Contains primarily North American documents. Basic keyword search with options to filter results. As of January 2014, contains 1,562 items and is temporarily closed to new submissions.

494 E-LIS: e-prints in library and information science. http://eprints.rclis. org/. AEPIC. Milan, Italy: AEPIC. 2003–

Z666
The largest open access digital repository for self-archived documents in library and information science. International in scope, with strongest representation from the Americas and Europe. Search interface is in English, and all documents carry English language abstracts. May be browsed by author, classified subject, country, year, or conference year and name. Offers a simple keyword search or an advanced search with 15 different parameters.

495 ERIC. http://www.eric.ed.gov/. U.S. Department of Education. Washington: U.S. Department of Education

National education database sponsored by the U.S. Department of Education. Presently the largest education database in the world, ERIC contains over one million citations covering research documents, journal articles, books, technical reports, program descriptions and evaluations, and curricular materials in the field of education. Also includes abstracts, citations, and selective full-text. Earlier print versions were available as *Current index to journals in education* and *Resources in education*. Electronic versions are available through several different vendors, as well as freely available through the government website. The *Thesaurus of ERIC descriptors* is embedded in each database.

496 IFLA library. http://library.ifla.org/. International Federation of Library Associations and Institutions. The Hague, The Netherlands: International Federation of Library Associations and Institutions. 2013-

The official digital repository of IFLA (564). Contains papers from its annual conferences and other materials. Browsable by activity or group; IFLA annual congress (2013-); author; and subject. In addition to a simple keyword search, an advanced search feature provides many options for refining and limiting retrieval.

497 Informed librarian online: professional reading for the information professional. http://www.informedlibrarian.com/. Infosources Publishing. Teaneck, N.J.: Infosources Publishing. 2002– 1061-3609
Z671

Monthly current awareness service. Compiles tables of contents from over 300 "domestic and foreign library and information-related journals, e-journals, magazines, e-magazines, newsletters and e-newsletters."— *Home Page* Current and archived issues are searchable by keyword. Provides complimentary access to about a dozen full-text articles in each issue. Some content is free; full access requires a paid "premium" membership, which includes notification of new issues by e-mail or RSS feed. "Premium members" may set up a profile to customize displays and notifications.

498 InfoSci-Books. http://www.igi-global.com/EResources/InfoSciBooks.aspx. [IGI Global]. Hershey, Pa.: IGI Global. [2000–]. 1946–1984
011

A searchable, full-text database of 2,400-plus monographs and reference works published by IGI Global since 2000. Covers information science and many related subjects, such as online education, business applications of information technology, e-government, health informatics, and library science. Continually updated. See also *InfoSci-Journals* (499), a companion database with the full text of articles in IGI Global journals.

499 Infosci-Journals. http://www.igi-global.com/EResources/InfoSciJournals.aspx. [IGI Global]. Hershey, Pa.: IGI Global. 2000s– 1947-9689
004

A searchable, full-text database of over 150 peer-reviewed journals published by IGI Global. Covers many topics related to information science and its applications in health care, business, education,

government, and library science. Continually updated. See also InfoSci-Books (498), a companion database with the full text of IGI Global monographs and reference books.

500 Librarian's e-library. http://www.google.com/coop/cse?cx=015271347771663724636%3Acmwvisovdsg. American Library Association. Chicago: American Library Association. 2006–

Customized Google Web search engine maintained by the American Library Association (ALA) library and volunteers. Searches some 250 selected sites. Recommended to search by using very specific terms, as retrieval is limited to 100 items.

501 Library, information science and technology abstracts. http://www.libraryresearch.com. EBSCO Publishing. Ispwich, Mass.: EBSCO Publishing. 2005–
Z699

On the EBSCOhost platform, but available free of charge. Indexes and abstracts articles from 600 plus journals in librarianship, classification, cataloging, bibliometrics, online information retrieval, information management, and similar fields. Also indexes some conference proceedings, books, and research reports. Coverage extends back to mid-1960s. Libraries subscribing to other EBSCOhost databases may add LISTA to their profile without charge.

In 2012, the publisher merged the full text subscription version of LISTA with *Library Literature & Information Science Full Text* (503) and additional content to create a new database, *Library & Information Science Source* (502). However, the two older titles, with their more selective but overlapping coverage, are still available by subscription separately.

No longer issued in print. Earlier print equivalents: *Documentation abstracts* (1966–68); *Documentation abstracts and information science abstracts* (1968); *Information science abstracts* (1969–2002); *Information science and technology abstracts* (2003–4). Publisher and frequency varied.

502 Library & information science source. http://www.ebscohost.com/academic/library-information-science-source. Ipswich, Mass.: EBSCO Publishing. 2012-
Z665

On the EBSCOHost platform. Created by merging content from *Library literature & information science full text* (503), *Library literature & information science retrospective* (504), and *Library, information science & technology abstracts* (501), with added coverage of journals not included in those databases. Indexes, either fully or selectively, articles and book reviews in over a thousand English and foreign-language periodicals. Provides full text of approximately 440 titles. Indexing coverage begins in 1905. Utilizes the subject thesaurus originally developed by the H.W. Wilson company for the *Library literature and information science* databases. Includes profiles of frequently-indexed authors.

503 Library literature and information science full text. http://www.ebscohost.com/academic/library-literature-information-science-full-text. Ipswich, Mass.: Ebsco
Informally known as *Library Lit*. Indexes journals, books, conference proceedings, library school theses, pamphlets, and book reviews, covering all aspects of library science. Earliest records are from 1984. Most entries include abstracts. Since 1997, includes full text of articles from over 175 periodicals. Updated daily.

Originally developed by the H.W. Wilson Company but now provided by Ebsco through its EbscoHost interface. In 2012 the new publisher merged *Library Lit* with its own database, *Library, Information Science & Technology Abstracts* (501), to form a single product, *Library & Information Science Source* (502), with full-text articles from over 440 journals.

The same database without full text is available with the title *Library Literature & Information Science Index*. A companion database, *Library Literature & Information Science Retrospective* (504), extends coverage back to 1905. Previously published in print by H.W. Wilson, beginning in 1921. Frequency varied; annual cumulative volumes.

504 Library literature and information science retrospective. http://www.ebscohost.com/academic/library-literature-information-science-retrospective. Ebsco. Ipswich, Mass.: EBSCO Publishing. 2007
Indexes journals in library literature and information science from 1905 to 1983. Incorporates indexing from *Library work* (1905–11), *Library journal* (1912–20), and *Library literature* (1921–83). Also includes

full text content of the influential *Wilson library bulletin* (1914–83), plus citations to book reviews, books, book chapters, and library school theses. Scope is international but emphasizes U.S. periodicals. Available on the EBSCOhost platform. See *Library Literature and Information Science Full Text* (503) for coverage from 1984 to present.

Since 2012, the content of this database is also included in *Library and information science source.* (502).

505 LISA: library and information science abstracts. http://www.proquest.com/en-US/catalogs/databases/detail/lisa-set-c.shtml. ProQuest, LLC. Bethesda, Md.: ProQuest, LLC. 1990s
016.02   Z666; Z671
Indexes and abstracts journal articles in librarianship, information science, online retrieval, publishing, and information technology. International scope. Covers over 440 periodicals. Article titles are given in the original language with English translation; abstracts are in English. Earliest records are from 1969. Updated online every two weeks. A companion product, *ProQuest Library Science*, provides full text of articles in over 190 titles that are indexed in *LISA*.

Previously issued in print. Continues *Library science abstracts* (1950-68).

Library History

Editor's Guide: This section cites reference works of historical scholarship. To identify primary source documents, consult Library Literature and Information Science Retrospective (504) or Library and Information Science Source (502) and the older bibliographies in Library and Information Science > General Works > Bibliography.

Bibliography

506 American Library Association archives. http://archives.library.illinois.edu/ala/. American Library Association. Urbana, Ill.: University of Illinois. 1997-
Z673
The University of Illinois Archives are the repository for the historical records of ALA. Houses official

records, correspondence, publications, photographs (including digitized images), sound recordings, films, and videotapes. Well-documented in finding aids that may be searched by keywords or browsed by collection title, subject, name, or classification. An open access repository for born-digital content, launched in January 2014, may be searched or browsed separately.

507 **American library history: A bibliography of dissertations and theses. 3rd ed.** Arthur P. Young, Michael H. Harris. Metuchen, N.J.: Scarecrow Press, 1988. x, 469 p. ISBN 0810821389
016.02   Z666.Y68

Revised and updated edition of *A guide to research in American library history*. An annotated subject guide to master's theses, doctoral dissertations, and some research reports. Describes more than 1,150 items through 1986. Author and subject indexes. For coverage of dissertations and theses since 1990, see the Bibliography of Writings on the History of Libraries, Librarianship, and Book Culture (510), as well as general online dissertation indexes, such as ProQuest Dissertations and Theses (163).

508 **American library history: A comprehensive guide to the literature.** Donald G. Davis, John Mark Tucker, Michael H. Harris. Santa Barbara, Calif.: ABC-CLIO, 1989. xxi, 471 p. ISBN 0874361427
027.073   Z731.D38

First ed., 1978, by Michael H. Harris and Donald G. Davis, Jr. Includes 7,150 unannotated entries for works published through 1986. In 15 sections: (1) Historiography and sources, (2) General studies, (3) Private libraries and reading tastes, (4) Predecessors of the public library, (5) Public libraries, (6) Academic libraries, (7) School libraries, (8) State libraries, (9) Special libraries, (10) Archival enterprise, (11) Education for librarianship, (12) Library associations, (13) Special aspects of librarianship, (14) Women in librarianship, (15) Biographies of individual librarians and library benefactors.

Short bibliographic essays introduce each chapter. Indexes of authors, institutions, and essays. For updates, the compilers recommend the biennial bibliographic essays titled, "The literature of American library history," published in the journal *Libraries &*

culture (now *Information & culture*). See also Bibliography of Writings on the History of Libraries, Librarianship, and Book Culture (510).

509 **Annual bibliography of the history of the printed book and libraries.** International Federation of Library Associations. Dordrecht, The Netherlands: Springer, 1970–2000. 31 v. 0303-5964
016.001552   Z117.A55

Publisher varies. At head of title: ABHB. Since 1989, edited by staff of the Koninklijke Bibliotheek (Royal Library of the Netherlands) under the auspices of the International Federation of Library Associations and Institutions. Lists scholarly books, articles, and dissertations about the history of (1) printed books, (2) the arts, crafts, techniques, and equipment of book manufacture, and (3) the economic, social, and cultural environment surrounding the production, distribution, conservation, and description of books. A classed list with name indexes. International, multilingual. Most citations include a few descriptive words. Includes section, "Libraries, librarianship, scholarship, institutions," arranged geographically. Each volume contains about 5,000 records. Continued by Book History Online (511).

510 **Bibliography of writings on the history of libraries, librarianship, and book culture.** http://www.ala.org/lhrt/popularresources/libhistorybib/libraryhistory. Ed Goedeken, American Library Association, Library History Round Table. Chicago: American Library Association. 1990–

Also available in the *LHRT newsletter* from the ALA Library History Round Table. Issued semi-annually. Cumulative editions: 1990–1995; 1995-1999; 2000-2004; 2005-2012. Early numbers arranged by author. Since Fall 1995, arranged by subject: A) United States; B) Non-U.S. Western Hemisphere; C) Europe; D) Asia, Africa, the Middle East and other; E) History of books, reading, and book culture; F) General, historiography, philosophy, library, and information science education. Cites books, articles, theses, and dissertations. Not annotated.

511 **Book history online.** http://bibliographies.brillonline.com/browse/book-history-online. Leiden, The

Netherlands: Brill. 1989–
016.001552   Z117.A55

Continues *Annual bibliography of the history of the printed book and libraries* (509), with similar scope and content, and duplicates its entries for 1990–2000. May be searched by authors, keywords and titles. "Included are monographs, articles and reviews dealing with the history of the printed book, its arts, crafts, techniques and equipment, its economic, social and cultural environment, as well as its production, distribution, preservation and description."—*Home Page.* Researchers who cannot access a library subscription may purchase short-term access to the database.

512   A brief history of the future of libraries: An annotated bibliography. Gregg Sapp. Lanham, Md.: Scarecrow Press, 2002. xi, 295 p. ISBN 0810841967
027.073   Z731.S26

Documents predictions within the profession about the effects of information technology on libraries and places them in historical context. Introductory chapter surveys writings about the future of libraries from 1876 to the mid-1970s. Four subsequent chapters (1978–84; 1985–89; 1990–94; 1995–99) open with essays that spotlight major themes, followed by annotated bibliographies arranged by author. Subject index.

513   Children's services in the American public library: a selected bibliography. Fannette H. Thomas. New York: Greenwood Press, 1990. xii, 151 p. ISBN 0313247218
027.625   Z718.2.U6T46

Lists over 600 articles and books from 1876 to 1976, with brief annotations. Arranged by broad topics: historical focus, professional staff, organizational scheme, philosophical perspective, client group, collection development, readers' services, story hour, interagency cooperation, and multi-media. Author and subject indexes.

Encyclopedias

514   A chronology of librarianship. Josephine Metcalfe Smith. Metuchen, N.J.: Scarecrow Press, 1968. 263 p.
020/.9   Z665.S58

Year-by-year listing of milestones in library history from the first century C.E. through 1959, emphasizing the United States. Cites sources for all facts. Subject and names indexes. Supplemented by *A chronology of librarianship, 1960-2000,* by Jeffrey M. Wilhite, which arranges entries by topic under each year.

515   Encyclopedia of library history. Wayne A. Wiegand, Donald G. Davis. New York: Garland Publ., 1994. xxxi, 707 p. ISBN 0824057872
020.3   Z721.E54

Signed articles, ranging from 200 to 6,000 words, on the historical development of libraries by country, type of library, and period. Also topical entries on library practices, services, user groups, and social issues, plus profiles of 60 major libraries. No biographical entries. Separate tables of content list entries by geographic location and by subject. Index to subjects and proper names.

516   Encyclopedia of the Library of Congress: For Congress, the nation and the world. John Young Cole, Jane Aikin, Library of Congress. Washington; Lanham, Md.: Library of Congress; Bernan Press, 2004. xxxi, 569 p., ill. (some color), ports. ISBN 0890599718
027.57303   Z733.U6E53

Entries emphasize the historical development of the Library of Congress. Part I: essays on major topics (e.g., the Library's international role), large units, and relations with other agencies. Part II: shorter articles on selected divisions, collections, buildings, functions, and individuals. Part III: chronologies of senior officials, legislative appropriations, collection growth, major gifts, and chairs of the Congressional Committee on the Library. Bibliography. Index. Heavily illustrated.

517   International dictionary of library histories. David H. Stam. Chicago: Fitzroy Dearborn Publishers, 2001. 2 v. (xxx, 1053 p.) ISBN 1579582443
027.009   Z721.I57

Introductory surveys of 34 types of libraries and 13 geographical regions, followed by 224 institutional histories. Includes only libraries that are still operating. Signed entries, each two to five pages long, contain contact data, founding date, holdings counts, and a bibliography, along with a list of special collections and a narrative history. Index.

518 Library world records. 2nd ed. Godfrey Oswald. Jefferson, N.C.: McFarland & Co., 2009. 327 p.
027   Z721.O79

Presents records, "firsts" and other facts related to: national libraries; public and subscription libraries; university and academic libraries; specialty libraries and archives; miscellaneous world records (such as notable people who have worked in libraries); books, periodicals, and bookstores; library buildings; library catalogs, databases, and technology; and LIS organizations and schools. The scope is international. Bibliography. Detailed index. Illustrated.

First ed., 2004.

Periodicals

Editor's Guide: *Ulrich's* (49) identifies more than four thousand English-language periodicals in the field of library & information science. The highly selective list here stresses:

 a. journals frequently ranked highly in bibliometric and qualitative studies of journal prestige;
 b. widely read trade magazines and newsletters;
 c. periodicals focused on reference work and allied specialities.

Except where web-only publication is indicated, these periodicals are available in both print and online formats.

519 The American archivist. http://www2 .archivists.org/american-archivist. Society of American Archivists. [Chicago]: Society of American Archivists. 1938-. 0360-9081
025.17/1   CD3020.A45

Semiannual. Online open access to the entire back file, except for the last six issues, which are available to Society of American Archivists members or by payment. The leading peer-reviewed journal of the archival profession "seeks to reflect thinking about theoretical and practical developments in the archival profession, particularly in North America;

about the relationships between archivists and the creators and users of archives; and about cultural, social, legal, and technological developments that affect the nature of recorded information and the need to create and maintain it."—*Home page*. Each issue features 8–12 research articles, book reviews, and occasional case studies, opinion pieces, and reprinted addresses.

For practical articles on archival practice and news from the field, see SAA's member magazine, *Archival outlook*.

520 Booklist online. http://www.booklist online.com/. American Library Association. Chicago: American Library Association. 2006–

Useful for reviews of current fiction, nonfiction, and reference materials, Booklist Online is a subscription database that "contains over 120,000 reviews and thousands of features dating back to 1992."—FAQ There is some free content, including feature articles, columns, and some current reviews. The bulk of the reviews are available only to subscribers. Reviews are arranged into broad categories of Adult Books, Books for Youth, Media, and Reference. Users can browse reviews in these areas by subject or use a variety of search tools to locate materials. Online content is derived from the long-running ALA publication *Booklist*.

521 Children & libraries. Association for Library Service to Children., American Library Association. Chicago: American Library Association, 2003-. 1542-9806
027.62 13   Z718.1 C46

Quarterly. As the official, refereed journal of ALA's (553) Association for Library Service to Children, "showcases current scholarly research and practice in library service to children and significant activities and programs of the Association," including its many book awards. —*Home page* Online publication will begin in spring 2014; print publication will continue. Ebsco databases also provide full text.

522 College and research libraries. http:// crl.acrl.org/. Association of College and Research Libraries. Chicago: Association of College and Research Libraries. 1939-. 2150-6701
027.705   Z671.C6

Bimonthly. The official, refereed journal of the Association of College and Research Libraries, a division of ALA (553), highly regarded and widely read by academic librarians. Bimonthly. Issued in print until 2013; now published as an open access e-journal. All back issues are available electronically. Each issue contains 5-6 peer-reviewed articles on varied aspects of academic librarianship and 5-6 book reviews.

523 College and research libraries news.
http://crln.acrl.org/. Association of College and Research Libraries. Chicago: Association of College and Research Libraries. 1967-. 2150-6698
020   Z671

Eleven/year. Published as an open access online newsletter, with back issue access from May 2004. Also issued in print. Older issues available online in several EbscoHost databases. "[P]rovides articles on the latest trends and practices affecting academic and research libraries." —*About C&RL News*. Serving as the official magazine of the Association of College and Research Libraries, a division of ALA (553), spotlights innovative programs and announces major acquisitions, grants, legislation, Internet resources, people in the news, and ACRL initiatives and publications.

524 Communications in information literacy. http://www.comminfolit.org/. s.l.: s.n. 2007-. 1933-5954
028.7   LB1044.87; ZA3075

Semiannual. "An open-access, independent, peer-reviewed journal on information literacy in institutions of higher education." —*Home page* A typical issue features a half dozen peer-reviewed articles focused on theory, research, or practical knowledge, plus non-referreed articles under the heading "Perspectives." Occasional theme issues.

525 D-Lib magazine. http://www.dlib.org/. Corporation for National Research Initiatives, D-Lib Forum, Federal High Performance Computing Program (U.S.). Reston, Va.: Corp. for National Research Initiatives. 1995-. 1082-9873
025 12   ZA4080

Bimonthly. One of the earliest online-only, open access periodicals in LIS, focusing on "digital library research and development, including new technologies, applications, and contextual social and economic issues."—*About D-Lib magazine*. A typical issue contains 5-6 articles and 1-2 conference reports. Indexes: author; title.

526 Information & culture: a journal of history. Austin, Tex.: University of Texas Press, 2012-. 2164-8034
027   Z671

Quarterly. Continues the numbering of *Journal of library history* (v.1-22, 1966-1987), *Libraries & culture* (v.23-41, 1988-2006), and *Libraries & the cultural record* (v.41-46, 2006-2011). Back issues, except the latest three years, available through JSTOR (360). Volume 36 to present available through Project Muse (386).

Each issue offers 4-6 peer-reviewed articles on information history, which encompasses library history. Book reviews are published on the journal's website: http://www.infoculturejournal.org/

527 Information processing & management. Amsterdam, The Netherlands: Elsevier, 1975-. 0306-4573
029/.05   Z699.A16

Bimonthly. Continues the numbering of *Information storage and retrieval* (v.1-10, 1963-1974). Features peer-reviewed research articles from around the world on "the generation, representation, organization, storage, retrieval, and use of information; the nature, manifestations, behavior, and effects of information and knowledge; communication and distribution of information and knowledge; and human information behavior."--*About this journal*. All issues available online in Science Direct.

528 Information research: an international journal. http://informationr.net/ir. Lund, Sweden: T.D. Wilson; Lund University Libraries. 1995-1368-1613 (online)

Quarterly. Open access. Contains "both refereed papers and working papers in the fields of information science, information management, information systems, information policy and librarianship."--*About the journal*. Also features reviews of books and software.

529 The information society.
London: Taylor & Francis, 1981-. 0197-2243
020/.5   Z668;TK5101.A1

5/year. "[A] multidisciplinary journal intended to answer questions about the Information Age."—*Aims & scope*. Approximately four peer-reviewed articles and six book reviews per issue cover topics in information policy, practice and theory; occasional issues are devoted to special themes. Available online from the publisher and, with an 18-month delay, through several Ebsco databases.

530   Information technology and libraries.
http://ejournals.bc.edu/ojs/index.php/ital/index. Library and Information Technology Association (U.S.). Chicago: Library and Information Technology Association. 1982-. 0730-9295
025.3/028/54   Z678.9.A1 53
Quarterly. The official journal of ALA's (553) Library & Information Technology Association. Publishes 4-5 peer-reviewed articles per issue related to "all aspects of information technology in all types of libraries." —*Home Page*. Since 2012, published only as an open access ejournal. At this writing, full text of issues is available on the journal website only back to 2005. Older back files available online, from various start dates, in databases from Ebsco, Gale, and ProQuest.

Preceded by *Journal of library automation* (1968-1981), which is completely and freely available on the *Information technology & libraries* website.

531   Journal of academic librarianship.
Amsterdam, The Netherlands: Elsevier, 1975-. 0099-1333
020/.5   Z671.J58
Bimonthly. Back issues from v.18 (1993) available in Science Direct. Focuses on problems and issues germane to college and university libraries. Contains peer-reviewed research, analysis, viewpoints, and reviews.

532   The Journal of documentation.
Aslib. Bingley, U.K.: Emerald Publ. Group, 1945-. 0022-0418
010.5   Z1007.J9
Bimonthly. The scope is "broadly information sciences, encompassing all of the academic and professional disciplines which deal with recorded information," including librarianship.—*About the journal*. Most of the peer-reviewed articles are categorized as "research papers" or "conceptual papers,"

with occasional case studies, technical papers, and reviews. Complete online back file available through Emerald.

533   Journal of education for library and information science.
Association for Library and Information Science Education. Chicago: Association for Library and Information Science Education, 1984-. 0748-5786
020/.5   Z671.J64
Quarterly. Continues the numbering of *Journal of education for librarianship* (v.1-24, 1960-1984). Back issues, except the last three years, available in JSTOR (360). Also available online, starting from various dates, in databases from Ebsco, Gale, and ProQuest.

The official, peer-reviewed journal of the Association for Library and Information Science Education. Each issue contains a half dozen research articles focused on teaching and learning for the information professions.

534   Journal of information science.
Institute of Information Scientists, Chartered Institute of Library and Information Professionals (Great Britain). Los Angeles: SAGE, 1979-. 0165-5515
020.5   Z1007.J95
Bimonthly. Approximately 10 peer-reviewed research articles per issue addresses information science theory, policy, application or practice. International scope. Most back issues are available online through the publisher.

535   Journal of the American Society for Information Science and Technology: JASIST. American Society for Information Science and Technology. New York: John Wiley & Sons, 2001-. 1532-2882
020 13   Z1007.A477
Monthly. Considered the leading information science journal within the field of LIS. Averages 12-15 peer-reviewed research articles per issue, focused on "the production, discovery, recording, storage, representation, retrieval, presentation, manipulation, dissemination, use, and evaluation of information and on the tools and techniques associated with these processes."—i}Aims and scope{/i}. Review articles

published in JASIST under the running title, "Advances in information science," continue the former *Annual review of information science and technology* (606).

Previous titles: *American documentation* (v.1-20, 1950-1969); *Journal of the American Society for Information Science* (v.21-51, 1970-2000). All back issues available by subscription or per-article payment from the Wiley Online Library and, for members of ASIS&T, through the ASIS&T digital library.

536   Knowledge quest: journal of the American Association of School Librarians. American Association of School Librarians. Chicago: American Library Association, 1997-.
1094-9046
027 13   Z675.S3; K67

Five per year. Continues the numbering of *School media quarterly* (v.1-9, 1972-1981) and *School library media quarterly* (v.10-25, 1982-1997). Official publication of the American Association of School Librarians, a division of ALA (553). Articles focus on the development of school library programs and services, and related trends in education, learning theory, and relevant disciplines.

Available as an electronic flipbook, for AASL members and subscribers, on AASL's eCollab website; and in various Ebsco, Gale, and ProQuest databases.

537   Library and information science research. Amsterdam, The Netherlands: Elsevier, 1983-. 0740-8188
020/.5   Z671

Quarterly. Continues numbering of *Library research* (v.1-4, 1979-1982). Since v. 16, available online in Elsevier's Science Direct database. Nine peer-reviewed research articles in each issue, covering a wide range of topics; occasionally includes book reviews.

538   Library collections, acquisitions, & technical services. London: Taylor and Francis Group, 1999-.
1464-9055
025.21 L697   Z689.L515

Quarterly. Serves as "a forum for the international exchange of ideas and experiences among members of the library collection management, technical services, vendor and publishing communities throughout the world."—*Aims & scope.* Each issue contains

6-9 peer-reviewed research articles; some issues contain book reviews. Complete backfile online through the publisher. Previous title: *Library acquisitions: practice and theory* (v. 1-22, 1977-1998), available in Elsevier's ScienceDirect.

539   Library journal. New York: Library Journal, 1876- 0363-0277

Twenty per year. Subscription includes print and iPad editions. The magazine's website, http://lj .libraryjournal.com, includes much of the magazine's recent content, plus additional features such as blogs by leaders in the field and the InfoDocket news service. Full-text back issues are available, starting from various dates, in databases from several aggregators, including EbscoHost, Gale, Lexis-Nexis, and ProQuest.

Each issue contains feature articles on library management, technology, policy, and other current issues, along with columns, opinion pieces, news, and book reviews. Over 8,000 sources are reviewed annually. Popular yearly features include a spotlight on library architecture, a survey of placements and salaries, profiles of "movers and shakers" in the field, and the "star libraries" (593) index of public library service.

LJ also publishes a number of free email newsletters on weekly, semi-monthly, and monthly schedules. A sign-up form is available on the website.

540   Library leadership & management. http://journals.tdl.org/llm/index.php/ llm/index. Chicago: American Library Association. 2009-

Quarterly. The official journal of the Library Leadership and Management Association of ALA (553). Continues the volume numbering of *Library administration and management* (v.1-22, 1987-2008). Focuses on "assisting library administrators and managers at all levels as they deal with day-to-day challenges." —*Focus and scope.* Includes referred research articles, columns offering practical advice, and interviews with leading practitioners. Published online only since v. 24 (2010). Open access to issues since v. 19 (2005) via LLAMA's website.

541   The library quarterly: information, community, policy. University of Chicago. Chicago: University of Chicago Press, 1931-. ill. 0024-2519
020.5   Z671.L713

Quarterly. Available online in JSTOR (360). One of the field's most prestigious, peer-reviewed journals. Covers a wide range of subjects, with an emphasis on "research that chronicles libraries as organizations that connect their communities to information."—*Publication information*. Each issue contains several research or review articles, plus 6-9 long book reviews.

542 Library resources & technical services. American Library Association, Association for Library Collections & Technical Services. Chicago: American Library Association, 1957-. 0024-2527

025.06273   Z671.L7154

Quarterly. The official journal of ALA's (553) Association for Library Collections & Technical Services. Publishes peer-reviewed articles (3-4 per issue) on collections, scholarly communication, preservation, acquisitions, continuing resources, and all aspects of cataloging, along with book reviews. Publisher provides full text online, v. 40 (1996) to present, by subscription. Also available in various Ebsco, Gale, and ProQuest databases; dates of coverage vary.

543 Library trends. University of Illinois, Urbana-Champaign. Graduate School of Library and Information Science. Baltimore: Johns Hopkins University Press, 1952-. 0024-2594

020.5   Z671.L6173

Quarterly thematic issues, each with a different guest editor, cover critical issues in professional librarianship of interest to practitioners and LIS educators. Published online through Project Muse (386). All back issues, except for the most recent two years, can be found in the University of Illinois institutional repository, IDEALS (http://www.ideals.illinois.edu).

544 Online searcher. Medford, N.J.: Information Today, 2013-. 2324-9684

025 15   Z699.A1 O546

Bimonthly. Formed by the merger of *Online* (1977-2012) and *Searcher* (1993-2012). Full-text available online in databases from Ebsco, Gale, and ProQuest. Illustrated magazine format. Features industry news, topical articles, and several recurring columns.

545 portal: libraries and the academy. Baltimore, Md.: Johns Hopkins University Press, 2001-. 1531-2542

020 13   Z675.U5; P82

Quarterly. Peer-reviewed articles cover topics in academic library administration, information technology, and information policy. Each issue includes 2-3 substantive articles and 3-4 brief book reviews. Complete online back file in Project Muse (386).

546 Public libraries. Public Library Association. Chicago: Public Library Association, 1978-. 1531-2542

027.4/73 x   Z731.P932

Bimonthly. Continues the numbering of the *PLA newsletter* (v.1-16, 1962-1977). Official magazine of ALA's (553) Public Library Association. Some of the print magazine's current content is also available openly on its companion website, *Public libraries online* - http://publiclibrariesonline.org. To retrieve issues more than 18 months old, use the site's search feature; older issues (2003-2009) are available as PDFs at http://www.ala.org/pla/publications/publiclibraries/pastissues, and in EbscoHost databases. Articles address a wide range of issues relevant to public librarians, such as funding, public policy, and programming.

547 Reference & user services quarterly. http://rusa.metapress.com. Reference and User Services Association. Chicago: American Library Association. 1997-. 1094-9054

025.5/2/0973   Z671.R23

Quarterly. As of v. 51 (2011), online only. Official journal of ALA's (553) Reference and User Services Association; available to non-members by subscription. Peer-reviewed articles deal with library service to adults, reference service, readers' advisory, and reference collection development for all types of libraries. Publishes the annual "Notable Books" list and various "best of" bibliographies and lists of recommended websites. Presents 12–18 reviews of reference books per issue, and 8-10 reviews of professional literature.

548 The reference librarian. New York:
Taylor & Francis, 1982-. 0276-3877
025.5/2   Z711.R444

Quarterly. Encompasses all aspects of reference
work in peer-reviewed research articles and practice-
focused columns. Frequent thematic or conference-
based issues. Complete electronic back file is
available from the publisher and in selected Ebsco-
Host databases, with an 18-month embargo.

549 Reference services review: RSR.
Bingley, U.K.: Emerald Publ. Group,
1973-. 0090-7324
011/.02/05   Z1035.1.R43

Quarterly. Presents peer-reviewed articles on reference and other aspects of user services in libraries.
Frequent thematic issues, including selected papers
from the biennial Library Instruction West conference. Annually since 1976, includes a bibliography
of the year's publications on library instruction and
information literacy. The complete backfile is available online from the publisher.

550 School library journal: SLJ.
New York: Media Source, 1954-. 0362-8930
027.8/05   Z675.S3; S29115

Monthly. Highly valued for its reviews of children's
books and media, which subscribers can access
online in the Book Verdict database at http://
bookverdict.com. *SLJ* also features articles on many
aspects of school library management and services,
as well as trends in publishing for young readers.
Full-text articles, from varied start dates, are available in Ebsco, Gale, and ProQuest databases, and
selected content is available free on the *SLJ* website,
http://www.slj.com.

551 Young adult library services.
American Library Association, Young Adult
Library Services Association. Chicago:
American Library Association, 2002-.
1541-4302
027 13   Z718.5.Y656

Quarterly. Official magazine of ALA's (553) Young
Adult Library Services Association (YALSA). Features
articles that showcase best practices, report news from
YALSA and other sources, and review professional literature. Full text available, with varying depth of back
files, in databases from Ebsco and Gale.

YALSA also sponsors an online, open access,
peer-reviewed publication, *Journal of Research on
Libraries and Young Adults.*

Professional Associations

Editor's Guide: The websites of professional associations are rich sources for information. In addition
to content about the associations and their activities,
many of the sites offer job postings, bibliographies,
directories, and various professional tools. This section spotlights associations with a wide focus (e.g.,
American Library Association, Special Libraries Association) and selected specialized associations relevant to most academic and public libraries. For a
fuller listing of LIS associations, see *World Guide to
Library, Archive, and Information Science Associations.*

**552 AIIM: the global community of
information professionals.** http://www
.aiim.org. AIIM (The Enterprise Content
Management Association). Silver Spring,
Md.: AIIM. 2003–
658.403806; 651.59

Former name: Association for Information and Image
Management International. Focuses on providing
"independent research, education and certification
programs to information professionals" including
"practitioners, technology suppliers, integrators and
consultants."—*About AIIM* Includes background on
the organization's structure and activities; "Solutions Provider Directory" (a categorized directory
of companies); job listings; industry reports and
white papers. Access to some content is restricted
to members.

553 ALA. http://www.ala.org/. American
Library Association. Chicago: American
Library Association

Official website of the American Library Association (ALA), the major professional group for
librarians and staff from many types of libraries.
Includes a wealth of information on careers in
librarianship, professional awards, scholarships,
social and political issues championed by librarians (e.g., intellectual freedom), and the internal
workings of the association, its conferences, and
its publishing arm.

A subsection of ALA's site, "Professional Resources: A to Z Index of Topics" (http://www.ala.org/ala/professionalresources/atoz/index.cfm), collates information from throughout the website concerning types of libraries, library operations and programs, and relevant topics such as banned books, diversity, green libraries, and vendors. Information about libraries for the general public can be found at a related site sponsored by ALA: http://www.ilovelibraries.org/. Subsites of particular reference value within the ALA website are separately entered and described in *Guide to reference* (52).

554   ALA handbook of organization.
http://www.ala.org/aboutala/governance/handbook. American Library Association. Chicago: American Library Association. 1972–. 0002-9769

Z673.A5

Requires American Library Association member login. Provides detailed information about the structure and governance of the association, including committee charges and membership; staff listings; conference dates and locations; policies; elected officers and Council members; awards and scholarships; and more. Published together with the *Member directory* (461), 1981–96. Published online only since 2009.

555   ALISE: Association for Library and Information Science Education. http://www.alise.org. Chicago: Association for Library and Information Science Education

Former name: Association of American Library Schools (1915-1983). A primary professional group for university faculty teaching in North American graduate programs in library and information science. Provides information on ALISE's history, structure, goals, awards, conferences, and publications, plus faculty job listings. Member login is required to access the detailed statistical report and searchable membership directory.

556   American Association of Law Libraries. http://www.aallnet.org/. American Association of Law Libraries. Chicago: American Association of Law Libraries

Official website of the major professional association for law librarians. Provides information about

the association, its chapters and committees, conferences, continuing education opportunities, publications, and more. The "Career Center" lists current vacancies. Some content available only to members. For historical information on the association and its officers, subunits, meetings, publications, and awards, see the annually updated loose-leaf service, *AALL reference book*, which is also in *HeinOnline*.

557   American Society for Indexing. http://www.asindexing.org/. American Society for Indexing. Wheat Ridge, Colo.: American Society for Indexing. 1968–

Z695.9

ASI is "the only professional organization in the United States devoted solely to the advancement of indexing, abstracting and database construction."— *Mission Statement* Known as the American Society of Indexers from its founding until 2008. Website details the association's structure and history, provides background on indexing as a vocation, and links to useful information for authors, editors, and professional indexers. Includes an "Indexer Locator," a directory of freelance indexers and abstractors, searchable by location, subject specialty, language, type of material, and software.

558   ARLIS/NA. http://www.arlisna.org/. Art Libraries Society of North America. Ottawa, Ont., [Canada]: Art Libraries Society of North America. 1995–

026.706

ARLIS/NA is the main professional association for art librarians and others interested in visual arts information. Content on its website includes history, mission, and internal structure of the association; awards and honors; event calendar; job postings; a roster of internships; conference proceedings; and numerous online publications, including book reviews, bibliographies, guidelines, and surveys.

559   Association of Research Libraries. http://www.arl.org. Association of Research Libraries. Washington: Assocation of Research Libraries

Official website of the Association of Research Libraries, an organization of 125 libraries at comprehensive, research-extensive institutions in the United States and Canada. Includes background on the association and its initiatives in such areas as copyright reform, diversity, leadership development, library assessment measures, and new models for scholarly communication. Also presents recent years of ARL Statistics (587) and ARL Annual Salary Survey (752). Lists publications such as *SPEC kits* (596), often with in-depth summaries, and offers full text of newsletters, press releases, issue briefs, etc.

560   Church and Synagogue Library Association. http://cslainfo.org/. Portland, Ore.: Church and Synagogue Library Association

CSLA provides practical information for congregational librarians, who are often non-professional volunteers. The website offers full-text, searchable book and media reviews, how-to publications and booklists for purchase, and information about the association's services, which include online workshops and mentoring. Some content is restricted to members.

561   CLA. http://www.cla.ca/. Canadian Library Association. Ottawa, Ont., Canada: Canadian Library Association. 1999–. ISBN 41667209

Website of the association that serves as the "national voice for Canada's library communities."—*Home Page* Provides background on the history, governance, organization, and finances of the association; staff contact data; awards and scholarships; current projects; job postings; position statements; online bookstore and boutique; and more.

562   Council on Library and Information: CLIR. http://www.clir.org/. Washington: Council on Library and Information Resources. 1998-
060; 004; 323.445;   Z673.C962
025.04; 027

Created by the merger of the Council on Library Resources (1956-1997) and the Commission on Preservation and Access (1986-1997). Sponsored and funded by academic libraries, CLIR focuses on "enhanc[ing] research, teaching, and learning environments in collaboration with libraries, cultural institutions, and communities of higher learning."— *Home Page* More than 150 published reports about key topics and trends are freely available on its

website. Describes CLIR's initiatives, history, fellowships, and publications; displays job postings; and supports an online community. The Digital Library Federation is a program of CLIR.

563   ICA: International Council on Archives. http://www.ica.org. International Council on Archives. Paris: International Council on Archives. 1996–
                                                    Z673

". . . dedicated to the effective management of records and the preservation, care and use of the world's archival heritage through its representation of records and archive professionals across the globe."—*About ICA* Includes information about the organization's mission, governance, and events; a resource center of digitized documents, including bibliographies and guidelines; and a members-only networking and communication site.

564   IFLA: International Federation of Library Associations and Institutions. http://www.ifla.org. International Federation of Library Associations and Institutions. The Hague, The Netherlands: International Federation of Library Associations and Institutions. 1995–
                                                    Z673.A54

The most prominent global library association. Includes background on the mission and structure of the federation; newsletters, reports, minutes, publications, and contact data for activities, divisions, sections, and special interest groups related to all aspects of the profession; full text of conference papers, guidelines, position papers, and other publications.

565   MLANET. http://www.mlanet.org/. Medical Library Association. Chicago: Medical Library Association (MLA). 1998–
Medical Library Association (MLA), since 1889, "a nonprofit, educational organization of more than 1,100 institutions and 3,600 individual members in the health sciences information field, committed to educating health information professionals, supporting health information research, promoting access to the world's health sciences information, and working to ensure that the best health information is available to all" (*MLA website*).

Searchable home page for MLA which provides a variety of resources for its members, such as professional standards and practices, discussion of information issues and policy, career information resources, professional credentialing, publications, etc. Also provides resources for health consumers, e.g., "A User's guide to finding and evaluating health information on the Web" (http://www.mlanet.org/resources/userguide.html), including "Deciphering MedSpeak," and MLA's guidelines on finding quality information on the Internet. Provides links to websites considered quality sites ("top ten") by MLA, such as: Cancer.gov, Centers for Disease Control (CDC), familydoctor.org (http://familydoctor.org)healthfinder®; HIV InSite, Kidshealth® (http://www.kidshealth.org/), Mayo Clinic, MedlinePlus. Some content is restricted to members only.

Currently 23 different MLA sections have their own webpages (http://www.mlanet.org/sections/sections.html). A prominent example of a section website is the Consumer and Patient Information Section of the Medical Library Association (CAPHIS).

566   Music Library Association. http://www.musiclibraryassoc.org/. Music Library Association. Middleton, Wis.: Music Library Association. 1998–

The MLA provides "a professional forum for librarians, archivists, and others who support and preserve the world's musical heritage."—*Mission Statement* The website supplies information about the association's history; committees and other sub-units; publications; grants and awards; and employment and education. Provides list of current job openings and other career resources. Links to a copyright guide for music librarians. Membership directory is restricted to members.

567   SLA: Special Libraries Association. http://www.sla.org. Special Libraries Association. Alexandria, Va.: Special Libraries Association

Website of the Special Libraries Association—an organization for information professionals who provide specialized information resources and services in corporate, academic, and government settings. Provides background on the association and its policy stances, describes the work of special librarians, and offers career development opportunities, job postings, and an online store of SLA publications. Access to much of the content on the site, including the membership directory, professional development tools, and links to information resources by subject, is restricted to members.

568   Society of American Archivists: SAA. http://www2.archivists.org/. Society of American Archivists. Chicago: Society of American Archivists. 1990s–

Official website of the major professional organization for archivists in the U.S. Provides background on the mission, governance, and internal workings of the society, as well as its public advocacy role. Presents information on archival careers (including job postings), continuing education, and events. Includes digital back issues of the society's newsletter and journal and an online store of its print publications. Access to some content is restricted to members. Includes A glossary of archival and records terminology (431).

569   State and regional chapters. http://www.ala.org/groups/affiliates/chapters/state/stateregional. American Library Association. Chicago: American Library Association. [n.d.]

Lists library associations in all fifty states, the District of Columbia, Guam, and the Virgin Islands, plus four regional US associations. Provides links to each association's website, address and contact information, officers' names and email addresses, and links to annual reports that provide data on membership, budget, programs, and more.

570   VRA. http://www.vraweb.org/. Eric Schwab. s.l.: Visual Resources Association. [2001–]

"The Visual Resources Association is a multidisciplinary, international professional organization dedicated to furthering research and education in the field of media management within the educational, cultural heritage, and commercial environments."—*About page*

In addition to documentation for *VRA core*, the leading metadata standard for visual images, the site includes background on the organization's history, projects, and publications; a job listing; and the Digital Image Rights Computator, a step-by-step program to assess the intellectual property status of art images.

571 World guide to library, archive, and information science associations. 3rd ed. Alexandra Meinhold, International Federation of Library Associations and Institutions. Berlin; New York: De Gruyter Saur, 2010. ISBN 9783110226379
020.62025   Z673.A1W67
Pt. 1: International associations, in alphabetical order. Pt. 2: National associations, organized by country. In addition to address, URL, officers, and other basic data, provides information on membership requirements, organizational structure, sources of financial support, major goals and objectives, activities, and publications. Indexes to association names, acronyms, official journals, officers, and subjects. Covers 603 associations. See also *Library associations around the world*, an online directory maintained by IFLA and ALA, for a selective list of major international, national and state associations, with contact information and links to their websites.

First edition, 1990, ed. by Josephine Riss Fang and Alice H. Songe. 2nd ed., 2005, ed. by Marko Schweizer. Succeeds *International guide to library, archival, and information science associations*, also ed. by Fang and Songe (1976, 1980).

Quotations

572 A book in hand is worth two in the library: Quotations on books and librarianship. Les Harding. Jefferson, N.C.: McFarland, 1994. vii, 119 p. ISBN 0899509339
002   PN6084.B65H37
Quotations on ten themes—libraries, librarians, books, bookworms, borrowing and lending, censorship, classics, reading, writing, and education—are strung together with the compiler's comments. Speaker/writer index. Keyword and subject index.

573 The librarian's book of quotes. Tatyana Eckstrand. Chicago: American Library Association, 2009. viii, 117 p., ill. ISBN 9780838909881
020   PN6084.L52E25
Presents approximately 200 quotations that celebrate libraries and librarians. Cites sources and identifies the authors by date and occupation. Lacks an index or subject categories but is formatted nicely for browsing.

574 Library quotes. http://libraryquotes.org/. Chicago: United for Libraries / American Library Association. [n.d.]
A database of quotes about "libraries, reading, books, literacy, and more."—*Home page*. Quotations are categorized by their sources: activists and benefactors; contemporary authors; entertainment and sports figures; historical figures; members of the library community; media figures and journalists; politicians; and other. All quotations are attributed, but full citations are not supplied. Simple and advanced searches are available, but not on the home page.

575 Quotations about libraries and librarians. http://www.ifla.org/I/humour/subj.htm. International Federation of Library Associations and Institutions. The Hague, The Netherlands: International Federation of Library Associations and Institutions. 2000
Z682.5
Over a hundred quotations, in English or English translation, arranged under 17 subject headings. Links to a parallel listing by author.

576 Speaking of information: the Library juice quotation book. Rory Litwin, Martin Wallace. Duluth, Minn.: Library Juice Press, 2009. xv, 154 p. ISBN 9780980200416
020   PN6084.L52; L58
Presents quotations, ranging from single sentences to full paragraphs, on various aspects of information. Arranged in fifteen categories, including: books and reading; libraries; information technology; information control; information overload; and librarians. Available as a print or e-book.

Research Methods

Editor's Guide: These handbooks emphasize applied research by practitioners but are also useful for students and beginning academic researchers. See also: Library and Information Science > Professional Practice > Assessment and Evaluation.

577 Applications of social research methods to questions in information and library science. Barbara M. Wildemuth. Westport, Conn.: Libraries Unlimited, 2009. vii, 421 p., ill.
ISBN 9781591585039
020.72   Z669.7.W55
Covers research-methods courses and serves as a guide for practitioners of research and evaluation. Discusses the process of developing a research question, designing a research project, sampling, collecting data, and analyzing data. Assesses the strengths and weaknesses of many methods and presents exemplary studies. The conversational tone and abundance of examples de-mystify the topic. Subject index; index to authors of exemplary studies.

578 Basic research methods for librarians. 5th ed. Lynn Silipigni Connaway, Ronald R. Powell. Santa Barbara, Calif.: Libraries Unlimited, 2010. xii, 370 p., ill.
ISBN 9781591588634
020/.72   Z669.7.P68
Introduces methodologies appropriate to research in librarianship: survey (i.e., questionnaires, interviews, focus groups, observation), experimental, qualitative, and historical. Also addresses research planning, hypothesis formulation, sampling, ethics, data analysis, statistics, and the writing of research proposals and reports.
    First ed., 1985.

579 Knowledge into action: research and evaluation in library and information science. Danny P. Wallace, Connie Jean Van Fleet. Santa Barbara, Calif.: Libraries Unlimited, 2012. x., 388 p., ill.
ISBN 9781598849752
025.0072   Z669.7.W35
Written to serve as a text for LIS research methods courses and a foundation for evidence-based practice. Describes and compares the processes of research and evaluation. Discusses ethical and political issues; publication and critical evaluation of research literature; project planning; funding; measurement and sampling. Explains specific methods: historical, descriptive (questionnaires, interviews, observations), experimental, and bibliometrics and citation analysis. Covers data analysis and presentation, and introduces descriptive and inferential statistics.

Glossary. Bibliography. See also the authors' earlier guide, which concentrates on evaluation in the work setting: *Library evaluation: A casebook and can-do guide*.

580 Practical research methods for librarians and information professionals. Susan E. Beck, Kate Manuel. New York: Neal-Schuman, 2007.
ISBN 155570591X
020.72   Z669.7
Discusses the steps in the research process—finding a topic, formulating questions, defining the population, selecting a research design, gathering data, interpreting the evidence, telling the story—and describes them in the context of specific methodologies: content analysis; interviews and focus groups; observation and usability; experimental research; bibliometrics; action research; and classroom research. Background readings and exemplary studies by practitioners are highlighted for each methodology. A separate chapter discusses common pitfalls in research.

581 Research methods in information. 2nd ed. Alison Jane Pickard. Chicago: Neal-Schuman, 2013. xxii, 361 p., ill.
ISBN 9781555709365
020.72   Z669.7
A thorough overview of the research process in LIS. Part 1, Starting the Research Process, describes major research paradigms, explains how to conduct a literature review, define a conceptual framework, write a proposal, take a sample, manage research data, and apply ethics to research. Part 2, Research Methods, covers case studies, surveys, experiments, usability testing, ethnography, Delphi studies, action research, historical research, and grounded theory. Part 3, Data Collection Techniques, explains interviews, questionnaires, observation, diaries, focus groups, and analysis of existing, externally created material. Part 4, Data Analysis and Research Presentation, covers qualitative and quantitative analysis, as well as research reporting. Glossary. Bibliography. Index.

Standards

Editor's Guide: See also various sections within Library and Information Science > Professional

Practice for standards related to specific areas of LIS work.

582   American Library Association standards and guidelines. http://www.ala.org/ala/professionalresources/guidelines/standardsguidelines/index.cfm#. American Library Association, Office of Research and Statistics. Chicago: American Library Association

List of all standards and guidelines promulgated by the American Library Association and its subunits. Arranged by subject. Most entries link to full text; others provide information for ordering print copies.

583   NISO standards. http://www.niso.org/standards/index.html. National Information Standards Organization. Bethesda, Md.: National Information Standards Organization. [1971–]

Z665.2.U6

The National Information Standards Organization (NISO) promulgates technical standards that "apply both traditional and new technologies to the full range of information-related needs, including retrieval, re-purposing, storage, metadata, and preservation."—*About NISO* Standards are alphanumerically coded; nearly all carry the designation Z39 followed by a decimal point and a unique number. Full-text PDF downloads are free. NISO also publishes "recommended practices" (designated with RP series numbers), which are often relevant to library operations; technical reports; and white papers.

584   Standards at the Library of Congress. http://www.loc.gov/standards/. Library of Congress. Washington: Library of Congress

Handy grouping of links to major standards used for library cataloging, access, and digital projects in the United States: resource description formats; digital library standards; and information resource retrieval protocols, etc.

Statistics

Editor's Guide: Most of the works included here provide statistical data in tabular form. For guidance on using statistical measures, see Library and Information Science > Professional Practice > Administration and Management > Assessment and Evaluation. For comparative data on salaries, see Library and Information Science > Professional Practice > Administration and Management > Human Resources.

585   Academic library trends and statistics. http://www.ala.org/acrl/publications/trends. Association of College and Research Libraries. Chicago: Association of College and Research Libraries. 1999–

Annual. Detailed statistics of nearly 1,500 libraries of American colleges and universities. Data covers size of collections and expenditures by type of material (including electronic resources), personnel, service points, hours, PhD degrees awarded, number of faculty, and student enrollments. Year-by-year summary tables, along with analysis of selected variables and trend charts. Print edition in three parts, covering institutions offering the associate degree, baccalaureate and master's degrees, and PhD. The same data, 2010-present, is available by subscription in *ACRLMetrics* (586), an interactive database.

Academic library trends and statistics are complemented by the ARL Statistics (587).

Previous title: *ACRL university library statistics* (1980–98).

586   ACRLMetrics. http://www.acrlmetrics.com/. Association of College and Research Libraries. Chicago: Association of College and Research Libraries. 2010–

Z675.U5

Subscription-only site. Searchable database of ACRL (585) and NCES (592) academic library statistics (2000 to present) plus a subset of IPEDS data specific to academic libraries. Presents annual summary tables, 2010 to present, broken out by Carnegie classification, for: holdings; expenditures; personnel; instruction, reference and circulation; Ph.D. degrees, faculty and enrollment; selected ratios; and electronic resources and ILL. Specific measures and trend data vary somewhat from year to year. Valuable resource for the ability to create, store, organize and publish complex customized reports, including peer comparisons, rankings and trend reports.

587   ARL statistics. http://www.arl.org/focus-areas/statistics-assessment/arl-statistics-salary-survey. Association of Research

Libraries. Washington: Association of Research Libraries

Detailed annual statistics on collections, interlibrary loan, personnel, and expenditures of the 125 members of the Association of Research Libraries. Specific statistics collected have varied over time. The Interactive Analytics database, available to members and to others by paid subscription, includes data from 1908 to the present. Allows users to compare institutions, generate ranked lists, and create summary tables and graphs. Data may be downloaded. Also issued annually in print: *Academic library statistics*(1963/64–1973/74) and *ARL statistics* (1974/75–present) (587). Data for the years 1907–08 through 1961–62, compiled by James Gerould, are available in print as well as online at http://www.arl.org/publications-resources/all-publications-resources/1888-the-gerould-statistics-190708-196162. Separate publications present statistics for academic health sciences and law libraries (from 1998–99), preservation (from 1999–2000), and miscellaneous supplementary topics (from 1996–97).

ARL statistics are complemented by the *ACRL university library statistics* (1980–98), *Academic Library Trends and Statistics* (585), and *ACRLMetrics* (586).

588 A bibliographical guide to a chronological record of statistics of national scope on libraries in the United States. http://faculty.libsci.sc.edu/bob/LibraryStatistics/LibraryStatisticsGuide.html. Robert V. Williams. [Columbia, S.C.]: University of South Carolina, School of Library and Information Science. 2008–

Two PDF files. Pt. I, 1829–99, 47 p. Pt. II, 1900–99, 228 p. Detailed bibliographic information about nationwide statistical studies of libraries of all types in the U.S. Arranged by date of study. Describes the purpose, types of libraries covered, variables measured, and method of data collection. Assesses the completeness and quality of the data, and cites the publication.

589 Hennen's American public library ratings (HAPLR). http://www.haplr-index.com. Thomas J. Hennen. Racine, Wis.: haplr-index.com. 1999–2010

Annual. Based on data gathered by the federal Institute for Museum and Library Services (595), ranks public libraries within population categories using 15 factors, including circulation, staffing, materials, reference service, and funding levels. The latest ranking (2010) of the top 100 libraries is available on the website. The HAPLR index was published annually in *American Libraries* through 2008; rating scores for individual libraries were organized by state. Custom reports may be purchased.

590 LibQual+: charting library service quality. http://www.libqual.org. Association of Research Libraries. Washington: Association of Research Libraries

LibQual+(TM) is a system used primarily by academic libraries to assess library-user expectations and opinions of service quality. Includes information on the survey instrument and its implementation, along with bibliographies of publications and presentations. Annual summary reports are available, as PDF documents, since 2002 for participating members of the Association of Research Libraries (559).

591 Library and information science education statistical report. ALISE Library and Information Science Education Statistics Committee, Association for Library and Information Science Education. State College, Pa.: ALISE, 1983–. 0739-506X

020.710973   Z668.L495

Annual. Presents extremely detailed statistical information on faculty, students, curriculum, income and expenditures, and continuing professional education activities of ALA-accredited LIS programs in North America. ALISE members may log in to access recent volumes on the association's website: http://www.alise.org/statistical-reports. Volumes for 1997 to 2004 are available openly at http://ils.unc.edu/ALISE. Non-members may purchase the print edition.

592 Library statistics program. http://nces.ed.gov/surveys/libraries/. National Center for Education Statistics. Washington: National Center for Education Statistics. 1990s–

Nationwide surveys of academic libraries (biennial) and school library media centers (quadrennial) cover many aspects of collections, revenue, expenditures, services, and staffing. Reports, available in PDF format, do not include data for individual libraries but present aggregate statistics (e.g., by type of institution for academic libraries). Data files and special reports are also available for download. The interactive "Compare Academic Libraries" feature will generate statistics for individual libraries and compare them to other specified libraries and to state and national averages and medians.

Prior to 2008, the NCES Library Statistics Program also surveyed public libraries and state library agencies. These surveys are now administered by the Institute of Museum and Library Services (595).

593 LJ index of public library service.
http://lj.libraryjournal.com/category/managing-libraries/lj-index/. Keith Curry Lance, Ray Lyons. New York: Library Journal. 2009–

Also known as "America's star libraries." Published annually in *Library Journal* (539). Presents rankings of public libraries based on data reported by public libraries to their state library agencies and compiled by the Institute of Museum and Library Services (595). Scores are computed from per capita measures of library visits, circulation, program attendance, and public Internet use. Libraries are ranked within expenditure categories and also listed state-by-state. Each year, accompanying articles spotlight shifts in the rankings and explain trends.

594 PLAMetrics. http://www.plametrics.org/. Public Library Association; Public Library Data Service. Chicago: Public Library Association. 2011-

Access restricted by password to subscribers. Continues the printed Public Library Data Service *Statistical report* (1988-2011). Updated annually. The database includes all the yearly PLDS data since FY2002 and IMLS data (595) since FY2000. The data, collected by survey, covers finances, resources, use, and technology at over 1,500 individual public libraries in the U.S. and Canada. In addition, one special topic is surveyed each year, e.g., young adult services in 2012, facilities in 2013. Allows customized creation of peer groups, sorting and reporting; templates are provided. Reports can be downloaded as Excel spreadsheets or charts, and results can be output as Word files.

595 Public libraries in the United States survey. http://www.imls.gov/research/public_libraries_in_the_united_states_survey.aspx. Institute for Museum and Library Services (U.S.). Washington: Institute for Museum and Library Services. [2007-]

Presents statistical data from annual surveys of public libraries. The reports (PDF files) include information on visitation, circulation, computing resources, staffing, library collections and services, and fiscal information such as operating revenue and expenditures. Data generally aggregated by state; reports do not include figures for individual libraries. Local data viewable by using the interactive "Search for Public Libraries" feature. The "Compare Public Libraries" feature permits the user to select individual libraries or peer groups for comparison on chosen variables.

Provides downloadable data files and links to earlier surveys conducted by the National Center for Education Statistics' Library Statistics Program (592).

596 SPEC kits. Association of Research Libraries. Washington: Association of Research Libraries, 1973–. 0160-3582
Z675.R45S63

These "kits" analyze survey data from ARL (559) member libraries, along with supporting documentation such as sample policies and forms. Full kits are available in print for purchase individually or by subscription to the series. Perpetual electronic access to individual kits may be purchased; the complete collection is available online through an annual subscription. Executive summaries and tables of contents only are available free on the Web at http://www.arl.org/resources/pubs/spec/complete.shtml. Recent surveys covered a wide range of currently important topics, including the changing role of senior administrators (no.331), scholarly communication services (no. 332), research data management (no. 334), digital image collections and services (no. 335), and print retention decision-making (no. 337). Six kits are published each year.

597 State library administrative agency survey. http://www.imls.gov/research/state_library_agency_survey.aspx. Institute for Museum and Library Services (U.S.). Washington: Institute for Museum and Library Services. [2007]–

Presents statistical data from surveys of library agencies for the 50 states and the District of Columbia. The data (collected annually from 1994 to 2010, biennially since 2010) include governance, public service hours, service outlets, collections, library service transactions, library development transactions, services to other libraries in the state, allied operations, staff, income, expenditures, and electronic services and information. Both PDF reports and data files are available for downloading.

User Guides to Library Research

Editor's Guide: The how-to-use-the-library guidebook is a traditional reference subgenre, designed to guide college students through the process of researching and writing a term paper. Such guides advise on how to choose a topic, find and evaluate published literature, organize the paper, write in an academic style, and cite sources in a bibliography. This section highlights guides that are devoted in large part to the information-seeking stage of the research process and that are general rather than discipline specific.

598   Archival information: How to find it, how to use it. Steven Fisher. Westport, Conn.: Greenwood Press, 2004. 180 p. ISBN 1573563897
027.073   CD3021.A38

Introduction to archives for general researchers. Individually authored chapters describe archival resources on American government, genealogy, science, religion, women's history, moving images and sound, fine arts, sports, business, and the military. Chapters vary in content and approach. Most chapters focus solely on American archives and provide full address information for major collections. Some chapters identify published primary source materials in micro- and electronic formats, major bibliographies, and other useful tools; some offer advice on using archives, as does the introduction. Index. Also available as an e-book.

599   Bookmarks: A guide to research and writing. 3rd ed. John J. Ruszkiewicz, Janice R. Walker, Michael A. Pemberton. New York: Longman, 2006. xix, 428 p., ill. ISBN 0321271343
                                 LB2369.R88

A thorough guide for college students to the research and writing process. Offers extensive advice on using library and online information resources, as well as choosing a topic, avoiding plagiarism, and evaluating sources. Also covers aspects of argumentation and rhetoric, presentation of findings in various formats, and standard citation systems for print and online sources. Companion website (http://wps.ablongman.com/long_ruszkiewic_bookmarks_3) includes links to information resources on the open Web, tutorials on the search process, and learning activities. Other excellent guides include *The Facts on File guide to research*, which cites thousands of specific print and web-based resources in the major disciplines, in addition to providing sound guidance on search techniques; and *Research strategies for a digital age*.

600   The college student's research companion: finding, evaluating, and citing the resources you need to succeed. 5th ed. Arlene R. Quaratiello, Jane Devine. New York: Neal-Schuman Publishers, 2011. xiii, 183 p.
025.5/24   Z710.Q37

Addressing first-year college students, this guide explains how to plan a library research project, evaluate information sources, and use and cite information correctly. Individual chapters focus on the Web, databases, library catalogs, periodicals, and ready reference sources. Appendixes include an annotated list of major subscription databases and sample citations in MLA, Chicago, and APA styles.

601   Concise guide to information literacy. Scott Lanning. Santa Barbara, Calif.: Libraries Unlimited, [2012]. xii, 99 p. ISBN 9781598849493
020   ZA3075.L36

Serves as a basic self-study guide for students or a simple text for library instruction courses. Covers how to define one's information need, understand the types of information sources, search databases and catalogs, and more. Includes vocabulary words, review questions, and an assignment for each step of the process.

602   The elements of library research: what every student needs to know. Mary W. George. Princeton, N.J.: Princeton University Press, 2008. xiv, 201 p., ill.
025.5/24   Z710.G44

Unlike many research guides that emphasize information resources, this guide, written in a conversational style, focuses on the nature of inquiry and the process of library research. Appendixes summarize the hints and maxims in the preceding chapters; suggest timelines for two-week, four-week, and six-week research projects; and recommend questions to ask one's professor or librarian. Glossary. Bibliography. Index.

603 The Oxford guide to library research. 3rd ed. Thomas Mann. New York: Oxford University Press, 2005. xx, 293 p., ill.
ISBN 9780195189971
025.524   Z710.M23

First ed., 1987, titled *A guide to library research methods*. 2nd ed., 1998. Focuses on methods and tools for subject searching and emphasizes the value of printed books and licensed databases in comparison to the open Internet. Dense narrative, abundance of examples, and sage but opinionated advice will speak best to serious adult researchers. Friendlier guides for novice library users are listed elsewhere in this section; also useful is *The research virtuoso: brilliant methods for normal brains*, a succinct guide for college-level students from the Toronto Public Library.

604 Research and documentation online. http://www.dianahacker.com/resdoc. Diana Hacker, Barbara Fister. Boston: Bedford/St. Martin's

ZA4375

Includes guidelines for documenting sources following MLA, APA, Chicago, and CSE styles, with sample student papers illustrating how citation styles are applied. Presents tips for evaluating sources and a glossary of terms related to literature searching. Discusses research in humanities, social sciences, history, and sciences and recommends standard reference sources.

Printed version offers additional guidance on formulating research questions, mapping search strategies, and finding and evaluating sources: *Research and documentation in the electronic age*, 5th ed.

605 Student guide to research in the digital age: How to locate and evaluate information sources. Leslie

F. Stebbins. Westport, Conn.: Libraries Unlimited, 2006. xiii, 202 p., ill.
ISBN 1591580994
025.524   ZA3075.S74

A well-organized guide to finding and critically evaluating information resources for college-level research: books and e-books, scholarly and popular articles, primary sources, biographies, legal information, and U.S. government documents and statistics. Also addresses general steps in research and citing sources. Appendixes: subject guide to journal article databases, glossary.

Yearbooks and Current Surveys

Editor's Guide: This section includes frequently updated factual sources and recurring collections of essays that survey current topics in the discipline.

606 Annual review of information science and technology. Carlos A. Cuadra, Martha E. Williams, Blaise Cronin, American Society for Information Science and Technology, American Society for Information Science, American Documentation Institute. Medford, N.J.: Information Today, 1966-2011. v.1–45.
0066–4200
029.708   Z699.A1A65

Presents 12 to 15 essays on "recent trends and significant developments" in selected areas of information science, with extensive bibliographies. Indexes. Volumes for 2002- available online through Wiley InterScience or by subscription to the ASIST Digital Library. Since ARIST ceased publication, current developments in information science and technology are treated in Advances in Information Science, a section of the Association's *Journal of Information Science and Technology* (JASIST) (535) that appears approximately six times year.

Vol. 1-2 issued by the society under its earlier name: American Documentation Institute. Ed. by Carlos A. Cuadra (v. 1–10), Martha E. Williams (v. 11–35), Blaise Cronin (v. 36–45).

607 British librarianship and information work. Ashgate. Aldershot, U.K.: Ashgate, 1976/80–. 1752-556X
020.941   Z666.F5; Z665.4.G7B75

Published with varying frequency by the Library Association as *Year's work in librarianship* (1928–50); *Five years' work in librarianship* (1951/55–1961/65); *British librarianship and information science* (1966/70–1971/75); and *British librarianship and information work* (1976/80–1986/90). Revived by Ashgate Publishing with volumes covering 1991–2000 and 2001-2005. The latest volume, 2006-1010, was self-published by the editor through lulu.com. Presents state-of-the-art essays on approximately 30 types of libraries or dimensions of librarianship in Great Britain. Topical index.

608   IFLA/FAIFE world report series.
http://www.ifla.org/faife/world-report. International Federation of Library Associations and Institutions. The Hague, The Netherlands: International Federation of Library Associations and Institutions. 2001–
Biennial issued in odd-numbered years as a PDF file. Compiled by IFLA's Committee on Freedom of Access to Information and Freedom of Expression (FAIFE). Country-by-country survey of libraries' and library users' freedom of access to information. Companion series, *Theme report*, issued in even-numbered years, covers such topics as lifelong literacy (2004) and "Libraries and the fight against HIV/AIDS, poverty and corruption" (2006). Also available in print until 2010, when it became a web-only publication.

609   Library and book trade almanac.
[Information Today, Inc.]. Medford, N.J.: Information Today, Inc., 2009– 2150-5446
020.5   Z731.A47
Title varies: 1956–58, American library annual [new series]; 1959–61, American library and book trade annual; 1962–88, The Bowker annual of library and book trade information; 1989-2008, The Bowker annual: Library and book trade almanac. Includes reviews of the year's events, trends, and legislation relevant to librarianship and publishing; reports from federal agencies and key organizations; statistics on placement and salaries of beginning librarians; scholarship and award winners; statistics on library expenditures, facilities, and rankings; statistics on publishing output and average prices of books; bibliographies of recent books in librarianship, bestsellers, and award-winning books; directories of library consortia and associations; and a calendar of conferences and book fairs. Indexes: organizations; subjects.

610   The whole library handbook 5: current data, professional advice, and curiosa about libraries and library services. 5th ed. George M. Eberhart. Chicago: ALA Editions, 2013. v, 528 p., ill. ISBN 9780838910900
020.973   Z665.2.U6
Eclectic compendium of facts and figures about libraries and librarians, along with "a selection of the most informative, practical, and entertaining" recent writings on libraries.—Pref. Organized by broad themes: libraries; people; the profession; materials; operations; users; advocacy; technology; issues; librariana. Reprints many short, practical articles that summarize professional topics and offer tips. Because each edition contains primarily new material, older editions remain useful. Index to subjects and authors. Similar volumes, *The whole digital library handbook* and *The whole school library handbook 2*, reprint short works and extracts from journal articles but have less value for ready reference.

First edition, 1991.

15 _Professional Practice_

Administration, Management, and Planning—General Works

611 ALA library fact sheets. http://www
.ala.org/ala/aboutala/offices/library/
libraryfactsheet/alalibraryfact.cfm.
American Library Association. Chicago:
American Library Association
Web-based fact sheets answer questions that are frequently posed by either practicing librarians or the
general public to the ALA Library's reference service.
Content and organization vary. Typical fact sheet
presents information, annotates and recommends
readings, and provides links to other websites. Representative topics: disaster response, weeding, library
fund-raising, how to market products to libraries, how
to set up your own library, and where to donate books.

612 ALA professional tips wiki. http://wikis
.ala.org/professionaltips/index.php/Main
_Page. American Library Association. Chicago:
American Library Association. [2006]
A service of the library at the American Library Association headquarters. Functions as a topical index to
information on the ALA website and elsewhere on
the Internet, and also cites print sources. Maintained
by ALA library staff; open to other contributors. Covers all aspects of the profession.

613 How-to-do-it manuals. Neal-Schuman.
New York: Neal-Schuman, 1989–

The one-hundred-eighty-plus books published in
this series (now absorbed by ALA Editions) address
the full spectrum of practical knowledge in librarianship. For example, recent volumes treat such topics
as e-book collections, lapsit programs for toddlers,
assistive technology, book repair, public relations
for archives, and metadata for digital collections.
Volumes typically include checklists, sample forms
and policies, references to print and Web resources,
and are written in an easily consulted outline format;
many are accompanied by CD-ROMs with files that
can be tailored for local use. Several individual numbers in the _How-to-do-it_ series are cited elsewhere in
the _Guide to reference_ (52).

**614 Library management 101: a practical
guide.** Diane L. Velasquez. Chicago:
ALA Editions, 2013. 366 p.
ISBN 9780838911488
025.1   Z678.L4725
Provides background on classical and modern management theories, as well as practical guidance on
the following topics: human resources management; strategic planning; leadership; communication; change management; organizational culture;
marketing; financial management; assessment and
evaluation; internal and external stakeholders; ethics; dealing with conflict; diversity; facilities management; information technology management; grants;
outsourcing; and future trends. Includes a glossary
of management terms and key laws.

Other useful works that treat the full breadth of library administration and management include *The accidental library manager*, *Management basics for information professionals* and *Library and information center management*.

615   The library's continuous improvement fieldbook: 29 ready-to-use tools. Sara Laughlin, Denise Sisco Shockley, Ray W. Wilson. Chicago: American Library Association, 2003. ix, 133 p., ill. ISBN 0838908594

025.1   Z678.L34

Step-by-step instructions for techniques of planning and implementing changes in libraries, with illustrations, lists of do's and don'ts, and success stories. Includes tools for stimulating thinking, analyzing information, reaching consensus, and more. The authors' follow-up book, *The quality library: A guide to staff-driven improvement, better efficiency, and happier customers*, describes in detail the steps of measuring process performance and instituting improvements.

616   Library success: a best practices wiki. http://libsuccess.org/. Meredith Farkas. [2000s-]

"This wiki was created to be a one-stop shop for great ideas and information for all types of librarians." --*Intro* Original content and links to external websites are organized under fourteen topical categories; most are further sub-divided. Because many contributors have built the wiki, its coverage and style is uneven, yet it contains much useful information.

617   Managing change: a how-to-do-it manual for librarians. Rev. ed ed. Susan Carol Curzon. New York: Neal-Schuman Publishers, 2005. xiv, 129 p. ISBN 9781555705534

025.1   Z678.C885

Lays out a step-by-step process for managing change in libraries, from initial vision, through planning and implementation, to evaluation. The text is structured around questions and answers, and each chapter ends with a summary checklist. Fifteen short scenarios are provided for use in training or teaching.

618   SPEC kits. Association of Research Libraries. Washington: Association of Research Libraries, 1973–. 0160-3582 Z675.R45S63

These "kits" analyze survey data from ARL (559) member libraries, along with supporting documentation such as sample policies and forms. Full kits are available in print for purchase individually or by subscription to the series. Perpetual electronic access to individual kits may be purchased; the complete collection is available online through an annual subscription. Executive summaries and tables of contents only are available free on the Web at http://www.arl.org/resources/pubs/spec/complete.shtml. Recent surveys covered a wide range of currently important topics, including the changing role of senior administrators (no.331), scholarly communication services (no. 332), research data management (no. 334), digital image collections and services (no. 335), and print retention decision-making (no. 337). Six kits are published each year.

619   Strategic planning for results. Fully rev. ed. Sandra S. Nelson, Public Library Association. Chicago: American Library Association, 2008. xvii, 291 p., ill., forms. ISBN 9780838935736

025.1974   Z678.N454

First ed., 1998, titled *Planning for results: A library transformation process*. Also titled *The new planning for results*.

Outlines a model for strategic planning in public libraries; provides examples of service responses to community needs; supplies a "tool kit" of techniques for group decision making, communication, and data presentation; and includes reproducible workforms. Subject index. A similarly organized companion volume, *Implementing for results* by Nelson, provides guidance on putting plans into action.

This is the keystone title in the *PLA results series*. Other volumes cover policy creation, technology, resource allocation, staffing, facilities, outcome measurement, and human resources. Each volume traces a step-by-step process, illustrated by a case study and accompanied by many ready-to-use workforms.

Archives and Special Collections

620   Archival and special collections facilities: guidelines for archivists,

librarians, architects, and engineers.
Michele F. Pacifico, Thomas P. Wilsted,
Society of American Archivists. Chicago:
Society of American Archivists, 2009. viii,
191 p. ISBN 1931666318
CD981.A695

In outline format, these guidelines treat: the building
site; construction; archival environments for different
types of records (paper, film, electronic); fire protection; security; lighting; materials and finishes; storage
equipment; and the design of spaces according to
function (e.g., loading dock, processing rooms, reading spaces). Glossary. Bibliography. Detailed index.

621 Archival fundamentals series II.
Society of American Archivists. Chicago:
Society of American Archivists, 2004–
2010. 7 v.

Replaces an earlier monographic series, *Archival fundamentals*, (1990-1993). Provides "the basic foundation for modern archival practice and theory."—*Series
Preface*. Provides an overview of archival practice and
addresses specific issues in volumes on management,
selection and appraisal, reference services, arrangement and description, and preservation. Also included in the series is *A glossary of archives and records
terminology* (431).

**622 Archival information: How to find it,
how to use it.** Steven Fisher. Westport,
Conn.: Greenwood Press, 2004. 180 p.
ISBN 1573563897
027.073   CD3021.A38

Introduction to archives for general researchers. Individually authored chapters describe archival resources
on American government, genealogy, science, religion,
women's history, moving images and sound, fine arts,
sports, business, and the military. Chapters vary in
content and approach. Most chapters focus solely
on American archives and provide full address information for major collections. Some chapters identify
published primary source materials in micro- and electronic formats, major bibliographies, and other useful
tools; some offer advice on using archives, as does the
introduction. Index. Also available as an e-book.

623 Archive finder. http://archives.chadwyck
.com. ProQuest (Firm). Ann Arbor, Mich.:
ProQuest. 2009–

Describes over 206,000 collections of primary source

material housed in nearly 6,000 repositories across
the United States, the United Kingdom, and Ireland.
Combines records from the former *ArchivesUSA* database (which were drawn from the *Directory of Archives
and Manuscript Repositories in the United States*,
National Union Catalog of Manuscript Collections
[NUCMC] and the index to the National Inventory of Documentary Sources in the United States
[NIDS]) and the National Inventory of Documentary
Sources in the UK and Ireland (NIDS UK/Ireland).
Also includes collection descriptions provided by
other repositories and some 6,000 links to online
finding aids. Keyword search results provide links to
repository directory information as well as descriptive and bibliographic data. Updated annually.

624 ArchiveGrid. http://www.archivegrid
.org/. Research Libraries Group, Online
Computer Library Center. Dublin, Ohio:
OCLC. 2006–
CD3022.A2

Continuously updated, open access, searchable database of collections held by thousands of
archives, museums and libraries, primarily in the
U.S. A typical entry indicates: size of the collection;
type of material; subjects, persons, and time periods
covered. Information drawn from web-based finding
aids and records in WorldCat. *Archive Finder* (624),
available by subscription, is a similar database that
covers the UK and Ireland as well as the U.S.

625 Archives: principles and practices.
Laura Millar. London: Facet Pub, 2010.
xxiii, 280 p.
027   CD950.M55

Summarizes archives and archival services, covering
both theoretical foundations and practical approaches to appraisal, acquisition, arrangement, description, preservation, and access. Addresses digital as
well as traditional archives and covers key concepts
such as provenance and *respect des fonds*. Bibliography. Glossary. Index.

**626 Articles describing archives and
manuscript collections in the United
States: An annotated bibliography.**
Donald L. DeWitt. Westport, Conn.:
Greenwood Press, 1997. xi, 458 p.
ISBN 0313295980
016.973   CD3022.A2D478

A companion volume to *Guides to archives and manuscript collections in the United States: An annotated bibliography*, by the same compiler. Identifies and briefly describes over 2,000 journal articles about collections of unpublished primary sources, which appeared between the 1890s and the mid-1990s. Topical arrangement with index to names, subjects, and repositories.

627 CoSA resource center. http:// rc.statearchivists.org/. Council of State Archivists. Albany, N.Y.: Council of State Archivists

An index to online resources developed by and for state archives and records programs. Includes a state-by-state directory of archives, accessed through a clickable map, with links to laws and other state-specific information; and a topical index to fee schedules, preservation guidelines, training materials, emergency plans, and more.

628 Describing archives: a content standard. http://files.archivists.org/pubs/ DACS2E-2013.pdf. Society of American Archivists. Chicago: Society of American Archivists. 2013. 978-1-931666-08-4
Z695.2
Part I: Describing Archival Materials (rules for describing archival collections of any material type and at any level of specificity from collection to item). Part II, Archival Authority Records (rules for persons, families, and corporate bodies). Appendices include a bibliography of related standards, and crosswalks of DACS data elements to other descriptive frameworks, including RDA.
209-page PDF. Also available in print. 1st ed., 2004.

629 Directory of Archival Organizations in the United States and Canada. http:// www2.archivists.org/assoc-orgs/directory. Society of American Archivists. Chicago: Society of American Archivists. [n.d.]
Previously issued in print. Includes contact information, membership size, dues, brief description, and links to websites of seventy archivists' organizations at the national, regional, state/provincial, and local levels.

630 Encoded archival description. http:// www.loc.gov/ead/. Society of American Archivists; Library of Congress; Network

Development and MARC Standards Office. Washington: Library of Congress. 2002
"The EAD Document Type Definition (DTD) is a standard for encoding archival finding aids using Extensible Markup Language (XML)" and is jointly maintained by the Library of Congress and the Society of American Archivists (568)—*Home Page.* Website provides background on EAD's development, as well as the current schema, DTD (document type definition), and tag library. For tools, help files, and a bibliography of writings about EAD, see: http://www2.archivists.org/groups/encoded-archival -description-ead-rou ndtable. A revised EAD schema is under review for adoption in 2014. See also the *Encoded Archival Context for Corporate Bodies, Persons, and Families (EAC-CPF)*, a companion standard.

631 A glossary of archival and records terminology. http://www.archivists.org/ glossary/index.asp. Richard Pearce-Moses. Chicago: Society of American Archivists. 2005
Also published in print in the *Archival fundamentals series II* (621). Defines over 2,000 English language terms found in the archival literature, with an emphasis on electronic records. Includes acronyms and organizations. Provides citations to usage and notes relationships among terms.

632 ICA: International Council on Archives. http://www.ica.org. International Council on Archives. Paris: International Council on Archives. 1996–
Z673
". . . dedicated to the effective management of records and the preservation, care and use of the world's archival heritage through its representation of records and archive professionals across the globe."—*About ICA* Includes information about the organization's mission, governance, and events; a resource center of digitized documents, including bibliographies and guidelines; and a members-only networking and communication site.

633 Multilingual archival terminology. http://www.ica.org/14282/multilingual -archival-terminology/multilingual-archival -terminology.html. International Council on Archives. Paris: International Council on Archives. [n.d.]

An interactive, online database of archival terms and definitions in 20 languages, including English.

634 Rare book librarianship: an introduction and guide. Steven Kenneth Galbraith, Geoffrey D. Smith. , 2012. xvii, 185 p., ill.
025.1/9609   Z688.R3G35

An overview of core topics in rare book librarianship, including: the history of rare book libraries; descriptive bibliography; history of printing; provenance; appraisal; proper handling; preservation; security; disaster preparedness; collection development; accessioning and cataloging; copyright; outreach; and continuing education. The final chapter lists selected reference sources by topic. Also available as e-book.

635 Rarebooks.info. http://rarebooks.info. Rarebooks.info. Boulogne, France: Rarebooks.info. 2000–

Includes more than 100 key bibliographies regarding rare books. Subjects include early printing, world literature, natural history, science, medicine, theology, cultural and area studies, Judaica, music, theology, art, and architecture, among others. Key bibliographies include standard reference works by Goff (incunabula), Brunet (Manuel), Sabin (Americana), Fairfax Murray (French and German books), and many more hard-to-find and out-of-print works.

Search options include: "Basic," "Advanced," "Browse works," "Browse topics," and "Search history." Allows full-text and keyword searching. Results are first displayed in summary format (with the number of results and hits listed at the top of the page), and entries are arranged by author and title (with the option to resort results).

Texts are scanned facsimiles of the actual books. Both individual and institutional subscriptions are available, along with free trials and a digital guided tour.

636 RBMS controlled vocabularies. http://www.rbms.info/committees/bibliographic_standards/controlled_vocabularies/index.shtml. Association of College and Research Libraries.; Rare Books and Manuscripts Section; Bibliographic Standards Committee. Chicago: Rare Books and Manuscripts Section, Association of College and Research Libraries. 2005-

"These thesauri provide standardized vocabulary for retrieving special collections materials by form, genre, or by various physical characteristics that are typically of interest to researchers and special collections librarians, and for relating materials to individuals or corporate bodies."--*Home page.* Separate, searchable thesauri present terms about binding, genres, paper, printing and publishing, provenance, and types, in both alphabetical and hierarchical displays.

637 Society of American Archivists: SAA. http://www2.archivists.org/. Society of American Archivists. Chicago: Society of American Archivists. 1990s–

Official website of the major professional organization for archivists in the U.S. Provides background on the mission, governance, and internal workings of the society, as well as its public advocacy role. Presents information on archival careers (including job postings), continuing education, and events. Includes digital back issues of the society's newsletter and journal and an online store of its print publications. Access to some content is restricted to members. Includes A glossary of archival and records terminology (431).

638 The special collections handbook. Alison Cullingford. London: Facet, 2011. xiv, 210 p.
025.17 23|025.17   Z688.A2C85

An overview of management topics in special collections, including: collection care; emergency planning; types of materials and formats; acquisitions; cataloging; legal and ethical issues; user services; marketing; outreach; and fund-raising. Each chapter also includes recommendations for further reading, pointers to examples and case studies, and URLs for useful websites. A brief appendix describes key reference sources for special collections. Bibl. Index. Also available as e-book.

Assessment and Evaluation

Editor's Guide: See also Library and Information Science > General Works > Research Methods.

639 Assessing service quality: satisfying the expectations of library customers. 2nd ed. Peter Hernon, Ellen Altman. Chicago: American Library Association, 2010. xi, 206 p., ill.

ISBN 9780838910214

025.5 22|025.5   Z711.H45

Discusses the concepts of service quality and customer satisfaction and their relevance to the library's mission. Explains various metrics for evaluation and assessment and compares the pros and cons of methods such as comment cards, surveys, and focus groups. Includes many charts, sample forms, and worksheets for gathering and analyzing data. Includes bibliography and index. Some of the same topics are covered in a complementary book, *Listening to the Customer* (645) (2011), which focuses on creating customer-focused libraries and methods for gathering feedback from both users and non-users.

1st ed., 1998.

640   Engaging in evaluation and assessment research. Peter Hernon, Robert E. Dugan, Danuta A. Nitecki. Santa Barbara, Calif.: Libraries Unlimited, 2011. xvii, 305 p., ill. ISBN 9781598845730

027   Z678.85.H46

Distinguishing evaluation from assessment (a subfield of evaluation), outlines a process of applied research as a tool for managerial decision-making in libraries. Includes practical advice on methods and data presentation.

641   Evaluating reference services: A practical guide. Jo Bell Whitlatch. Chicago: American Library Association, 2000. vi, 226 p. ISBN 0838907873

025.52   Z711.W45

Practical guide to evaluating traditional reference services. Covers planning for an evaluative study, strengths and weaknesses of common methods, issues in the collection and analysis of data, and advice on communicating the findings. Presents sample forms, questions, and checklists. Of particular value is the 100-page selective bibliography keyed to the topical chapters. Many of the entries were previously published in the *Reference assessment manual* but appear here in revised form alongside newer entries. Combined index to subjects in the narrative chapters and authors in the bibliography.

642   Knowledge into action: research and evaluation in library and information science. Danny P. Wallace, Connie Jean Van Fleet. Santa Barbara, Calif.: Libraries

Unlimited, 2012. x., 388 p., ill. ISBN 9781598849752

025.0072   Z669.7.W35

Written to serve as a text for LIS research methods courses and a foundation for evidence-based practice. Describes and compares the processes of research and evaluation. Discusses ethical and political issues; publication and critical evaluation of research literature; project planning; funding; measurement and sampling. Explains specific methods: historical, descriptive (questionnaires, interviews, observations), experimental, and bibliometrics and citation analysis. Covers data analysis and presentation, and introduces descriptive and inferential statistics. Glossary. Bibliography. See also the authors' earlier guide, which concentrates on evaluation in the work setting: *Library evaluation: A casebook and can-do guide.*

643   LibQual+: charting library service quality. http://www.libqual.org. Association of Research LIbraries. Washington: Association of Research Libraries

LibQual+(TM) is a system used primarily by academic libraries to assess library-user expectations and opinions of service quality. Includes information on the survey instrument and its implementation, along with bibliographies of publications and presentations. Annual summary reports are available, as PDF documents, since 2002 for participating members of the Association of Research Libraries (559).

644   Library data: empowering practice and persuasion. Darby Orcutt. Santa Barbara, Calif.: Libraries Unlimited, 2010. x, 302 p., ill. ISBN 9781591588269

025.007/23   Z669.8.L54

A collection of 18 essays intended to help academic librarians make data-driven decisions. Includes assessment recommendations and case studies about reference, collection development, serial acquisitions, institutional repositories, website design, interlibrary loan, and bibliographic instruction. Several of the essays focus on e-resource management and use.

645   Listening to the customer. Peter Hernon, Joseph R. Matthews. Santa Barbara, Calif.: Libraries Unlimited, 2011. xiii, 201 p., ill. ISBN 9781598847994

025.10973   Z678.85.H475

Discusses the value of customer feedback and explains many methodologies for obtaining, analyzing, and reporting it. Presents examples from public and academic libraries.

646 Practical evaluation techniques for librarians. Rachel Applegate. Santa Barbara, Calif.: Libraries Unlimited, 2013. ix, 232 pages. ISBN 9781610691598
027.0029 Z678.85.A67

A detailed guide to evaluating operations, collections, and programs in any type of library. Covers "personal" techniques (surveys, interviews, focus groups, usability testing, instructional evaluation, observational tallying, unobtrusive observation, mystery shopping) and "impersonal" techniques (list-checking, citation analysis, collection mapping, use analysis, materials availability checking, process evaluation, transaction log analysis). Explains how to create an evaluation plan, select the right techniques, draw samples, analyze data, and prepare reports.

647 A practical guide to information literacy assessment for academic librarians. Carolyn J. Radcliff. Westport, Conn.: Libraries Unlimited, 2007. xiii, 180 p., ill. ISBN 9781591583400
028.70711 ZA3075.P73

Explains nine techniques for assessing college students' information literacy, such as in-class assessment, surveys, and portfolios. Provides examples and lists reasons to use (or not use) each technique. Also gives advice on analyzing data and working with the results. References. Index.

648 Statistics, measures, and quality standards for assessing digital reference library services. http://quartz.syr.edu/rdlankes/Publications/Books/Quality.pdf. Charles R. McClure, R. David Lankes, Melissa Gross, Beverly Choltco-Devlin, School of Information Studies, Information Use Management and Policy Institute, Florida State University., Information Institute of Syracuse, School of Information Studies, Syracuse University. Syracuse, N.Y.; Tallahassee, Fla.: Syracuse University; Florida State University. [2002]
025.040727 Z711.45

One hundred and four page PDF document. Outlines 35 ways to evaluate digital reference services (e.g., live chat, e-mail, instant messaging), including descriptive statistics, log analysis, user satisfaction measures, cost, and staff time expended. For each, provides a definition, rationale, data collection procedure(s), and brief discussion of issues and considerations. Sample forms and instruments in appendix.

649 Viewing library metrics from different perspectives: inputs, outputs, and outcomes. Robert E. Dugan, Peter Hernon, Danuta A. Nitecki. Santa Barbara, Calif.: Libraries Unlimited, 2009. xv, 346 p., ill. ISBN 9781591586654
025.5/877 Z669.8.D84

Designed to help librarians, especially academic librarians, use metrics to increase accountability and improve services. Individual chapters discuss metrics from the perspectives of the library, its customers, the institution, and stakeholders. Extensive appendices list examples of metrics used by libraries: input and output numbers and ratios; process, trend, and qualitative metrics; metrics for benchmarking and marketing; and more. Many of this book's basic concepts are presented more simply in *Getting started with evaluation*.

Budgeting and Fundraising

650 The ALA book of library grant money. 8th ed. Ann Kepler, American Library Association. Chicago: American Library Association, 2012–
Z683.2.U6B54

Alphabetic listing of grant sources with contact information, basic description, financial summary, typical recipients, types and amounts of grants, restrictions, and list of recent grants. Indexes: grantors by total grant value; grantors by state; named grants; professional library organization grantors. See also *Grants for libraries and information services* (654). Also available as an e-book.

Previous editions were titled *The big book of library grant money*,

651 Balancing the books: accounting for librarians. Rachel A. Kirk. Santa Barbara,

Calif.: Libraries Unlimited, 2013. xiii, 134 p., illustrations
2013 025.1/1 23   Z683.K57
Emphasizes the unique accounting issues related to the acquisition of library materials. Explains the current state of accounting knowledge in the field; necessary skill sets; general accounting principles for different types of libraries; basic classification, reporting, and reconciliation; and the budget process. Includes bibliography. Also available as an e-book.

652   Beyond book sales: the complete guide to raising real money for your library. Susan Dowd, Library Strategies, Saint Paul Public Library. Chicago: ALA Editions, 2014. 160 p.
ISBN 9781555709129
025.1/1   Z683.2.U6; B49
Practical advice and encouragement directed at librarians, trustees, and members of friends groups. Part 1 focuses on assessment, planning, and team- and relationship-building. Part 2 goes into detail about types of fundraising activities, including: annual and special appeals; membership programs; tributes and memorials; major gifts; planned giving; fundraising events; online giving; business underwriting and sponsorships; grants; and capital campaigns. Appendix A: sixty-page "tool kit" containing sample forms, letters, checklists, step-by-step procedures, and other aids for launching a fundraising effort, recruiting donors, lobbying, accepting gifts, sponsoring events, garnering corporate sponsorships, and applying for grants. Appendix B: gallery of fundraising brochures, posters, etc. Detailed index.

653   Fundraising for libraries: 25 proven ways to get more money for your library. James Swan. New York: Neal-Schuman, 2002. xiii, 409 p.
ISBN 1555704336
025.110973   Z683.2.U6S93
Part 1, "Fundamentals of fundraising," covers basic principles and attitudes, with chapters devoted to increasing government funding, writing grants, funding capital projects (through bond issues, capital campaigns, large gifts, and large grants), soliciting donations, selling goods, raising money passively through good public relations, and enlisting outside help. Part 2, "Proven fundraising techniques," describes 25 specific strategies and provides hints,

a checklist, and an annotated bibliography for each. Appendixes: examples of bylaws for a library friends group and a library foundation. Index. Aimed at public librarians; includes a section in each chapter on the applicability of the strategy to school and academic libraries. For a more succinct introduction to library fundraising, see *Becoming a fundraiser: The principles and practice of library development*.

654   Grants for libraries and information services. http://marketplace.
foundationcenter.org/Publications/
Digital-Grant-Guides/Grants-for-Libraries-
Information-Services-2013-Digital-Edition.
[New York]: Foundation Center. 2013
001.44   Z716.5
Originally issued annually in print, but now available only in a digital edition (PDF). 2013 is the final volume. "Covers grants to public, academic, research, school, and special libraries, and to archives and information centers for construction, operations, equipment, acquisitions, computerization, and library science education. Also included are grants for citizen information and philanthropy information centers." --Introd. Information is culled from the online database maintained by the Foundation Center (300). Arranged by state. Identifies foundations, notes limitations on funding, and lists recent grants with purpose and amount. Includes several charts analyzing giving by foundation, location, subject, type of support, recipient, and population served. Indexes: recipient name, recipient location, and subject. See also the *The ALA book of library grant money* (650).

655   Grassroots library advocacy. Lauren Comito, Aliqae Geraci, Christian Zabriskie. Chicago: American Library Association, 2012. xi, 62 p., ill. ISBN 9780838911341
021.70973   Z716.3.C66
Practical advice for all librarians, not just administrators, on planning and implementing a campaign to raise public awareness about the impact of library budget cuts.

656   Librarian's handbook for seeking, writing, and managing grants. Sylvia D. Hall-Ellis. Santa Barbara, Calif.: Libraries Unlimited, 2011. xvi, 313 p., ill.
025.1/122   HD69.P75L533

An in-depth guide for grant seekers and grant administrators. Part 1 covers grant development, with chapters on planning, project design, project narrative, personnel, evaluation, budget development, and grant application appendices. Part 2 addresses implementation and management of successful grants. Includes checklists, worksheets, glossary of terms, selective bibliography, and index. Also available as an ebook.

657   The library grants center. http://
       salempress.com/store/grants/grants.htm.
       Hackensack, N.J.: Salem Press. 2011–
A database of grant sources for libraries provided free by Salem Press. Provides varied options for searching and browsing national and state-level grant opportunities. Includes a tutorial on how to apply for grants, an FAQ, and many links to additional resources.

**658   Managing budgets and finances: A
       how-to-do-it manual for librarians.**
       Arlita Hallam, Teresa R. Dalston. New
       York: Neal-Schuman, 2005. xv, 233 p., ill.
       ISBN 1555705197
       025.11   Z683.2.U6H355
Readable introduction to budgets and budget processes. Special topics covered: outsourcing; protecting library property (insurance, fines, etc.); capital projects; contracts and RFPs; alternative funding sources. Many checklists, examples, and pointers to further information in sidebars and appendixes. Index. For more extensive treatments of library budgeting see *Accounting for libraries and other not-for-profit organizations* and *Managerial accounting for libraries and other not-for-profit organizations*.

**659   Winning grants: a how-to-do-
       it manual for librarians with
       multimedia tutorials and grant
       development tools.** Pamela H. MacKellar,
       Stephanie K. Gerding. New York: Neal-
       Schuman Publishers, 2010. xxi, 242 p., ill.
       025.1/1   Z683.2.U6M33
Updated and expanded edition of *Grants for libraries*.
   A practical, step-by-step guide to project planning, grant research, and proposal writing, including profiles of successful grants. Accompanying DVD reproduces checklists, planning worksheets, and templates found in the book, and includes videos keyed to each chapter. Bibliography. Glossary.

Index. A similar handbook tailored for school library media specialists is *Grants for school libraries* by Hall-Ellis and Jerabek.

Cataloging and Classification

**660   Cataloging correctly for kids: an
       introduction to the tools. 5th ed.** Sheila
       S. Intner, Joanna F. Fountain, Jean Riddle
       Weihs, Association for Library Collections
       & Technical Services. Chicago: American
       Library Association, 2011. xiii, 224 p, ill.
       025.3/2   Z695.1.C6 C37
First edition, 1989. Authors of earlier editions vary. The classic guide to cataloging books and other materials for children and young adults. Chapters are devoted to standards, children's search behavior, AACR2 and MARC21, copy cataloging, RDA, authority control, LC and Sears subject headings, Dewey Decimal classification, materials, and more. Bibliography. Glossary of abbreviations and acronyms.

Classification

661   BISAC subject headings. https://
       www.bisg.org/bisac-subject-codes. Book
       Industry Study Group. New York: Book
       Industry Study Group, Inc. [n.d.]
Hierarchical subject classification system used in many bookstores and some public libraries to shelve materials and facilitate browsing. BISAC stands for "book industry standards and communications." Updated annually in the fall.

**662   Bliss bibliographic classification. 2nd
       ed.** Henry Evelyn Bliss, J. Mills, Vanda
       Broughton, Valerie Lang. London; Boston:
       Butterworths, 1977–. v. , port.
       ISBN 0408708212
       025.4   Z696.B6
First ed., 4 v., 1940–53. Publisher varies; now published by K.G. Saur. To date, 15 of the projected 23 volumes of the 2nd edition have been issued: Introduction and auxiliary schedules; A/AL, Philosophy and logic; AM/AX, Mathematics, statistics, and probability; AY/B, Science, technology, and physics; C, Chemistry and materials; H, Physical anthropology, human biology, and health sciences; I,

Psychology and psychiatry; J, Education; K, Society (includes social sciences, sociology, and social anthropology); P, Religion, the occult, morals, and ethics; Q, Social welfare and criminology; R, Politics and public administration; S, Law; T, Economics, management of economic enterprises; W, The Arts. Seldom used in North American libraries, the Bliss system is applied in some British libraries and is taught in LIS programs as an example of a fully faceted classification scheme.

663 **Cataloger's desktop.** http://www.loc
.gov/cds/desktop/index.html. Library
of Congress. Washington: Library of
Congress. 1994–. 1073-4929
025   Z693

Available by paid subscription on the Web. Assembles more than 250 reference sources for catalogers, including such important basic tools as the *Library of Congress rule interpretations*, *Subject heading manuals* (708), MARC 21 formats (694), and the latest editions of all MARC code lists (694), along with many specialized guides, thesauri, authority lists, and other documentation. Since March 2013, the *Anglo-American cataloguing rules (AACR2)* (674) may be accessed via Cataloger's Desktop only by those who also subscribe to the *RDA toolkit* (686). Searches may be limited to selected resources or to a type of material (text, music, electronic resources, etc.), type of activity (descriptive cataloging, subject headings, etc.), method of distribution or special classes (monographs, continuing resources, archives, etc.), or materials for cataloging education. Users may add bookmarks and local notes and may save searches. Updated periodically.

664 **Classification in theory and practice.**
Sue Batley. Oxford, U.K.: Chandos, 2005.
xi, 181 p. ISBN 9781843340836 (pbk.);
025.42   Z696.A4

A basic introduction to classification, with chapters devoted to schemes for general collections (Dewey Decimal and Library of Congress) and specialist collections (Universal Decimal and Dewey and faceted systems). A separate chapter covers classification of electronic resources and the use of thesauri, taxonomies, and ontologies.

665 **Classification web.** http://classification
web.net/. Library of Congress. Washington:
Library of Congress. [2002]–

Available by paid subscription. Enables browsing and searching of the full text of the Library of Congress Classification (LCC) schedules and Library of Congress Subject Headings (LCSH). Features a calculator that combines tables and schedule data, then displays fully calculated numbers together with their corresponding captions. Supplies correlations between Dewey and LC classification numbers, and between Dewey numbers and LC subject headings. Updated daily. Users may add and save their own notes.

The complete LC classification schedules, previously distributed in print, are now issued as PDF files (670). Weekly updates are posted online at http://www.loc.gov/aba/cataloging/classification/weeklylists/.

666 **Conversion tables. 3rd ed.** Mona
L. Scott. Westport, Conn.: Libraries
Unlimited, 2006. 3 v. ISBN 1591583489
025.433   Z696.U4S36

First edition, 1993. Second edition, 1999. Based on the 22nd edition of the *Dewey decimal classification* , the latest editions (as of 2006) of the various Library of Congress classification schedules, and *Library of Congress subject headings*. Vol. 1, LC to Dewey, and vol. 2, Dewey to LC, list detailed class numbers with corresponding numbers in the other system and the matching Library of Congress subject headings. Vol. 3 lists LC subject headings alphabetically with matching Dewey and LC class numbers.

667 **Dewey decimal classification and
relative index. 23rd ed.** Melvil Dewey,
Joan S. Mitchell, Julianne Beall, Rebecca
Green, Giles. Martin, Michael Panzer.
Dublin, Ohio: OCLC Online Computer
Library Center, Inc., 2011. 4 v.
ISBN 9781910608814
025.4/31   Z696.D52

Vol. 1 provides an overview of the DDC, major changes since the last edition, a glossary, a "manual" with advice on classifying difficult subjects, and tables of standard subdivisions, geographic areas, literary genres, languages, ethnic groups, etc. Vols. 2–3 present detailed schedules of class numbers with notes and cross-references. Vol. 4 is the "Relative Index," an A–Z list of topics mapped to class numbers.

Available from OCLC through subscription to

the online *WebDewey* (673). Libraries holding under 20,000 titles may prefer the one-volume abridgment of the DDC (15th ed., 2012). Some basic information from these publications is available openly on OCLC's *Resources for teachers and students of the DDC* website (http://www.oclc.org/dewey/resources .en.html), including a detailed summary of the Dewey schedule.

First published anonymously in 1876 under the title, *A classification and subject index.* Second to the fourteenth eds., published under the title, *Decimal classification and relative index.*

668 Dewey decimal classification: Principles and application. 3rd ed.
Lois Mai Chan, Joan S. Mitchell. Dublin, Ohio: OCLC, 2003. xi, 216 p.
ISBN 0910608725
025.431   Z696.D7C48
First (1994) and 2nd (1996) eds. titled *Dewey decimal classification: A practical guide.* Explains the principles and structure of the 22nd ed. of the *DDC*, with instructions and examples for locating, assigning, and synthesizing class numbers. Glossary. Selected bibliography. Index.

669 A guide to the Library of Congress classification. 5th ed. Lois Mai Chan.
Englewood, Colo.: Libraries Unlimited, 1999. xviii, 551 p. ISBN 1563084996
025.433   Z696.U4C47
First edition, 1968, and second edition, 1971, titled *A guide to Library of Congress classification* by John Phillip Immroth. Third edition, 1980, and fourth edition, 1990, titled *Immroth's guide to the Library of Congress classification*, by Lois Mai Chan. Introduces the principles, structure, and format of the LC classification system. Explains notation, tables, and general policies for assigning class numbers. Numerous examples for individual classes and special types of materials. Appendixes: general tables; models for sub-arrangement in classes D, H, Q, and R. Bibliography. For the actual LC class schedules, see Classification Web (665) and its print counterparts.

670 Library of Congress Classification PDF Files. http://www.loc.gov/aba/ publications/FreeLCC/freelcc.html. Washington: Library of Congress Cataloging Distribution Service. [2008-]

Previously issued in 42 printed volumes; now being converted to PDF-only distribution as print supplies are exhausted and schedules are updated. The LC classification schedules provide a detailed outline of LC class numbers, including cross-references and usage notes. Also available in *Classification web* (665). Weekly updates are posted online at http://www .loc.gov/aba/cataloging/classification/weeklylists. For a simpler outline of LC classes and subclasses see http://www.loc.gov/catdir/cpso/lcco.

671 Superintendent of Documents (SuDocs) Classification scheme. http:// www.fdlp.gov/catalogingandclassification/ cataloging-articles/1791-superintendent-of -documents-sudocs-classification-scheme. Federal Depository Library Program (FDLP). Washington: Federal Depository Library Program. 2010
Briefly explains the history and structure of SuDocs numbers, which are used by the Government Printing Office to classify federal documents. Also available as a 6-page PDF.

672 UDC online. http://www.udc-hub.com/ index.php. UDC Consortium. The Hague, The Netherlands: UDC Consortium. 2005–
In contrast to the *Dewey decimal classification* (667), the Universal Decimal Classification is designed for the purpose of information retrieval rather than shelf location. Available by subscription in several languages; current languages are English, Czech, German, French, Croatian and Dutch, with more to be added. The English *UDC Online* contains more than 70,000 current classes and over 11,000 records of historical UDC data (canceled numbers). Users may search, browse, parse, validate, and build numbers. The UDC Consortium's website, http://www.udcc .org/index.php, presents background on the UDC's history, structure, and use.

673 WebDewey. http://www.oclc.org/dewey/ versions/webdewey/. OCLC. Dublin, Ohio: Forest Press. 2002– 025.431
Available by subscription. Integrates Dewey Decimal Classification (DDC) (667) and related information with searching and browsing capabilities. Maps *Library of Congress subject headings (LCSH)*, *BISAC subject headings* (661), and selected *Medical subject*

headings (MeSH) (705) to Dewey numbers. Includes a work area for building DDC numbers, and allows creation and retention of local notes in the database. Links to local online catalog for searching DDC numbers. Includes many Relative Index terms and built numbers not available in the printed version (667). Updated continuously.

Descriptive Cataloging

674   Anglo-American cataloguing rules. 2nd ed., 2002 revision ed. Joint Steering Committee for Revision of AACR, American Library Association. Ottawa, Ont., Canada; Chicago: Canadian Library Association; American Library Association, 2002. 1 v. (loose-leaf). ISBN 083893529X

025.32   Z694.15.A56A53

Part I, "Description," devotes chapters to general rules; books, pamphlets, and printed sheets; cartographic materials; manuscripts; music; sound recordings; motion pictures and videorecordings; graphic materials; electronic resources; artefacts and realia; microforms; continuing resources; and analytics. Part II, "Headings, uniform titles, and references," addresses choice of access points and covers headings for persons, places, corporate bodies, and uniform titles. Appendixes present rules for capitalization, abbreviations, numerals, and initial articles. Glossary. Index.

For usage guidelines and examples of applying the rules, consult *Maxwell's handbook for AACR2* and *Cataloging with AACR2 & MARC21*. For an abridgment suitable for small general libraries and beginning catalogers, see *The concise AACR2*.

The Joint Steering Committee for Revision of AACR produced a new standard, *RDA: Resource description and access* (685), which was released in 2010. The full text of AACR2 is included in the online *RDA Toolkit* (686).

First edition, 1967. 2nd ed., 1978. Revised in 1988, 1998, and 2002. Kept current with annual updates, of which 2005 is the last. Included in Cataloger's Desktop (663).

675   Cataloger's desktop. http://www.loc.gov/cds/desktop/index.html. Library of Congress. Washington: Library of Congress. 1994–. 1073-4929

025   Z693

Available by paid subscription on the Web. Assembles more than 250 reference sources for catalogers, including such important basic tools as the *Library of Congress rule interpretations*, *Subject heading manuals* (708), MARC 21 formats (694), and the latest editions of all MARC code lists (694), along with many specialized guides, thesauri, authority lists, and other documentation. Since March 2013, the *Anglo-American cataloguing rules (AACR2)* (674) may be accessed via Cataloger's Desktop only by those who also subscribe to the *RDA toolkit* (686). Searches may be limited to selected resources or to a type of material (text, music, electronic resources, etc.), type of activity (descriptive cataloging, subject headings, etc.), method of distribution or special classes (monographs, continuing resources, archives, etc.), or materials for cataloging education. Users may add bookmarks and local notes and may save searches. Updated periodically.

676   Demystifying serials cataloging: a book of examples. Fang Huang Gao, Heather Tennison, Janet A. Weber. Santa Barbara, Calif.: Libraries Unlimited, an imprint of ABC-CLIO, LLC, [2012]. xxi, 345 p., ill. ISBN 9781598845969

025.3/432   Z695.7; G36

Using real-world examples, illustrates the unique issues that arise in the cataloging of serials, such as choice of main entry, enumeration, chronology, title and publisher changes, multiple formats, supplements, special issues, and the like. See also *Notes for serials cataloging*, 3rd ed. by Genereux and Moeller, for more examples from actual serials records.

677   Describing electronic, digital, and other media using AACR2 and RDA: a how-to-do-it manual and CD-ROM for librarians. Mary Beth Weber, Fay Angela Austin. New York: Neal-Schuman Publishers, [2011]. ISBN 9781555706685

025.3/4   Z695.66.W435

Explains the essential components of RDA and the FRBR framework. Provides instructions for cataloging cartographic resources, sound recordings, videos, electronic resources, electronic integrating resources, microforms, multimedia kits and mixed materials. Supplies examples of metadata in MARC, MODS and Dublin Core formats. Companion website: http://www.neal-schuman.com/describingmedia

Rev. ed. of *Cataloging nonprint and internet resources: a how-to-do-it manual for librarians* by Mary Beth Weber (Neal-Schuman, 2002).

678 Functional requirements for authority data: a conceptual model. http://www .ifla.org/node/5849. Glenn E. Patton. The Hague, The Netherlands: International Federation of Library Associations and Institutions. 2009
025.4/7   Z666.63.F77
Defines in detail the attributes and relationships of authority records for names and titles, and maps them to user tasks. For further information, see *Demystifying FRAD* by Qiang Jin, which features examples of entity relationship diagrams and maps between FRAD and RDA (685). See also *Functional requirements for subject authority data* (701).
IFLA series on bibliographic control,v. 34. A 60-page PDF document; also available in print (Munchen: K.G. Saur, 2009).

679 Functional requirements for bibliographic records. http://www.ifla .org/VII/s13/frbr/frbr.pdf. IFLA Study Group on the Functional Requirements for Bibliographic Records; International Federation of Library Associations and Institutions; Section on Cataloguing; Standing Committee. Munich, Germany: K. G. Saur. 1998. ISBN 359811382X
                                         Z699
UBCIM publications, new ser., v. 19. A 144-page PDF document; also available in print. Sets forth "a framework that identifies and clearly defines the entities of interest to users of bibliographic records, the attributes of each entity, and the types of relationships that operate between entities."—*Introd.* For a succinct explanation of FRBR, see Barbara Tillett's eight-page *What is FRBR?*. Lengthier explanations include *FRBR: A guide for the perplexed*; and *Understanding FRBR*.

680 Introducing RDA: a guide to the basics. Chris Oliver, American Library Association. Chicago: American Library Association, 2010. vii, 117 p., ill. ISBN 9780838935941
025.3/2   Z694.15.R47; O45
An introduction to *Resource Description and Access (RDA)*, a cataloging standard designed for library

materials and other content in all formats, including digital. Summarizes FRBR (*Functional Requirements for Bibliographic Records*, 679) and FRAD (*Functional Requirements for Authority Data*), the conceptual models that underlie RDA. Explains how RDA aligns with, and differs from, its predecessor, AACR (*Anglo-American Cataloging Rules*, 674). Discusses the implementation of RDA, use of the *RDA Toolkit* (686), and the advantages of RDA for users, institutions, and catalogers. Topically arranged bibliography. For in-depth instructions on using RDA, with examples, see *RDA: strategies for implementation* or the massive *Maxwell's handbook for RDA resource description and access* (683).

681 ISBD: International Standard Bibliographic Description. Consolidated ed. International Federation Of Library Associations and Institutions, International Federation of Library Associations and Institutions. Berlin; Boston: De Gruyter Saur, 2011. xvii, 284 p. ISBN 9783110263794
025.3/24   Z694.15.58 82
IFLA series on bibliographic control, v.44. The ISBD guides cataloging by national libraries and other libraries that share bibliographic data, by prescribing the elements of bibliographic description and the order in which they should be presented. This edition merges and updates the latest editions for various types of materials: general; older monographic publications (antiquarian); cartographic materials; serials and other continuing resources; electronic resources; monographic publications; non-book materials; printed music. IFLA's ISBD Review Group issued a multilingual supplement, *Full ISBD examples*, as a 161-page PDF at http://www.ifla.org/files/ assets/cataloguing/isbd/isbd-examples_2013.p df.

682 Library of Congress authorities. http:// authorities.loc.gov/webvoy.htm. Library of Congress. Washington: Library of Congress. 2002–
Searchable database of Library of Congress authority records for subjects, names, titles, and name/ title entries. Updated daily. Does not offer keyword searching, only left-anchored searching for terms and phrases. Records may be downloaded in MARC format for use in library catalogs. Includes authority records for *Library of Congress subject headings*. Also

included in the omnibus *Cataloger's desktop* (663), which requires a paid subscription.

683 Maxwell's handbook for RDA resource description and access: explaining and illustrating RDA: resource description and access using MARC21. Robert L. Maxwell. Chicago: ALA Editions, 2014. x, 900 p. ISBN 9780838911723

025.32   Z694.15.R47; M39

"[D]esigned to assist experienced catalogers as well as library school students in the application of the most commonly used RDA guidelines . . ."—*Preface* Organized in the same order as the RDA code, which should be used alongside it. By means of examples, illustrates the rules for: manifestations and items; persons; families; corporate bodies; geographic entities; works; expressions; and relationships. Appendices outline processes for record creation for specific resource formats: printed books and sheets; cartographic resources; unpublished manuscripts and manuscript collections; notated music; audio recordings; moving image resources; two-dimensional graphic resources; three-dimensional resources and objects; digital resources; microform resources; serials and integrating resources; analytical description. Detailed index. *RDA: strategies for implementation* likewise relies on examples to demonstrate the application of RDA rules. *Introducing RDA: a guide to the basics* (680) provides a conceptual overview, sans examples.

684 Practical cataloguing: AACR, RDA, and MARC21. Anne Welsh, Sue Batley. New York: Neal-Schuman Publ., 2012. xvi, 217 p., ill. ISBN 9781555707439

025.3/2   Z694.W425

Aimed at students of cataloging and practicing librarians trained in AACR2 who must transition to RDA. Covers the history of cataloging standards, FRBR principles, bibliographic elements, access points and headings, plus chapters devoted to RDA, AACR and MARC 21. Includes examples of works cataloged to RDA standards.

685 RDA: Resource description & access. Canadian Library Association., Chartered Institute of Library and Information Professionals (Great Britain), Joint Steering Committee for Development of RDA. Chicago: American Library Association, 2010–. ISBN 9780838910931, 2167-325X

14|025.3/2   Z694.15.R47; R47 025.3

New standards for descriptive cataloging, developed by a Joint Steering Committee representing the American Library Association (ALA), Canadian Library Association (CLA), Chartered Institute of Library and Information Professionals (CILIP, UK), Deutsche Nationalbibliothek, Library of Congress (US), Library and Archives Canada, British Library, and National Library of Australia. Based on FRBR (*Functional requirements for bibliographic data*) (679) and FRAD (*Functional requirements for authority data*) (678) and designed for all resource formats, including digital. Included in the *RDA Toolkit* (686), an online, interactive resource that can be customized for local workflows. A new revision of RDA in print and e-book formats was released in 2013, with annual updates anticipated after that.

686 RDA toolkit: resource description & access. http://www.rdatoolkit.org/. Canadian Library Association, Chartered Institute of Library and Information Professionals (Great Britain), Joint Steering Committee for Development of RDA, American Library Association. Chicago: American Library Association. 2010–. 2167-3241

025.3   Z694.15.R47

A subscription-based, online, interactive collection of cataloging-related documents and resources, including the full text of *RDA: Resource Description and Access* (685). Local workflows can be incorporated into the toolkit. Includes the complete text of RDA, which can be searched or browsed; the complete text of the *Anglo-American Cataloguing Rules (AACR2)* (674), with links to parallel content in RDA; mappings between RDA, MARC (694) and MODS (698); RDA element sets for FRBR (679) and FRAD (678); Library of Congress-Program for Cooperative Cataloging policy statements; a glossary; and more. Updated eight times a year.

General Works

687 Cataloging and classification: An introduction. 3rd ed. Lois Mai Chan,

Theodora L. Hodges. Lanham, Md.: Scarecrow Press, 2007. xix, 580 p., ill. ISBN 9780810859449

025.3   Z693.5.U6C48

First ed., 1981; 2nd ed., 1994.

Basic text for students of cataloging. Covers the theory and major standards for resource description, authority control, subject access, and classification, as well as MARC formats and other encoding schemes. Includes glossary, bibliography, and detailed index. See also *Introduction to cataloging and classification* by Arlene G. Taylor (10th ed., 2006), which covers much of the same information and also discusses the organization and management of cataloging work.

688 Practical strategies for cataloging departments. Rebecca L. Lubas. Santa Barbara, Calif.: Libraries Unlimited, 2011. xv, 117 p., ill. ISBN 9781598844924

025.3   Z693.P73

Unlike other books, focuses on the management of cataloging operations and the transition to new tools and systems. Separately authored chapters treat the transition from AACR2 to RDA, changes in Library of Congress cataloging policies, standards and workflows for digital cataloging, training issues, cataloging by vendors, new uses for MARC, and more.

689 Standard cataloging for school and public libraries. 4th ed. Sheila S. Intner, Jean Riddle Weihs. Westport, Conn.: Libraries Unlimited, 2007. xii, 286 p., ill. ISBN 9781591583783

025.3   Z693.56

An introductory text covering description, access points, subject headings (Sears and LC), classification (Dewey and LC), and MARC, plus a brief chapter on management of the catalog department. Glossary; multiple indexes.

First ed., 1990. As the current edition is based on AACR2, a new edition based on RDA is anticipated.

Metadata

690 Describing electronic, digital, and other media using AACR2 and RDA: a how-to-do-it manual and CD-ROM for librarians. Mary Beth Weber, Fay

Angela Austin. New York: Neal-Schuman Publishers, [2011]. ISBN 9781555706685

025.3/4   Z695.66.W435

Explains the essential components of RDA and the FRBR framework. Provides instructions for cataloging cartographic resources, sound recordings, videos, electronic resources, electronic integrating resources, microforms, multimedia kits and mixed materials. Supplies examples of metadata in MARC, MODS and Dublin Core formats. Companion website: http://www.neal-schuman.com/describingmedia

Rev. ed. of *Cataloging nonprint and internet resources: a how-to-do-it manual for librarians* by Mary Beth Weber (Neal-Schuman, 2002).

691 Dublin core metadata initiative (DCMI). http://www.dublincore.org/. Dublin Core Metadata Initiative. Dublin, Ohio: DCMI. 1995–

025.344   Z699.24

The most important information on this website is the set of metadata terms for describing digital resources known widely as "the Dublin Core." These are also published as NISO (583) standard Z39.85-2007. Besides the terms, the site offers extensive documentation, background materials, and news. See also the DCMI Wiki at http://wiki.dublincore.org/index.php/Main_Page, especially the User's Guide.

692 Encoded archival description. http://www.loc.gov/ead/. Society of American Archivists; Library of Congress; Network Development and MARC Standards Office. Washington: Library of Congress. 2002

"The EAD Document Type Definition (DTD) is a standard for encoding archival finding aids using Extensible Markup Language (XML)" and is jointly maintained by the Library of Congress and the Society of American Archivists (568)—*Home Page.* Website provides background on EAD's development, as well as the current schema, DTD (document type definition), and tag library. For tools, help files, and a bibliography of writings about EAD, see: http://www2.archivists.org/groups/encoded-archival-description-ead-rou ndtable. A revised EAD schema is under review for adoption in 2014. See also the *Encoded Archival Context for Corporate Bodies, Persons, and Families (EAC-CPF)*, a companion standard.

693   Information resource description: creating and managing metadata.
Philip Hider. Chicago: ALA Editions, 2012.
xix, 220 p., ill. ISBN 9780838912010
025.3   Z666.7
Neither a manual for working with metadata nor a guide to particular metadata schemas, but rather a broad overview of the nature and uses of metadata. Describes the attributes of information resources; the tools and systems which employ metadata; sources for metadata; issues associated with metadata quality and sharing; domain-specific standards; vocabularies; and future directions.

694   MARC standards. http://www.loc.gov/marc/. Library of Congress, Network Development and MARC Standards Office. Washington: Library of Congress, Network Development and MARC Standards Office. 1900s–
Standards for "the representation and communication of bibliographic and related information in machine-readable form."—*Home Page* Presents the latest annual edition of the concise MARC formats for bibliographic, authority, holdings, classification, and community data; MARC code lists for countries, geographic areas, languages, organizations, relators; and other value lists for codes and controlled vocabularies. Also provides links to background on MARC, tutorials, mappings to other metadata standards, and information on vendors, systems, and tools that support MARC21.

The MARC formats are also available online in Cataloger's Desktop (663). They are no longer published in print.

695   Metadata. Marcia Lei Zeng, Jian Qin. New York: Neal-Schuman Publishers, 2008. xvii, 365 p., ill. ISBN 9781555706357
025.3   Z666.7.Z46
Designed to serve as both a textbook and a self-study guide for practitioners. Covers the theory of metadata; current standards; the "building blocks" of metadata schemas and records; metadata services; and research directions. Provides exercises and reading lists in each chapter. Appendixes: annotated list of metadata standards; annotated list of value encoding schemes and content standards; glossary;

bibliography. A second edition is forthcoming in summer 2014.

696   Metadata encoding and transmission standard. http://www.loc.gov/standards/mets/. Library of Congress, Network Development and MARC Standards Office, Digital Library Federation. Washington: Library of Congress. 2003–
Joint effort of the Network Development and MARC Standards Office of the Library of Congress and the Digital Library Federation. "The METS schema is a standard for encoding descriptive, administrative, and structural metadata regarding objects within a digital library, expressed using the XML schema language of the World Wide Web Consortium."—*Home Page*

Website includes complete documentation, links to software tools, a registry of projects, a primer and reference manual (148-page PDF document), and more.

697   Metadata for digital collections: a how-to-do-it manual. Steven J. Miller. New York: Neal-Schuman Publ., 2011. xxiii, 343 p., ill. ISBN 9781555707460
025.3   Z695.24.M55
A basic introduction to concepts, practices, and standards for the creation, implementation, and documentation of metadata schemas to describe digital content. Concentrates on the Dublin Core (691) element set; also covers MODS (698) (Metadata Object Description Schema) and VRA (Visual Resources Association core categories) (570). Addresses controlled vocabularies, XML encoding, metadata interoperability, and linked data. Many tables and examples accompany the text. Bibliography. A companion website (http://www.neal-schuman.com/metadata-digital-collections) presents chapter-by-chapter questions for review and discussion, recommended resources, and exercises; links to metadata standards, examples, and other resources; glossaries of terms and acronyms; and more.

698   Metadata object description schema (MODS). http://www.loc.gov/standards/mods/. Library of Congress. Washington: Library of Congress. [2003–]
Documents a bibliographic metadata element set using the XML schema and provides guidelines for

applying it. MODS "is intended to be able to carry selected data from existing MARC 21 records as well as to enable the creation of original resource description records."—*Uses and Features*. New versions are posted periodically; version 3.5 was released in July 2013. In addition to the schema itself, the site provides mappings to other standards (e.g. MARC, RDA, Dublin Core), user guidelines, tools, and other resources. For a full picture of evolving MARC XML resources see http://www.loc.gov/standards/marcxml.

699 Understanding metadata. http://www.niso.org/standards/resources/UnderstandingMetadata.pdf. National Information Standards Organization. Bethesda, Md.: NISO Press. 2004. ISBN 1880124629

025.316   Z699

First edition, 2001, titled *Metadata made simpler: A guide for libraries*. Recommended by experts as the best concise explanation of metadata and its uses. Describes the most common metadata schemas. Glossary. List of websites. For a more in-depth introduction, see Priscilla Caplan's *Metadata fundamentals for all librarians* or Introduction to Metadata: Pathways to Digital Information, version 3.0; both works contain examples and glossaries. See also *Information resource description: creating and managing metadata*.

Subject Headings

700 Cataloger's desktop. http://www.loc.gov/cds/desktop/index.html. Library of Congress. Washington: Library of Congress. 1994–. ISBN 1073-4929

025   Z693

Available by paid subscription on the Web. Assembles more than 250 reference sources for catalogers, including such important basic tools as the *Library of Congress rule interpretations*, *Subject heading manuals* (708), MARC 21 formats (694), and the latest editions of all MARC code lists (694), along with many specialized guides, thesauri, authority lists, and other documentation. Since March 2013, the *Anglo-American cataloguing rules (AACR2)* (674) may be accessed via Cataloger's Desktop only by those who also subscribe to the *RDA toolkit* (686). Searches may be limited to

selected resources or to a type of material (text, music, electronic resources, etc.), type of activity (descriptive cataloging, subject headings, etc.), method of distribution or special classes (monographs, continuing resources, archives, etc.), or materials for cataloging education. Users may add bookmarks and local notes and may save searches. Updated periodically.

701 Functional requirements for subject authority data (FRSAD): a conceptual model. http://www.ifla.org/node/5849. Marcia Lei Zeng, Maja. Žumer, Athena Salaba, IFLA Working Group on the Functional Requirements for Subject Authority Records (FRSAR). The Hague, The Netherlands: International Federation of Library Associations and Institutions. 2011

025.4/7   Z666.63.F77; F86

Outlines a model within the FRBR framework for expressing "aboutness" of works. See also *Functional requirements for authority data* (678), which treats name and title authority data.

IFLA series on bibliographic control, v.43. A 75-page PDF document; also available in print (Berlin: DeGruyter Saur, 2011).

702 Library of Congress authorities. http://authorities.loc.gov/webvoy.htm. Library of Congress. Washington: Library of Congress. 2002–

Searchable database of Library of Congress authority records for subjects, names, titles, and name/title entries. Updated daily. Does not offer keyword searching, only left-anchored searching for terms and phrases. Records may be downloaded in MARC format for use in library catalogs. Includes authority records for *Library of Congress subject headings*. Also included in the omnibus *Cataloger's desktop* (663), which requires a paid subscription.

703 Library of Congress Subject Headings PDF Files. http://www.loc.gov/aba/publications/FreeLCSH/freelcsh.html. Library of Congress, Policy and Standards Division. Washington: Library of Congress. 2013–

025.4/9   Z695.Z8

The list of subject headings most widely used in U.S. libraries, commonly referred to as "LCSH."

Alphabetical arrangement, with separate PDF files for each letter, and for free-floating subdivisions, genre/form terms, and children's subject headings. Employs the usual abbreviations used in thesauri, i.e., BT (broader term), NT (narrower term), RT (related term), UF (use for), and SA (see also). Includes scope notes and LC classification numbers. Use and interpretation of the headings may require consulting the *Subject heading manual* (708) or Lois Mai Chan's *Library of Congress subject headings: Principles of structure and policies for application*.

Kept up-to-date by monthly lists (posted at http://www.loc.gov/aba/cataloging/subject/weeklylists/). Also available in Classification Web (665), a subscription-based online service.

Thirty-fifth edition (6 vols.) was the last to be published in print. The printed sets (1975-2013) were commonly known as "the red books."

704 Library of Congress subject headings: principles and application. 4th ed.
Lois Mai Chan. Westport, Conn.: Libraries Unlimited, 2005. xvi, 549 p.
ISBN 1591581540
025.49   Z695.Z8L5226

Introduces basic principles of LC subject headings and the forms of headings, subdivisions, and cross-references. Provides many examples of headings applied to special material types and subject areas. Discusses LCSH in the electronic environment and the FAST (Faceted Application of Subject Terminology) metadata schema derived from LCSH. Appendixes include free-floating subdivisions; MARC 21 coding for subject information; and rules for abbreviation, capitalization, and punctuation within headings. Glossary. Bibliography. For a concise overview of the LCSH system, see Chan's *Library of Congress subject headings: Principles of structure and policies for application*. Chan's work must be used with the official *Library of Congress subject headings* compilation, which is available online as PDF files (703) or as part of the subscription service, Classification Web (665). For a newer treatment of this topic, which also includes numerous examples, a glossary, and brief chapters on Classification Web and open access online LC databases, see *Essential Library of Congress subject headings*, by Vanda Broughton.

First edition, 1978. Second edition, 1986. Third edition, 1995.

705 MeSH: medical subject headings.
http://www.nlm.nih.gov/mesh/MBrowser .html. National Library of Medicine (U.S.). Bethesda, Md.: U.S. National Library of Medicine. 1975–
Z695.1.M48

MeSH®; MeSH Browser; National Library of Medicine (NLM).

"MeSH is the National Library of Medicine's controlled vocabulary thesaurus. It consists of sets of terms naming descriptors in a hierarchical structure that permits searching at various levels of specificity. MeSH descriptors are arranged in both an alphabetic and a hierarchical structure . . . 26,853 descriptors in 2013 MeSH . . . 213,000 entry terms . . . 214,000 headings called 'Supplementary concept records' (formerly 'Supplementary chemical records') within a separate thesaurus." -*MeSH fact sheet* (http://www. nlm.nih.gov/pubs/factsheets/mesh.html).   Many cross-references help in locating the most appropriate MeSH heading. MeSH is used for indexing, cataloging, and searching biomedical and health-related information and documents.

Access points to MeSH are available via the MeSH browser, which contains the full contents of the vocabulary and the MeSH website (http://www.nlm .nih.gov/mesh), which provides additional information about MeSH and for obtaining MeSH in different electronic formats.

MeSH subject descriptors appear in MEDLINE®/ PubMed®, the NLM catalog, and elsewhere. Related pages are the Unified medical language system (UMLS®) and the NLM classification.

Supplement to index medicus®, commonly known as "black and white" MeSH, combines the alphabetic arrangement and the tree structures in a single publication. It was published in print format each Jan. through 2007. Other separate MeSH publications (*Annotated alphabetic MeSH*, the *MeSH trees structures*, and the *Permuted MeSH*) ceased publication in 2004. A brief history of MeSH and other introductory material can be found at http://www .nlm.nih.gov/mesh/intro_preface2007.html. "MeSH is 50 years old http://ojs.med.utah.edu/index.php/ esynapse/article/view/166/278 (*eSynapse* v.26 (1), 2011), includes links to historical information about MeSH, i.e., a videocast and presentation remarks by Robert M. Braude ("50 years of medical subject headings: Past, present, and future impact on biomedical information").

706 Sears list of subject headings. http://
www.ebscohost.com/academic/sears-list
-of-subject-headings. EBSCO Publishing.
Ipswich, Mass.: EBSCO Publishing. 2013–
025.4/9   Z695.Z8
Online version of the classic print tool published until
2010 by the H. W. Wilson Company and subsequent-
ly by Grey House Publishing, *Sears list of subject headings* (707). Suggests subject headings for the catalogs
of small and medium-sized libraries. Includes scope
notes, class numbers from the *Abridged Dewey Decimal Classification* (667), and copious cross-references.
Intended for both adult and juvenile collections.

**707 Sears list of subject headings. 20th
ed.** Joseph Miller, Susan McCarthy, Minnie
Earl Sears. New York: H.W. Wilson Co.,
2010. liii, 847 p. ISBN 9780824211059
025.4/9   Z695.Z8; S43
In thesaurus format, suggests subject headings
for the catalogs of small and medium-sized libraries. Includes scope notes, class numbers from the
Abridged Dewey Decimal Classification, and copious
cross-references. Intended for both adult and juvenile collections. A separately published *Canadian
companion* provides supplementary headings pertaining to Canada. The most recent Spanish language
edition, *Sears lista de encabezamientos de materia*, was
released in 2008.

First to fifth editions (1923–44) titled *List of subject headings for small libraries*. New editions appear
approximately every three years; the 21st ed. will be
published in spring 2014.

708 Subject heading manual. http://www
.loc.gov/aba/publications/FreeSHM/
freeshm.html. Library of Congress,
Acquisitions and Bibliographic Access
Directorate. Washington: Library of
Congress. 2013–
A set of freely available PDF files. Explains the rules
that govern the formulation of Library of Congress
subject headings and defines and explains the use
of terms in these headings and their sub-divisions,
with illustrative examples. Glossary. Also available as
part of *Cataloger's Desktop* (663). The last printed,
looseleaf editionappeared in 2008.

**709 Subject headings for school and
public libraries. Bilingual 4th ed.**

Joanna F. Fountain. Santa Barbara, Calif.:
Libraries Unlimited, 2012. lxix, 414 p.
ISBN 9781591586388
025.4/68088/99282   Z695.Z8;L523518
A thesaurus of simplified subject terms for children's
materials, based on the *Library of Congress Subject
Headings* (703) and LC's Children's and Young
Adult Cataloging Program. Includes names of people and corporate bodies as well as topics, arranged
alphabetically by English term. Identifies relationships among terms (USE, UF, BT, NT, RT) and supplies Spanish equivalents. Includes instructions on
using free-floating sub-divisions. Spanish-language
indexes: topical and geographic headings; name and
title headings.

First edition, 1996. Previous eds. were sub-
titled "An LCSH/Sears companion," and the 3rd ed.
(2001) remains useful for libraries switching from
Sears (707) to LCSH.

Collection Development and Acquisitions

**710 Children's books: a practical guide
to selection.** Phyllis J. Van Orden,
Sunny Strong. New York: Neal-Schuman
Publishers, 2007. xv, 239 p., [16] p. of
plates, col. ill. ISBN 9781555705848
025.2/187625   Z718.1.V335
A guide to the selection of printed children's books
for school and public libraries. Part I covers the selection process, general criteria, diversity issues, and
selection tools. Part II discusses specific criteria for
genres (picture books, fiction, folk literature, poetry).
Part III covers information and reference books, as
well as particular subjects, such as alphabet books
and biographies. Includes annotated lists of recommended titles. Appendices: glossary; annotated list
of resources; directory of organizations; resources
for writing collection policy statements. Separate
author, illustrator, title, and subject indexes.

**711 Collection development and
management for 21st century library
collections: an introduction.** Vicki
L. Gregory. New York: Neal-Schuman
Publishers, 2011. xvii, 261 p., ill.
025.2/1   Z687.G68

Opens with a chapter on the impact of new technologies on collection development and management. Subsequent chapters cover user needs, policies, selection, acquisitions, budgets, assessment/ evaluation (including weeding), consortial collection development, legal issues, professional ethics, and preservation. Each chapter lists key vocabulary and recommends further readings. An accompanying CD contains 21 sample collection policies and a directory of nearly 400 publishers, distributors and wholesalers. For another useful overview, see *Fundamentals of collection development and management* (714).

712   CREW: a weeding manual for modern libraries. https://www.tsl.texas.gov/ld/ pubs/crew/index.html. Jeanette Larson. Austin, Tex.: Texas State Library and Archives Commission. 2012

025.216   Z703.6

One-hundred-and-eight-page PDF. A widely-used guide to deselection. Outlines rationales, criteria, and processes for continuous review, evaluation and weeding (CREW) of library collections, including print books, e-books, reference works, nonprint media, and juvenile materials. Provides detailed guidelines by Dewey class. Training materials are available on the website.

First edition: *The CREW manual: a unified system of weeding, inventory, and collection-building for small and medium-sized public libraries*, by Joseph P. Segal (1976).

713   Developing and managing electronic collections: the essentials. Peggy Johnson. Chicago: ALA Editions, 2013. vii, 186 pages; 23 cm

025.2/84   Z692.C65; J64

Provides practical information on evaluating e-resources, ordering, licensing, doing business with e-content and service suppliers, managing access, and budgeting. Suggests readings on each topic. Glossary. Detailed index. *Managing electronic resources: a LITA guide* covers the same basic topics in separately authored chapters.

714   Fundamentals of collection development and management. 2nd ed. Peggy Johnson. Chicago: American Library Association, 2009. xiii, 407 p., ill.

ISBN 9780838909720

025.2/1   Z687.J64

Thorough overview covering organization and staffing; policy, planning, and budgets; developing collections; managing collections; marketing, liaison, and outreach activities; collection analysis; cooperative collection development; and scholarly communication. Suggested readings at end of each chapter. Appendices list professional resources, selection aids, model collection policy statements, and contract and license terms. Glossary. Index. Also available as an e-book. A third edition is forthcoming in 2014.

For other useful overviews, see *Collection development and management for 21st century library collections* (711), and the classic, frequently revised textbook, *Collection management basics* by Evans and Saponaro (1st-5th editions titled *Developing library and information center collections*).

715   Fundamentals of managing reference collections. Carol A. Singer. Chicago: ALA Editions, 2012. 167 p. ISBN 978-0-8389-1153-2

025.21   Z711

With balanced attention to both electronic and print resources, this practical guide covers: reference collection development policies; staffing models for managing reference collections; selection of materials; acquisitions, budgets and licenses; collection maintenance; weeding; consortial collection management; and discovery and access. Includes a collection development policy template. *Reference collection development: a manual* by Perez is an older but still useful work with examples of collection policies.

716   Gifts for the collections. http://www .ifla.org/VII/s14/nd1/Profrep112.pdf. Kay Ann Cassell, Sharon Johnson, Judith Mansfield, Sha Li Zhang. The Hague, The Netherlands: International Federation of Library Associations and Institutions. 2008. ISBN 9789077897324, 0168-1931

025.26   Z689

IFLA professional reports, no. 112. 21-page PDF, also issued in print. A concise set of guidelines for evaluating, accepting and processing gift materials, applicable to most types of libraries. Includes a sample donor agreement. See also *Crash course in library gift programs* by Roberts.

717 Guide to out-of-print materials. Narda Tafuri, Anna Seaberg, Gary Handman, Association for Library Collections and Technical Services. Lanham, Md.: Scarecrow Press, 2004. iv, 46 p. ISBN 0810849747
025.21 Z689.A2746; Z692.O95

Succinct guide, in outline form, to acquiring out-of-print books, serials, and audiovisual materials. Identifies both traditional and web-based resources and techniques. Glossary. Bibliography. Appendix: URL resource list.

718 Handbook on the international exchange of publications. 5th ed. Kirsti Ekonen, Paivi Paloposki, Pentti Vattulainen, International Federation of Library Associations. Munchen, Germany: K.G. Saur Verlag, 2006. 158 p. ISBN 9783598117527
021.8

First ed., 1950. Explains current practices used by libraries to acquire materials through exchange, with examples from several countries. Includes directory of national exchange centers.

719 The Kovacs guide to electronic library collection development: essential core subject collections, selection criteria, and guidelines. 2nd ed. Diane K. Kovacs. New York: Neal-Schuman Publ., 2009. xxiii, 303 p., ill. ISBN 9781555706647
025.2/84 ZA4080.5.K685

Part I opens with a discussion of general collection development principles for e-resources and an extensive list of online tools. Topics related to organization, maintenance, and licensing of electronic content are also covered. Part II presents strategies and tools for building collections in the following areas: ready-reference sources and government documents; jobs and employment, consumer information, and genealogy; business; law; medicine; biology; engineering, computer sciences, and mathematics; physical and earth sciences; social sciences; education and homework e-resources; arts and humanities. Identifies core resources, recommends selection tools, and profiles an "e-library success story" for each subject area.

First edition, 2004, by Diane K. Kovacs and Kara L. Robinson.

720 LIBLICENSE: licensing digital content - a resource for librarians. http://liblicense.crl.edu/. Chicago: Center for Research Libraries. 1997–
070.5797; 341.7582 Z286.E43

Founded by Ann Okerson and originally hosted by the Yale University Library, this searchable website provides resources to assist academic and research libraries in negotiating electronic licensing agreements. Includes a glossary of common license terms, a bibliography (last updated in 2009), sample clauses with commentary, links to other websites, links to full text of publishers' and authors' licenses, and downloadable software for step-by-step license creation.

721 Library collection development policies: Academic, public, and special libraries. Frank W. Hoffmann, Richard J. Wood. Lanham, Md.: Scarecrow Press, 2005. xv, 329 p. ISBN 0810851806
025.21 Z687.2.U6H64

Updates the authors' earlier guide, *Library collection development policies: A reference and writers' handbook* (1996). Explains 25 components of collection development policies (target audience, evaluative criteria, weeding, intellectual freedom, etc.), with illustrative extracts from actual policies. Devotes separate chapters to online resources and resource sharing. An appendix reprints various statements on intellectual freedom by the American Library Association. A companion volume, Library collection development policies: School libraries and learning resource centers, covers similar policy components, provides extracts from school library policies, and includes a chapter on polices that define acceptable use of the Internet.

722 Licensing digital content: a practical guide for librarians. 2nd ed. Lesley Ellen Harris. Chicago: American Library Association, 2009. xviii, 161 p.
346.7304/8 KF3024.C6H368

First ed., 2002. Thoroughly covers the licensing of electronic resources by libraries, including when to license, the negotiation process, and specialized concepts and terms. Explains the meaning of and reasons for typical license clauses. Appendices reprint sections of the U.S. Copyright Act governing fair use and interlibrary loan and provide a checklist of licensing clauses. Glossary. Index. Also available as e-book.

723 No shelf required: e-books in libraries. Sue Polanka. Chicago: American Library Association, 2011. xiii, 182 p. ISBN 9780838910542
025.17/4   Z716.6.N62

Nine separately authored chapters provide an overview of e-book publishing, acquisition, preservation, and use. Includes chapters focused on school, public, and academic libraries. Detailed index. A follow-up book, *No shelf required 2*, focuses on library use and management of e-books, with sixteen chapters on various topics, including accessibility, cataloging, weeding, the library as e-book publisher, and the place of e-books in education. For the latest developments, consult the editor's blog of the same name. For another practical view of the e-book landscape, see *Building and managing e-book collections: a how-to-do-it manual for librarians*.

724 Serials acquisitions glossary. http://www.ala.org/alcts/resources/collect/serials/acqglossary. Association for Library Collections & Technical Services, Serials Section, Acquisitions Committee. Chicago: American Library Association. 2005
                          Z1006.S5

First edition, 1993. Defines terms used by librarians, vendors, and publishers of serials, with special attention to electronic publishing. Fifty-one page PDF file.

Digitization, Digital Libraries, and Information Technologies

Editor's Guide: See also Library and Information Science > Professional Practice > Cataloging and Classification > Metadata. For guides to acquiring and organizing digital content from external sources, see Library and Information Science > Professional Practice > Collection Development and Acquisitions.

725 The accidental systems librarian. 2nd ed. Nicole C. Engard, Rachel Singer Gordon. Medford, N.J.: Information Today, 2012. xxiii, 302 p., ill.
025.00285   Z682.4.S94 E54

Provides guidance on managing IT services in a library, including mastering software and web applications and applying basic library science principles to IT-related work. Topics treated include troubleshooting technical problems, evaluating technologies for purchase, training staff and patrons, creating a technology plan, migrating to a new library system, and more. Discusses career management and continuing education as well. Bibliography. Chapter-by-chapter list of websites. Index.

726 Archiving websites: A practical guide for information management professionals. Adrian Brown. London: Facet, 2006. xiv, 238 p., ill.
ISBN 9781856045537
025.284   Z701.3.W43B76

Well-organized overview of all aspects of archiving websites, including selection; collection methods; quality assurance and cataloging; preservation; delivery to users; legal issues; managing a web archiving program; and future trends. Appendixes include a list of software tools and models for a permission form, test script, problem log, and job description. Glossary. Bibliography. Index.

727 Assistive technologies in the library. Barbara T. Mates, William R. Reed. Chicago: American Library Association, 2011. xiv, 206 p., ill.
027.6/63   Z711.92.H3; M323

Overviews topics such as accessible web design, with specific recommendations of software, equipment, and services for users with particular disabilities. Addresses staff development, funding, and marketing. Appendixes offer annotated lists of vendors, web-based information resources, and grant opportunities.

728 The best 100 free apps for libraries. Jim Hahn. Lanham, Md.: Scarecrow Press, 2013. viii, 217 p., ill.
ISBN 9780810885820
005.3   Z680.5.B47

Recommends mobile apps that can be downloaded free-of-charge onto smartphones and tablets. For each, displays a screenshot, describes the app's function, suggests how it can be used in the context of library services or a librarian's work, and predicts future directions for apps of that type. The selections include utility apps (e.g., barcode scanners), augmented reality apps that interact graphically with the environment, productivity apps (e.g., news sources and web search engines), and social apps.

729 Building digital libraries: A how-to-do-it manual. Terry Reese, J. Kyle Banerjee. New York: Neal-Schuman Publ., 2008. ISBN 9781555706173

025.00285 ZA4080

A step-by-step guide to acquiring, processing, organizing, and managing a local digital collection. Addresses repository architecture, metadata, federated searching, and access management; includes workflow charts and screenshots. Index.

Another step-by-step guide, illustrated with a case study, is *Creating digital collections: A practical guide*. For a more detailed introduction that uses the open source Greenstone Digital Library Software as an example, see *How to build a digital library*, 2nd ed.

730 The complete library technology planner: a guidebook with sample technology plans and RFPs on CD-ROM. John M. Cohn, Ann L. Kelsey. New York: Neal-Schuman Publ., 2010. xxiv, 161 p., ill. ISBN 9781555706814

025.00285 Z678.9.A4; U622

A step-by-step overview of the elements of a library technology plan, the process for developing one, and aspects of working with a plan, evaluating it, and keeping it up-to-date. Includes sample worksheets. Each chapter concludes with a brief annotated bibliography; additional sources on the Web are cited in a separate list. An accompanying CD-ROM reproduces technology plans and requests for proposals (RFPs) from 32 public, academic, school, and special libraries. *Technology for results* by Mayo (2005) is an older but still useful source for similar information.

731 The cybrarian's web: an A-Z guide to 101 free Web 2.0 tools and other resources. Cheryl Ann Peltier-Davis. Medford, N.J.: Information Today, 2011. xxv, 486 p., ill.

025.042/2 ZA4225.P44

Describes the functions and features of selected Web-based tools that librarians can use to accomplish their work and enhance library services. Provides examples of successful uses of blog publishing

services, social networks, search engines, video and photo hosting sites, wikis, social bookmarking services, digital libraries, and more, as well as a wide range of productivity tools. Index. Find updates and links on the companion website, http://www.cybrariansweb.com.

732 Digital curation: a how-to-do-it manual. D. R. Harvey. New York: Neal-Schuman Publishers, 2010. xxii, 225 p.

025.00285 ZA4080.H37

Defines conceptual models for data curation and explains the role of curators. Addresses major components of the digital curation process, including description and representation information (i.e., metadata) and preservation policies. Introduces the best practices in data design, creation, appraisal, selection, ingestion, organization, preservation, and storage, as well as issues associated with data access, use and re-use. A companion website contains templates for forms, checklists, etc. and links to online resources: http://www.neal-schuman.com/nealschuman/companionwebsite/curation

733 A framework of guidance for building good digital collections. http://www.niso.org/publications/rp/framework3.pdf. NISO Framework Working Group. Bethesda, Md.: NISO Press. 2007. ISBN 1880124742; 9781880124741

ZA4080.5

First ed., 2000; 2nd ed., 2004. One hundred-page PDF document. "The Framework establishes principles for creating, managing, and preserving digital collections, digital objects, metadata, and projects."—*Home Page* Includes hundreds of links to relevant guidelines and documentation of best practices.

734 Handbook of research on digital libraries: design, development, and impact. Yin-Leng Theng. Hershey, Pa.: Information Science Reference, 2009. xxxix, 649 p., ill., map ISBN 9781599048796

025.00285 ZA4080.H36

Comprised of fifty-eight research-based articles, spanning the design and development of digital libraries; information processing and content management; users, interactions and experiences; case studies and applications; and digital library education and future trends. All articles cite references and define key terms.

735 Information industry directory. Gale Research, Thomson Gale (Firm). Detroit: Gale Research, 1991–. 1051-6239

025.040294   Z674.3.E53

Comprehensive, international directory of database producers and other firms and organizations "involved in the production and distribution of information in electronic form."—*Title page* Descriptive listings, arranged alphabetically, provide contact data, company information, and details about individual products and services. Indexes include master name and keyword; function/service classifications; personal name; geographic; subject. A searchable online version of this directory is included in the *Gale directory library*.

Annual, in 2 vols. First through tenth editions, (1971–90) had title *Encyclopedia of information systems and services*.

736 Integrated library systems: planning, selecting, and implementing. Desiree Webber, Andrew Peters. Santa Barbara, Calif.: Libraries Unlimited, 2010. xii, 183 p. ISBN 9781591588979

025.00285   Z678.93.I57; W43

Lays out the process of selecting and implementing an integrated library system (ILS) from start to finish, including comparing products, determining hardware needs, considering add-on modules, crafting a request for proposals (RFP), developing a project timeline, working with sales consultants, evaluating demonstrated products, preparing a technology plan, drafting a budget and justification; and, finally, installing and going live with the chosen system. Appendices include a grid for comparing vendors and features, sample plans, and a sample RFP. Glossary. Bibliography.

737 Library technology reports. American Library Association. Chicago: American Library Association, 1976–. ill. 0024-2586

022.9   Z684.L75

Continues the supplementary material to American Library Association Library Technology Program, *Library technology reports* (1965–75) and continues its volume numbering. As of 2008, eight issues per

year. A typical issue is 50 pages long, offers a state-of-the-art overview of a current topic, and is authored by an expert librarian. For example, recent issues have treated linked data, web analytics, ebook platforms, and electronic resource management. Electronic full text available with print subscription, or through a subscription to ALA TechSource Online (http://www.alatechsource.org), bundled with *Smart Libraries Newsletter*. Also available through several databases licensed from Ebsco, Gale, and ProQuest.

738 Mobile technology and libraries. Jason Griffey. New York: Neal-Schuman Publ., 2010. xi, 115 p., ill. ISBN 9781555707118

004.1675   Z680.5.G75

A basic introduction for libraries aiming to develop services using mobile technology. Covers platforms, planning, marketing, and evaluation. Provides instructions, including simple code, for online catalog access, instructional resources, library tours, SMS (texting) services, and more. Bibliography. *Using mobile technology to deliver library services: a handbook* is another good overview with an emphasis on academic library uses. For more technical information, see *Building mobile library applications* and *Going mobile: developing apps for your library using basic HTML programming*.

739 Neal-Schuman library technology companion: a basic guide for library staff. 4th ed. John J. Burke. Chicago: ALA Neal-Schuman, 2013. 264 p. ISBN 9781555709150

025.00285   Z678.9.B85

A broad introduction to the technologies used in libraries. Part 1, Library Technology Basics, introduces the history of library technology and suggests resources for keeping up to date and evaluating equipment and systems. Part 2, Technology Tools, examines hardware, software, and the Internet. Part 3, How Libraries Put Technology to Work, considers both patron and staff uses. Part 4, Building and Maintaining the Technology Environment, addresses such topics as security, troubleshooting, and ergonomics. Part 5, Where Library Technology is Going and How to Get There, focuses on technology planning and the future. Most chapters include brief bibliographies. Glossary.

740   No shelf required: e-books in libraries. Sue Polanka. Chicago: American Library Association, 2011. xiii, 182 p. ISBN 9780838910542
025.17/4   Z716.6.N62

Nine separately authored chapters provide an overview of e-book publishing, acquisition, preservation, and use. Includes chapters focused on school, public, and academic libraries. Detailed index. A follow-up book, *No shelf required 2*, focuses on library use and management of e-books, with sixteen chapters on various topics, including accessibility, cataloging, weeding, the library as e-book publisher, and the place of e-books in education. For the latest developments, consult the editor's blog of the same name. For another practical view of the e-book landscape, see *Building and managing e-book collections: a how-to-do-it manual for librarians*.

741   SHERPA-RoMEO: publisher copyright policies and self-archiving. http://www.sherpa.ac.uk/romeo/. University of Nottingham. Nottingham, U.K.: University of Nottingham; University of Lund. [n.d.]

Database of journal publishers' policies concerning the digital archiving of articles by their authors. Color-coded to indicate whether a publisher permits the archiving of preprints, post-prints, both, or neither. Of particular use to university libraries hosting institutional repositories. Covers 22,000 journals. May be searched by publisher name, journal title, or ISSN.

742   Technology for the rest of us: a primer on computer technologies for the low-tech librarian. Nancy Courtney. Westport, Conn.: Libraries Unlimited, 2005. viii, 184 p., ill. ISBN 1591582334
025/.00285   Z678.9.T415

The intent of the expert contributors to this volume "is not to turn readers into IT practitioners, but to improve their technological literacy about topics currently of interest in the library community so that they can communicate effectively with systems personnel."—*Back cover* Similar to the *Tech Set* series but more condensed. Separately authored chapters explain such technologies as wireless networks, OpenURL, RFID, blogs, XML, institutional repositories, adaptive technologies, and more. A follow-up volume, *More technology for the rest of us*, introduces Web services, digital data curation, cloud computing, learning management systems, authentication/authorization, content management systems, data visualization, digital preservation systems, open source software, and metadata repurposing using XSLT. The final chapter focuses on communication with IT staff. Glossary.

743   TechSoup for libraries. http://www.techsoupforlibraries.org. TechSoup Global. [San Francisco]: TechSoup Global. [n.d.]

Resources to help public libraries provide computer access and support. The site offers downloadable "cookbooks" (tips and techniques for planning and maintaining technology-based services), profiles of successful library programs, a blog, and other resources. The parent organization, TechSoup, connects non-profit organizations with companies that donate hardware and software.

Education and Continuing Professional Development

744   Directory of LIS programs and faculty in the United States and Canada. http://www.alise.org/lis-programs--faculty. Association for Library and Information Science Education. Chicago: Association for Library and Information Science Education. 2005– 1555-9092
                                Z668.D55

A complete listing of the faculty of 60 North American schools of library and information science, along with the teaching and research areas of each faculty member keyed to ALISE's LIS Research Areas Classification Scheme (http://www.alise.org/classification-scheme). Now published only online. Available to ALISE members and to others upon payment. Similar information for earlier years in *Directory of the Association for Library and Information Science Education* (1983–2004), *Directory of the Association of American Library Schools* (1971–1982), and the fall or winter issue of the *Journal of education for librarianship* (1960–1970).

745   The librarian's career guidebook. Priscilla K. Shontz. Lanham, Md.: Scarecrow Press, 2004. xix, 565 p. ISBN 0810850346
020.23   Z682.35.V62L53

In short readable chapters, delivers practical advice from information professionals on more than 60 topics pertaining to library education, job hunting, entry-level jobs, basic skills such as time management, professional development, and balancing work with other aspects of life. Subject index. Author maintains a website on the same subject at http://liscareer.com. Education for librarianship and related fields is covered in several recent career guides, such as *The new information professional: your guide to careers in the digital age* and *Information nation: education and careers in the emerging information professions*.

746   Top library and information studies schools. http://grad-schools.usnews .rankingsandreviews.com/best-graduate -schools/top-library-information-science -programs. U.S. News & World Report. Washington: U.S. News & World Report
This ranking, issued periodically by the magazine, *U.S. News & World Report*, is based on a survey of LIS deans, program directors, and senior faculty members at ALA-accredited schools. The 2013 release also includes rankings of several specialization areas: archives and preservation; digital librarianship; health librarianship; information systems; law librarianship; school library media; and services for children and youth. The publisher provides additional information on the individual programs in its online tool, *Grad Compass*, available by subscription, and in an annual print publication, *Best graduate schools*.

747   WebJunction. http://www.webjunction .org. OCLC. Dublin, Ohio: OCLC. 2003–
Z668
An open, online learning community for librarians. Maintained by OCLC. Offers webinars, self-paced online courses, discussion forums, and many short documents with practical tips on patron services, library management, and technology. Access to some features requires registration.

748   What they don't teach you in library school. Elisabeth Doucett. Chicago: American Library Association, 2011. viii, 149 p. ISBN 9780838935927
020.23   Z665.D685
Supplements formal coursework in LIS. Offers tips for developing practical skills in a sixteen areas, including networking, getting familiar with a new

community, managing problem patrons, teamwork, marketing, and managing facilities and finances.

749   World guide to library, archive and information science education. 3rd ed. Axel Schniederjürgen. München, Germany: K.G. Saur, 2007. 560 p. ISBN 9783598220357, 0344-6891
Z668
First ed., 1985, titled *International guide to library and information science education*, edited by Josephine Riss Fang and Paul Nauta. 2nd ed., 1995, edited by Josephine Riss Fang, Robert D. Stueart, and Kuthilda Tuamsuk. Arranged by country. Profiles of institutions and their programs include street address, phone number, e-mail address, and URL; director's name; year founded; sources of funding; tuition rate; financial aids; numbers of staff, students, and graduates; requirements for foreign students; continuing education programs; accreditation; and details of degrees offered, including admission requirements, objectives, and content areas. Indexes: place names; names of schools.

Consult individual schools' websites for more current information. For lists of accredited North American schools, visit the websites of the American Library Association (553), and for school library media programs specifically, the National Council for Accreditation of Teacher Education (http://www .ncate.org).

Human Resources

750   Achieving diversity: a how-to-do-it manual for librarians. Barbara I. Dewey, Loretta Parham. New York: Neal-Schuman Publ., 2006. x, 245 p., ill. ISBN 1555705545
027.6/3   Z711.8.A25
A practical guide for academic libraries. Brings together papers and case studies in three sections— how to create a successful diversity plan; how to recruit and retain a diverse workforce; and how to improve diversity through services, collections, and collaborations — plus samples of diversity documents. For another perspective on services for multicultural academic library users, see *Librarians serving diverse populations: challenges and opportunities* (869).

751   ALA-APA library salary database.
http://ala-apa.org/improving-salariesstatus/
resources/ala-apa-librarian-and-library
-worker-salary-surveys/. American Library
Association-Allied Professional Association.
Chicago: American Library Association-
Allied Professional Association. 2006–

Data gathered from annual surveys, 2006-2010;
biennial surveys, 2012-. Previous print title: *ALA
survey of librarian salaries*. Frequency varied: biennial,
1982–88; annual, 1989–2005. Current title also
produced in separate print volumes covering public
and academic library positions that require an ALA-
accredited master's degree (issued annually 2006-
2010 and now biennially) and non-MLS positions
(last issued in 2007). Provides statistical data on salaries for six librarian positions: Directors/deans; dep-
uty/associate/assistant directors; department heads/
coordinators/senior managers; managers/supervisors
of support staff; librarians who do not supervise and
beginning librarians; and 62 non-MLS positions.

Tables may be generated from public library data
based on position title, size of population served,
region, and/or state, and from academic library data
based on position title, type of institution (two-year
college, four-year college, university), region, and/or
state. For salary data on special librarians see the *SLA
annual salary survey and workplace study* (758).

752   ARL annual salary survey. http://www
.arl.org/focus-areas/statistics-assessment/
arl-statistics-salary-survey. Association of
Research Libraries. Washington, D.C.:
Association of Research Libraries

Volume for 1966/67 issued as *ARL newsletter*,
no. 23; 1967/68 as part of its *Academic library statistics*;
first published separately in 1973, covering 1972/73.
Available in PDF format. Compiles data from libraries of major North American research institutions. In
addition to aggregate data on salary levels and trends,
provides ranked data on average, median, and beginning salaries at individual institutions. Includes some
year-to-year comparisons. Various charts present variables such as gender, position, years of experience,
type of institution (i.e., public or private), total staff,
and geographic region. Separate tables for university
medical librarians and university law librarians.

**753   Developing library leaders: a how-
to-do-it manual for coaching, team**

building, and mentoring library staff.
Robert D. Stueart, Maureen Sullivan. New
York: Neal-Schuman Publishers, 2010. xii,
106 p.
023/.3   Z682.S89

Discusses theories and models of leadership development as applied to libraries and other information organizations. Focuses on exerting influence,
facilitating teams, managing projects, coaching,
mentoring, and succession planning. Includes many
checklists, self-assessment tools, and recommended
books and websites. Aspiring leaders will find additional advice in *Leadership basics for librarians and
information professionals*.

**754   Fundamentals of library supervision.
2nd ed.** Joan Giesecke, Beth McNeil.
Chicago: American Library Association,
2010. x, 189 p., ill.
ISBN 9780838910160
023.9   Z682.2.U5G54

Succinctly addresses all aspects of managing library
employees, including communication; work climate
and motivation; teamwork; diversity; policies and the
legal environment; hiring and interviewing; orientation
and training; planning and organizing work; managing
performance; budgeting; managing facilities; meetings;
rewards; project management; and career management. Subject index. Available as an e-book. *Supervis-
ing staff: A how-to-do-it manual for librarians* presents
similar content with numerous checklists, bullet
points, Q and A sidebars, glossary, and bibliography.

755   Library job postings on the Internet.
http://www.libraryjobpostings.org.
Sarah L. Johnson. 1995-

Presents links to websites with library job postings.
For each site, describes its scope, sponsor, and
update schedule. Includes the following browsing
options: academic positions; archives/records management; federal libraries; individual library sites;
placement services; school library media; and special libraries/subject specialists. A clickable map
facilitates access to job information by geographic
location. Also recommended is the job listings
maintained by ALA at http://joblist.ala.org; and the
extensive lists of ads for information professionals,
librarians, and knowledge managers, plus advice on
job searching, at the INALJ (I Need a Library Job)
website, http://inalj.com.

756 **Managing library employees: a how-to-do-it manual.** Mary J. Stanley. New York: Neal-Schuman Publ., 2008. xi, 247 p. ISBN 9781555706289

023/.9   Z682.S76

Intended as "a basic orientation in human resources management for librarians"—*Pref.* Covers federal laws; recruitment and selection of staff; training, retention, and professional development; compensation and benefits; performance appraisal; problem employees; conflict resolution and discipline; communication; technology in human resources management; and change management. Includes sample forms, checklists, and bibliographic references. More specialized works on employee relations include *Managing student assistants: a how-to-do-it manual for librarians* and *Managing library volunteers*, Second edition.

757 **The no-nonsense guide to training in libraries.** Barbara Allan. London: Facet Publ. x, 212 p. ISBN 9781856048286

023.8   Z668.5.A643

Broadly addresses both user instruction and employee training. Presents practical techniques for designing and delivering training in both face-to-face and online settings. The final chapter, arranged in A-Z order, briefly describes more than 90 ideas for workplace training in particular. Examples and case studies appear throughout the book.

758 **SLA annual salary survey.** Special Libraries Association. Washington: SLA Publishing. ill. ISBN 1543-9240

331.28102   Z682.4.S65

Previous titles: *SLA triennial salary survey*, 1982–89; *SLA biennial salary survey*, 1991–95; *SLA annual salary survey*, 1997–2004; *SLA annual salary survey and workplace study*, 2005-2009. Data for 1959, 1967, 1970, 1973, 1976, and 1979 published in the magazine *Special libraries*. Frequency varies. Based on surveys of U.S. and Canadian members of the Special Library Association. Charts provide median, mean, and percentile salaries according to geographic region, education, years of experience, gender, type of employer, and many other factors. Detailed statistical charts by primary job responsibility, covering over 20 professional specializations. Also includes data on employee benefits. Canadian and U.S. statistics are treated separately. Separate survey of human resources professionals, 2005-2008, provides data

for the "Workplace Study," covering trends in staffing, organizational structure, outsourcing, evaluation of services, budgets, required skill sets, and more. SLA members may log in to access survey data and an online salary calculator through the association website (http://www.sla.org).

759 **Staff development: a practical guide. 4th ed.** Andrea Stewart, Carlette Washington-Hoagland, Carol T. Zsulya, Library Leadership and Management Association. Chicago: American Library Association, 2013. viii, 219 p. ISBN 9780838911495

023/.8   Z668.5.S7

In 17 chapters by experienced library managers, addresses planning, designing, delivering, and assessing staff development programs, with attention to topics such as core competencies and succession planning. Includes many checklists and step-by-step recommendations.

First edition, 1988.

Indexing and Abstracting

760 **The accidental taxonomist.** Heather Hedden. Medford, N.J.: Information Today, 2010. xxix, 442 p., ill.

025   Z666.5.H43

Defining "taxonomy" broadly to include many types of structured knowledge organization systems, this book explains the principles of controlled vocabularies, relationships among terms, software for creating and managing taxonomies, and taxonomy structures and displays. Treats the role of taxonomies in both human and automated indexing. Describes the steps in planning, designing, creating, implementing and revising a taxonomy, and offers advice on working as a professional taxonomist. Glossary. Recommended readings and websites.

761 **American Society for Indexing.** http://www.asindexing.org/. American Society for Indexing. Wheat Ridge, Colo.: American Society for Indexing. 1968–

                          Z695.9

ASI is "the only professional organization in the United States devoted solely to the advancement of indexing, abstracting and database construction."—*Mission*

Statement Known as the American Society of Indexers from its founding until 2008. Website details the association's structure and history, provides background on indexing as a vocation, and links to useful information for authors, editors, and professional indexers. Includes an "Indexer Locator," a directory of freelance indexers and abstractors, searchable by location, subject specialty, language, type of material, and software.

762   Glossary of terminology in abstracting, classification, indexing, and thesaurus construction. 2nd ed. Hans H. Wellisch. Medford, N.J.: Information Today, 2000. vii, 77 p. ISBN 1573870943
025.3014   Z695.9.W435

First ed., 1996, titled *Abstracting, indexing, classification, thesaurus construction: A glossary.* Defines terms used in standards and professional texts, as well as terms for common types of documents and their parts. Many entries include examples of usage.

763   Handbook of indexing techniques: a guide for beginning indexers. 5th ed. Linda K. Fetters. Medford, N.J.: Information Today, 2013. xi, 178 pages
025.3   Z695.9.F45

First edition, 1994. A concise guide for the novice indexer, covering books, periodicals, and electronic documents. Includes both an alphabetical bibliography and a bibliography classified by topic.

764   Indexing books. 2nd ed. Nancy C. Mulvany. Chicago: University of Chicago Press, 2005. xiv, 315 p. ISBN 0226552764
025.3   Z695.9.M8

Introduction to the principles and techniques of back-of-the-book indexing, written for novices. Well formatted for reference use, with a thorough index of its own and detailed tables of contents for each chapter. Covers the structure and arrangement of entries, forms of names, formatting, and more. *The indexing companion* by Browne and Jermey presents a more expansive overview that addresses both book and "collection" indexing (e.g., bibliographic databases, library catalogs, websites), with attention to metadata, indexing software, and special formats, subjects, and genres. Appendix identifies relevant websites.

765   Introduction to indexing and abstracting. 4th ed. Donald Cleveland, Ana Cleveland. Santa Barbara, Calif.: Libraries Unlimited, 2013. xiii, 384 p.
025.3   Z695.9.C592

Encyclopedic treatment of indexing and abstracting—their history, theoretical underpinnings, techniques, and professional practice. Of particular value for reference are Chapter 8, which describes two dozen types of indexes, and Chapter 22, a directory of resources and aids, including books about indexing and abstracting, background sources, software, professional organizations, and more. Covers indexing of journals, books, images, and the Internet. Glossary. First ed. 1983

Information Literacy Instruction

766   The Big6: information & technology skills for student success. http://www.big6.com/. Michael B. Eisenberg, Robert E. Berkowitz. Fayetteville, N.Y.: Big6 Associates. 2001–

The Big6, a trademarked approach to teaching information and technology literacies, is used in elementary through college classrooms and libraries. The website provides examples of how the Big6 has been applied, lesson plans and materials, research reports, an online store, and more. Several books have been published about the Big6, including *Achieving educational standards using the Big6* and *The Big6 workshop handbook*, now in its fourth edition.

767   Fundamentals of library instruction. Monty L. McAdoo. Chicago: American Library Association, 2012. x., 112 p. ISBN 9780838911419
025.5/677   Z711.2; M33

Intended as a general introduction to library instruction. Covers core topics such as who should be responsible for instruction, how students learn, and what to teach, along with practical considerations of place and time. Provides tips for effective instruction and assessment. Information basics for college students by Sobel also provides a concise overview, specifically focused on teaching first-year students.

768   A guide to teaching information literacy: 101 practical tips.

Helen Blanchett, Chris Powis, Jo Webb. London: Facet Publ., 2012. ix, 262 p., ill. ISBN 9781856046596

025.524   ZA3075

A compendium of tips and techniques, organized alphabetically by topic under the broad themes of planning (e.g., needs analysis, learning outcomes), delivery (e.g., body language, managing questions), and learning activities (e.g., discussions, games, mind maps). Describes each technique, the situations in which it works best, and its drawbacks.

769   Information literacy competency standards for higher education.
http://www.ala.org/acrl/standards/informationliteracycompetency. Association of College and Research Libraries. Chicago: Association of College and Research Libraries. 2000
027.70218

Outlines standards for information literacy of college students. Each standard is accompanied by performance indicators and outcomes. Introductory sections define information literacy in the contexts of higher education, information technology, and pedagogy. Includes a link to a PDF version. An ACRL task force aims to issue updated standards early in 2015. Librarians working with K–12 populations should consult *Standards for the 21st-century learner* (http://www.ala.org/aasl/standards-guidelines/learning-standards).

770   Information literacy instruction that works: a guide to teaching by discipline and student population. 2nd ed. Patrick Ragains. Chicago: Neal-Schuman, 2013. 342 pp.
028.7071/1   ZA3075.I537

Practical programmatic strategies and teaching techniques from librarians who have used them successfully. Part I covers planning and faculty-librarian collaboration. Part II focuses on specific audiences: college and university freshmen, community college students, students with disabilities, and online and distance learners. Part III zeroes in on the disciplines of English literature; art and art history; film studies; music; history; psychology; anthropology; scientific literacy; agricultural sciences; engineering; and business. Part IV covers specialized legal, government, and patent information

literacy. Detailed index. Additional resource lists and samples of print, video and slide teaching materials on companion website: http://www.alaeditions.org/web-extra-information-literacy-instruction- works. First ed. 2008.

771   Information literacy instruction: theory and practice. 2nd ed. Esther S. Grassian, Joan R. Kaplowitz. New York: Neal-Schuman Publ., 2009. xxvii, 412 p. ISBN 9781555706661
025.5/24/071   ZA3075.G73

Overviews the concepts and methods of information literacy instruction in any type of library. Covers the history of library instruction, the psychology of learning, planning and instructional design issues, assessment, and modes of teaching. Lengthy bibliography. An accompanying CD-ROM includes supporting materials, such as sample mission statements and lessons. First edition, 2001. For guidance on managing a library instruction program, see the authors' companion work, *Learning to lead and manage information literacy instruction*.

772   Information literacy resources. http://www.ala.org/acrl/issues/infolit. Association of College and Research Libraries, Information Literacy Advisory Committee. Chicago: Association of College and Research Libraries. [2003–]

A "gateway to resources on information literacy." —*Home Page*. Presents the Information Literacy Competency Standards for Higher Education (769), along with a toolkit for adapting and applying them. Offers selected links to other websites on curriculum, accreditation, discipline-specific standards, and more.

773   Library instruction and information literacy 2012. Anna Marie Johnson, Claudene Sproles, Robert Detmering, Reference Services Review. Bingley, U.K.: Emerald, 2013. 0090-7324

Bibliography published in: *Reference Services Review* (549), v.41, no.4, pp.675-784. First compiled by Hannelore Rader in 1973, this annual annotated bibliography appears in the fourth quarterly issue of *RSR* and cites articles, monographs, and audiovisual publications related to library instruction and information literacy. The 2012 bibliography (published in 2013) includes 546 items, categorized by type of library (academic, public, school, special, and other), preceded by a short review of trends in the literature.

774   LIRT top twenty. http://www.ala.org/lirt/top-twenty. American Library Assocation, Library Instruction Round Table. Chicago: American Library Association. 1994–

Annual annotated bibliographies of the best articles on library instruction and information literacy, chosen by a committee of the American Library Association Library Instruction Round Table. Published in the June issue of the *LIRT news*.

775   LOEX. http://www.emich.edu/public/loex/index.html. LOEX Clearinghouse for Library Instruction. Ypsilanti, Mich.: LOEX Clearinghouse for Library Instruction

Founded in 1971 as the Library Orientation Exchange. Provides links to exemplary information literacy curricular materials, such as online tutorials, and other resources for librarian-teachers. LOEX also publishes newsletters and sponsors conferences.

776   The no-nonsense guide to training in libraries. Barbara Allan. London: Facet Publ. x, 212 p. ISBN 9781856048286

023.8   Z668.5.A643

Broadly addresses both user instruction and employee training. Presents practical techniques for designing and delivering training in both face-to-face and online settings. The final chapter, arranged in A-Z order, briefly describes more than 90 ideas for workplace training in particular. Examples and case studies appear throughout the book.

777   A practical guide to information literacy assessment for academic librarians. Carolyn J. Radcliff. Westport, Conn.: Libraries Unlimited, 2007. xiii, 180 p., ill. ISBN 9781591583400

028.70711   ZA3075.P73

Explains nine techniques for assessing college students' information literacy, such as in-class assessment, surveys, and portfolios. Provides examples and lists reasons to use (or not use) each technique. Also gives advice on analyzing data and working with the results. References. Index.

778   Practical pedagogy for library instructors: 17 innovative strategies

to improve student learning. Douglas Cook, Ryan Sittler. Chicago: Association of College and Research Libraries, 2008. vii, 184 p, ill. ISBN 9780838984581

025.5/677   Z711.25.C65 P73 2008

Presents fully-explained innovative techniques for teaching information literacy concepts and skills. "Cases exemplifying direct instruction" offer ideas for presenting large amounts of information, reviewing information presented, and presenting complex ideas. "Cases exemplifying student-centered instruction" recommend the use of dialogue, simulation, and students' own experiences.

779   PRIMO: peer-reviewed instructional materials online. http://www.ala.org/cfapps/primo/public/search.cfm. Association of College and Research Libraries, Instruction Section, PRIMO Committee. Chicago: Association of College and Research Libraries. [n.d.]

Maintained by a committee of the ACRL Instruction Section as a selective directory of "instructional materials created by librarians to teach people about discovering, accessing and evaluating information in networked environments." —*Home page.* As of spring 2013, the directory holds nearly 300 descriptive records linked to tutorials, lesson plans, and other online learning tools. Options for access include the following: browsing by title, author, category, or date; searching by title, author, category, description or keyword; or searching a subset of records that include data on creation, such as the number of employees involved, source of funding, time expended, etc.

780   Research within the disciplines: foundations for reference and library instruction. Peggy Keeran. Lanham, Md.: Scarecrow Press, 2007. xi, 267 p., ill. ISBN 9780810856882

020.72   Z710.R47

Intended for the novice librarian or LIS student; also useful to librarians assuming reference or instruction responsibility for unfamiliar disciplines. Individually-authored chapters describe research practices, key information sources, and information literacy competencies in several broad and specialized fields: humanities; music; history; social sciences; business; sciences; and engineering. A separate chapter covers government documents across the disciplines. Concludes with a chapter on integrating discipline-based library instruction into the college curriculum, and another that reflects on the nature of disciplinary and interdisciplinary research. A second edition is forthcoming in spring 2014. For those who seek more than an overview, the ALA *Guide to reference* (52) recommends discipline-specific research guides in almost every subject category.

781 Teaching information literacy: 50 standards-based exercises for college students. 2nd ed. Joanna M. Burkhardt, Mary C. MacDonald, Andrée J. Rathemacher. Chicago: American Library Association, 2010. xi, 138 p., ill.
ISBN 9780838910535
028.7071/1   ZA3075.B87
Fifty ready-to-use lessons with accompanying exercises, based on the ACRL Information Literacy Competency Standards for Higher Education (769). Addresses the nature of information, research preparation, issues such as plagiarism and privacy, and strategies for searching catalogs, periodical indexes, and the Web. Describes the semester-long "Paper Trail Project" at the University of Rhode Island as a model for in-depth instruction.
First edition, 2003.

782 Web-based instruction: a guide for libraries. 3rd ed. Susan Sharpless Smith, American Library Association. Chicago: American Library Association, 2010. xviii, 236 p., ill. ISBN 9780838910566
025.5/60785   Z711.2.S59
Addresses the pedagogical, technological, and design issues in web-based library instruction. Includes glossary and extensive resource list of publications and websites, arranged by topic. Accompanying website links to tools and information sources: http://www.alaeditions.org/web-extra-web-based-instruction
First edition, 2001.

Knowledge Management

Editor's Guide: Reference tools and periodicals dealing with management information systems (MIS) may be found in the online Guide to Reference (www.guidetoreference.org) under Social and

Behavioral Sciences > Economics and Business > Functional Areas of Business.

783 Encyclopedia of knowledge management. 2nd ed. David G. Schwartz, Dov Te'eni. Hershey, Pa.: Information Science Reference, 2011. 2 v. (lx, 1574, 18 p.), ill.
ISBN 9781599049311
658.4/03803   HD30.2.E53
Covers theory, processes, technologies, organizational aspects, social aspects, managerial aspects, and specific applications of knowledge management in 149 chapters. The alphabetical arrangement by chapter title is unhelpful. Instead, consult the topical index and/or the hierarchical table of contents by category. Signed chapters, typically six to twelve pages long, include bibliographic references and definitions for key terms, which are separately indexed. Also available as an e-book and as part of the InfoSci-Books (498) database.

784 Knowledge management: an introduction. Kevin C. Desouza, Scott Paquette. New York: Neal-Schuman Publ., 2011. xvi, 351 p., ill.
ISBN 9781555707200
658.4/038   HD30.2.D469
A textbook approach to knowledge management. Covers key concepts, processes (creation, organization, transfer, application), and practical strategies for building a knowledge management program. Glossary. Detailed index.

Library Facilities

785 Archival and special collections facilities: guidelines for archivists, librarians, architects, and engineers. Michele F. Pacifico, Thomas P. Wilsted, Society of American Archivists. Chicago: Society of American Archivists, 2009. viii, 191 p. ISBN 1931666318
CD981.A695
In outline format, these guidelines treat: the building site; construction; archival environments for different types of records (paper, film, electronic); fire protection; security; lighting; materials and finishes; storage equipment; and the design of spaces

according to function(e.g., loading dock, processing rooms, reading spaces). Glossary. Bibliography. Detailed index.

786 Building blocks for planning functional library space. 3rd ed. Library Leadership and Management Association. Chicago; Lanham, Md.: American Library Association; Scarecrow Press, 2011. 148 p., ill. ISBN 9780810881044

022/.9   Z679.55.B85

After presenting advice on the space planning process for libraries, this unique guide provides formulas with illustrations for calculating the square footage required for various types of shelving, service points, reading areas, computer stations, offices, etc. Includes brief bibl.

787 Building science 101: a primer for librarians. Lynn M. Piotrowicz, Scott Osgood. Chicago: American Library Association, 2010. x, 123 p., ill.

022/.31   Z679.2.U6 P56

While most books about library facilities are concerned with designing and furnishing new spaces, this one focuses on maintaining older buildings and improving their energy efficiency. Explains the major structural components (e.g. windows) and building systems (e.g. heating). Offers guidance on contracting with architects, engineers, designers, and others.

788 Checklist of library building design considerations. 5th ed. William W. Sannwald. Chicago: American Library Association, 2009. viii, 211 p. ISBN 9780838909782

727.8   Z679.2.U54S36

First ed., 1988.

A useful, detailed workbook for planning and evaluating library spaces. Covers site selection, sustainable design, exterior and interior layouts, ADA compliance, telecommunications and electrical wiring, furnishings, shelving, security, disaster planning, maintenance, and more. Includes bibliography.

789 Countdown to a new library: managing the building project. 2nd ed. Jeannette A. Woodward. Chicago: American Library Association, 2010. vii,

272 p., ill.

022/.3   Z679.2.U6W66

Practical, in-depth guidance in the planning, design, and construction of new library buildings and library additions, with particular emphasis on working with architects and contractors.

790 The green library planner: what every librarian needs to know before starting to build or renovate. Mary M. Carr. Lanham, Md.: Scarecrow Press, 2013. xv, 136 p.

022/.3   Z679.85.C37

Overviews choices that affect the sustainability of library buildings, including siting, energy, lighting, materials, indoor environmental quality, water, construction management, and building maintenance. Includes checklists, examples, and annotated resource lists. For in-depth treatment of this topic, see *How green is my library?* by Sam McBane Mulford and Ned A. Himmel.

791 Interior design for libraries: Drawing on function and appeal. Carol R. Brown. Chicago: American Library Association, 2002. viii, 143 p., [8] p. of color plates, ill. ISBN 0838908292

727.80973   Z679.5B76

Discusses various aspects of designing and furnishing academic, public, school, and special libraries, such as floor plans, furniture, color schemes, and signage. Many photographs and color plates. Appendix lists questions for library staff to inform the design process. Brief bibliography. Index. See also *Library furnishings: A planning guide.*

792 The library renovation, maintenance, and construction handbook. Donald A. Barclay, Eric D. Scott. New York: Neal-Schuman Publishers, Inc, 2011. xix, 212 p., ill.

022/.3   Z679.2.U54 B37

Covers many aspects of library facility planning and management. Part I, "The basics of construction and renovation," explains: the stages of a building project; building systems (structural, electrical, etc.); architectural plans; codes and standards; and the various construction professions. Part II treats "Library-specific construction and renovation," including interior spaces (stacks areas, reading rooms, children's rooms, workspaces, etc.) and furnishings. A chapter is devoted to wayfinding and signage. Part III, "Maintaining an existing library building," addresses: security;, green building design and operation; running a library during a remodeling project; and routine and preventative maintenance. Accompanying CD-ROM includes a sizable, searchable glossary; photographs illustrating construction technique; sample building plans; and more. Older, but still useful: *The librarian's facility management handbook*, by Carmine and Marcia Trotta.

793 Libris Design planning documentation. http://www.librisdesign .org/docs/index.html. Cerritos, Calif.: Libris Design Project. 2001-2005

Detailed, illustrated guides, each 20-30 pages long, covering 17 aspects of library facilities planning, such as acoustics, furniture, collection storage, security, technology infrastructure, and wayfinding. Created by the Libris Design Project, which has as its centerpiece a Microsoft Access database for creating public library building programs, these guides are useful even without access to the database.

794 Planning academic and research library buildings. 3rd ed. Philip D. Leighton, David C. Weber. Chicago: American Library Association, 1999. xxx, 887 p., ill., maps. ISBN 0838907474

022.317   Z679.5.L45

First ed., 1965, by Keyes D. Metcalf. 2nd ed., 1986.

Extremely detailed guidance on planning library sites and buildings, working with architects and consultants, developing written programs of requirements (for collections, readers, and staff), budgeting, developing design schematics, and managing the construction process. Appendixes add to the reference value by presenting examples of building program documents, formulas, standards, environmental guidelines, and more. Bibliography. Glossary. Index. Newer sources should be consulted when space planning involves information technology infrastructure and furnishings.

795 The school library media facilities planner. Thomas L. Hart. New York: Neal-Schuman, 2006. xiii, 253 p., ill. ISBN 1555705030

027.8   Z675.S3H2674

Provides step-by-step advice for planning and building a new school library. Includes guidelines, floor plans, formulas, checklists, glossary, and samples of a planning document, contract, and request for bids. Index.

Marketing, Advocacy, and Public Relations

796 Advocacy, outreach, and the nation's academic libraries: a call for action. William C. Welburn, Janice Welburn, Beth McNeil. Chicago: Association of College and Research Libraries, 2010. xii, 210 p., ill. ISBN 9780838985496

021.7   Z675.U5; A4145

Not a how-to book per se, but a collection of essays, literature reviews, and case studies that provide inspiration and ideas for academic libraries to reach out to their users, stakeholders, and surrounding communities.

797 Bite-sized marketing: realistic solutions for the overworked librarian. Nancy Dowd, Mary Evangeliste, Jonathan Silberman. Chicago: American Library Association, 2010. xi, 140 p., ill. ISBN 0838910009

021.7   Z716.3.D69

Offers "tangible ideas that can be done in bite-sized chunks." —*Intro.* Covers word-of-mouth marketing, telling the library's story, marketing electronic resources, press releases, trade show booths, political advocacy, Web 2.0 tools, graphic design, and branding. Concludes with advice on marketing best practices.

798 Even more great ideas for libraries and friends. Sally Gardner Reed, Beth Nawalinski, Friends of Libraries U.S.A. New York: Neal-Schuman Publ., 2008. xxi, 285 p., ill. ISBN 9781555706388

021.7   Z681.7.U5; R45

Patterned on an earlier work, *101+ great ideas for libraries and friends*, this guide prepared by Friends of Libraries USA (FOLUSA) suggests proven ways for public, academic, and school libraries to connect with their communities through programs, fundraisers, advocacy, public relations campaigns, and more.

Includes forms, publicity materials, and other customizable content.

799 Grassroots library advocacy. Lauren Comito, Aliqae Geraci, Christian Zabriskie. Chicago: American Library Association, 2012. xi, 62 p., ill. ISBN 9780838911341
021.70973   Z716.3.C66
Practical advice for all librarians, not just administrators, on planning and implementing a campaign to raise public awareness about the impact of library budget cuts.

800 The library marketing toolkit. Ned Potter. London: Facet Publishing, 2012. xxii, 218 p., ill. ISBN 9781856048064; 1856048063
021.7   Z716.3
An introduction to marketing concepts and techniques for all types of libraries. Addresses strategic marketing, the library brand, the library building, online marketing, social media, new technologies, marketing through people, internal marketing, and library advocacy. One chapter is dedicated to special collections and archives. Includes numerous case studies.

801 Library public relations, promotions, and communications: A how-to-do-it manual. 2nd ed. Lisa A. Wolfe. New York: Neal-Schuman, 2005. xv, 326 p. ISBN 9781555704711
021.7   Z716.3.W58
Chapters in Part I, "Planning and evaluation," discuss the purpose of public relations, the library's message, and the planning and evaluation of PR programs. Chapters in Part II, "Strategies and methodologies," explain specific approaches, such as building a brand, handling media interviews, working with technology, creating effective print communications, and planning special events. Includes many sample planning tools and products.

Policies, Procedures, and Legal Issues

Editor's Guide: For guidance on collection development policies in particular, see Library and Information Science > Professional Practice > Collection Development and Acquisitions.

802 The academic library manager's forms, policies, and procedures handbook with CD-ROM. Rebecca Brumley. New York: Neal-Schuman Publ., 2007. xxv, 499 p., ill., 1 CD-ROM. ISBN 9781555705978
027.7   Z675.U5B8527
Hundreds of exemplary policies, forms, and procedures from college and university libraries. Organized by subject: administrative policies and guidelines; facilities and equipment; collection development; traditional reference service; virtual reference service; circulation; government documents; legal and ethical concerns; information literacy and library instruction; interlibrary loan and document delivery; Internet and electronic resources; and university repositories. Subject index. All documents are also included on accompanying CD-ROM. The same format is used in *The public library manager's forms, policies, and procedures handbook.*

803 Copyright advisory network. http:// librarycopyright.net/. American Library Association, Office for Information Technology Policy. Chicago: American Library Association. 2002-
"This web site is a way for librarians to learn about copyright and seek feedback and advice from fellow librarians and copyright specialists." —*Home page*
Although the discussion forums have fallen into disuse, the Copyright Genie, Fair Use Evaluator tool, and Section 108 Spinner remain useful for decision-making regarding use of copyrighted materials.

804 Copyright crash course. http://copyright .lib.utexas.edu/. Georgia Harper. Austin, Tex.: University of Texas System. 2001-
346.0482   KF2995
An extensive introduction to copyright, fair use, and intellectual property for creators and users, with an emphasis issues in higher education. Includes a section on "copyright in the library" that covers fair use (including reserve collections and electronic copies), reproduction and distribution (including archiving and interlibrary loan), and other (including digital libraries and licensing). Provides a tutorial and test, and links to other information sources on the Web.

805 Copyright law for librarians and educators: creative strategies and practical solutions. 3rd ed. Kenneth D. Crews. Chicago: American Library Association, 2012. xii, 192 p., ill., forms

346.7304/8202402   KF2995.C74

Basic information on copyright and fair use in the library context, presented in short chapters. Appendixes include selected provisions from the U.S. Copyright Act, checklists for fair use and compliance with the TEACH Act (for use of copyrighted materials in distance education), and a model letter for permission requests. Bibliography. Index. Available as an e-book.

First edition, 2000, was titled *Copyright essentials for librarians and educators*. Other sources useful for reference purposes include *Complete copyright: An everyday guide for librarians*, which features colorful cartoons and narrative vignettes; *The complete copyright liability handbook for librarians and educators*, which features in-depth explanations and real-world examples with legal analyses; *Copyright for Teachers and Librarians in the 21st Century*, which includes decision flowcharts for numerous situations; *Technology and copyright law*, which discusses the history of copyright legislation, as well as current issues; and *The Digital Librarian's Legal Handbook*, which provides an in-depth introduction to intellectual property rights.

806 The essential friends of libraries: fast facts, forms, and tips. Sandy Dolnick. Chicago: American Library Association, 2005. xv, 99 p.

021.7   Z681.7.U5D65

Distills advice from the *Friends of the libraries sourcebook* in an alphabetical, ready-reference format. Topics covered include board membership, meetings, book sales, fiscal management, programs, and more. Accompanying CD includes sample documents, policies, forms, etc.

807 Intellectual freedom manual. 8th ed. American Library Association. Chicago: American Library Association, 2010. ISBN 9780838935903

025.213   Z711.4.I57

First ed., 1974.

Intended as a desk reference for librarians. Reprints the "Library Bill of Rights," ALA-approved interpretations of it, guidelines, policies, and other relevant documents, all accompanied by historical commentary. Covers all aspects of "the freedom to read," including library patron privacy, minors' rights to information, and access to the Internet. Offers extensive advice on handling censorship disputes. Indexed. Similar information appears on the ALA's Office of Intellectual Freedom website: http://www.ala.org/offices/oif.

808 The library's legal answer book. Mary Minow, Tomas A. Lipinski. Chicago: American Library Association, 2003. x, 361 p. ISBN 0838908284

344.73092   KF4315.M56

In question-and-answer format, explains legal issues affecting libraries: copyright; web page content and links; Internet filtering; digital resources for patrons with disabilities; library records and privacy; meeting rooms and displays; professional liability; employment issues; and rules governing non-profit organizations. For a more extensive treatment of these and other topics, see Bryan Carson's *The law of libraries and archives*. Both works contain extensive references to statutes, case law, and legal opinions and have subject indexes. Two handbooks by Lee Ann Torrans address particular types of libraries: *Law and libraries: The public library*; and *Law for K–12 libraries and librarians*. Authors have degrees in both law and library science. Also available as an e-book.

809 Privacy and confidentiality issues: a guide for libraries and their lawyers. Theresa Chmara. Chicago: American Library Association, 2009. iii, 98 p. ISBN 9780838909706

344.73/092   KF4315.C47

Succinct coverage of the First Amendment and other legal considerations related to privacy and confidentiality for library patrons, including minors, and staff. Appendix summarizes state statutes. Although composed in Q&A format, chapters are written to be read straight through.

810 The public library policy writer: A guidebook with model policies on CD-ROM. Jeanette C. Larson, Herman L. Totten. New York: Neal-Schuman Publishers, 2008. xxi, 280 p. ISBN 9781555706036

025.1974   Z704.L37

With small and medium-sized public libraries in mind, presents over 60 model policies to cover varied aspects of personnel and employment practices; staff conduct; access to library services; use of materials; collection development; reference and information services; access and use of facilities; and patron conduct. Provides background and identifies key issues for each policy area. The full text of the policies is included on an accompanying CD-ROM and may be downloaded and adapted. Another useful source, which likewise comes with a CD-ROM, is *The public library manager's forms, policies, and procedures handbook. Creating policies for results*, while not presenting actual policies, provides checklists of questions to ask when developing policies in three dozen areas of public librarianship.

811 **The school library media specialist's policy & procedure writer.** Elizabeth Downs. New York: Neal-Schuman Publishers, Inc., 2010. xviii, 195 p., ill. ISBN 9781555706210

025.178   Z675.S3D7485

Sample policies, procedures, and forms that school librarians can adapt are reproduced in this book and on the accompanying CD-ROM. Covers all areas of school library media center management, including mission, collections, equipment, technology, staff, and users.

812 **SHERPA-RoMEO: publisher copyright policies and self-archiving.** http://www.sherpa.ac.uk/romeo/. University of Nottingham. Nottingham, U.K.: University of Nottingham; University of Lund. [n.d.]

Database of journal publishers' policies concerning the digital archiving of articles by their authors. Color- coded to indicate whether a publisher permits the archiving of preprints, post-prints, both, or neither. Of particular use to university libraries hosting institutional repositories. Covers 22,000 journals. May be searched by publisher name, journal title, or ISSN.

813 **The successful library trustee handbook. 2nd ed.** Mary Y. Moore. Chicago: American Library Association, 2010. ix, 110 p. ISBN 9780838910030

021.820973   Z681.7.U5M66

A succinct guide for public library board members, outlining their roles and responsibilities. *The complete*

library trustee handbook presents similar information, along with sample policy documents.

Preservation and Conservation

814 **Bibliographic database of the Conservation Information Network.** http://www.bcin.ca/English/home_english.html. Conservation Information Network (CIN), Canadian Heritage Information Network (CHIN), Getty Conservation Institute. Hull, Québec, Canada: Canadian Heritage Information Network. 2002–

Z5133.P73; CC135

Cultural-property electronic index of nearly 200,000 articles on conservation and restoration of art objects and architecture. Includes the *Art and archaeology technical reports*. Covers books, periodicals, technical papers, and unpublished sources from a variety of major worldwide agencies, including the Smithsonian, Getty Conservation Institute, Canadian Conservation Institute, and museum conservation organizations.

815 **Book repair: a how-to-do-it manual. 2nd ed. rev. ed.** Kenneth Lavender, Artemis BonaDea. New York: Neal-Schuman Publishers Inc, 2011. xiv, 265 p, ill. ISBN 9781555707477

025.8/4   Z701.L32

First ed., 1992; second ed., 2001. Lists decision factors, specifies supplies, and describes and illustrates procedures for cleaning paper, treating water-damaged books, removing mold, mending paper, repairing hinges and spines, and constructing protective enclosures. Directory of suppliers. Bibliography. Index. Glossary. Many library conservation experts still recommend the classic Books, their care and repair by Jane Greenfield, which is still in print. Sharon McQueen's newer In-house bookbinding and repair focuses only on torn pages and damaged bindings. All feature copious illustrations of equipment and techniques. An engagingly written manual for the general reader, unfortunately lacking illustrations, is The care and feeding of books old and new: A simple repair manual for book lovers.

816 **Conservation online (CoOL): resources for conservation professionals.**

http://cool.conservation-us.org/.
Stanford University Libraries, Preservation
Department. Foundation of the American
Institute for Conservation of Historic and
Artistic Works (FAIC). 1994–
Extensive set of links to web-based information on
the conservation of library, archives, and museum
materials, including full-text documents, organizations, directories of people and suppliers, and e-mail
list archives. May be searched by keyword (including
full text of documents) or browsed by topic.

817 Digital Curation Centre (DCC). http://
www.dcc.ac.uk/. [s.l.]: Digital Curation
Centre. [2004-]

ZA4080

Focused on the preservation of digital data in the UK
higher education sector, but offering many free information resources, including how-to guides, a glossary, and a comprehensive *Curation reference manual*
(in progress).

**818 Disaster planning: a how-to-do-it
manual for librarians with planning
templates on CD-ROM.** Deborah D.
Halsted, Richard P. Jasper, Felicia M. Little.
New York: Neal-Schuman Publishers,
2005. xx, 247 p., ill., 1 CD-ROM
ISBN 1555704867
025.82   Z679.7.H35

Part 1 outlines the steps of disaster planning, such
as forming a team, assessing risks, securing the
building, and stocking supplies. Part 2 focuses
on 14 common natural and man-made disasters,
detailing what to do before, during, and after the
crisis. Part 3 identifies and annotates resources on
the Web. Part 4 presents "quick guides," including
a directory of agencies and consultants and a prevention checklist. Bibliography. Index. On accompanying CD-ROM: templates for a written disaster
plan and a disaster mitigation website. A newer
work, *Emergency planning and response for libraries,
archives and museums* by Emma Dadson, focuses on
salvaging and restoring damaged collections. See
also *Disaster response and planning for libraries* (3rd
ed.) (819).

**819 Disaster response and planning for
libraries. 3rd ed.** Miriam B. Kahn.

Chicago: American Library Association,
2012. xvii, 158 p. ISBN 9780838911518
025.8/2   Z679.7.K38

Presents practical instructions on responding to
many types of disasters, with an emphasis on restoration of service and remediation of physical damage.
Also covers prevention and planning. Appendices:
Forty-three checklists and forms that can be copied
or adapted for local use; directory of associations,
organizations and companies, categorized by specialty; bibliography. See also *Disaster planning: a how-
to-do-it manual for librarians* (818).
First ed., 1995.

**820 Northeast Document Conservation
Center (NEDCC).** http://www.nedcc.
org/. Northeast Document Conservation
Center. Andover, Mass.: Northeast
Document Conservation Center
025.1714028

A conservation laboratory specializing in the treatment of paper and parchment, and "a trusted resource
for information on the preservation of paper-based
collections."—*Home page*. Free information on the
website includes some 60 downloadable leaflets on a
range of topics such as the environment, storage and
handling, and reformatting, and an online tool for
writing library disaster plans. Provides free preservation advice by phone and e-mail. Similar information
is available in the Preservation Toolbox by LYRASIS
(http://www.lyrasis.org).

**821 Practical digital preservation: a
how-to guide for organizations of
any size.** Adrian Brown. Chicago: Neal-
Schuman, 2013. xvi, 336 p., ill. ISBN
9781555709426
025.84   Z701.3.C65

Intended to guide "smaller memory institutions, such
as libraries, archives, museums and galleries" in planning and implementing digital preservation solutions.
Explains how to make the case, understand requirements, and choose a model for a digital preservation
service. Covers the selection, acquisition, accessioning,
ingestion, and description of digital objects, as well as
preservation and access strategies. Appendices include
a template for a digital asset register and an annotated
guide to systems, tools, and services, including commercial products. Glossary. Bibliography.

822   Preservation and conservation for libraries and archives. Nelly Balloffet, Jenny Hille, Judith A. Reed. Chicago: American Library Association, 2005. xix, 214 p., ill. ISBN 0838908799

025.84   Z701.B234

An illustrated introduction to techniques in preserving and conserving library and archival materials. Covers basic measures such as environmental monitoring and disaster planning, equipping a work area, rehousing materials, conserving paper, conserving books, designing exhibits, and caring for photographs. Appendixes list suppliers and organizations. Glossary. Bibliography. Index. Also available as an e-book.

823   Preserving digital materials. 2nd ed ed. D. R. Harvey. Berlin ; Boston: De Gruyter Saur, 2012. ix, 251 p. ISBN 9783110253689

025.8/4   Z701.3.C65H37

Aims to provide information professionals and students with an introduction to the principles, strategies and practices of digital preservation. Discusses the selection of material for preservation; the attributes of digital materials; various approaches to preserving technology versus preserving objects; national and international initatives; and future challenges. Not a how-to manual. First ed., 2005.

Readers' Advisory

824   eSequels: the online guide to series fiction. http://www.esequels.com/. Janet Husband, Jonathan Husband. Brewster, Mass.: Novel Data. 2002-

A database of "the best, most enduring, and most popular novels in series that might appeal to today's adult readers." —*Scope note* Based on the print reference book, *Sequels*, but continually updated. Limited to English-language works. Browsable by author, title, character, location, or subject, and searchable by keywords in the full text. The basic organization is by author, with a summary of their oeuvre, identification of separate series, and briefly annotated lists of works within those series, in reading order. Available by subscription.

825   Genreflecting: a guide to popular reading interests. 7th ed. Cynthia Orr, Diana T. Herald. Santa Barbara, Calif.: Libraries Unlimited, 2013. xxii, 622 p. ISBN 9781598848403

016.813009   PS374.P63; R67

A classic guide to books that appeal to adult readers, organized by genres and sub-genres. Following several chapters on the practice of readers' advisory, sections by various contributors highlight works of historical fiction, mysteries, thrillers, westerns, romance, women's fiction, fantasy, horror, science fiction, "mainstream" fiction, nonfiction, inspirational/Christian fiction, urban fiction, and graphic novels. Indexes: name; subject; title. Following the same formula, *Teen genreflecting* recommends books for young adult readers, and *Primary genreflecting* highlights picture books and easy readers.

First ed., 1982.

826   NoveList plus. http://www.ebscohost. com/novelist. EBSCO. Ipswich, Mass.: EBSCO Pub. 1994–

Requires paid subscription. Supplies information on over 200,000 works of fiction and non-fiction for all ages. Includes full-text book reviews, discussion guides, thematic and genre-based reading lists, and popularity rankings. Popular features include "author read-alike" lists, lists of award-winning and "best" titles in various categories, and recommendations from librarians. Searchable or browsable by author, title, series, Dewey number, appeal factors such as genre and tone, and more. Users may create a personal login to save title lists and to establish and manage alerts. A companion database, NoveList K–8 Plus, focuses on works for young readers. Both databases and more are available in the NoveList Complete package.

827   The readers' advisory guide to genre fiction. 2nd ed. Joyce G. Saricks. Chicago: American Library Association, 2009. xii, 387 p. ISBN 9780838909898

025.5/4   Z711.5.S27

First edition, 2001. Organizes suggested works by the nature of their appeal to readers: adrenaline genres (adventure, romantic suspense, suspense, thrillers); emotions genres (gentle reads, horror, romance, and women's lives and relationships); intellect genres (literary fiction, mysteries, psychological suspense, and science fiction); and landscape genres (fantasy, historical fiction, and Westerns). Each chapter defines a genre and explains its characteristics, identifies key authors, discusses the preferences of that genre's fans, and gives advice on readers' advisory interviewing. Index to titles, authors, subjects, and series. Available as a print or e-book.

828 The readers' advisory handbook.
Jessica E. Moyer, Kaite Mediatore Stover. Chicago: American Library Association, 2010. xi, 220 p. ISBN 9780838910429
025.5/4 2   Z711.55.R44
Short, practical chapters by various authors, often incorporating worksheets and checklists, on many aspects of readers' advisory work. Includes the following topics: techniques for rapidly getting familiar with books and other materials; advice on writing reviews; suggestions for marketing and promoting materials; recommendations for programming; and ideas for extending readers' advisory services to new audiences.

829 Readers' advisory service in the public library. 3rd ed. Joyce G. Saricks. Chicago: American Library Association, 2005. xi, 211 p. ISBN 0838908977
025.5/4   Z711.55.S27
Elucidates the philosophy of readers' advisory work, provides tips for evaluating readers' advisory reference sources, recommends key sources, and expounds on the elements that constitute a book's appeal. Advises on how to interview patrons about their leisure reading preferences, develop broad knowledge of popular literature, and market readers' advisory services. Appendices briefly list popular fiction and nonfiction authors by genre and suggest "sure bets." Short bibliography. Author and subject indexes.
First ed., 1989.

Reference and Information Retrieval

830 ARBAonline. http://www.arbaonline.com/. Westport, Conn.: Libraries Unlimited. 2003–
Database of librarian-authored reviews of reference books and electronic reference tools, 1997 to date.

Updated monthly. Search interface offers multiple options, plus browsing by subject or latest monthly update. Access restricted to subscribers. Also issued in print since 1970 as *American reference books annual*.

831 Best free reference web sites. http://www.ala.org/rusa/sections/mars/marspubs/marsbestindex. American Library Association, Reference and Adult Services Association, Machine-Assisted Reference Section, Best of Free Reference Web Sites Committee. Chicago: American Library Association. 1999–
Cumulative alphabetical list of websites judged annually by librarians to be among the best free information sources. Links to reviews; changes and cessations are noted.

832 Conducting the reference interview: A how-to-do-it manual for librarians. 2nd ed. Catherine Sheldrick Ross, Kirsti Nilsen, Marie L. Radford. New York: Neal-Schuman Publishers, 2009. xiv, 290 p., ill. ISBN 9781555706555
025.52   Z711.R64
First ed, 2004. A thorough guide to reference interviewing, grounded in research and offering many real-life examples, both good and bad. Explains the purpose of the reference interview and presents techniques for opening and ending reference interactions, as well as skills for eliciting details from information-seekers. Addresses special topics such as telephone reference, questions posed by children, virtual reference, and readers' advisory. Devotes the final chapter to policy and training issues. Extensive annotated references in each chapter. For additional insights into interactions between librarians and information seekers, see Susan Knoer's *The reference interview today* (2011).

833 Dialog database catalog. http://support.dialog.com/publications/dbcat/. ProQuest. Ann Arbor, Mich.: ProQuest. [2002–]
025   Z699.4.D18
Frequency and title varies. Describes over 600 databases available through the Dialog and DataStar online information retrieval services. Lists databases by name and under 18 subject categories. Provides brief descriptions that note the provider, subjects, type (bibliographic, full text, directory and/or

numeric), language(s), years covered, and frequency of updates. Indexes: Dialog database number; Data-Star database label.

More extensive descriptions of individual databases, including field codes and search techniques, can be found in the "Dialog bluesheets" at http://library.dialog.com/bluesheets/. Search aids, tutorials, and other documentation are also available, in addition to information about Dialog's migration to ProQuest in 2013.

834 Evaluating reference services: A practical guide. Jo Bell Whitlatch. Chicago: American Library Association, 2000. vi, 226 p. ISBN 0838907873

025.52   Z711.W45

Practical guide to evaluating traditional reference services. Covers planning for an evaluative study, strengths and weaknesses of common methods, issues in the collection and analysis of data, and advice on communicating the findings. Presents sample forms, questions, and checklists. Of particular value is the 100-page selective bibliography keyed to the topical chapters. Many of the entries were previously published in the *Reference assessment manual* but appear here in revised form alongside newer entries. Combined index to subjects in the narrative chapters and authors in the bibliography.

835 The Extreme Searcher's Internet Handbook: A Guide for the Serious Searcher. 4th ed. Randolph Hock. , 2013. xxi, 315 p., ill. ISBN 9781937290023

025.04252   ZA4226.H63

First ed., 2004. Aimed, as the subtitle states, at "the serious searcher," but also useful for less-experienced seekers of online information. Covers the basics of Web searching; directories and portals; search engines; discussion groups, forums, and newsgroups; online reference tools; images, audio, and video; news resources; products and shopping sites; and Internet publishing.

Companion website, http://extremesearcher.com/handbooklinks.html, aggregates links to resources mentioned in the book.

836 Fundamentals of managing reference collections. Carol A. Singer. Chicago:

ALA Editions, 2012. 167 p. ISBN 978-0-8389-1153-2

025.21   Z711

With balanced attention to both electronic and print resources, this practical guide covers: reference collection development policies; staffing models for managing reference collections; selection of materials; acquisitions, budgets and licenses; collection maintenance; weeding; consortial collection management; and discovery and access. Includes a collection development policy template. *Reference collection development: a manual* by Perez is an older but still useful work with examples of collection policies.

837 Fundamentals of reference. Carolyn M. Mulac. Chicago: American Library Association, 2012. 131 p. ISBN 9780838910870

025.5   Z711

A basic introduction to library reference works. Part 1 covers print and electronic reference sources: encyclopedias; websites; dictionaries; almanacs, handbooks, and yearbooks; indexes; directories; geographical sources; biographical sources; and statistical sources. Part 2 covers aspects of reference service: the reference interview; in-person reference; telephone reference; online reference; service to children and young adults; reference in special subjects; policies; standards; evaluation. Bibl. Index. For more in-depth treatment of these topics, consult the standard textbooks: *Reference and information services: an introduction*,ed. by Richard E. Bopp and Linda C. Smith (4th ed., 2011); and *Reference and information services: an introduction*,by Kay Ann Cassell and Uma Hiremath (3rd ed., 2013).

838 Gale directory of databases. Gale Research. Detroit: Gale Research, 1993–. ISBN 1066-8934

025.040296   QA76.9.D32G36

Contents: v. l, pt. 1-3, Online databases; v. 2, pt. 1-3, Portable databases. Formed by the merger of *Computer-readable data bases*; *Directory of online databases*; and *Directory of portable databases*. Vol. 1 consists of an alphabetical list of online databases, with separate directories of producers and online services. Database entries include database name; producer with address and telephone number; contact person or department; type of database (e.g., full text, numeric); description of content; subject coverage; frequency of updating; options for online access. Indexes: geographic; subject; master (i.e., current and former names of databases, producers, and services). Vol. 2 consists of separate alphabetical directories by format (CD-ROM, DVD, diskette, magnetic tape, handheld, and batch access database products); content and organization are similar to v. 1. Also available online through Gale's Ready Reference Shelf, the Gale Directory Library, and Proquest's Dialog database catalog (833).

839   Google search secrets. Christa Burns, Michael P. Sauers. Chicago: ALA Neal-Schuman, 2014. x, 211 p., ill., maps. ISBN 9781555709235

025.04252   ZA4234.G64; B87

Provides advice on using Google's advanced features to search the Web and to find images, news, videos, maps, blogs, scholarly works, patents, and books. Also covers Google alerts and other "tips and tricks." Copiously illustrated with screenshots.

840   Guide to reference books. 11th ed. Robert Balay, Vee Friesner Carrington, Murray S. Martin. Chicago: American Library Association, 1996. 2020 p. ISBN 0838906699

011.02   Z1035.1.G89

The most recent precursor to the present Guide to Reference database, often referred to simply by the editor's surname as "Balay." 1st ed.: *Guide to the study and use of reference books: A manual for librarians, teachers and students*, 1902. Title varies by edition; the American Library Association has always been the publisher. Past editors: Alice Bertha Kroeger (1st–3rd eds.), Isadore Gilbert Mudge (4th–6th eds.), Constance M. Winchell (7th–8th eds.), Eugene P. Sheehy (9th–10th eds.). Supplements issued irregularly. Accompanying the present database as a PDF file, Balay remains useful for identifying older printed reference works judged most important and useful by practicing librarians. Covers general works, the humanities, social and behavioral sciences, history and area studies, and science, technology, and medicine. Comprehensive index.

For a history of the *Guide* through its 10th edition, see the essay by Stuart W. Miller in *Distinguished classics of reference publishing.*

841   ipl2. http://www.ipl.org/div/subject/. University of Michigan School of Information, Drexel Univ. College of Information Science and Technology, Florida State Univ. College of Information, The IPL Consortium. Philadelphia: Drexel University iSchool. [1995–] 028.7; 001.4

A subsection of ipl2, which was formed by the merger of the Internet Public Library and the Librarians' Internet Index. Presents thousands of annotated links to freely-available websites, arranged in broad subject categories and subcategories. Many of the topical websites can be useful in responding to reference question.

The actual "Reference" category (http://www.ipl. org/IPLBrowse/GetSubject?vid=13&tid=6996& parent=0) covers general sources and sources that provide "quick answers to factual questions": almanacs; associations and organizations; biographies; calculation and conversion tools; calendars; census data and demographics; dictionaries; encyclopedias; experts and how-to; genealogy; geography; grammars; news and current events; periodical directories; quotations; search engines; style and writing guides; telephone and address; time and weather; trivia; web directories. Also links to German and Italian ready reference collections.

842   Know it all, find it fast: an A-Z source guide for the enquiry desk. 3rd ed. R.J. Duckett, Peter Walker, Christinea Donnelly. London: Facet Publ., 2008. xvi, 480 p. ISBN 9781856046527

025.52   ZA3050

Intended to help reference librarians quickly find answers to patrons' questions. For more than 160 subject areas (e.g. animals, companies, fairy tales), presents typical questions, considerations for conducting the reference interview, print and online sources, and tips and pitfalls when dealing with the topic. Nearly all cited sources are British, but most North American libraries will hold equivalent sources, and the other suggestions transcend nationality. Subject index.

The same concept is followed in two more recent, specialized handbooks, *Know it all, find it fast for academic librarians* (843) and *Know it all, find it fast for youth librarians and teachers.*

843   Know it all, find it fast for academic librarians. Heather Dawson. London:

Facet Pub., 2012. 387p.
ISBN 1856047598; 9781856047593
025.52   ZA3075

Following the model of the more general *Know it all, find it fast: an A-Z source guide for the enquiry desk* (842), this guide helps academic reference librarians quickly find answers to patrons' questions. For approximately a hundred subject areas related to academic study and research practices and to major academic fields, this handbook presents typical questions, considerations for conducting the reference interview, and annotated references to print and online sources. The majority of the recommended sources are British, but many US and international sources are included also. Subject index.

844 **Librarian's guide to online searching. 3rd ed.** Suzanne S. Bell. Santa Barbara, Calif.: Libraries Unlimited, an imprint of ABC-CLIO, LLC, [2012]. xviii, 286 p. ISBN 9781610690355
025.04   ZA4460.B45

First ed., 2006. Explains database structure and basic search concepts such as Boolean logic and controlled vocabulary. Provides in-depth sample searches of a dozen commonly-used bibliographic and numerical databases. Additional chapters address information-seeking behavior, the reference interview, choosing the right database, evaluating databases, and teaching database searching to others. Bibl. Index.

845 **The new Walford guide to reference resources: Volume 1: Science, technology, and medicine. 9th ed.** Ray Lester. London: Facet, 2005–. xix, 827 p., ill. ISBN 1856044955
011.02   Z1035.1

"This book is the first volume of a series that succeeds *Walford's guide to reference material*, published . . . 1959 and 2000 by Library Association Publishing." The scope and format of this guide is much different from the "old Walford," and thus it would behoove librarians to keep both eds. on the shelf. This version concentrates on websites and on general interest resources, including many that aren't specific to science and technology. Includes current awareness sources and many monographs that aren't traditional reference sources, but rather are popular introductions to topics.

Volume 2: The social sciences (846) was published

January 2008; and *Volume 3: Arts, humanities, and general reference* is expected in 2015. For more information, see publisher's page at http://www.facet publishing.co.uk/title.php?id=4998.

846 **The new Walford guide to reference resources: Volume 2: The social sciences.** Ray Lester. London: Facet, 2008. xvi, 699 p., ill. ISBN 9781856044981

This new ed. of a classic publ. has added coverage of numerous web-based information sources and is intended as "a carefully structured guide to examples of the various types of reference sources germane to communication in the social sciences"—*Preface*. The emphasis is on discovery by students and researchers, rather than the cataloging of reference titles. Nearly 6,000 entries date from mid-2007 and are organized around the major subjects of psychology; sociology; social work and social welfare; politics; government; law; finance, accounting, and taxation; industries and utilities; business and management; education and learning; sport; media and communications; and information and library sciences. Entries provide annotations and complete citations, including ISBN and price for books, with URLs for web-based sources. A significant number of websites are included for associations, research institutes, NGOs, and publishers. Indexes by topic and author/title.

847 **Recommended reference books for small and medium-sized libraries and media centers. 28th ed.** Shannon Graff Hysell. Littleton, Colo.: Libraries Unlimited, 1981–. 0277-5948
011.02   Z1035.1.R438

A compilation of best titles reviewed in *American Reference Books Annual (ARBA) Online* (33) and recommended for purchase by small and medium-sized academic, public, or school libraries. Each annual edition features approximately 500 critical, signed reviews of print and electronic reference sources taken from ARBA and published in the previous two years. The reviews are in a classified arrangement by subject area with author/title and subject indexes. The focus is on materials that are both affordable and useful.

848 **The reference librarian's policies, forms, guidelines, and procedures handbook: With CD-ROM.** Rebecca Brumley. New York: Neal-Schuman, 2006.

339 p., 1 CD-ROM. ISBN 1555705693
025.52   Z711.R4444

Similar to the compiler's compendia of policies from academic (802) and public libraries, but focused on reference services. Covers mission statements and service philosophies, as well as policies and processes concerned with personnel, collections, circulation, interlibrary loan, types of queries, reference resources, in-person and virtual assistance, and reference services for children. Index.

849 Reference research review. http://
connect.ala.org/node/64439. Chicago:
RUSA Reference Services Section, Research
& Statistics Committee. [1999-]

Annual annotated bibliography of research studies of reference. 1999-2009 editions are on the RUSA RSS Research & Statistics Committee website, http://www.ala.org/rusa/sections/rss/rsssection/rsscomm/rssresstat/res earchstatistics. Editions since 2009 are in the committee's ALA Connect collaborative web space; locate them by searching the phrase "reference research review."

**850 Reference sources and services for
youth.** Meghan Harper. New York: Neal-
Schuman Publishers, 2011. xx, 307 p., ill.
025.52778   Z675.S3 H266

Discusses the basic components of reference service for children and young adult users of public libraries and school library media centers. Topics include: developmentally appropriate practice; youth with special needs; communication; information literacy; collection development; online sources; government resources; evaluation of services; marketing; and management. Includes recommended core reference collections for grades K-4, 5-8, and 9-12. Glossary. Index to reference sources. Subject index.

**851 Reference sources for small and
medium-sized libraries. 7th ed.** Jack
O'Gorman. Chicago: American Library
Association, 2008. ISBN 9780838909430
011.02   Z1035.1.A47

The 7th ed. of this long-running guide is all new and "includes the best of the best and most affordable resources, web sites, CD ROMS, and electronic databases, as well as print."—*Back cover* Chapters are arranged by subject area, each with an introduction to scholarship in that area. Each chapter begins by reviewing general sources (directories, bibliographies, databases, almanacs, etc.) and then looks at resources for specific subcategories. Title selections are annotated and include complete bibliographic information. The guide focuses on resources useful and affordable for libraries serving populations under 100,000 users. Author/title index.

**852 Research within the disciplines:
foundations for reference and library
instruction.** Peggy Keeran. Lanham, Md.:
Scarecrow Press, 2007. xi, 267 p., ill.
ISBN 9780810856882
020.72   Z710.R47

Intended for the novice librarian or LIS student; also useful to librarians assuming reference or instruction responsibility for unfamiliar disciplines. Individually-authored chapters describe research practices, key information sources, and information literacy competencies in several broad and specialized fields: humanities; music; history; social sciences; business; sciences; and engineering. A separate chapter covers government documents across the disciplines. Concludes with a chapter on integrating discipline-based library instruction into the college curriculum, and another that reflects on the nature of disciplinary and interdisciplinary research. A second edition is forthcoming in spring 2014. For those who seek more than an overview, the ALA *Guide to reference* (52) recommends discipline-specific research guides in almost every subject category.

**853 Statistics, measures, and quality
standards for assessing digital
reference library services.** http://
quartz.syr.edu/rdlankes/Publications/
Books/Quality.pdf. Charles R. McClure,
R. David Lankes, Melissa Gross, Beverly
Choltco-Devlin, School of Information
Studies, Information Use Management and
Policy Institute, Florida State University.,
Information Institute of Syracuse,
School of Information Studies, Syracuse
University. Syracuse, N.Y.; Tallahassee,
Fla.: Syracuse University; Florida State
University. [2002]
025.040727   Z711.45

One hundred and four page PDF document. Outlines 35 ways to evaluate digital reference services (e.g., live chat, e-mail, instant messaging), including descriptive statistics, log analysis, user satisfaction measures, cost, and staff time expended. For each, provides a definition, rationale, data collection procedure(s), and brief discussion of issues and considerations. Sample forms and instruments in appendix.

854   Training paraprofessionals for reference service: a how-to-do-it manual for librarians. 2nd ed. Pamela J. Morgan, Julie Ann McDaniel. New York: Neal-Schuman Publishers, 2009. xiii, 201 p. ISBN 9781555706432

025.5/2071173   Z711.2.M36

Reviews the arguments for and against staffing a reference desk with paraprofessionals and explains how to create a training plan and structure orientation. Presents modules for training in basic and advanced information retrieval skills, ready reference knowledge, and communication skills. Concludes with chapters on performance management and evaluation. Includes bibliographies, checklists, exercises, and sample documents. Index.

855   Virtual reference best practices: tailoring services to your library. M. Kathleen Kern. Chicago: American Library Association, 2009. viii, 148 p., ill. ISBN 9780838909751

025.5/2   Z711.45.K47

Aims to help libraries follow RUSA's "Guidelines for implementing and maintaining virtual reference services" (http://www.ala.org/rusa/resources/guidelines/virtrefguidelines) by offering straightforward advice on determining needs, setting policies, selecting software, developing a staffing model, training, marketing, evaluating, and more. Similar information can be found in *IM and SMS reference services for libraries*.

Resource Sharing

856   Interlibrary loan and document delivery: Best practices for operating and managing interlibrary loan services in all libraries. Lee Andrew Hilyer. New York: Haworth Information Press, 2006. xix, 150 p., ill. ISBN 0789031280

025.62   Z713.H447

Also published in print and online as vol. 16, no. 1/2 (2006) of *Journal of interlibrary loan, document delivery and electronic reserve*. A basic primer on ILL operations, with chapters devoted to policies and codes, borrowing, lending, copyright, and management. Includes extensive annotated bibliography of print and electronic information resources. Appendixes reprint the national interlibrary loan code (857) and examples of a statewide code (TexShare), a reciprocal agreement, and e-mail and print forms.

857   Interlibrary loan code for the United States. http://www.ala.org/rusa/resources/guidelines/interlibrary. Interlibrary Loan Committee, Reference and User Services Association. Chicago: American Library Association. 2008

Spells out the responsibilities of both the requesting and supplying libraries when providing loans or copies of materials. Supplemented by a point-by-point explanation of the Code's provisions.

First edition, 1994.

858   Interlibrary loan policies directory. 7th ed. Leslie R. Morris. New York: Neal-Schuman, 2002. viii, 1275 p. ISBN 1555704239

Z713.5.U6M67

First ed., 1975. Sets forth the interlibrary loan policies of some 1,500 academic, public, and special libraries in the United States and Canada and approximately 200 foreign libraries. Arranged by state and nation. Entries include address and telephone number; DocLine, Ariel, and Internet addresses; acceptable methods of transmission; average turnaround time; charges and billing procedures; loan regulations; duplication services; URLs for full policies where available; and much more. Every data element in the entries is indexed, permitting the identification of libraries that loan overseas, use OCLC's payment system, share government documents or dissertations, etc. For up-to-date information, consult individual libraries' websites.

859   Interlibrary loan practices handbook. 3rd ed. Cherié L. Weible, Karen L. Janke. Chicago: American Library Association, 2011. ix, 131 p., ill. ISBN 9780838910818

025.62   Z713.5.U6B68

First ed., 1984, and 2nd ed., 1997, by Virginia Boucher.

Covers the history and future of interlibrary loan, basic workflows for borrowing and lending operations, U.S. copyright, management issues, technology, and Web 2.0.

860   ShareILL. http://www.shareill.org/.
Mary Hollerich, Linda Frederiksen. [s.l.]: ShareILL. 2007–

Wiki, international in scope, with information on many aspects of interlibrary loan, document delivery, and resource sharing among libraries. Replaces earlier website, ILLWeb (2001–06), which is no longer available. Linked resources include finding aids and verification tools (e.g., national libraries, online union catalogs, directories, and commercial and nonprofit document suppliers); management tools (e.g., codes, guidelines, library networks and consortia, software, background on copyright and licensing, and training materials); and sources for keeping current (e.g., conferences, discussion lists, blogs, projects, professional associations, and recommended print publications). After registering, users of ShareILL can contribute or edit content.

Services to Special and Diverse Populations

861   Access to libraries for persons with disabilities: checklist. http://www.ifla.org/publications/ifla-professional-reports-89. Birgitta Irvall, Gyda Skat Nielsen. The Hague, The Netherlands: International Federation of Library Associations and Institutions. 2005
027.663

"IFLA Professional reports," no. 89. A simple checklist covering physical access, media formats, and service and communication. Librarians in the United States should also consult the specific requirements of the Americans with Disabilities Act and other federal and state laws. Although dated, especially in its discussions of adaptive technologies, *The Americans with Disabilities Act: Its impact on libraries: The library's responses in "doable" steps* remains useful for its very detailed guidelines on physical access. See also guidelines for library services to the deaf, people

with mental illnesses, people with developmental disabilities, and others, published in booklet format by ALA's Association of Specialized and Cooperative Library Agencies; these are listed at http://www.ala.org/ascla/asclaprotools/asclastandards/standards guidelines.

862   Achieving diversity: a how-to-do-it manual for librarians. Barbara I. Dewey, Loretta Parham. New York: Neal-Schuman Publ., 2006. x, 245 p., ill.
ISBN 1555705545
027.6/3   Z711.8.A25

A practical guide for academic libraries. Brings together papers and case studies in three sections—how to create a successful diversity plan; how to recruit and retain a diverse workforce; and how to improve diversity through services, collections, and collaborations — plus samples of diversity documents. For another perspective on services for multicultural academic library users, see *Librarians serving diverse populations: challenges and opportunities* (869).

863   Assistive technologies in the library. Barbara T. Mates, William R. Reed. Chicago: American Library Association, 2011. xiv, 206 p., ill.
027.6/63   Z711.92.H3; M323

Overviews topics such as accessible web design, with specific recommendations of software, equipment, and services for users with particular disabilities. Addresses staff development, funding, and marketing. Appendixes offer annotated lists of vendors, web-based information resources, and grant opportunities.

864   Bienvenidos! = Welcome!: a handy resource guide for marketing your library to Latinos. Susannah Mississippi Byrd. Chicago; El Paso, Tex.: American Library Association; Cinco Puntos Press, 2005. xiii, 110 p., ill.
027.6/3   Z711.92.H56; B97

Guide to extending public library services to Latino populations. Covers demographics and community assessment, collection development, services, programming, and publicity. About half the book is devoted to a directory of Spanish-language vendors and print and media publishers. For an exhaustive guide, with worksheets for planning, see *Hola, amigos! A plan for Latino outreach.*

865   Guidelines for library services to prisoners. http://www.ifla.org/VII/s9/nd1/iflapr-92.pdf. Vibeke Lehmann, Joanne Locke. The Hague, The Netherlands: International Federation of Library Associations and Institutions. 2005. ISBN 9077897070

027.665   Z675.P8

No. 92 in series, *IFLA professional reports.* 1st ed., 1992, and 2nd ed., 1995, ed. by Frances E. Kaiser. Outlines standards, many of them quantitative, addressing all aspects of prison libraries. Includes bibliography, international in scope, spanning 1990 to 2005. For guidance on the provision of legal information to prisoners, consult *Werner's manual for prison law libraries.*

866   50+ library services: innovation in action. Diantha Dow Schull. Chicago: ALA Editions, 2013. xxvii, 335 p. ISBN 9780838911198

027.62/2   Z711.92.A35; S38

Describes public library programs for midlife and older patrons, with copious examples grouped under the following themes: work, careers and service; reflections and transitions; health and wellness; information technology and social media; creativity; information and community connections; lifelong learning; intergenerational programs and services; financial planning and business development. Other guides to serving older adults include *5-star programming and services for your 55+ library customers* and *Serving seniors: A how-to-do-it manual for librarians.*

867   International directory of libraries for the blind. http://ifla.jsrpd.jp/. Misako Nomura, Mayu Yamada, International Federation of Library Associations and Institutions; Section of Libraries for the Blind. [Tokyo]: Japanese Society for Rehabilitation of Persons with Disabilities (JSRPD). 2000

Searchable database. Provides contact information, holdings data (by type of material), and lending policies. Also available in print.

868   International resource book for libraries serving disadvantaged persons. Joanne Locke, Nancy M. Panella,

Margaret Girolami, International Federation of Library Associations and Institutions. München, Germany: K.G. Saur, 2001. xii, 249 p. ISBN 3598218265

016.027663

Detailed chronology with lists of conference papers and reports that document the work of the IFLA Section of Libraries Serving Disadvantaged Persons (now called the Library Services to People with Special Needs Section, http://www.ifla.org/lsn) between 1931 and 2001. Also includes multilingual, unannotated bibliographies on library services to the deaf and to the elderly, the use and development of easy-to-read publications, hospital patient libraries, and prison libraries, covering the period 1970-2000. Indexes: author; subject. A supplement covers 2001-2008 and is available as an open-access PDF on the IFLA website.

IFLA publications, no. 96.

869   Librarians serving diverse populations: challenges and opportunities. Lori Mestre, Association of College and Research Libraries. Chicago: Association of College and Research Libraries, 2010. xviii, 211 p., ill. Z682.4.M85; M47 027.6/3. ISBN 9780838985120

Reports on a research study of academic librarians in positions dedicated to serving diverse or multicultural users. Describes the challenges of such work and suggests ways for individuals and organizations to succeed. Contains an extensive list of web-accessible information resources, as well as a bibliography.

870   Library services for multicultural patrons: strategies to encourage library use. Carol Smallwood, Kim Becnel. Lanham, Md.: Scarecrow Press, 2013. xiii, 338 p. ISBN 978-0-8108-8722-0

027.6/3   Z711.8.L5285

Presents 37 "success stories" from academic, public, school, and special libraries that have designed services, programs, and collections to serve diverse patrons. The chapters, filled with practical ideas, are organized in seven thematic sections, including a section devoted to reference services. Also available as an e-book.

871 Multicultural communities: guidelines for library services. http://www.ifla.org/publications/multicultural-communities-guidelines-for-library-services-3rd-edition. IFLA Section on Library Services to Multicultural Populations. The Hague, The Netherlands: International Federation of Library Associations and Institutions. 2009

"These guidelines promote fairness and equity of access in library services to multicultural communities." —*Overview.* This 33-page PDF makes recommendations regarding the mission, planning, services, collections, and staffing of public libraries serving multicultural populations. Presents best practices from several countries.

872 Office for Literacy and Outreach Services (OLOS), American Library Association. http://www.ala.org/offices/olos. American Library Association, Office for Literacy and Outreach Services. Chicago: American Library Association
331.71206; 374.012; 027

The American Library Association's Office for Literacy and Outreach Services "focuses attention on services that are inclusive of traditionally underserved populations, including new and non-readers, people geographically isolated, people with disabilities, rural and urban poor people, and people generally discriminated against based on race, ethnicity, sexual orientation, age, language and social class."—*Home Page* Offers fact sheets and links to resources and ALA policies.

873 Professional tools. http://www.ala.org/glbtrt/publications. American Library Association. Gay, Lesbian, Bisexual, and Transgender Round Table. Chicago: American Library Association. Gay, Lesbian, Bisexual, and Transgender Round Table

Provides links, organized by type of resource, pointing to bibliographies and other tools for serving gay, lesbian, bisexual, and transgender patrons, including annual lists of winners of the Stonewall Book Awards (1971-), and annotated bibliographies of recommended books for children and teens (*Rainbow Book List,* 2008-) and adults (*Over the Rainbow Book List,* 2011-).

874 Serving Latino communities: A how-to-do-it manual for librarians. 2nd ed. Camila A. Alire, Jacqueline Ayala. New York: Neal-Schuman, 2007. xiii, 229 p., ill. ISBN 9781555706067
027.63   Z711.92.H56A44

Provides background on Latino culture and demographics. Addresses community needs assessment, outreach, collection development, workforce issues, and funding. Includes a "resource directory" of websites, books, periodicals, library organizations, and conferences; other reference content appears in appendixes to chapters (e.g., directory of book distributors; service guidelines; key Spanish words and phrases). Bibliography. Index.

An older work, *Library service to Spanish speaking patrons* by Moller, remains useful for its focus on age groups (preschool to early elementary, middle grades, teenage years, adults) and its more extensive listings of periodicals, publishers, and distributors, although some information is out-of-date.

875 Serving LGBTIQ library and archives users: essays on outreach, service, collections and access. Ellen Greenblatt. Jefferson, N.C.: McFarland & Company, Inc., Publ., [2011]. xi, 346 p. ISBN 9780786448
Z711.92.S49; S47 027.6/3

An eclectic collection of essays about the needs of LGBTIQ (lesbian, gay, bisexual, transgender, intersex, and queer/questioning) library users, with recommendations for collection development, patron services, programs, and bibliographic access. Also addresses censorship and workplace issues for LBGTIQ librarians. Covers public, academic, and school libraries, as well as archives, and includes personal reflections, memoirs, and profiles of libraries, archives, publications, and more. Young adult librarians should consult *Serving lesbian, gay, bisexual, transgender, and questioning teens: a how-to-do-it manual for librarians.*

876 Successful community outreach: a how-to-do-it manual for librarians. Barbara Blake, Robert S. Martin, Yunfei Du. New York: Neal-Schuman Publ., 2011. viii, 104 p. ISBN 9781555707729
021.2   Z711.7.B58

"Outreach programs or services are designed to connect, educate, and serve nontraditional or underserved communities and populations"—(p.35). Explains how to profile the community and the public library, assess needs and assets, and create an outreach plan. Includes 24 worksheets, state-by-state directory of data sources on libraries and communities, bibliography, and numerous examples of outreach programs in and outside the library building. Accompanying CD-ROM includes all worksheets, directory of data sources with web links, and seven exemplary plans.

877 That all may read . . . National Library Service for the Blind and Physically Handicapped (NLS). http://www.loc.gov/nls/index.html. Library of Congress, National Library Service for the Blind and Physically Handicapped. Washington: Library of Congress. 1998–
                                    Z5347.L52

The Library of Congress's National Library Service (NLS) for the Blind and Physically Handicapped produces and lends braille and audio materials through a network of libraries. Website outlines services and eligibility requirements and provides a searchable directory of cooperating libraries. Also links to an online catalog, new book lists, and a sizable number of reference circulars, directories and resource lists, including a 2006 bibliography on library services for the disabled.

878 Tribal libraries, archives, and museums: preserving our language, memory, and lifeways. Loriene Roy, Anjali Bhasin, Sarah K. Arriaga. Lanham, Md.: Scarecrow Press, 2011. xix, 247 p. ISBN 9780810881945
025.5/4   E97.8.T75

Comprised of 25 essays that describe exemplary tribal library and archival services, address standard library practices like collection development and cataloging in the tribal context. Offers advice for tribal librarians on marketing, staff development, and other subjects. Index.

Type of Library

879 Academic librarianship. Camila A. Alire, G. Edward Evans. New York: Neal-Schuman Publ., 2010. xvi, 383 p. ISBN 9781555707026
027.70973   Z675.U5; A427

An overview of academic libraries in the context of the history and current concerns of American higher education. Addresses campus-wide topics that impact libraries in chapters focused on faculty, students, curriculum, governance, funding, facilities, technology, and accountability. Covers library-specific issues including collections, services, staffing, career development, current themes, and future challenges. Bibliographies in each chapter; detailed index. For another practical text on academic libraries from a British perspective, see Peter Brophy's *The academic library*, 2nd ed.

880 The American public library handbook. Guy A. Marco. Santa Barbara, Calif.: Libraries Unlimited, 2012 ISBN 9781591589105
027.473   Z731.M29

A one-volume encyclopedia of American librarianship. Includes 65 topical articles on the history, issues, and daily operations of public libraries, with bibliographic references; 75 biographies of persons who died before 2000; and brief profiles of 1,200 libraries. Alphabetical arrangement. Detailed name and subject index.

881 The basic business library: core resources and services. 5th ed. Eric J. Forte, Michael R. Oppenheim. Santa Barbara, Calif.: Libraries Unlimited, 2012. xi, 227 p. ISBN 9781598846119
016.0276/9   Z675.B8

Reference resources are presented in the context of essays on topics such as core collections, investment sources, start-ups, government information, and marketing research. Tips and advice for working with library users. Updated since the 4th edition of 2002, to reflect the growing importance of online tools in the last decade.

882 Basic manual series. Music Library Association. Lanham, Md.: Scarecrow Press, 2002–

Set of handbooks on various aspects of music librarianship. Published to date: v. 1, classification; v. 2, binding and care of printed music; v. 3, instruction; v. 4, acquisitions; v. 5, audio and video equipment; and v. 6, performance libraries.

Most volumes provide thorough coverage of their topics. For example, v. 4 describes music publishing (including numbering systems for scores and recordings), identifies major vendors, outlines pre-order and ordering procedures, treats special topics such as out-of-print music (but not downloadable online music), and includes a glossary and bibliography. The Music Library Association (566) also produces a *Technical reports series* (1973–) on a wide range of practical yet specialized subjects.

883 Best practices for corporate libraries.
Sigrid Kelsey, Marjorie J. Porter. Santa Barbara, Calif.: Libraries Unlimited, 2011. xiii, 337 p., ill. ISBN 9781598847376
025.1/9769   Z675.C778; B47
Not a management manual, but a collection of 16 essays and case studies, grouped under the headings: Services and facilities; Communication and networking; Management; Marketing and demonstrating value; Change management and reorganization; and Current state of libraries. Specific topics include: the pre-computer-age history of the corporate library; intellectual property and information sharing; outsourcing; and assessment. Brief glossary of business terms.

884 The changing academic library: operations, culture, environments. 2nd ed. John M. Budd. Chicago: Association of College and Research Libraries, 2012. 412 p. ISBN 9780838986127
027.70973   Z675.U5; B866
ACRL publications in librarianship, no. 65. Presents the academic library in the context of the history, organizational culture, and governance of higher education. Surveys contemporary issues in management, funding, collection development, staffing and more, and situates the academic library within the larger domains of scholarly publishing and electronic information. Bibliography. First ed., 2005.

885 Fundamentals of school library media management: a how-to-do-it manual.
Barbara Stein Martin, Marco Zannier. New York: Neal-Schuman Publishers, 2009. xii, 172 p., ill. ISBN 9781555706562
025.1/9780973   Z675.S3; M27345
Intended for the first-time school library media specialist. Explains the basic tenets of managing a school library and recommends best practices for

the librarian in her roles as administrator, information specialist, and teacher. Reprints the Library Bill of Rights and related documents, provides exemplary acceptable use policies, and presents sample forms and screenshots. Includes directories of review sources and suppliers of materials and equipment.

886 Guidelines for library services to prisoners. http://www.ifla.org/VII/s9/nd1/iflapr-92.pdf. Vibeke Lehmann, Joanne Locke. The Hague, The Netherlands: International Federation of Library Associations and Institutions. 2005 ISBN 9077897070
027.665   Z675.P8
No. 92 in series, *IFLA professional reports*. 1st ed., 1992, and 2nd ed., 1995, ed. by Frances E. Kaiser. Outlines standards, many of them quantitative, addressing all aspects of prison libraries. Includes bibliography, international in scope, spanning 1990 to 2005. For guidance on the provision of legal information to prisoners, consult *Werner's manual for prison law libraries.*

887 Handbook for community college librarians. 2013 ed. Michael A. Crumpton, Nora J. Bird. Santa Barbara, Calif.: Libraries Unlimited. xiv, 172 p. ISBN 9781610693455
027.7   Z675.J8; C78
Provides wide-ranging advice for community college librarians on the following topics: administration, reference, accreditation standards, information literacy, instructional design, planning, budgeting, facilities, collection development, technology, diversity, supervision, assessment, and "managing yourself," i.e. personal productivity. An appendix reports findings from a survey of community college librarians.

888 The handbook of art and design librarianship. Amanda Gluibizzi, Paul Glassman. London: Facet Publ., 2010. 330 p., ill. ISBN 9781856047029
026   Z675.A85
Twenty-one chapters by various authors address a range of topics relevant to academic art libraries, including administration, liaison work, collection management, electronic resources, cataloging, outreach, and library spaces. Several chapters address information and visual literacies. An appendix

contains brief profiles of 17 libraries. For background on libraries in art museums, see *Art museum libraries and librarianship* by Benedetti.

889   The IALL international handbook of legal information management.
Richard A. Danner, Jules Winterton, International Association of Law Libraries. Farnham, Surrey, U.K.; Burlington, Vt.: Ashgate, 2011. xviii, 392 p., ill.
ISBN 9780754674771
026/.34   KZ1234.15
Separately authored chapters take stock of the current state of law librarianship and legal information management globally, covering topics such as education and training, copyright, information literacy, digitization, the open access movement, commercial legal publishing, collection development, and electronic resources. A section on "Law librarianship around the world" profiles India, Moldova, Nigeria, the Philippines, Turkey, and Vietnam. Includes lists of journals, research centers, and associations focused on comparative law. Detailed index.

890   Introduction to health sciences librarianship. M. Sandra Wood. Binghamton, N.Y.: Haworth Information Press, 2008. xvii, 494 p., ill. (some col.)
ISBN 9780789035
026.61   Z675.M4.I58
Contents: sec. 1, "Introduction/overview"; sec. 2, "Technical services"; sec. 3, "Public services"; sec. 4, "Administration"; sec. 5, "Special topics."
Overview of health sciences librarianship and the different types of health sciences libraries, reflecting current trends in the health care field; the important influence of many organizations, particularly the Medical Library Association (MLA), the Association of Academic Health Sciences Libraries (AAHSL), and the National Library of Medicine (NLM); and the pervasive role of advances in information technology. Addresses concepts such as information literacy, evidence-based librarianship, and health informatics. Glossary; index. Also available as an e-book.

891   Introduction to public librarianship. 2nd ed ed. Kathleen de la Peña McCook. New York: Neal-Schuman Publishers, 2011. xx, 523 p., ill.
027.473   Z731.M355

This textbook covers the history of public libraries in the United States, including their legal basis, administration, staffing, structure, infrastructure, services and community connections. The final chapters cover international issues and the role of public libraries in advancing human rights in the present and future. The appendices have particular value for reference purposes. The first appendix is a bibliography of more than a hundred pages, listing books, articles and websites keyed to each chapter. Additional references on adult and youth services are organized by the specific service responses outlined in Strategic planning for results (619). Another appendix contains a complete listing of national statistics on American public libraries since 1850.

892   The Medical Library Association guide to managing health care libraries. 2nd ed. Margaret Bandy, Rosalind F. Dudden, Medical Library Association. New York: Neal-Schuman Publishers, 2011. xxiii, 424 p., ill. ISBN 9781555707347
026.61   Z675.M4M5
First ed., 2000 (based on *Hospital library management,* 1983).
Contents: Ch. 1, Introduction: Libraries in health care settings (Margaret Moylan Bandy, Rosalind Farnam Dudden); ch. 2, The health care environment (Margaret Moylan Bandy, Barbara Jahn); ch. 3, Topics in management (Jacqueline Donaldson Doyle, Kay E. Wellek); ch. 4, Financial management (Mary Fran Prottsman); ch. 5, Human resources management (Dixie A. Jones); ch. 6, Evaluation and improvement management (Rosalind Farnam Dudden); ch. 7, Collection planning management (Craig C. Haynes); ch. 8, Collection technical management (Gretchen Hallerberg, Michelle Kraft, Marlene Englander, Marian Simonson); ch. 9, Library space management (Elizabeth Connor); ch. 10, On-site and web-based information services (Susan Lessick); ch. 11, Educational services (Lisa K. Traditi); ch. 12, Information practice (Michele Klein-Fedyshin); ch. 13, Knowledge services (Lorri Zipperer); ch. 14, Health information for patients and consumers (Michele Spatz); ch. 15, Associated services (Hope Leman, Donna Beales, Daniel Sokolow, Alison Aldrich, Marlene Englander); ch. 16, Solo librarian (Jerry Carlson).
This revised edition presents an overview of current trends in health sciences libraries and highly relevant topics in health sciences librarianship.

Accompanying CD-ROM with MLA policy statements, policy and procedure templates, bibliographies, and various other resources. Intended as a resource and practical guide for librarians in different types of healthcare libraries and for library & information sciences students.

893 Public libraries in the 21st century.
Ann E. Prentice. Santa Barbara, Calif.: Libraries Unlimited, 2011. viii, 222 p., ill.
027.473   Z731.P924
Provides an overview of public library administration, with such topics as governance and trusteeship; laws and policy; leadership; demographics; the library as virtual and physical place; innovation and planning; decision making; organizational structures; technology; services and programs; staffing; marketing and public relations; program evaluation; and finances. Each chapter includes a brief reading list.

894 Resources for school librarians. http://www.sldirectory.com/. Linda Bertland. Philadelphia: Linda Bertland. [n.d.]
Under subject categories, points to hundreds of websites and books related to information skills instruction, school library collections, program administration, technology, and career issues. Also searchable by keywords.

895 Small public library management.
Jane Pearlmutter, Paul Nelson. Chicago: American Library Association, 2012. viii, 139 p., ill. ISBN 9780838910856
025.1/97   Z675.S57; P43
A concise guide to all aspects of small public library administration, including: governance; planning; finances; personnel; facilities; collection management; services and programs; advocacy; and more.

896 Special libraries: a survival guide.
James M. Matarazzo, Toby Pearlstein, Sylvia R. M. James. Santa Barbara, Calif.: Libraries Unlimited, 2013. xv, 167 p., ill. ISBN 9781610692670
025.1/96   Z675.A2; M375
A collection of essays by Matarazzo, Pearlstein and others aimed at stemming the flood of corporate library closures. Several case studies complement the essays, which cover such subjects as evaluation, outsourcing, scenario-planning, and education for special librarianship.

897 Tribal libraries, archives, and museums: preserving our language, memory, and lifeways. Loriene Roy, Anjali Bhasin, Sarah K. Arriaga. Lanham, Md.: Scarecrow Press, 2011. xix, 247 p. ISBN 9780810881945
025.5/4   E97.8.T75
Comprised of 25 essays that describe exemplary tribal library and archival services, address standard library practices like collection development and cataloging in the tribal context. Offers advice for tribal librarians on marketing, staff development, and other subjects. Index.

Youth Services

Editor's Guide: Works about children's and young adult literature are not included here but may be found in the the online Guide to Reference (www.guidetoreference.org) under Humanities > Literature > Children's Literature.

898 The Big6: information & technology skills for student success. http://www.big6.com/. Michael B. Eisenberg, Robert E. Berkowitz. Fayetteville, N.Y.: Big6 Associates. 2001–
The Big6, a trademarked approach to teaching information and technology literacies, is used in elementary through college classrooms and libraries. The website provides examples of how the Big6 has been applied, lesson plans and materials, research reports, an online store, and more. Several books have been published about the Big6, including *Achieving educational standards using the Big6* and *The Big6 workshop handbook*, now in its fourth edition.

899 Cataloging correctly for kids: an introduction to the tools. 5th ed. Sheila S. Intner, Joanna F. Fountain, Jean Riddle Weihs, Association for Library Collections & Technical Services. Chicago: American Library Association, 2011. xiii, 224 p, ill.
025.3/2   Z695.1.C6 C37
First edition, 1989. Authors of earlier editions vary. The classic guide to cataloging books and other materials for children and young adults. Chapters

are devoted to standards, children's search behavior, AACR2 and MARC21, copy cataloging, RDA, authority control, LC and Sears subject headings, Dewey Decimal classification, materials, and more. Bibliography. Glossary of abbreviations and acronyms.

900   Children's books: a practical guide to selection. Phyllis J. Van Orden, Sunny Strong. New York: Neal-Schuman Publishers, 2007. xv, 239 p., [16] p. of plates, col. ill. ISBN 9781555705848
025.2/187625   Z718.1.V335

A guide to the selection of printed children's books for school and public libraries. Part I covers the selection process, general criteria, diversity issues, and selection tools. Part II discusses specific criteria for genres (picture books, fiction, folk literature, poetry). Part III covers information and reference books, as well as particular subjects, such as alphabet books and biographies. Includes annotated lists of recommended titles. Appendices: glossary; annotated list of resources; directory of organizations; resources for writing collection policy statements. Separate author, illustrator, title, and subject indexes.

901   Children's services in the American public library: a selected bibliography. Fannette H. Thomas. New York: Greenwood Press, 1990. xii, 151 p.
ISBN 0313247218
027.625   Z718.2.U6T46

Lists over 600 articles and books from 1876 to 1976, with brief annotations. Arranged by broad topics: historical focus, professional staff, organizational scheme, philosophical perspective, client group, collection development, readers' services, story hour, interagency cooperation, and multi-media. Author and subject indexes.

902   Connecting young adults and libraries: A how-to-do-it manual. 4th ed. Michele Gorman, Tricia Suellentrop, Patrick Jones. New York: Neal-Schuman Publishers, 2009. xxxiii, 389 p.
ISBN 9781555706654
027.626   Z718.5.J66

Hefty guide for librarians who serve teenagers, in an easy-to-consult outline and Q&A format. Covers all aspects of young adult librarianship. Includes a glossary of terms, acronyms, organizations, and key individuals. The accompanying CD-ROM offers a toolkit of editable policies, forms, and planning documents. Bibliographies in each chapter. Index.

903   Dictionary for school library media specialists: a practical and comprehensive guide. Mary Maude McCain, Martha Merrill. Englewood, Colo.: Libraries Unlimited, 2001. xiii, 219 p. ISBN 1563086964
020.3   Z1006.M43

Intended as a comprehensive dictionary covering all aspects of library work in K-12 schools. Includes computer terminology and educational jargon. Numerous cross-references. Also available as ebook. For a more succinct and slightly newer dictionary, see *The essential school library glossary*.

904   Empowering learners: guidelines for school library media programs. American Association of School Librarians. Chicago: American Association of School Librarians, 2009. 64 p., ill. ISBN 9780838985199
027.8   Z675.S3

Addresses the roles of school library media specialists as teachers, managers, and leaders. Should be used in conjunction with *Standards for the 21st-century learner* (http://www.ala.org/aasl/standards-guidelines/learning-standards) and *Standards for the 21st-century learner in action*. Taken together, these standards and guidelines replace *Information power*.

905   Fundamentals of children's services. 2nd ed. Michael Sullivan. Chicago: American Library Association, 2013. xx, 359 p.
027.62/50973   Z718.2.U6; S85

Overviews children's services in public libraries. Twenty-seven chapters treat the mission of the library, the collection, services, programming, and management. Bibliography. Index. Appendices reprint key ALA documents, including "Competencies for librarians serving children in public libraries," which is also available at http://www.ala.org/alsc/edcareeers/alsccorecomps. For a broader view of children's services across all library types, see *Managing children's services in libraries* (909).

First ed. 2005.

906 Fundamentals of school library media management: a how-to-do-it manual.
Barbara Stein Martin, Marco Zannier. New York: Neal-Schuman Publishers, 2009. xii, 172 p., ill. ISBN 9781555706562
025.1/9780973   Z675.S3; M27345
Intended for the first-time school library media specialist. Explains the basic tenets of managing a school library and recommends best practices for the librarian in her roles as administrator, information specialist, and teacher. Reprints the Library Bill of Rights and related documents, provides exemplary acceptable use policies, and presents sample forms and screenshots. Includes directories of review sources and suppliers of materials and equipment.

907 Guide to reference materials for school library media centers. 6th ed.
Barbara Ripp Safford. Santa Barbara, Calif.: Libraries Unlimited, 2010. xiv, 236 p.
011.62   Z1037.1.S34
Recommends and describes over 700 positively reviewed reference books and online resources for K-12 school libraries. Part 1, Library Tools (e.g., review journals and bibliographies); Part 2, General Reference; Part 3, Social Sciences; Part 4, Humanities; Part 5, Science and Technology. Within parts, arranged by subject and type of resource. Bibliography. Prices listed. Annotations indicate grade levels. Author, title, and subject indexes.

First edition, 1973, through 4th ed., 1992, titled *Guide to reference books for school library media centers*.

908 Library service to children: a guide to the history, planning, policy, and research literature. Phyllis Van Orden, Patricia Pawelak-Kort. Lanham, Md.: Scarecrow Press, 2005. xiii, 139 p.
ISBN 0810851695
016.027625   Z718.1.V336
Previous ed.: *Library service to children: a guide to the research, planning, and policy literature* (ALA, 1992). Over 400 references to English-language works about public library services to children and children's librarianship. Emphasizes "policy statements, reports, and research studies not readily identified

in any one source"—*Introd*. Listed alphabetically by author; indexed by title, subject, research method, funding source, and type of literature.

909 Managing children's services in libraries. 4th ed. Adele M Fasick, Leslie Edmonds Holt. Santa Barbara, Calif.: Libraries Unlimited, 2013. xix, 225 p.
ISBN 9781610691000
025.1/97625   Z718.2.U6; F37
A general guide to children's services in public, school, and special libraries in museums, hospitals, etc. After presenting background on today's children and their library needs, focuses on strategic planning, evaluation, funding, and facilities. Other sections address: developing and managing collections (including intellectual freedom issues); programs and services (including outreach and marketing); and the work environment (including supervision, leadership, and communication). Recommends readings on each topic.

Previous editions (1991, 1998, 2008) titled *Managing children's services in the public library* were narrower in scope.

910 Pioneers and leaders in library services to youth: a biographical dictionary. Marilyn L. Miller. Westport, Conn.: Libraries Unlimited, 2003. xvi, 267 p. ISBN 1591580285
027.626092B   Z720.A4P56
Intended to compensate for inadequate inclusion of youth services for librarians in *The dictionary of American library biography* (407). Reprints 40 profiles from the *DALB* and its supplements, and adds 57 new ones. All subjects are deceased. Signed essays cover family background, education, professional career and contributions, and includes a bibliography. Index to names and subjects.

911 Reference sources and services for youth. Meghan Harper. New York: Neal-Schuman Publishers, 2011. xx, 307 p., ill.
025.52778   Z675.S3 H266
Discusses the basic components of reference service for children and young adult users of public libraries and school library media centers. Topics include: developmentally appropriate practice; youth with special needs; communication; information literacy; collection development; online sources; government

resources; evaluation of services; marketing; and management. Includes recommended core reference collections for grades K-4, 5-8, and 9-12. Glossary. Index to reference sources. Subject index.

912 Resources for school librarians. http://www.sldirectory.com/. Linda Bertland. Philadelphia: Linda Bertland. [n.d.]

Under subject categories, points to hundreds of websites and books related to information skills instruction, school library collections, program administration, technology, and career issues. Also searchable by keywords.

913 The school library media facilities planner. Thomas L. Hart. New York: Neal-Schuman, 2006. xiii, 253 p., ill. ISBN 1555705030

027.8   Z675.S3H2674

Provides step-by-step advice for planning and building a new school library. Includes guidelines, floor plans, formulas, checklists, glossary, and samples of a planning document, contract, and request for bids. Index.

914 The school library media specialist's policy & procedure writer. Elizabeth Downs. New York: Neal-Schuman Publishers, Inc., 2010. xviii, 195 p., ill. ISBN 9781555706210

025.178   Z675.S3D7485

Sample policies, procedures, and forms that school librarians can adapt are reproduced in this book and on the accompanying CD-ROM. Covers all areas of school library media center management, including mission, collections, equipment, technology, staff, and users.

915 Special collections in children's literature: an international directory. 3rd ed. Dolores Blythe Jones, Association for Library Service to Children. Chicago: American Library Association, 1995. xxiii, 235 p., ill. ISBN 0838934544

026.808899282   Z688.C47S63

Describes 300 collections in the United States and 119 in other countries. The main listing of U.S. collections is arranged by state and city and supplies contact information and a brief summary of the collection's size and highlights. The subject listing serves as an index by authors' names and topics to the main listing. A separate geographic listing, without subject access, covers non-U.S. collections. The final index is a name index to all collections. Although some contact information is out-of-date, there is no more recent guide of similar depth to special collections of children's literature.

First edition, *Subject collections in children's literature* (N.Y.: Bowker, 1969), and 2nd ed., *Special collections in children's literature* (Chicago: A.L.A., 1982), compiled by Carolyn W. Field.

916 Voya's five-foot bookshelf: essential books for professionals who serve teens 2000 to 2012. 1st ed. RoseMary Hornold. Bowie, Md.: VOYA Press, 2013. 92 p. 9781617510106

Bibliography of recommended books for young adult librarians, including both library professional literature and books on adolescent development from related disciplines. Reprints reviews from *VOYA* [Voice of Youth Advocates] magazine. Arranged alphabetically by main entry, with an author/title index.

917 Young adults deserve the best: YALSA's competencies in action. Sarah Flowers, Young Adult Library Services Association. Chicago: American Library Association, 2011. viii, 126 p. ISBN 9780838935873

Z682.4.Y68; F58 027.62/6

Practical advice organized around the seven areas of the ALA Young Adult Library Services Association's "Competencies for librarians serving youth": Leadership and professionalism; knowledge of client group; communication, marketing & outreach; administration; knowledge of materials; access to information; service. Appendixes include documents such as the *Library bill of rights* and the YALSA/RUSA *Guidelines for library services to teens*.

INDEX

Note: Numbers in bold refer to entry numbers. Numbers in roman type refer to mentions in annotations of other works.